Best Places to Stay in the Pacific Northwest

The Best Places to Stay Series

Best Places to Stay in America's Cities
Kenneth Hale-Wehmann, Editor

Best Places to Stay in Asia
Jerome E. Klein

Best Places to Stay in California
Anne E. Wright

Best Places to Stay in the Caribbean
Bill Jamison and Cheryl Alters Jamison

Best Places to Stay in Florida
Christine Davidson

Best Places to Stay in Hawaii
Kimberly Grant

Best Places to Stay in Mexico
Bill Jamison and Cheryl Alters Jamison

Best Places to Stay in the Mid-Atlantic States
Dana Nadel Foley

Best Places to Stay in the Midwest
John Monaghan

Best Places to Stay in New England
Christina Tree and Kimberly Grant

Best Places to Stay in the Pacific Northwest
Marilyn McFarlane

Best Places to Stay in the Rockies
Roger Cox

Best Places to Stay in the South
Carol Timblin

Best Places to Stay in the Southwest
Anne E. Wright

Best Places to Stay in the Pacific Northwest

Marilyn McFarlane

Bruce Shaw, Editorial Director

Fifth Edition

HOUGHTON MIFFLIN COMPANY

BOSTON • NEW YORK

Fifth Edition

ISSN: 1048-5465
ISBN: 0-395-76339-8

Printed in the United States of America

Maps by Charles Bahne
Design by Robert Overholtzer

This book was prepared in conjunction with Harvard Common Press.

QUM 10 9 8 7 6 5 4 3 2 1

To John

Contents

Introduction

If you plan to travel in the Pacific Northwest and like to stay at out-of-the-ordinary, top-quality, interesting places, this book is for you. It's for families looking for vacations they can enjoy together, for couples yearning for a romantic weekend, for skiers seeking cozy inns near powdery slopes. It's for sailors and history buffs, wine lovers and hikers in search of lodgings that suit their varied moods and pocketbooks.

The fifth edition of *Best Places to Stay in the Pacific Northwest* is divided by state or province and by the city or town where each hotel or inn is located. There are many new lodgings, a few deletions, and numerous changes — the result of months of personally investigating hundreds of inns. Again, the best were selected. That does not mean they're the most elegant or expensive. What I look for are comfortable accommodations, cleanliness, a commitment to hospitality, an interesting setting, and personality. These criteria apply to every lodging in the book.

At the beginning of each section, the hotels and inns are listed under categories that can help you decide if this is the type of place you're looking for: a wilderness retreat, a country inn, a resort, an island getaway, or any of several other categories. In addition, the book has brief descriptions of each region, maps, and a recommended reading list.

"What's What," at the end of the book, is a handy cross reference for special interests, such as who accepts pets, has cooking facilities, provides wheelchair access, or offers fine dining; and it indicates where sports and recreation are available.

The inns are not rated; each has its own merits and your choice depends upon the type of place you want. If it's in this book, you can assume it is among the best of its kind. *None of the inns paid to be included.*

You may not agree with all the choices. Some fine places were excluded not because of their quality but by necessity (the inn may be changing ownership, for example, with its future in doubt). You won't find many chain hotels here because, with a few outstanding exceptions, they differ very little between locales.

Your comments are welcome. If you know of a special place that is not described here, or if you've had an unsatisfactory experience at an inn listed, please let us know. Your suggestions will help with future editions and allow us to provide you and other travelers with accurate information. Send your comments to:

>Chris Paddock
>*Best Places to Stay in the Pacific Northwest*
>The Harvard Common Press
>535 Albany Street
>Boston, MA 02118

Rates and Taxes

Please note that the rates given applied at press time and are subject to change without notice. Taxes are not included, for the most part, so the total cost may be slightly higher than listed. Unless otherwise noted, rates cited are for one night. "Single" is the cost for one person, "double," the cost for two. Be sure to ask about discount packages, corporate and family rates, and off-season and midweek discounts. These are frequently offered, and you may save a substantial amount.

Rates for all lodgings in Canada are shown in Canadian dollars and marked (Cd).

Meals

Breakfasts are described as full, Continental, or expanded Continental. A full breakfast connotes a hot entrée; a Continental meal is a light repast, usually coffee, rolls, and fruit; while expanded Continental falls between the two, often including cereal, yogurt, or an assortment of cheeses. Coffee and tea are usually not mentioned in breakfast descriptions. You can assume that they are always served.

Booking a Room

Explain your needs clearly when you make a hotel reservation (do you prefer a private bath, a view, quiet surroundings, a firm bed?), and they are likely to be met. If you are not satisfied, request a change. Every hotel has less desirable rooms, but you should never have to accept a room you don't like.

The information in this guidebook is as current and accurate as possible, but changes inevitably occur. I recommend asking about rates and policies before you check in. I also strongly urge making reservations. But if you haven't made reservations, try anyway! Innkeepers are delighted to fill rooms that are suddenly empty because of cancellations.

Best Places to Stay in the Pacific Northwest is the most comprehensive compilation of outstanding lodgings for the region. I hope you enjoy reading and using it as much as I've enjoyed the research and writing. Happy travels!

Marilyn McFarlane
Portland, Oregon
January 1998

DEFINITIONS OF CATEGORIES

Intimate City Stops

This group includes small hotels and bed-and-breakfast inns that combine sophisticated urban amenities with personal style and attention to detail. They may have as few as four rooms; none has more than a hundred.

Grand City Hotels

Famous historic landmarks and hotels of contemporary opulence are included in this category.

Country Inns and B&Bs

When you're looking for a peaceful retreat from urban bustle, a country inn or homey bed-and-breakfast is the ideal choice. Those described here are not all in rural areas, but each has a distinct country inn atmosphere and offers a change of pace.

Family Favorites

If you've wanted a vacation spot for the whole family, possibly offering programs for children, these inns, lodges, and ranches are your answer. They fit other categories, too, but they have perfected the art of providing fun for every age, and their rates often favor families.

Inns and Cottages by the Sea

Resorts, condominiums, lodges, private homes, and old-fashioned beach hotels are described here. Most are right on the shore, with views of the Pacific, while some are a few blocks inland in seaside towns. Each has a setting that focuses on the ocean.

Island Getaways

There are hundreds of islands in Washington and British Columbia, some connected to the mainland by bridges and others accessible only by boat or plane.

On a Budget

These inns are included not only for their unusually low rates but for other qualities such as an outstanding view, a quaint atmosphere, or a prime location.

Resorts

If a resort offers a wide variety of recreational activities and all meals and is a destination rather than a stopping place, we consider it a full-service resort that belongs first in this category.

Romantic Hideaways

These retreats for romantics offer scenic beauty, privacy, and enchanting atmosphere. They're ideal not only for honeymooners but for any vacationers seeking quiet and seclusion.

Wilderness Retreats

If a lodge or resort is in the forest or on a mountainside or river-bank removed from most habitation, it's a wilderness retreat. Some inns, deep in the wild, are inaccessible by road. Others are mere yards off a highway, but they, too, offer opportunities to leave civilization behind and enter a primeval world.

Wine Region Inns

Most of these inns are in two wine regions, Washington's Yakima Valley and Oregon's Willamette Valley. There are other wine-producing areas in the Northwest, particularly in eastern Washington and western Idaho, the Hood River area, and the Umpqua Valley of southern Oregon.

Pacific Northwest

British
Columbia

Washington

Oregon

Idaho

Babue '92

British Columbia

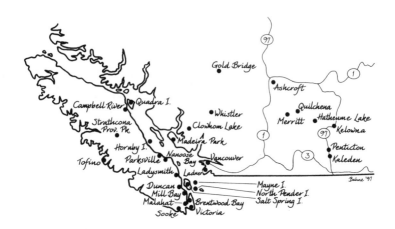

Ashcroft
Sundance Ranch, 11
Brentwood Bay
The Boathouse, 13
Campbell River
Painter's Lodge, 14
Clowhom Lake
Clowhom Lodge, 15
Duncan
Fairburn Farm Country Manor, 17
Grove Hall Estate, 18
Gold Bridge
Tyax Mountain Lake Resort, 20
Hatheume Lake
Hatheume Lake Resort, 22
Hornby Island
Sea Breeze Lodge, 23
Kaleden
Ponderosa Point Resort, 25
Kelowna
Hotel Eldorado, 26
Ladner
River Run Floating Cottages, 27
Ladysmith
Yellow Point Lodge, 29

Madeira Park
Lowe's Resort, 30
Malahat
The Aerie, 32
Mayne Island
Fernhill Lodge, 33
Oceanwood Country Inn, 35
Merritt
Corbett Lake Country Inn, 36
Mill Bay
Pine Lodge Farm, 38
Nanoose Bay
Pacific Shores Nature Resort, 39
Parksville
Bayside Inn, 40
Tigh-Na-Mara, 42
Pender Island
Cliffside Inn On-the-Sea, 43
Penticton
Clarion Lakeside Resort, 45
Quadra Island
April Point Lodge, 46
Tsa-Kwa-Luten Lodge, 48
Quilchena
Quilchena Hotel, 49

Best Intimate City Stops

Best Grand City Hotel

Best Country Inns and B&Bs

Best Family Favorites

Best Inns by the Sea

Best Island Getaways

Best Resorts

Best Romantic Getaways

Best Wilderness Retreats

Ladysmith
Strathcona Provincial Park

The dominant feature of western British Columbia is water. Lakes, rivers, streams, waterfalls, fjords, inlets, and bays riddle this huge, ocean-lapped chunk of Canada, feeding a rich green landscape and creating a recreational paradise for boating, fishing, and water sports. There are more than 8,000 trout-filled lakes in Cariboo country alone, a region that sprawls across central B.C.

This 366,000-square-mile province, twice the size of California, has a terrain of astounding variety within its borders. Between Vancouver's city lights and the shimmering northern lights lie hundreds of miles of unbroken wilderness and jagged mountain ranges, lush farmlands, Indian villages with weathered totem poles, ice fields, mist-cloaked islands, and vast cattle ranches.

Much of British Columbia's natural beauty may be seen in its 333 provincial parks and five national parks, which contain some of the most magnificent scenery in Canada. Most parks have well-developed facilities for visitors, but one out of ten is a wilderness area, largely untouched and frequented mostly by backpackers and mountaineers. Historic parks include restorations of 19th-century gold rush towns and an abandoned Haida Indian village, a UNESCO World Heritage Site.

Exploring, sightseeing, fishing, hunting, boating, hiking and nearly every other outdoor activity is available in B.C. The skiing is superb, whether it's just out the door of a luxury resort or high on slopes accessible only by helicopter. You can cross-country ski, showshoe, skate, go snowmobiling, and even golf in the snow in this land that extends farther north than parts of Alaska.

Fewer than 2.5 million people live in British Columbia, and most of them reside in the extreme southwest corner. In contrast to the rest of the province, that corner is highly urbanized, sparkling with charm and vitality. Almost without exception, the people welcome visitors warmly. The English reserve that is their heritage is enlivened with a western spirit of hospitality and spiced by the cultures of emigrants from many parts of the world, particularly Asia.

Cosmopolitan **Vancouver** is well known for its excellent restaurants, fine shops, restored historic district, active nightlife, secluded beaches, and pockets of untouched woodland. Rugged, snowclad mountains with ski slopes and hiking trails rise from the city's doorstep. Cruise ships sail from the harbor to Alaska and other ports.

In 1886, in an act of amazing foresight, Vancouver's first city council set aside 150 acres to be preserved as a park. At a time when there was so much forest, establishing a wild area near the heart of the city must have seemed a redundancy at best. Today Stanley Park, now 1,000 acres of forest, lake, and playground, is one of Vancouver's prime attractions.

Spectator sports include hockey, baseball, horseracing, and football in B.C. Place Stadium, a 60,000-seat covered arena. Granville Island, on False Creek, is a special corner of Vancouver, filled with art galleries, restaurants, and water views. Its delightful farmer's market is a great place to shop.

B.C.'s biggest city and the large island off the coast bear the same name: Vancouver, after the British sea captain and explorer. The slightly confusing nomenclature clears with a personal visit. No one who's seen the cities of Vancouver, on the mainland, and **Victoria,** perched on the southern tip of Vancouver Island, would confuse the two.

Shreds of the British Empire cling to Victoria, happy with its "bit of Olde England" label. But the lively, sunny city, famous for its magnificent flower displays and gardens, and the only city in Canada where you can golf year-round, is not a museum piece. It has outstanding restaurants, shops chic and antique, and many beaches and parks.

Major attractions are the grand Empress Hotel, facing Inner Harbour; the much-acclaimed Royal British Columbia Museum; the artfully landscaped Butchart Gardens; and the elegant Parliament Buildings (Victoria is the capital of the province).

Vancouver Island, spreading north from Victoria for 280 miles, has thick forests punctuated by lakes, small towns, farms, and resort communities, such as **Parksville,** that hug the coastline. **Duncan** has gained fame for its totem poles and Native art; **Campbell River** is internationally known for its sport fishing. Among the Gulf Islands, in the Strait of Georgia east of Vancouver Island, **Salt Spring, Mayne,** and **North Pender** are havens for artists and vacationers.

One main, east-west road crosses the island to a rugged and isolated west coast, where the Pacific Rim National Park is located. The little town of **Tofino** offers fishing and whale-watching charters.

Other parts of British Columbia seem like a different world. East of the Cascades, far from the city streets and brooding rain forest, is dry, sagebrush-covered rangeland. Mines, canyons, ridges, hot springs, and great lakes and long rivers form a varied terrain all the way to the Rocky Mountains. Cowboys and guest ranches, barbecues, roundups and rodeos invite visitors to join in the hearty life of the West. Orchards and vineyards flourish in the fertile valleys of Okanagan country. The friendly towns of **Penticton, Kelowna, Kaleden,** and **Vernon** cluster near Okanagan Lake, several smaller lakes, and hills that rise to snowy ski slopes.

Travelers are welcomed everywhere in "Super, Natural B.C.," as promoters of the province call it. Whatever adventure you seek, you are likely to find it here. And whatever you find, even if you weren't looking for it, you'll never be bored.

For more information on travel in British Columbia, contact Tourism British Columbia, 720 Olive Way, Seattle, Washington 98101, or Tourism British Columbia, Parliament Buildings, Victoria, B.C., Canada V8V 1X4 (phone: 800-663-6000).

Ashcroft

Sundance Ranch

Box 489
Ashcroft, B.C., Canada V0K 1A0
604-453-2422
604-453-2554
Fax: 604-453-9356
sundance@mail.netshop.net

A dude ranch with an Old West flavor

Proprietors: Stan and Vicki Rowe. **Accommodations:** 28 rooms (all with private bath). **Rates:** (Cd) March, April, and October, $120–$136 per adult; $105, ages 15–18; $80, ages 8–14; $10, ages 3–7. Summer months, $148–$168 per adult; $120, ages 15–18; $95 ages 8–14; $10 ages 3–7. **Included:** All meals and activities. **Minimum stay:** None. **Payment:** MasterCard, Visa. **Children:** Under age 3, free with a parent. **Pets:** Not allowed. **Smoking:** Allowed. **Open:** Open in winter for group functions only.

➤ **A corral has horses for youngsters (the minimum riding age is 8), children are served meals before adults, and babysitting can be arranged in summer.**

At Sundance, there are more than 80 horses to take you riding on trails with names like Bad Lands, Two Pines, and Sioux Lookout. When you tire of riding, you can relax by the heated swimming pool, play tennis on the regulation-size court, watch movies, or join the crowd in the BYOB lounge singing "Home on the Range." A sound system pipes country music everywhere on the ranch, including the stables.

The rooms are air-conditioned, to counter the summer heat of the Thompson River Valley in south-central B.C. Most accommodations have natural wood interiors and queen-size and twin beds; some have fireplaces and king-size beds. The layout of the ranch house–style buildings is unusual and blends well with the dry, hilly surroundings dotted with verdant meadows and wooded canyons.

Sundance Ranch goes back to 1867, when a cattle ranch was founded to provide meat for the Cariboo miners. For nearly a century, it raised and marketed cattle. In 1957, it opened as a guest ranch known as the Bar Q. By 1978 the ranch had gone downhill; Stan and Vicki Rowe bought it and began its renovation.

Their efforts have created a vacation wonderland for dudes dreaming of riding the range, just as Stan dreamed as a child in Alberta. He grew up to become a successful salesman and has turned much of that expertise into operating one of the most popular guest ranches in B.C., a four-hour drive from Vancouver. If you wish to fly in by private plane, someone from the ranch can pick you up at the landing strip at Cache Creek.

Meals include steak barbecues and cookout rides featuring good, hearty fare: hamburgers, chili, beans, watermelon, beer, lemonade, and homemade pies. Home-bred buffalo is occasionally on the menu. In the saddle shop you can rent boots, which are required for horseback riding, along with hats, gloves, bolo ties, belt buckles, and bandannas. Many of the holiday cowhands speak English with foreign accents, for one fourth of the guests come from far afield; European, Australian, and Japanese visitors go home in their cowboy hats, happily laden with frontier artifacts and memories of ranching in style.

Brentwood Bay

The Boathouse

746 Sea Drive, R.R. 1
Brentwood Bay, B.C., Canada V8M 1B1
250-652-9370

| **A secluded cottage at water's edge** |

Proprietors: Jean and Harvey Merritt. **Accommodations:** 1 cottage. **Rates:** $130 double. **Included:** Continental breakfast. **Minimum stay:** None. **Payment:** MasterCard, Visa. **Children:** Not appropriate. **Pets:** Allowed by arrangement. **Smoking:** Not allowed. **Open:** Year-round.

➤   **Nearby Clinkers Galley serves a good meal. Butchart Gardens is within easy walking distance or you can row around the inlet. Victoria is a 20-minute drive south.**

This charming spot is an idyllic getaway for two. Once a boathouse on the shore of Brentwood Bay, Vancouver Island, it has been transformed into comfortable lodgings overlooking the water and a nearby private island. The owners, who rebuilt the boathouse, live on the hill above. Every evening they bring a Continental breakfast down the long wooden staircase and store it in the boathouse refrigerator so guests can enjoy a leisurely meal whenever they choose.

The cottage is small. Its one large room is painted a crisp blue and white and has a queen-size sleeper sofa that faces the lovely view. Cooking facilities are limited to a toaster oven, a refrigerator, and a coffeemaker. A barbecue is available.

A corner nook, with two big soft rockers and shelves of books, is ideal for bird-watching. Binoculars are provided, along with cribbage and backgammon boards. Once you settle in here, you'll never want to leave.

The boathouse has electric baseboard heat. The bathroom is a few steps away in a modern, immaculate bathhouse. There are other homes in the area, but there's a strong sense of privacy in this woodsy setting. This is a place to relax completely. You can swim off the dock, throw darts at the dartboard on the porch, or take the rowboat out on the water. As a visitor wrote in the guest book, "the serenity and quaintness here are only surpassed by your gracious hospitality."

Campbell River

Painter's Lodge

1625 MacDonald Road
Campbell River, B.C., Canada V9W 5C1
250-286-1102
800-663-7090
Fax: 250-598-1361

A luxury fishing resort on Vancouver Island

Manager: Jim Evasiuk. **Accommodations:** 84 rooms and cabins. **Rates:** (Cd) Rooms, $144–$189 double; $15 additional person; cabins, $199–$325 (up to 6 people); fly-in packages available. **Minimum stay:** None. **Payment:** Major credit cards. **Children:** Under age 12, free. **Pets:** Not allowed. **Smoking:** Allowed. **Open:** April to mid-October.

▶ **Discovery Pier is a popular fishing spot, with facilities for children and wheelchairs, weather protection, fish-cleaning stations, and night fishing.**

Sixty-odd years ago, Painter's was a rustic lodge on Vancouver Island's east coast, catering to anglers who knew that Campbell River was a prime spot for salmon fishing. In 1985, the lodge burned to the ground. Now a sprawling hotel stands above the shore, its picture windows overlooking Discovery Passage and the Strait of Georgia. It has a swimming pool and hot tub, gift shop, restaurant, lounge, and outdoor dining terrace.

The guest rooms, most in the main lodge and three separate buildings, are furnished in contemporary style with double and queen-size beds. A few older cabins have knotty pine walls. The rooms with the best views are in the lodge and Redonda Wing, near the pier and fishing center, where boat charters and rentals and fishing licenses are available.

Though there's a sleek, corporate flavor to today's lodge, fishing is still the focus. Professional guides will take you out in well-equipped Boston whalers to find the fighting chinook salmon, perhaps hooking a tyee — one weighing 30 pounds or more. The Quinsam and Campbell rivers, rich spawning streams that empty into fast-flowing Discovery Passage, make the area highly productive for sports fishing.

The town of Campbell River has an information-packed visitors center and an interesting museum of Native artifacts and masks.

Clowhom Lake

Clowhom Lodge

Clowhom Lake, B.C., Canada
Mailing address:
P. O. Box 2720
Portland, OR 97208
503-226-4044

An isolated fishing lodge in western B.C.

Reservations Manager: Joy Gerttula. **Accommodations:** 6 rooms in lodge (one with private bath, others share 2 baths), 3 rooms plus bunkroom in cabin (share 2 baths). **Rates:** $130 (U.S.) per person; 30% discount in early May and after September 21; group rates available. **Included:** All meals and use of boats. **Minimum stay:** None. **Payment:** Major credit cards. **Children:** Under age 12, half-price. **Pets:** Allowed. **Smoking:** Allowed. **Open:** Mid-April to mid-October.

➤ **Three boats are available for saltwater fishing in the inlet, six boats for freshwater fishing in the lake behind Clowhom Dam. To fly-fish, go beyond the lake, up the Clowhom River.**

The west coast of mainland Canada is fringed with hundreds of inlets that reach east toward the mountains. One of them is Salmon Inlet, extending from Sechelt, 40 miles north of Vancouver, to Clowhom Lake. At the remote end of the inlet, between tree-covered hills and ridges, there are two signs of human habitation: a logging camp, bustling during the week and silent on weekends, and Clowhom Lodge.

There are no roads to the isolated lodge; you arrive by boat or seaplane. Clowhom's caretaker will bring a boat to pick you up at Poise Cove Moorage for the 23-mile ride up the inlet (there's an additional charge for this service).

The cedar-shake two-story lodge stands on a slope above the water, its pitched roof pierced by skylights and its windows overlooking a deck, lawn, fruit trees, and the original cabin — still used by guests — on the 23-acre property. Across the inlet is the logging camp, backed by steep, forested hills.

Despite its remote location, the lodge has every convenience. The kitchen has modern appliances, movies and a VCR are supplied, there's a wet bar, and rooms have queen-size beds. The guest rooms, four with private entrances to a patio, are on the lower level; they are furnished with firm beds, pine chests, and carpeting. Bathrooms contain tubs and showers; the fireplace suite has a private bath. Laundry facilities are provided. A cook on the premises prepares all the meals.

In the expansive living room, most of one wall is filled by a granite fireplace. There are foosball and bumper-pool tables, a stereo, and a long dining table of pine by windows that overlook the inlet.

Those who prefer something more rustic feel at home in the four-bedroom, tin-roofed cabin. It's simple, but it has character, with its stone fireplace, metal beds, slightly seedy furniture, and a fully equipped kitchen.

Although Clowhom Lodge is far off the beaten path, don't expect pristine wilderness here. The logging camp can be noisy, and a constant stream of smoke drifts down the canyon from the slash pile. The dam across the way and the occasional clearcut hillside are further reminders of human presence. But most people who come here simply want to fish. They get their gear together, take a boat out, and soon are surrounded by silence on limpid waters that reflect towering mountains.

Duncan

Fairburn Farm Country Manor

3310 Jackson Road
R.R. 7
Duncan, B.C., Canada V9L 4W4
250-746-4637

> **A classic working farm with hospitable hosts**

Proprietors: Anthea and Darrel Archer. **Accommodations:** 6 rooms . **Rates:** (Cd) $100–$135 single or double, $20 additional person, 10% discount for week-long stays. **Included:** Full breakfast. **Minimum stay:** 2 nights. **Payment:** MasterCard, Visa. **Children:** Welcome. **Smoking:** Outdoors only. **Open:** Easter to mid-October.

➤ **The Archers also have a self-contained cottage for rent ($750 per week for four), which has a kitchen with microwave and dishwasher.**

Here's an idyllic farm, reminiscent of a simpler day, on the east side of Vancouver Island, 5 miles from Duncan. When you're feeling nostalgic about rural joys or when you want the family to learn what country life is like, Fairburn Farm is the place to go. On its 130 acres are a 19th-century farmhouse and barn, organic vegetable gardens, a meandering stream, walking paths, and animals — sheep and lambs, cows, pigs, chickens, a horse, and a sheepdog.

Guests are invited to collect eggs, feed animals, and help gather the harvest from the garden and orchard. There are lambs to pet, a swing set and sandbox, kayaks by the creek, hiking trails, and, in winter, sleigh rides.

Anthea and Darrel, who have a blended family of six children, churn butter, grind wheat, and bake bread. The ham served at breakfast comes from pigs they raised, the milk, from their cows.

Theirs is a nonstop working farm, yet the Archers seem unhurried and are happy to stop and visit.

The white frame house, Darrel's home since his parents bought it in 1955, is aging gracefully. It has a welcoming verandah with a porch swing, two comfortable parlors with fireplaces, and a large dining room. On sunny mornings, light streams through the bay window and skylights in an addition, where tables are set for breakfast. As you might expect, meals are hearty. Range eggs, homemade berry jams, and teas from farm-grown herbs are a few specialties. The innkeepers have menus from nearby restaurants and will make dinner reservations for you.

The guest rooms in the old-fashioned, well-worn (but refurbished) house are light and airy, with long windows and high ceilings. The queen-size or twin beds are spread with flower-patterned quilts or crocheted coverlets. Two rooms have fireplaces and Jacuzzis.

Most rooms overlook the orchards, cornfields, or the yard, where linens flap on the clothesline, and the pasture, where the Morgan horse browses. In the distance are wooded hills and the Koksilah Mountains.

Grove Hall Estate

6159 Lakes Road
Duncan, B.C., Canada V9L 4J6
250-746-6152

| A secluded estate
overlooking a lake

Innkeeper: Judy Oliver. **Accommodations:** 3 rooms (1 with private bath) and cottage. **Rates:** (Cd) $135–$165 single, $155–$185 double. **Included:** Full breakfast in main house. **Minimum stay:** 2 nights in cottage. **Payment:** Cash or check. **Children:** Not appropriate. **Pets:** Not allowed. **Smoking:** Outdoors only. **Open:** Year-round.

➤   **The 1-bedroom cottage, tucked away beyond the secret garden, has a living room and kitchen and a touch of Art Nouveau in its furnishings.**

To reach Grove Hall, on the east coast of Vancouver Island, drive a lane bordered with chestnut trees, past meadows with grazing deer, until you reach the half-timbered inn that resembles an English manor house. It's surrounded by 17 acres of gardens and woodlands beside Quamichan Lake.

From the porte cochere, covered by a stained glass dome, you enter the foyer and remove your shoes. For the rest of your stay, you'll pad about the house in slippers provided by the innkeeper to protect the floors. Despite the classical formality of the turn-of-the-century mansion, with its antiques and Oriental carpets, the atmosphere is warm and casual.

Judy and Frank Oliver are world travelers and have filled their inn with exquisite furniture and art. Carved Chinese screens, delicate perfume bottles, elephant tables, and an antique French clock are among the items on the walls and mantels.

The least expensive room is the Siamese Suite, which has no lake view. It has twin beds, a private balcony, and white wicker furniture that lends a tropical touch. The Indonesian Suite, with a queen-size bed, is decorated with batiks and art objects from Indonesia. There's a private balcony, with a wide view of the grounds and lake. The Singapore Room features an antique carved and painted Chinese wedding bed, one of the many items Judy found when she was a nurse in Singapore.

The house the Olivers bought in the early 1980s was designed by the gifted architect Sam Maclure, whose distinctive style can be seen in many B.C. buildings. There are mullioned casement windows, tile fireplaces, a coffered ceiling, and a billiards room with an antique snooker table. (This room also has a piano, stereo, and TV.)

In the afternoon, Judy serves "tea and dainties," which might include a B.C. wine, matrimonial cakes, and macaroons. Fresh fruit and flowers are placed in all the rooms, and if it's your honeymoon you'll be given champagne. Breakfast is served at the time you request in the dining room, where Victorian lace curtains hang at windows that overlook the lawn and garden.

This peaceful, quiet retreat has a tennis court and walking paths that wind through the garden, trees, and crumbling grape arbor to the edge of the lake. Swans, geese, and bald eagles are frequently seen. Recommended restaurants nearby are the Inglenook and Quamichan Inn.

Grove Hall, 38 miles from Victoria, is a short distance from the Mill Bay ferry, which will take you to the world-famed Butchart Gardens, and the Crofton ferry, which sails to Salt Spring Island.

Gold Bridge

Tyax Mountain Lake Resort

Tyaughton Lake Road
Gold Bridge, B.C., Canada V0K 1P0
250-238-2221
Fax: 250-238-2528

A log lodge in the wilderness

President: Gus Abel. **Accommodations:** 29 rooms and 5 chalets. **Rates:** (Cd) Winter, rooms $96 single, $104 double, $20 additional person; chalets $180–$220. Summer, rooms $103 single, $115 double; chalets $250–$380 (up to 12 people). Packages available. **Minimum stay:** 2 nights. **Payment:** Major credit cards. **Minimum stay:** 2 nights. **Children:** Welcome. **Pets:** By prior arrangement, in winter only. **Smoking:** Allowed in designated areas. **Open:** Year-round.

➤ **Crisp, clear winter days combined with powder snow bring skiers who cross-country ski on groomed trails or go heli-skiing on 10,000-foot mountains.**

The lodge at Tyax Resort, said to be the largest log structure in western Canada, is deep in the wilderness but boasts first-class accommodations. Its spacious rooms have solid pine furniture and eiderdown quilts, balconies, and views of Tyaughton Lake and the Chilcotin Mountains. There are immense stone fireplaces, a dining room overlooking the lake and forest, a lounge and western-style bar, conference rooms, a sauna, and a children's playroom.

Tyax also offers five cozy log chalets, four with their own beach and 2 acres of woodland. They have three to six bedrooms, kitchens, and fireplaces. The largest chalet, behind the lodge, has a hot tub, laundry facilities, and a deck with a view of the lake.

The lodge is a 4-hour drive from Vancouver via Hurley Pass, which is open only in summer. The winter route is a 6-hour drive. Or you can go by train on B.C. Rail to Lillooet; the Tyax shuttle will pick you up. The fastest way is to take the lodge's airplane.

Outdoor recreation is constant all year round in this area, which is known for its sunny, dry weather. In summer, you can hike through lush alpine meadows, canoe or sail on the sparkling lake, play tennis, hunt for fossils, pan for gold, ride the trails on horseback. Try archery or trap-shooting, or take the floatplane into the mountains for a bird's-eye view of vast, ancient glaciers.

Nearby lakes and streams offer good fishing, and you can ride the floatplane to a remote lake filled with trophy-size rainbow trout. Tyaughton, which means "lake of the jumping fish," is virtually on your doorstep, and there's no charge to use a rowboat.

Winter recreation includes skiing, sleigh rides, sledding, and ice skating.

Some guests prefer to simply relax on the big sun deck. One of the main attractions of the lodge is its great variety. After the day's adventures, you might relax with a massage and a soak in the whirlpool tub before a hearty meal in the dining room. The chef prepares popular dishes such as baked ham with pineapple, stuffed roast turkey, prime rib, and B.C. salmon. He'll cook your own catch, if you prefer, or you can take your fish to the grill on the beach, where guests like to gather for music and singalongs.

Hatheume Lake

Hatheume Lake Resort

P.O. Box 490
Peachland, B.C., Canada V0H 1X0
250-767-2642

A fishing resort in the central B.C. wilderness

Innkeepers: Sean Imrie and Bev Davis. **Accommodations:** 6 cabins. **Rates:** (Cd) $110–$130 double, $15 per additional person; group and weekly rates available. **Minimum stay:** 2 nights. **Payment:** Major credit cards. **Children:** Under age 12, free. **Pets:** By arrangement. **Smoking:** Not allowed. **Open:** Year-round.

➤ **When you want a break from fishing, mountain bikes are available. You can go bird-watching, explore deserted homesteads, or listen to the call of the loons.**

The committed fisher is always ready to go far afield for a prime fishing spot. If it means staying in a comfortable cottage in a gorgeous mountain setting and meeting interesting people, in addition to battling the hefty Kamloops trout, so much the better. Flycasters don't hesitate to drive the bumpy road to Hatheume Lake — they know what awaits them.

The lake and resort lie on a high (4,600 feet) forested plateau between the Cascades and the Canadian Rockies, in the Okanagan country of south central B.C. The hand-hewn lodge and cluster of log cabins face sparkling Hatheume Lake, fringed by trees and filled with fish.

The resort changed owners in 1996. The new owners remodeled the cabins and installed modern appliances; guests now bring food and do their own cooking. Cabins have one or two bedrooms, decks, and views of the lake.

After a good night's sleep in the crisp mountain air, it's time to rent one of the resort's boats and go in search of the spirited Kamloops. This strain of rainbow trout is strong, grows rapidly, and does not surrender without a fight — an irresistible combination to fishers in search of action. Fly-fishing at this resort is unusual, perhaps unique. Guests have exclusive use of eight lakes, each with a pier and boats. Trucks transport guests to the various lakes. Hatheume, the largest lake, is strictly catch-and-release, but you may keep your limit from the other lakes. Your hosts have a fish table where you may clean your catch for a fresh trout dinner.

In the winter, you can go ice-fishing, skiing, and snowmobiling.

Hornby Island

Sea Breeze Lodge

Big Tree 3-2
Hornby Island, B.C., Canada V0R 1Z0
250-335-2321
Fax: 250-335-2321
seabreez@mars.ark.com

A quiet island getaway in the Georgia Strait

Innkeepers: Suzie and Steven Bishop. **Accommodations:** 14 cabins. **Rates:** (Cd) Summer: $92–$118 per person per day; children 13–17, $64; 7–12, $48; 2–7, $38; weekly rates available. Off-season: housekeeping cabins, $70–$116 double. **Included:** All meals in summer. **Minimum stay:** None. **Payment:** Visa, MasterCard. **Children:** Welcome. **Pets:** Not allowed. **Smoking:** Outdoors only. **Open:** Year-round.

➤ **Along the road, foxglove and lupine bloom beside neatly fenced orchards and farms. There are hiking trails in the woodlands and many artists' studios.**

To reach this lodge from the B.C. mainland, you have to take three ferry rides — one to Vancouver Island, a 10-minute ride to Denman Island, and another 10 minutes across the channel to Hornby Island. By the time you reach the north shore of Hornby, the cares of the world are far behind you.

The guest cabins lie on a broad swath of lawn on the 12-acre property. Some are separate units; others, duplexes. With light colors, modern furnishings, fireplaces (in a few), and plenty of windows, the lodgings offer cheery accommodations. Families return year after year, and sometimes their children grow up to join the staff.

Eagle's Nest is the most private cottage, tucked off to the side under arbutus and fir trees. The view from the deck is stunning.

A glass-paneled, tile and cedar room with a hot tub is perched at the edge of the bluff. It's open to guests who like to soak while they gaze at the seascape below.

Meals, served in the dining room of the main house, have achieved a fame of their own. In this room of old oak, with its stone fireplace and comfy couches, guests gather to sip chablis and eat oysters on the half-shell, and then to feast on Suzie's Madras curry, salmon, turkey, and beef dinners. If you collect and shuck oysters or clams, she will prepare them. Children eat at 5:30 and adults at 7 P.M.

Lunch might be quiche or chili or a picnic packed for hikers. All breads are homemade. In the spring and fall the dining room is open for dinners on Friday and Saturday and for Sunday brunch.

Activities at Sea Breeze include playing tennis on a grass court, kayaking, and hiking up Mount Geoffrey or in Helliwell Provincial Park, at the northeastern tip of the island.

Kaleden

Ponderosa Point Resort

Box 106
Kaleden, B.C., Canada V0H 1K0
250-497-5354

A cluster of cottages overlooking a lake

Innkeepers: Peter and Jean Spooner. **Accommodations:** 26 cottages. **Rates:** (Cd) Summer, $895–$1,290 per week, 2–6 people; spring and fall, 25% off. **Minimum stay:** 1 week in summer, 3 days other seasons. **Payment:** No credit cards. **Children:** Welcome (cribs available). **Pets:** Not allowed. **Smoking:** Outdoors preferred. **Open:** May through October.

➤ **The Okanagan country is rich in fertile valleys, clear lakes, and frontier history, with museums to tour, wines and peaches to taste, and water sports.**

Snug log cabins and A-frames stand under tall pines on the shore of Skaha Lake in the Okanagan, a few miles south of Penticton. There are 6 acres of landscaped grounds, and every cabin has a view of the lake.

Named for regional trees (Fir, Hawthorne, Cedar, Elm, Dogwood), the cabins have one, two, and three bedrooms. All contain sturdy furniture of good quality and well-equipped kitchens. Everything in them is spotlessly clean and polished to a shine. The staff does not enter the cottages once they're occupied, though clean linens are supplied after a week's stay.

Although the resort is jumping with activities in summer, it's a quiet place, largely because cars park near the road, not by the cabins. You can relax on your private deck and enjoy the serene setting, reserve tennis courts (lighted at night), rent a canoe, go water skiing, or take the resort's rowboat or paddleboat out. There's a playground, and children's supervised events include a weekly video night, hot dog and marshmallow roasts, and games in the park.

Kelowna

Hotel Eldorado

500 Cook Road Kelowna, B.C., Canada V1W 3G9 250-763-7500 Fax: 250-861-4779	**A lakeside hotel with a deco flavor**

Owner: Jim Nixon. **Accommodations:** 20 rooms. **Rates:** (Cd) $125–$165 single or double, rates vary seasonally. **Minimum stay:** None. **Payment:** Major credit cards. **Children:** Not appropriate. **Pets:** Not allowed. **Smoking:** Allowed. **Open:** Year-round.

➤ **Pioneer Market Country Store is an old-fashioned Kelowna market, with jams, wine jellies, grapevine wreaths, pies, and local handicrafts.**

In 1926, an Austrian countess had an English Tudor hotel built on the shore of Okanagan Lake. The Eldorado Arms became a landmark, but in 1989 was threatened with destruction. To save it, Jim Nixon had it floated by barge to a new site a quarter of a mile away. Once in place, it burned to the ground.

Still, the dream didn't end. A new hotel was put up on the site, this one a small, elegant country inn that savors the old while embracing the new. Its rooms contain period pieces from the 1930s along with today's hair dryers, telephones, and television. Most have queen-size beds. The best views are on the lake side of the three-story, salmon-colored stucco building.

There's a deco touch in the lounge on the main floor, with its black tiled fireplace, curved bar, and colorful oil paintings of seaside scenes. The dining room, above the boardwalk and lake, emphasizes seafood prepared with imagination (prawns with papaya, salmon fillet with saffron sauce) as well as standard beef, chicken, and lamb. For dessert, you'll be tempted by homemade Italian ge-

```
           THE HOMING INSTINCT
           1622 QUEEN ANNE AVE N
           SEATTLE        WA 98109


DATE: 05/21/00
MERN: 342600128348            TERM: 0001
           S-A-L-E-S  D-R-A-F-T


REF= 0002   BCH= 949
CD TYPE= VI
TR TYPE= PR
AMOUNT:                  $186.79


ACCT: 4673064911654014    EXP: 0601
AP:   021334
NAME: JAY A          LEVINGER
   CARDMEMBER ACKNOWLEDGES RECEIPT OF
  GOODS AND/OR SERVICES IN THE AMOUNT OF
   THE TOTAL SHOWN HEREON AND AGREES TO
 PERFORM THE OBLIGATIONS SET FORTH BY THE
 CARDMEMBER'S AGREEMENT WITH THE ISSUER
        THANK YOU FOR USING VISA


X_____
 TOP COPY-MERCHANT BOTTOM COPY-CUSTOMER
```

lato and a palette of pastries made by the award-winning pastry chef.

There are two golf courses nearby. In Kelowna you can tour the buildings of the early settlement at Pandosy's Museum, cruise on the *Fintry Queen* paddlewheeler, visit the B.C. Orchard Industry Museum, and attend performances by the Okanagan Symphony Orchestra and Sunshine Theatre.

Ladner

River Run Floating Cottages

4551 River Road West
Ladner, B.C., Canada V4K 1R9
604-946-7778
Fax: 604-940-1970
riverrun@direct.ca

Private homes on the water

Proprietors: Bill and Janice Harkley and Terry and Deborah Millichamp. **Accommodations:** 4 cottages. **Rates:** (Cd) $90–$150 double, $20 additional person; reduced rates January–March. **Included:** Full breakfast. **Minimum stay:** None. **Payment:** MasterCard, Visa. **Children:** Not appropriate. **Pets:** Not allowed. **Smoking:** Outdoors only. **Open:** Year-round.

➤ **Ladner offers a waterfowl refuge and an excellent French restaurant, La Belle Auberge. Uncle Herbert's is very British, serving good fish 'n' chips; Sharkeys is known for seafood and generous portions.**

South of Vancouver, where the fingers of the Fraser River spread to form a broad delta, the River Run cottages offer unusual and delightful lodgings. One is the Waterlily, a floating cottage, or houseboat, with flower-filled window boxes and a private deck. Inside, it's a snug room with a wood-burning stove, skylights, a little galley with a hot plate and toaster oven, and a bench by windows overlooking the river and a wooded island.

The atmosphere is warm, with exquisitely crafted woodwork in teak, mahogany, bird's-eye maple, and yellow cedar. There's a built-in aquarium, a loft with a bed by a round stained glass window, and a roomy bath in white tile. This is an idyllic getaway for two.

Cross over the bridge and you reach the Northwest Room, which has a fireplace, a four-poster log bed, and French doors that open to a deck. The Keepers Quarters also has a fireplace, along with a handmade driftwood bed and a Jacuzzi.

The Net Loft is a suite with a spiral staircase leading to a loft bedroom containing a peeled log four-poster bed. There are skylights and views of the river, a kitchenette with a microwave oven, and an immaculate bath in white tile and bright florals. Outside on the deck is a Japanese style two-person soaking tub. Finally, the River Room is a quaint, cozy hideaway with a deck by the river. All the cottages have phones, refrigerators, and CD players. Wood for the stoves is provided and breakfast is delivered at the time you request.

The personable owners will lend a boat if you want to paddle on the river or a bicycle if you'd like to explore the area. Ask them about the shortcut to the ferry landing for Vancouver Island; you can ride there in 20 minutes, take your bike on board the ferry, and spend a day bicycling on Vancouver Island or one of the Gulf Islands.

Ladysmith

Yellow Point Lodge

Yellow Point Road
R.R. 3
Ladysmith, B.C., Canada V0R 2E0
250-245-7422
Fax: 250- 245-7411

**A waterside retreat on
Vancouver Island**

Innkeeper: Richard Hill. **Accommodations:** 52 rooms (some with private baths, some shared). **Rates:** (Cd) $110–$177. **Minimum stay:** 2 nights on weekends, 3 nights on holiday weekends. **Included:** All meals and activities. **Payment:** MasterCard, Visa. **Children:** Age 16 and older welcome. **Pets:** Not allowed. **Smoking:** Allowed in designated areas only. **Open:** Year-round.

➤   **In the evenings, new friends sing around the campfire, play table tennis, or gather in the big lounge to play cards, board games, and darts.**

About 60 years ago, an extraordinary lodge opened at the tip of a peninsula on the east coast of Vancouver Island. It was built of hand-hewn logs by Gerry Hill, a World War I veteran who dreamed of such a place while he was imprisoned overseas. When he returned home, Gerry created Yellow Point, a retreat that quickly gained a dedicated following.

In 1985, the great lodge burned to the ground, leaving only the massive stone fireplace. The ashes had hardly cooled when reconstruction began and, with the help of a volunteer organization, Friends of Yellow Point, a replica of the original went up and opened a year later. A few modernizing changes were made, but the distinctive character remained.

Shaded by arbutus trees, the lodge hugs a mass of sloping sandstone and faces a panorama of the Strait of Georgia, tree-covered islands, and snow-peaked mountains. It's at the edge of 180 acres of forest and meadow, an island wilderness inhabited by deer and squirrels and eagles.

On the grounds you'll find a 200-foot saltwater swimming pool built against rock, two tennis courts, a horseshoe pit, a copse-sheltered hot tub and sauna, and miles of paths winding through the woods and by the water. Scattered about the property are several cabins, some with all the usual conveniences and others rustic (no running water; outdoor toilets and showers). The most ram-shackle cabins (used only in summer) are always reserved months in advance, probably because they are quaint and inexpensive and they stand directly on the beach, with nothing to interrupt the stunning scenic views.

If you stay in the lodge, request a room on the water side so you'll have a view and avoid the sound of vehicles on the gravel road.

Eating is a communal affair, in the dining room or outdoors. Three hearty meals, morning and evening snacks, and afternoon tea guarantee that you'll never go hungry. Wine can be purchased at the lodge office.

Madeira Park

Lowe's Resort

P.O. Box 153
Madeira Park, B.C., Canada V0N 2H0
604-883-2456
800-870-9055
Fax: 604-883-2474

A bayside resort that's a family favorite

Proprietors: Davina and Reg Morton. **Accommodations:** 17 rooms and cottages. **Rates:** (Cd) $75–$95 double, $10 additional person, $5 ages 6–12. **Minimum stay:** None. **Payment:** MasterCard, Visa. **Children:** Under age 5, free with parents. **Pets:** Not allowed. **Smoking:** Allowed. **Open:** Year-round.

➤ **Fishing licenses, bait, and equipment are sold in the tackle shop, which also has divers' tanks and weight belts to rent.**

On B.C.'s Sunshine Coast north of Vancouver, nestled against the protected shore of Gerran's Bay, Lowe's Resort offers an array of activities that almost guarantees a satisfying family vacation. Thirty rental boats, from 9.9 to 70 horsepower, lie at the marina, ready to be taken out on fishing trips in Pender Harbour and beyond. There are canoes, kayaks, a small sandy beach, and rocky coves and inlets to explore. You can swim in the enclosed harbor, where a mermaid reposes. Similar to the Hans Christian Andersen mermaid of Copenhagen, she's most visible at low tide.

Guided fishing trips and charters are available. Steve Morton, the innkeepers' son, has been fishing these waters since he was three years old and often takes guests out to fish for salmon, lingcod, flounder, and snapper. Or you can dangle a line from the wharf and catch piling perch.

Youngsters like the sand castle contests and summer Fun Days, when games and face painting and other activities take place. And when they tire of digging in the sand and clambering over rocks, there's a playground at a nearby school.

Lodgings, scattered under the hemlock trees, have one, two, and three bedrooms. They vary from adjoining motel units to trim blue and white cottages with hanging flower baskets. They're simply furnished, with paneled walls and a twin or double bed in each bedroom. All have kitchens and access to a laundromat. Camping facilities are also available.

You're welcome to use the barbecue pit, which is surrounded by benches, flower boxes, and cedar trees. Geese wander up and down the grassy slope, apparently as happy as the guests are to be in such a pleasant spot.

Malahat

The Aerie

P.O. Box 108
Malahat, B.C., Canada V0R 2L0
250-743-7115
Fax: 250-743-4766

| An elegant villa on Vancouver Island |

Innkeepers: Leo and Maria Schuster. **Accommodations:** 23 rooms. **Rates:** (Cd) Summer, $195–$395; winter, $150–$295. **Included:** Full breakfast. **Minimum stay:** None. **Payment:** Major credit cards. **Children:** Not appropriate. **Pets:** Not allowed. **Smoking:** Not allowed. **Open:** Year-round.

➤ **Leo's culinary skills have established the Aerie as a trustworthy place for fine dining, while Maria's gracious welcome makes visitors feel at home.**

High on a wooded hill above Malahat Summit, 30 miles north of Victoria, the Aerie is one of British Columbia's most luxurious, romantic lodgings. With a white stucco exterior and red tile roof, it resembles a Mediterranean villa, but the spectacular view is purely Canadian. Almost every window overlooks a panorama of forested hills and valleys, Finlayson Arm, and the Strait of Juan de Fuca, with Washington's Olympic Mountains on the far horizon.

Leo Schuster says the view reminds him of his native Austria, but here it's more expansive — and has the ocean. The Schusters brought years of experience to their guesthouse, which opened in 1991. Leo is a classically trained chef; Maria managed hotels in Europe and owned and ran an exclusive resort in the Caribbean.

Fifteen acres of trees, wildflowers, and inviting paths surround the Aerie. Inside, on the main floor, is a small parlor, a conference room overlooking a pond and waterfall, and a restaurant that earns rave reviews. The menu changes every few days; entrées include black tiger prawns, roasted duckling with scented geranium glaze, and grilled medallions of veal with red onion marmalade. Black porcelain on white linen, fresh flowers, a crackling blaze in the fireplace, and a pianist playing light classics create an elegant ambience.

The dining room, recently expanded, is open daily and breakfast is served here. Fruits and berries, cereals, and scrambled eggs with salmon are typical dishes. Lunch is available for guests.

The rooms are decorated in pastels and furnished in several styles. There are Victorian white iron and brass beds, hand-carved furniture with multicolored designs, Chinese carpets, and plush, deco chairs. Some rooms have private Jacuzzis and reading nooks. The most opulent have fireplaces, covered balconies, king-size beds, and windows that frame stunning views.

The rooms do not have TV, and writing space is limited. This is a place for romance rather than work, but it is a good spot for an executive retreat or seminar. Guests are welcome to use the hot tub, sauna, and exercise room. The inn's little chapel next door is a popular spot for weddings.

What you'll find at the Aerie is European attention to detail and impeccable service, with the warmth of innkeepers who love their work.

Mayne Island

Fernhill Lodge

C-4, RR 1, Fernhill Road
Mayne Island, B.C., Canada V0N 2J0
250-539-2544
Fax: 250-539-2544

| **A hilltop home on a pastoral island**

Innkeepers: Mary and Brian Crumblehulme. **Accommodations:** 7 rooms. **Rates:** (Cd) $75–$124 single, $90–$149 double, $20 additional person, $15 ages 5–12. **Included:** Full breakfast. **Minimum stay:** None. **Payment:** MasterCard, Visa. **Children:** Under age 5 free. **Pets:** Allowed by arrangement. **Smoking:** Not allowed. **Open:** Year-round.

➤ **Fortunately for visitors, the Crumblehulmes have chosen to share their interests: history, cooking, gardening, and innkeeping.**

The Crumblehulmes, who have lived on this beguiling island since 1978, know its every lane, nook, and corner and can pull out a map and mark the best beaches and walking paths. But, they remind you, "Mayne is not a place to do, it's a place to be."

Their hilltop lodge is the perfect spot to do nothing but relax. You can walk the paths through the gardens, under arbors and trellises, to a stone bench at cliff's edge, watch eagles soar and swallows swoop; play Medieval Skittles; or sit in the swing on the deck. The herb gardens are among the most extensive in B.C. From them come the piquant flavors that enhance Fernhill's famous dinners (by reservation).

Guest room themes carry out their names: Jacobean Room holds 17th-century furniture, Colonial Room has a four-poster bed and plank floors, French Provincial Room contains gilded white furnishings, and Japanese Room has tatami mats and a serene, timeless mood.

Mary and Brian have a library of books on herbs, games, bicycles to lend, and a light-filled sun room. Their extensive breakfast menu includes juice, hot scones and muffins with jam, and omelets.

Oceanwood Country Inn

630 Dinner Bay Road
Mayne Island, B.C., Canada V0N 2J0
250-539-5074
Fax: 250-539-3002
oceanwood@gulfislands.com

| **A secluded island haven** |

Innkeepers: Marilyn and Jonathan Chilvers. **Accommodations:** 12 rooms. **Rates:** (Cd) Summer, $130–$295; spring and fall, $120–$275. **Included:** Full breakfast. **Minimum stay:** 2 nights on weekends. **Payment:** MasterCard, Visa. **Children:** Under age 16, not appropriate. **Pets:** Not allowed. **Smoking:** Not allowed in rooms or dining room. **Open:** March through November.

➤ **Miners Bay, the island's main town, has stores and eateries. Check Island Cottage for gift items, quilts, china, and twig furniture. At Spring-water Lodge, enjoy a view of the water with your lunch.**

One of the Gulf Islands sprinkled across the Strait of Georgia, peaceful, pastoral Mayne Island lies 10 miles southwest of B.C.'s mainland. Just 4 miles long, Mayne offers a restful retreat when you're looking for country walks and pretty beaches.

Oceanwood is a haven befitting the relaxed island character. It opened in early 1990, when the Chilverses left the advertising and public relations world in Vancouver to realize their dream of running a country inn. Their Tudor estate, originally built by a sea captain, stands on 10 acres of wooded and landscaped grounds at the edge of a cove overlooking Navy Channel. Grapevines and wisteria clamber over the long arbor at the entrance, where a circular driveway rings a group of London plane trees.

The inn's common rooms include a living room with a fireplace, a Games Room, and a library that shares a double-sided fireplace with the adjacent Garden Room. Oceanwood has gained renown for its restaurant. The 30-seat dining room, overlooking the water through four sets of French doors, serves a four-course dinner nightly. It features Northwest-style cookery and a West Coast wine list. Oceanwood guests receive a hearty breakfast of fruit, home-made granola, yogurt, and a main dish such as an omelet or sour-dough pancakes with prosciutto and melon. Afternoon tea is served in the Games Room.

The guest rooms, each named for a local flower or bird, are in the main house and new wing. Daffodil, the least expensive, is the only one without a water view; it overlooks the garden. It's sunny in yellow and white, with a skylighted bathroom. Rose Room contains a whirlpool tub from which you can watch the firelight flicker in the marble fireplace. Ivy and Iris have fine ocean views, and Geranium boasts a rooftop deck with a soaking tub. Most rooms have queen-size beds; one has twins. Wisteria Suite is a de-luxe accommodation with French doors opening onto decks and spectacular views down Navy Channel. There's a sunken living room with a fireplace and daybed. All the rooms include good lighting, extra pillows, fluffy robes, and easy chairs. Eight rooms have fireplaces and nine have soaking or jetted tubs.

The Chilverses have incorporated facilities for small conferences into their inn, which is a 5-minute drive from the ferry landing.

Merritt

Corbett Lake Country Inn

P.O. Box 327
Merritt, B.C., Canada V1K 1V8
250-378-4334

A rustic country hideaway by the lake

Innkeeper: Peter McVey. **Accommodations:** 3 lodge rooms, 10 cottages. **Rates:** (Cd) Cottages, $87–$100 per person; lodge rooms, $66–$76 per person. **Included:** Full dinner; breakfast for lodge room guests. **Minimum stay:** None. **Payment:** Visa. **Children:** Under age 9, half price. **Pets:** Allowed on leash. **Smoking:** Allowed. **Open:** May to mid-October, and December 24 to January 5.

➤ **Peter McVey custom-designs bamboo fly rods, an art he learned in England. "Making fly rods by hand is like resurrecting a dinosaur," he says.**

This sturdy, red-trimmed log lodge, set among aspens on sloping green lawns, has been a popular hideaway for years. A short distance off the Coquihalla Highway in south-central B.C., it's a 3-hour drive from Vancouver. Those who appreciate the joys of fly-fishing, bird-watching, and fine cuisine return regularly.

When Peter McVey came to Canada from England, where he'd been chef to the Lord Mayor of London, he wanted to operate a guest house where visitors could enjoy a wilderness experience and dine as well as his former employer had. Twelve miles south of Merritt, Peter found 305 acres that had a crumbling lodge and two overfished and stagnating lakes. He restocked the lakes with rainbow trout, remodeled the lodge, and began serving memorable meals.

The set-menu dinners draw praise from gourmands. They're included in the room rate and available to others by reservation for $35 (Cd.). On a typical evening you might be served vichyssoise, coquilles St. Jacques, rack of lamb, and oranges Grand Marnier; and you can choose from several European, Australian, and American wines. Breakfasts ($8.50) are feasts that fortify you for a hard day's fishing, hiking, or watching for the elusive mountain bluebird.

In the wide-windowed dining room that overlooks lawn and lake, antlers and a cougar skin hang on one wall, while brilliantly colored pheasants decorate another. Fishing creels and hand-tied flies with evocative names like Golden Demon, Ratface McVey, and McLeod Ugly attest to the owner's outdoor interests.

Fly-fishing only is the rule on McVey's two lakes. Motors aren't allowed, nor are campers or trailers. Rowboats are available for $22 a day.

Each of the cedar cabins overlooks a pristine lake. They're furnished with braided rugs and kitchens, and some have stone fireplaces. The lodge rooms (with no kitchen) are simple but comfortable, befitting a rustic hideaway. Daily maid service is provided.

Mill Bay

Pine Lodge Farm

3191 Mutter Road
Mill Bay, B.C., Canada V0R 2P0
250-743-4083
Fax: 250-743-7134

A peaceful country home filled with antiques

Innkeepers: Cliff and Barbara Clarke. **Accommodations:** 7 rooms. **Rates:** (Cd) $80–$90 single or double. **Included:** Full breakfast. **Minimum stay:** None . **Payment:** MasterCard, Visa. **Children:** Over age 7, welcome. **Pets:** Not allowed. **Smoking:** Not allowed. **Open:** April–October.

➤   **At the end of May, Mill Bay celebrates with a foot-stomping Country Music Festival and Jamboree, which includes fiddlers, square dancers, and cloggers.**

Entering this bed-and-breakfast on a hill in the countryside north of Victoria is like stepping into an antiques shop — not a surprise, since the Clarkes are collectors and once owned a shop. Their 6,000-square-foot home, designed and built by Cliff, is full of furniture from several periods and places; polished antiques from England mix with rustic pieces and walls of rough pine.

Red velvet couches on Oriental carpets face the massive stone fireplace in the living room, a large open space with a piano, an organ, shelves of whiskey bottles and Toby jugs, a wooden gramophone, and a tea cart with delicate china, among many other items. The bedrooms, off the loft above the main room, are furnished with antique armoires and bedsteads and old English prints. Those facing Satellite Channel have the best views, looking past the deck and red bark of madrone trees to the waters traversed by ferries from Vancouver. The silence is palpable; you are virtually guaranteed a peaceful night.

Breakfast, prepared by your ebullient host, is eaten in the dining room, where a butter churn, spinning wheel, woodstove, and pewter collection set the tone of a farm of long ago. Cliff cooks brown eggs, fresh from the henhouse, in any style requested and presents them with bacon or sausage, hotcakes, and berries picked by Barbara.

The landscaping of the 30-acre property is a major attraction. There are colorful flower beds, trout ponds, walking paths that descend to lovely woods, and fields where deer graze and cats and a dog gambol.

There's a golf course nearby, and fishing charters are available at Cowichan Bay. Most visitors, Cliff says, just want to walk, look at the view, and rest.

Come to Pine Lodge if you love antiques and want to be close to Victoria but stay in the country (the city is a 40-minute drive away).

Nanoose Bay

Pacific Shores Nature Resort

1655 Strougler
R.R. #1, Box 50
Nanoose Bay, B.C., Canada V0R 2R0
250-468-7121
Fax: 250-468-2001

A time-share resort on Vancouver Island

Owners: Susan and Andrew Pearson. **Accommodations:** 55 condos. **Rates:** $60–$260, 2–8 people; $15 additional adult; rates vary seasonally. **Minimum stay:** 2 nights on weekends preferred. **Payment:** Major credit cards. **Children:** Under age 16, $10 per night. **Pets:** Not allowed. **Smoking:** Allowed. **Open:** Year-round.

➤ **The Eco-Med Wellness Spa & Clinic at Pacific Shores offers mud baths, body wraps, and various naturopathic treatments.**

The only vacation-ownership resort on Vancouver Island, Pacific Shores is on a peninsula that juts into Craig Bay, 100 miles north of Victoria. Most of the units in the gray two-story buildings have views of the sea or estuary and are scattered over 18 acres, with part of the property beautifully landscaped and part left in a natural state. The owners, committed to protecting the environment, consulted with an expert on plant and animal preservation when they built the resort in 1990; the result is a harmonious blend of attractive buildings, native vegetation, and open space for wildlife habitat. The bay is frequented by seals, sea lions, and orca whales, and a section of the peninsula is a bird refuge. Some 250 species of birds fly through or live in the area.

The condos, tastefully furnished and roomy, have one or two bedrooms, sitting and dining areas, and full kitchens. Most units have a double-sided gas fireplace in the master bedroom and a Jacuzzi in the bath.

In this parklike setting, paths wind over lawns, under cedar and Douglas fir trees, and along a pebbled beach to a gazebo and hot tub with a view across the water to Rath Trevor Provincial Park. Five golf courses are within a 20-minute drive of the resort, and many water activities are available, including windsurfing, canoeing, kayaking, fishing, sailing, and scuba diving.

Parksville

Bayside Inn

P. O. Box 1720
240 Dogwood Street
Parksville, B.C., Canada V9P 2H5
250-248-8333
800-663-4232
Fax: 250-248-4689

A full-service resort on the Vancouver Island shore

Manager: Lou Roelofsen. **Accommodations:** 59 rooms and suites. **Rates:** (Cd) Summer, $109–$149; winter, $99–$109 double; $10 additional person; suites $155–$185; tour and group rates available. **Minimum stay:** 3 nights on holidays. **Payment:** Major credit cards. **Children:** Under 12, free with parents. **Pets:** Small dogs allowed. **Smoking:** Nonsmoking rooms available. **Open:** Year-round.

➤ **The Parksville area is known for its scenic hiking trails. Most famous is the path up 6,000-foot Mount Arrowsmith. Other paths lead to Little Qualicum Falls and Englishman River Falls.**

When the Bayside opened in 1985, tourism in the Parksville area promptly increased. The easy location was ready for a resort that would appeal to travelers seeking a bit of luxury during their visit to Vancouver Island's east coast. Parksville is a half-hour's drive from the ferry at Departure Bay in Nanaimo and less than two hours from Victoria. If you fly in, the resort's van will pick you up at Qualicum Airport.

The Bayside specializes in packages (except during July and August). The Golf Getaway, for example, includes 18 holes of play at any of three golf clubs, two nights' lodging, two breakfasts and one dinner, one court time for racquetball or squash, and unlimited use of other recreational facilities (tiled indoor swimming pool, sauna, and weight room). There are also honeymoon, racquet court, and holiday packages.

All this takes place at a three-story hotel situated above a sandy beach, with a view over Parksville Bay to the Strait of Georgia and the mountains on the mainland. Many of the rooms have balconies with views; the honeymoon/executive suite has two. The suite also has a queen-size bed and wet bar. Other rooms are comfortable and well furnished, if not as spacious. Woods are light-toned and on the white walls hang tasteful seascapes and landscapes in shadowy pastels.

At Herons, Bayside's three-tiered restaurant, the fresh seafood is exceptional. Order Baby Coho Bayside, for example, and you'll be served two fillets of coho salmon stuffed with scallop mousse and spinach, all wrapped in pastry.

If you're feeling romantic, request a window table for two. The tables are in small alcoves that give a sense of seclusion as well as an enjoyable view of Parksville Bay. With dark green carpets and pillars on three levels, brass railings, and pink linens, Herons has an atmosphere of light sophistication. Music is played on Saturday nights and at Sunday brunch.

Tigh-Na-Mara

1095 East Island Highway
Parksville, B.C., Canada V9P 2E5
250-248-2072
800-663-7373

One of B.C.'s best seaside inns

Managers: Joe and Jackie Hirsch. **Accommodations:** 142 rooms and cottages. **Rates:** (CD) Summer and holidays, $94–$179 single or double; winter, $72–$139; $10 additional adult; $5 children. **Minimum stay:** 2 nights on winter weekends, 3 nights in summer and on holiday weekends. **Payment:** Major credit cards. **Children:** Under age 2, free with parents (cribs $4). **Pets:** Allowed in cottages except in July and August. **Smoking:** Allowed. **Open:** Year-round.

➤ **In your room is a booklet filled with information about scenic spots, golf courses, fishing charters, boat rentals, and art galleries.**

Tigh-Na-Mara is a Scottish Gaelic name meaning "house by the sea," appropriate for a resort that's snug against the shore on Vancouver Island's east coast. The first cottage, still on the property, was built in 1946. More were added over the years, and now it's a condominium resort with 25 cottages and numerous lodge rooms. Most rooms have water views.

The big log lodge holds a conference center and restaurant with a varied menu. Tigh-Na-Mara has an indoor swimming pool, a ten-person Jacuzzi, a tennis court, and barbecue grills. The well-designed condo apartments and log cottages are in groves of madrone (arbutus), alder, and fir trees, spread over 22 acres. Housekeeping units have kitchens and stone fireplaces. The one- and two-bedroom cottages, most with queen-size beds, are nestled in the forest, while Oceanside is a three-story log complex overlooking the water. It stands on a bluff above the pebbly beach.

On Oceanside's top floor, the carpeted rooms have both knotty pine and white walls, vaulted ceilings with log beams, and private balconies. In each, the hearth is laid with kindling and more firewood is stacked outside the door. These are among the touches that make Tigh-Na-Mara special and well-known for its hospitality.

A staircase leads down to the safe swimming beach. From here or from your own balcony you can watch the sun rise over the mountains on the mainland.

Pender Island

Cliffside Inn On-the-Sea

P.O. Box 50
Pender Island, B.C., Canada V0N 2M0
250-629-6691

> **A clifftop inn with a spectacular view**

Innkeeper: Penny Tomlin. **Accommodations:** 4 rooms and cottage (all with private bath). **Rates:** (Cd) Rooms: summer, $135–$195 single or double; winter, $110–$145; $25 additional person. Cottage: $100–$195. Reduced rates for longer stays. **Minimum stay:** 3 nights on holiday weekends. **Included:** Full breakfast. **Payment:** MasterCard, Visa. **Children:** Under age 16, not appropriate. **Pets:** Allowed by arrangement. **Smoking:** Outdoors only.

> ➤ **From the beach at the end of Gowlland Point Road, you may spot a pod of orca whales, arcing and diving as they swim past the cove.**

From almost every aspect of the Cliffside Inn, including the hot tub on the deck, the view is remarkable. Cliffside stands at the edge of a 100-foot cliff above the shore, overlooking Navy Channel, Mayne and Saturna islands, and Mount Baker on the U.S. mainland. Shorebirds and eagles are regular visitors, and a river otter nests at the base of the cliff.

Penny Tomlin's family has lived on this 3-acre oceanfront site for 80 years. There are large vegetable and herb gardens, a raspberry patch, and sweetly scented hawthorne and magnolia trees on the lawn. The setting is serene and private, and Penny works to keep it that way. She offers warm hospitality, seclusion, and luxurious amenities — an ideal combination for a romantic retreat.

Each guest room has individual charm, a private entrance, and a patio or deck. The Garden Fireplace Suite has a queen-size bed and a fireplace. Ocean Queen, the smallest room, has a brass bed with a down comforter. Channel View is the deluxe, secluded honeymoon suite, 9 feet from the edge of the cliff. With a country French theme, it has a fireplace, bar, refrigerator, and a private brick patio. In Rosehip Room, glass doors slide open to a lawn and patio. Edgewater Cottage, next door, has two bedrooms, a fireplace, a kitchen, and a grand view.

The front door of the inn, off a flower-filled porch, opens to a small foyer; beyond it lies the Cliffhanger Solarium, a glass-walled dining room where multi-course dinners are served three nights a week. Candlelight, soft music, a gentle fire, and a view of the sunset on Mount Baker add to the romance. The imaginative cuisine includes fresh vegetables and herbs, buttermilk biscuits, seafood, lamb, and quiche. When it comes to keeping her guests happy, nothing escapes Penny's notice. The cheerful innkeeper will see that you're picked up at the ferry landing if you're traveling on foot, arrange for low-cost boat or mountain bike rentals, and take care of your laundry if you're staying for three days or more.

Pender, a 90-minute ferry ride from Tsawassen, is known as the island of beaches. Ask Penny about nearby walking trails; she can direct you to several that lead to quiet beaches. Many of her guests are bicyclists, out to travel the level byways of Pender Island. When you return from a long day of activity, you can reserve a private session in the hot tub on the cliff, overlooking the water.

One of Cliffside's most popular packages is the Two-Day Escape, including two nights' lodging, two breakfasts, and a four-course dinner. The cost is $340–$530 for two.

Penticton

Clarion Lakeside Resort

21 Lakeshore Drive West Penticton, B.C., Canada V2A 7M5 250-493-8221 800-663-9400 Fax: 250-493-0607	**A lakeside resort designed for recreation**

Manager: David Prystay. **Accommodations:** 204 rooms, 10 suites. **Rates:** (Cd) Rooms, $80–$170 double; $15 additional person; suites, $192; rates vary seasonally. **Minimum stay:** None. **Payment:** Major credit cards. **Children:** Under age 16, free with parents. **Pets:** Small pets allowed ($20). **Smoking:** Most rooms nonsmoking. **Open:** Year-round.

➤ **The resort has a summer children's program of arts and crafts. Babysitting, children's clubs, and family tours are available.**

The Lakeside is a full-service resort on the shore of Lake Okanagan, in south-central B.C. All the rooms in the six-story hotel have patios or balconies, most with views of the 72-mile-long lake. Standard rooms are furnished in a comfortable, contemporary style; suites are supplied with extras such as refrigerators, robes, and oversize bathrooms. Most expensive are the executive suites, which feature additional amenities (Gucci toiletries, for example).

Lakeside's restaurant, the Okanagan Surf and Turf Co., is a casual dining spot behind glass block walls off the open, light lobby. It features steak, seafood, and pasta. Outside, on the terrace, grilled foods and light meals are served when the weather permits. Outdoor lunches are popular, since the Penticton area is sunshine country, claiming more sunny days per year than Los Angeles, Bermuda, and Tahiti. There's also a lounge, the Barking Parrot.

Recreation is the major draw here. In addition to the attractively tiled indoor swimming pool, there is a well-designed fitness center (with Nautilus equipment), a jogging track, shuffleboard, tennis courts, and a sandy beach. Volleyball and basketball are available. Four nearby golf courses allow the resort to offer several golf packages. The resort has a gift shop and hair salon.

These, plus touring wineries, boating, and aquatic sports keep visitors occupied. When you take the kids out on the lake, you can tell them to watch for the legendary serpent-monster, Ogopogo, said to reside deep in Okanagan's waters.

Quadra Island

April Point Lodge

P.O. Box 1
Campbell River, B.C., Canada V9W 4Z9
250-285-2222
888-334-3474
Fax: 250-285-2411

A top-quality fishing resort on an island

Innkeepers: The Peterson family. **Accommodations:** 38 rooms, suites, and guest houses. **Rates:** (Cd) $99–$395 double, $25 additional person; 50% discount October through April. **Minimum stay:** None. **Payment:** Major credit cards. **Children:** Under 16, free with a parent. **Pets:** Allowed (limited basis). **Smoking:** Allowed. **Open:** Year-round.

➤ **A unique aspect of Quadra Island is its native Kwakiutl Indian art.**

Since 1944, when the Petersons bought and developed 100 acres of land on this point of Quadra Island, off the east coast of Vancouver Island, those who know fishing and salmon have carved vacation trips around April Point.

You reach the lodge by ferry from Campbell River, a logging, fishing, and tourist town about 125 miles north of Nanaimo (where the ferry from Vancouver drops you). When you get to April Point, you quickly realize that this is pure luxury, though the atmosphere is informal. The waterfront property overlooks Discovery Passage to Vancouver Island and has a one-mile marina.

Phyllis Peterson and her two sons, Eric and Warren, have developed a full array of facilities to please both fishers and those in search of a relaxing getaway. Everything connected with April Point is of the highest quality: the accommodations, the food, and the friendly service. Expert guides are available to take you fishing in Boston Whalers. Fishers here reel in coho salmon and 20-pound chinook regularly.

The staff will freeze or cool your catch, can it or smoke it. You can have your salmon made into lox and packed in vacuum-sealed bags, or make a paper print of it, using a Japanese technique called *gyotaku.*

If you want to be near the boating action on the harbor, book a room in the lodge, which has four units upstairs and two downstairs. These rooms have kitchenettes with coffeemakers, toasters, and microwave ovens. The accommodations spread over the wooded grounds range from one-bedroom Harbour Studios to the secluded Deluxe Guest Houses, with one to five bedrooms. Northwest art graces the walls of the well-appointed rooms. Each has a satisfying view, most include fireplaces and sun decks, and a few have Jacuzzi tubs. One cedar suite with a panoramic view has a square grand piano in the living room.

Morning coffee is set out in the dining room and the menu offers a variety of breakfast fare. A box lunch will be packed upon request; if you're not fishing you might take a boat to a cove with a pebbled beach where you can watch bald eagles fly while you picnic. The resort has bicycles to rent.

The dining room, which overlooks flowers and lawn at the ragged shore edge, features fresh seafood every night, plus several other entrées. These are often classic standards like prime rib or lamb, and they're simply and perfectly prepared. Wine is available.

Tsa-Kwa-Luten Lodge

P.O. Box 460
Quathiaski Cove, B.C., Canada V0P 1N0
250-285-2042
800-665-7745
Fax: 250-285-2532

| **An impressive Native resort by Discovery Passage** |

Manager: Graeme Bryson. **Accommodations:** 29 rooms and 4 cabins. **Rates:** (Cd) $115–$450 single or double, $20 additional person; packages available. **Minimum stay:** None. **Payment:** Major credit cards. **Children:** Welcome. **Pets:** Not allowed. **Smoking:** Nonsmoking rooms available. **Open:** May to mid-October.

➤ **Quadra Island, a diver's heaven, has abundant marine and animal life; occasionally wolves and cougar are seen, and orca whales pass by.**

The Native people of Cape Mudge on Quadra Island, which is off the east coast of Vancouver Island, have created Canada's first resort based on Pacific Coast Indian traditions. Built of Douglas fir, the imposing lodge — the Big House — is in a 1,100-acre forest on bluffs overlooking Discovery Passage. Across the water is Campbell River, known as one of the world's greatest salmon fishing areas.

The Big House, built to represent Indian architecture of the past, contains the main foyer, an open lounge, an 80-seat restaurant, and most of the guest rooms. Walls of windows provide expansive views of the forest, mountains, and water.

Some of the spacious guest rooms have lofts and fireplaces; all have queen-size or twin beds, decks or patios, and views. The seaside cottages and the larger guest house, which has a Jacuzzi and fireplace, are popular with groups and those seeking more seclusion. There's also a small fitness facility with a sauna and Jacuzzi.

The resort's name comes from the ancient village site at Cape Mudge, Tsa-Kwa-Luten, meaning "gathering place" in Kwakwala. The Indians of the island were known for their hospitality and intend to maintain that reputation with their lodge. They offer fishing packages, with guides and equipment, and cruises around the outer islands where eagles, ospreys, sea otters, sea lions, and birds can be seen. Whale-watching, kayaking, hiking on the island trails, and beachcombing are also popular.

The most unusual aspect of the resort is its attention to coastal Indian culture. You're invited to visit nearby petroglyphs and purchase stone rubbings, and there's a remarkable collection of masks and ceremonial regalia in the Kwagiulth Museum in the village of Cape Mudge. Delicately carved masks, cedar baskets, and jewelry can be found in the resort's gift shop.

The restaurant, serving three meals a day, offers Continental fare. You can get to Tsa-Kwa-Luten by driving to Campbell River and taking the ferry to Quadra Island, or travel by seaplane from Seattle. Sound Flight (206-255-6500) offers direct service to the lodge dock.

Quilchena

Quilchena Hotel

Highway 5
Quilchena, B.C., Canada V0E 2R0
604-378-2611

A homey, old-fashioned inn on a cattle ranch

Innkeepers: Guy and Hilda Rose. **Accommodations:** 16 rooms (2 with private bath, others share 2 baths). **Rates:** (Cd) $69–$79 double, $8.50 additional person. **Minimum stay:** None. **Payment:** MasterCard, Visa. **Children:** Welcome (crib available). **Pets:** Not allowed. **Smoking:** Outdoors and in saloon only. **Open:** April to mid-October.

➤ **You can fish and sail on Nicola Lake, play tennis and golf, and trace the footsteps of early explorers and miners.**

In the dry, rolling hills of south-central British Columbia, 250 miles northeast of Vancouver, this 66,000-acre ranch has a history. It started in 1857, when three brothers from Grenoble, France, came to California to prospect for gold and followed the gold rush into Canada. They decided they might do better selling goods to other miners, so gradually the Guichon brothers invested in livestock and developed a major ranch. In 1906, one brother, Joseph Guichon, built a hotel on the ranch. A grand opening was held for the Quilchena in 1908, with a feast and all-night ball drawing visitors from miles around. Ever since, tourists have stopped for shelter and refreshment on their way through the province.

The gray and white inn is still part of a working cattle ranch, the largest in B.C. that takes in guests. Guy Rose, a Guichon descendant, updates the guest facilities now and then but maintains the Victorian atmosphere. The furniture in the parlor is dark and elaborately carved, with red velvet cushions. Long windows reach to high ceilings, a writing table stands in one corner, and sentimental 19th-century paintings hang on the walls. Flowers and candelabra stand on the piano, a clock ticks softly. It hasn't always been so peaceful here; note the bullet holes in the bar of the saloon next to the parlor.

Across the hall, the dining room has a calico touch, and the tables hold candles and wildflowers. Quilchena's restaurant is open to the public, serving three meals a day, with beef the main item on the menu.

Guest rooms, up the wide, branching stairway, overlook a neatly fenced yard, hills parched in summer, and a 9-hole golf course. Each room has a different antique decor and double or twin beds. The Ladies' Parlour also boasts a sun room with couch, wicker chairs, and views through windows on three sides. The Senator's Suite has two double beds and can hold up to four people.

The few bathrooms might be a problem for some guests, but the pace of life is so deliberately slow, no one seems to feel rushed about being first into the clawfoot tub. Most of the guest rooms have sinks.

Time stretches and takes on less importance here, though there is enough activity for guests. You can rent a bicycle, play tennis, and fish. Several horses are available for wrangler-guided riding in the hills.

Salt Spring Island

Hastings House

Box 1110
Ganges, B.C., Canada V0S 1E0
250-537-2362
800-661-9255
Fax: 250-537-5333
hasthouse@saltspring.com

| A luxurious country resort on an island |

Managers: Judith Hart and Mark Gattaes. **Accommodations:** 12 rooms and suites. **Rates:** (Cd) $255–$490 double, $80 additional person. **Included:** Full breakfast. **Minimum stay:** 2 nights on weekends. **Payment:** Major credit cards. **Children:** Age 16 and older, welcome. **Pets:** Not allowed. **Smoking:** Not allowed in dining room. **Open:** Mid-March to December.

➤ **The resort has a white shell beach and 1,000 feet of water frontage. In Ganges there are art galleries and, on Saturdays, a farmer's market.**

At the head of Ganges Harbour on Salt Spring Island, Hastings House stands on grassy, wooded slopes, a peaceful enclave of grace and tradition. Several handsome buildings, containing the guest rooms, are scattered over the resort's 20 acres of lawn, orchard, and forest.

The Manor House, on a bluff above the harbor, is a half-timbered lodge with climbing vines and roses that looks as if it belongs in Tudor England. In fact, it was built in 1942 by Warren Hastings as a duplicate of his 11th-century home in Sussex. Its atmosphere is enhanced by the 20-ton stone fireplace and leaded casement windows.

The inn's restaurant, open to the public, is on the first floor of The Manor House. Upstairs are two suites, each with two bedrooms, a fireplace, and a view of the harbor.

The Farm House in the meadow is one of the old homes on the island; the Hastings family lived there while building the Manor House. Now it has two parlor suites, each with a king-size bed in an upstairs bedroom and a queen-size sofa bed on the lower level. The suites, with two baths, open brick fireplaces, and wet bars, can hold up to four people.

The Post, a former Hudson's Bay trading post that was moved onto the property, is an individual cottage in the orchard, with a queen-size bed, a woodstove, and a wet bar. The Barn has four units on two levels, with varying views of the meadow, orchard, and sea. Greenhouse, on the ground floor, has a large, sunny living room with wicker furniture and plants.

The newest unit, tucked away in the forest against an ivy hillside above the harbor, has two apartments with views. Ivy, on the lower level, has a queen-size bed. Upstairs, two-bedroom Cliffside is considerably larger. Its contemporary furnishings, light and colorful decor, and kitchen make it popular as a business hospitality suite.

All the suites feature eiderdown quilts made on the island, oversize towels, fresh flowers, fireplaces laid with kindling, and private phones. An unusual touch typical of the resort's attention to detail is the personalized card on each door.

In this inn devoted to service, you'll receive all sorts of attention, from bed turndown and evening chocolates to elegant picnic baskets. Hastings House caters to small business groups, as well as individuals, and provides a meeting place in The Mews with audio-visual equipment.

Dinner, at $65 per person, is a major event. Jackets are required. First come aperitifs by the fire in the sitting room, and then you are seated in the dark-beamed dining room for one of the lodge's justly famed meals. The cuisine tends toward West Coast contemporary, with French and Asian influences. A full breakfast is served in the dining room.

Salt Spring, one of the Gulf Islands in the Strait of Georgia, offers many recreational possibilities. Sea kayaking and salmon fishing are popular, as are bicycling, tennis, and golf.

The Old Farmhouse

1077 North End Road
Salt Spring Island, B.C.
Canada V8K 1L9
250-537-4113

An old-fashioned country home

Innkeepers: Gerti and Karl Fuss. **Accommodations:** 4 rooms. **Rates:** $150 double, $30 additional person. **Included:** Full breakfast. **Minimum stay:** 2 days on holiday weekends. **Payment:** MasterCard, Visa. **Children:** Not appropriate. **Pets:** Not allowed. **Smoking:** Outdoors only. **Open:** Year-round.

➤ **Salt Spring is the most populated of the Gulf Islands, but it retains its rural ambience and woodsy charm. For a great view, hike up Mount Maxwell, an ideal spot for a picnic.**

The Old Farmhouse represents the best a bed-and-breakfast lodging has to offer, combining tradition with up-to-date flair. It has an idyllic location, with 3 acres of lawns, gardens, and old arbutus and fir trees. The Fusses love to pamper guests, and their breakfasts are known throughout the island for their size and quality.

Gerti's European background in the hotel and restaurant business is evident in the warmth and professionalism at the Old Farmhouse. This former cooking school teacher rises early to bake fresh croissants and muffins. When the aromas from the kitchen draw hungry guests, she and Karl serve such dishes as apple strudel, blueberry-stuffed nectarines, and crêpes with asparagus, ham, and tomato coulis.

The dining room and a cozy living room with a cushioned window seat in the bay window are in the original, century-old farmhouse. The guest rooms, with private entrances, are in a new wing. Each is named for its dominant color — blue, peach, pink, and rose. Bright fabrics, plenty of space, and private balconies or patios make these rooms especially inviting. They overlook daisy-starred lawns under the trees and hanging boxes filled with petunias.

The Old Farmhouse is a quiet country place, set back from the road near St. Mary Lake. Guests like to canoe on the lake, fish, bicycle, and visit the art galleries in Ganges. Tennis and golf are within walking distance.

Spindrift

255 Welbury Drive
Salt Spring Island, B.C.
Canada V8K 2L7
250-537-5311

A quiet resort at the water's edge

Innkeepers: Sharon McCollough and Maureen Bendick. **Accommodations:** 6 cottages. **Rates:** (Cd) Summer, $80–$165 double, $10–$20 additional person; winter, $75–$130. **Included:** Continental breakfast on first day. **Minimum stay:** 2 nights. **Payment:** Cash or check. **Children:** Not appropriate. **Pets:** Allowed (on leash) by prior arrangement. **Smoking:** Not allowed. **Open:** Year-round.

➤ **Bird-watchers come to spot some of the 200 species that fly through every year; the island is on the Pacific Flyway migratory path.**

On a secluded 6-acre point of land on Salt Spring Island, there's a place of quiet beauty, where people and other animals live in harmony. Every year deer come to a grove just a few yards from Spindrift's oceanfront cottages to bear their fawns. Rabbits bound through the bushes, otters play by the shore, seals and eagles are seen regularly, and whales are sighted occasionally. The human visitors tend to be peaceable, too, most of them looking for a relaxing few days in an out-of-the-way spot.

All the cottages are set above the water at cliff's edge; the rest of Welbury Point has been left in its natural state, with paths winding through the arbutus and fir trees to private white sand beaches and cozy coves. It's easy to launch a canoe or kayak, and clamming is excellent. The property faces 4,000 feet of waterfront.

The cottages all have sun decks, electric heat, carpeting, well-equipped kitchens, pottery and paintings by local artists, and fireplaces. Firewood is available for a nominal fee.

Each cottage is named for an admired woman: Amelia Earhart, Constance Litton, Charlotte Whitton, and the English suffragists Emily and Sylvia Pankhurst. Henrietta's Rose Cottage, honoring a Canadian heroine, is on a secluded quarter-acre. It has two bedrooms, one and a half baths, a living room with stone fireplace, and a 50-foot deck on the water.

Two log cabins were built by Sharon and Maureen with the aid of an instruction manual. The innkeepers, formerly in the mental health field in Vancouver, came to Salt Spring to try something different. Their strong interest in preserving the natural environment led them to create this retreat.

The Spindrift attitude is typified by the sign in the parking area: "Please check under your car for rabbits before leaving."

Weston Lake Inn

813 Beaver Point Road
Fulford Harbour, B.C.
Canada V0S 1C0
250-653-4311

A B&B estate at the south end of the island

Innkeepers: Susan Evans and Ted Harrison. **Accommodations:** 3 rooms. **Rates:** (Cd) $80–$100 single, $95–$115 double, $25 additional person; discounts for longer stays. **Included:** Full breakfast. **Minimum stay:** 2 nights on holiday weekends. **Payment:** MasterCard, Visa. **Children:** Over age 14, welcome. **Pets:** Well-behaved outdoor dogs allowed. **Smoking:** Not allowed. **Open:** Year-round.

➤   **For an exciting ride and views of the area from the water, ask Ted about a sailing charter on his 36-foot sloop, the *Malaika* (Swahili for "angel").**

This inn sits on a hillside above Weston Lake, at the southern end of Salt Spring Island in the Strait of Georgia. On the 10-acre farm, well-tended gardens provide the produce and fruit and berries for ample breakfasts; chickens supply the eggs. Breakfast is served in an antique-filled dining room.

The guest rooms, each with its own theme, are stylishly decorated and have queen-size beds. Sailboat, the smallest, has a brass bed and sailing photographs on the walls. Petit Point is named for Ted's finely detailed needlework on display. Heritage features Native art and is the only room that accommodates more than two people.

On the lower floor, guests like to gather in the sitting area, which has a fireplace, soft couches, books, a television and VCR, musical instruments from Zaire, and an array of information on the island. Sherry, tea, and coffee are served here, and there's a refrigerator guests may use. The favorite activities, though, are relaxing on the wisteria-draped terrace, strolling among the flowering trees, and soaking in the hot tub.

Sidney

The Latch Country Inn

2328 Harbour Road
Sidney, B.C., Canada V8L 2P8
250-656-6622
Fax: 250-656-6212
latch@leaphere.com

A timber lodge close to Swarz Bay

Innkeepers: Heidi and Bernd Rust. **Accommodations:** 5 suites. **Rates:** (Cd) Summer, $125–$155 single or double, less in other seasons. **Included:** Continental breakfast. **Minimum stay:** None. **Payment:** Major credit cards. **Children:** Welcome in one suite. **Pets:** Not allowed. **Smoking:** Not allowed. **Open:** Year-round.

➤ **Golf courses, a sailing marina, and the world-famed Butchart Gardens are a short distance from the inn.**

A well-known architect from Victoria, Sam Maclure, designed this lodge-like home in the 1920s as the summer residence of the lieutenant governor of British Columbia. Maclure was told to design "something unusual" from B.C. wood species. This unique home has hosted elegant parties and visiting royalty and now welcomes tourists; it was renovated in 1995 as an inn. The exterior is covered with fir slabs with the bark left on. Porches and balconies are made of tree trunks; it took ten men to raise the large bark-covered boards that conceal the eaves. Inside, the walls are paneled with fir and ornamental carvings from the main hall to the dining room.

Set at the edge of a marina and close to the Swarz Bay ferry landing on Vancouver Island, The Latch is a 25-minute drive from Victoria. On the main floor is a restaurant with views of the gardens and a terrace overlooking Van Isle Marina, the biggest yacht and sailing harbor on Vancouver Island. The popular restaurant is known for Continental cuisine with an Austrian influence; the Rusts came to Canada from Austria.

The suites, on the second floor, are individually decorated with Canadian furnishings and original art. They all have phones, TV, and a queen- or king-size bed. The Governor's Suite is the only one with an extra bed for a child. It also has the home's original bath, in black and white tile with a shower with ten nozzles. In the Maclure Room, hand-painted panels on the walls look like silk hangings. The Miraloma is the largest suite and has a fireplace with seating area and a balcony. A central common room on the second floor is reserved for guests, and breakfast is served here by the stone fireplace.

Sooke

Hartmann House

15262 Sooke Road
Sooke, B.C., Canada V0S 1N0
250-642-3761
Fax: 250-642-756

> **An enchanting cottage on an acre of gardens**

Innkeepers: Ray and Ann Hartmann. **Accommodations:** 3 rooms. **Rates:** (Cd) $100–$180 single or double. **Included:** Full breakfast. **Minimum stay:** None. **Payment:** Visa. **Children:** Not appropriate. **Pets:** Not allowed. **Smoking:** Not allowed. **Open:** Year-round.

➤ **The Good Life Bookstore and Café serves tasty meals in a casual, pleasant setting.**

The Hartmanns spent ten years renovating this English cottage and planting an acre of trees and flowers. Visitors who find this place, a 35-minute drive west from Victoria, are charmed by the results. The guest books gush with praise, for every visitor raves about the gorgeous garden, the hospitality, the food, and the extra attention to detail.

From the wide wooden gate, which marks the entrance, you walk up a path and stone steps, where herbs and flowers grow in profusion, to the kitchen door. Ray and Ann greet you warmly and show you past the hanging dried flowers to your room, where a tray of fruit, cheese, and a small bottle of champagne await. Ann will ask what you had for breakfast so it won't be repeated the next morning, and she'll show you the sitting room. This is a cozy room with walls lined with books, a piano, a snifter of brandy, and a fire laid in the huge stone fireplace.

The Bay Window Room and the Garden Room are in the main house, while the newer Honeymoon Suite is a separate cottage, tucked behind a rose arbor. The suite has a hand-hewn red cedar four-poster bed (made by Ray, an artist with wood), wicker chairs, a private courtyard, and a see-through brick fireplace. Breakfast is delivered to the cottage, and there's a microwave, bar sink, and refrigerator for storing drinks and picnics. If you're staying in the main house, you'll have breakfast at the kitchen table. Light streams through multi-paned windows as Ann serves homemade breads, blueberry pancakes, fruit, and other dishes.

Gardeners revel in strolling the paths and admiring the lily ponds, vine-covered trellises, fruit trees, colorful blooms, and water views. The kindness of the hosts, along with the mini-paradise they've created, makes this place extraordinary.

Ocean Wilderness Country Inn

109 West Coast Road
Sooke, B.C., Canada V0S 1N0
250-646-2116
800-323-2116
Fax: 250-646-2317

A seaside home with a garden setting

Innkeeper: Marion Rolston. **Accommodations:** 9 rooms. **Rates:** (Cd) $85–$175 single or double, $15–$25 additional person. **Included:** Full breakfast. **Minimum stay:** None. **Payment:** MasterCard, Visa. **Children:** Welcome. **Pets:** Allowed by arrangement. **Smoking:** Not allowed. **Open:** Year-round.

➤ **As part of the inn's focus on romance, Marion Rolston suggests that if you are visiting on your honeymoon or anniversary, you plant a Douglas fir memory tree on the property.**

This romantic inn overlooking the sea stands on five acres of forest, lawn, and gardens. A trail leads down from the bluff to a pleasant beach with tide pools and sandstone cliffs. In one corner of the property there's a hot tub in a Japanese gazebo; guests are invited to sign up for private time in the tub. Watching the sunset or moonlight on the water from this pretty spot ranks high in the romance category.

The suites have queen- or king-size canopy beds and down comforters, antiques, and views of the ocean or gardens. Several suites have skylights and balconies or patios. The rooms are comfortable, but they're not examples of contemporary luxury; rather, they have an eclectic mix of furnishings, like an old-fashioned country manor.

In the morning, coffee or tea are served at your door on a silver tray; breakfast follows half an hour later in your room or in the dining room. The log dining room is part of the original homestead, but the table is far from rustic. White linens, silver, and candles make the meal elegant. Breakfast might include an omelet, French toast, or homemade cinnamon rolls and jams.

Point-No-Point Resort

1505 West Coast Road, R.R. 2
Sooke, B.C., Canada V0S 1N0
250-646-2020

A complex of cabins with panoramic ocean views

Proprietors: Stu and Sharon Soderberg. **Accommodations:** 20 cabins. **Rates:** (Cd) $85–$160 double, $8 additional person. **Minimum stay:** 2 nights on weekends, 3 nights in summer and on holiday weekends. **Payment:** Major credit cards. **Children:** Welcome. **Pets:** Allowed ($5 per night). **Smoking:** Allowed. **Open:** Year-round.

➤ **Hardy hikers trek the famous West Coast Trail, which begins about 25 miles north of Point-No-Point. The challenging wilderness trail was first created as an escape route for survivors of shipwrecks. Allow 5 days for the hike; September is the best month to try it.**

On the far southwest coast of Vancouver Island, 15 miles west of the village of Sooke, Point-No-Point Resort stands on 60 acres of woodland, facing south to the Strait of Juan de Fuca. Point-No-Point, a surveyors' term, refers to the coastal outcropping that can be seen as a point of land from the west but not from the east.

The duplex, fourplex, and individual cabins and chalets in this pristine setting offer a retreat into a world of natural beauty far from the city's clamor. There are no televisions, radios, or telephones — nothing but the squirrels and birds and surf to disturb the quiet.

All the cabins have fireplaces, kitchens, and ocean views — some of them breathtaking. They range from a spacious two-bedroom, two-bath log cabin to a studio apartment. One pine-paneled bungalow, a remodeled bunkhouse, has a loft with a queen-size bed reached by a spiral staircase.

The cabins have a rustic quality, but they're well equipped, and daily maid service is provided. Some firewood is supplied, and more may be purchased at the office. The newest cabins have decks with Jacuzzis.

At the resort entrance, perched on the bluff, is the Tea House, one of the first restaurants in the area. Now operated by the Soderbergs, who have owned the resort since 1982, it offers light lunches, dinners, and traditional English tea. The room is small, the view immense.

Paths lead from the Tea House and the cabins through bracken eight feet tall and under the arching branches of alder trees to emerge at the edge of a cliff. If you continue down to a ravine and walk over the red bridge, high above the water to the glacier-scored basaltic cliffs, you may spot sea lions, otters, mink, whales, and cormorants.

There are several isolated beaches at the resort. One has a picnic shelter with a cooking spit. Picnicking, kayaking, and whale-watching are favorite activities among visitors, along with lounging on the beach with a book.

Sooke Harbour House

1528 Whiffen Spit Road
Sooke, B.C., Canada V0S 1N0
250-642-3421
800-889-9688
Fax: 250-642-6988
shh@islandnet.com

A luxurious and unique seaside inn on Vancouver Island

Innkeepers: Frederica and Sinclair Philip. **Accommodations:** 13 rooms. **Rates:** (Cd) $260–$360 double, $35 additional person. **Included:** Full breakfast and lunch. **Minimum stay:** None. **Payment:** Major credit cards. **Children:** Under age 12, free. **Pets:** Allowed (extra charge for large dogs). **Smoking:** Not allowed. **Open:** Year-round.

➤ **The inn's garden continually amazes visitors. From its tidy beds come 300 different vegetables and as many herbs and edible flowers, all used in the restaurant.**

"The best months to visit Vancouver Island are September and October," says Frederica Philip, an innkeeper of verve and charm. "But for the quietest getaway, come between November and April." The crowds at Sooke Harbour are gone then, but the views are just as wide and the cuisine as outstanding.

On the southwestern shore of the island, 23 miles from Victoria, this white clapboard inn perches on a bluff over Whiffen Spit. The original house, which has welcomed guests since 1932, offers three rooms, all furnished with beauty and flair. Sea Song, for example, has a slate fireplace, a king-size bed under a floral quilt, and a two-person Jacuzzi. Double doors open to a deck with a priceless view of the harbor and sea. Each room in the annex, which is reached by a short path near the garden, has an ocean view, a balcony or terrace, and a fireplace. Some feature wet bars, whirlpool spas, outdoor hot tubs, or oversize clawfoot tubs. One room is designed for the disabled.

The largest is the Victor Newman Longhouse room. Its king-size bed, vaulted ceiling, and bathtub for two add to the sense of magnitude, and the view of the ocean brings the outdoors in. The room is decorated with original West Coast Indian masks, drawings, and paintings.

Open to the public for dinner, the Sooke Harbour House dining room has received international acclaim for its imaginative cuisine. "The entire surrounding landscape and waters are edible," claims Sinclair, a scuba diver who regularly collects fresh bounty from the Pacific, such as sea urchins, sea asparagus, periwinkles, scallops, oysters, mussels, squid, and fish. The menu changes daily. A lengthy wine list includes B.C. and other Northwest labels.

Candles and fresh flowers grace the tables that overlook the harbor, the Strait of Juan de Fuca, and the Olympic Mountains across the water in Washington.

Strathcona

Strathcona Park Lodge

Strathcona Provincial Park, B.C.
Mailing address:
P.O. Box 2160
Campbell River, B.C., Canada V9W 5C9
250-286-8206
Fax: 250-286-6010

> **A lodge in the heart of a wilderness park**

Proprietor: Myrna Boulding. **Accommodations:** Chalets and housekeeping cabins. **Rates:** (Cd) Cabins, $95–$170 (2–12 people); chalet rooms, $70–$110 (2–4 people); 8-bedroom chalet, $525. **Minimum stay:** Cabins: 3 nights in summer, 2 nights in winter. **Payment:** MasterCard, Visa. **Children:** Ages 3–12, half-price; under 3, free. **Pets:** Not allowed. **Smoking:** Outdoors only. **Open:** Year-round.

➤ **Ask about the lodge's Getaway Package. It includes lodging, meals, snacks, and unlimited use of canoes or kayaks.**

Strathcona Park, a rugged mountain wilderness in the center of Vancouver Island, is the oldest provincial park in British Columbia. Snow-mantled peaks, old-growth forests, wildlife and wildflowers, lakes and streams make it a place of extraordinary beauty. On its northeastern edge, nestled in a privately owned, 160-acre forest overlooking Upper Campbell and Buttle lakes, is Strathcona Park Lodge.

The lodge is not only a rustic retreat, it's a center for outdoor education, for the staff has a wealth of expertise in wilderness adventure and leadership. Since 1960 they've been teaching survival skills, whitewater canoeing, sea kayaking, rock climbing, and mountaineering to school groups, individuals, and Elderhostel groups. A flexible array of classes ranged from a 1-hour introduction to kayaking to a week of mountain climbing.

You need not take one of the courses to stay at the lodge and enjoy the fresh air and scenery. The park has numerous hiking trails along creeks and ascending to subalpine meadows. You can swim, fish for trout, sail or sailboard in the lakes, and go cross-country skiing or snowshoeing in the winter. Kayaks and canoes are available for rent. A protected paddling bay is an easy place to practice and take lessons.

The rooms are clustered in cedar chalets and lakefront cabins, some with kitchens. All are clean and well-furnished, and most have views of the long, blue lake and 6,815-foot Kings Peak. The largest is a 9-bedroom, 4-bath chalet.

One spacious room, on the top floor of the Haig-Brown building, is considered to be the honeymooners' favorite — a gabled hideaway under the eaves with both king-size and twin beds. The room has a white wicker table and chair, a desk, and a small balcony overlooking the treetops, the lake, and the shadowed mountains.

A typical cabin, which sleeps five, has rough plank walls, a kitchenette, a separate bedroom with a queen-size bed, a living room with two twins, and a mattress in the loft. It contains a wood stove; firewood is stacked on the porch.

Simple but hearty, flavorful meals are served buffet style in the dining room. In summer, adults may choose to dine in the smaller, quieter restaurant on the second floor of the main building, where wine and beer are served and it is possible to eat on an outdoor deck. From March to June and in September and October, visiting school groups fill the lodge with youthful exuberance. If you're looking for serenity, come at another time of the year or on a weekend.

Tofino

Pacific Sands Beach Resort

P.O. Box 237
Tofino, B.C., Canada V0R 2Z0
250-725-3322
800-565-2322
Fax: 250-725-3155

An ocean-facing resort on Vancouver Island's west coast

Proprietors: The Pettinger family. **Accommodations:** 64 rooms and cabins. **Rates:** (Cd) Summer and holidays, $115–$200 single or double; winter, $75–$140; $20 additional person. **Minimum stay:** 2 nights on weekends, 3 nights in summer. **Payment:** Major credit cards. **Children:** Ages 3–16, $5 per night; under age 3, free. **Pets:** Not allowed. **Smoking:** Nonsmoking rooms available. **Open:** Year-round.

➤ **Tofino has a few good casual restaurants, but you'll find some of the best food on the island at The Pointe, at Wickininnish Inn.**

The west coast of Vancouver Island is a rugged stretch of inlet-fringed shore, where a wild surf pounds beaches strewn with driftwood. South of the picturesque village of Tofino, in a protected cove facing Cox Bay, is Pacific Sands Beach Resort. Owned by the Pettingers since 1972, the resort has been expanded and remodeled in recent years until it now offers a wide variety of lodgings.

All the rooms have kitchens, and most have fireplaces. Because of the angled design of the two- and three-story buildings, every room has an ocean view. Two-bedroom cedar beach cottages, with double beds and a sofa bed in the living room, can hold up to six people. They have compact kitchens and big picture windows, but no fireplaces or TV. The cottages are almost on the beach, surrounded by salal and driftwood.

In the building of condominium suites, those on the second floor are for adults only. Vaulted ceilings, tile fireplaces, and full kitchens appeal to those looking for a bright, contemporary atmosphere. The suites share a long balcony that faces the sea.

Rooms called light housekeeping suites have a cozy charm. In a section for adults only, they have kitchens with combined refrigerator and stove (no oven), microwave ovens, TV, and wood-burning fireplaces. The one bedroom contains a queen-size bed, and there's a sofa bed in the living room. Glass doors lead to a small balcony, just right for watching the surf and sunset. The newest building has studio rooms and one- and two-bedroom units, two with hot tubs.

Tall spruce trees dot the green lawns at Pacific Sands, and a mile-long beach is a few yards from your door. To the south is world-famed Long Beach, part of Pacific Rim National Park. In Tofino, north of Pacific Sands, you'll find cafés, marinas, shops, and galleries of Indian art — especially notable is the Eagle Aerie Gallery.

The village draws tourists interested in scenic beauty, boating, fishing, and whale-watching, for more than 19,000 gray whales migrate through these waters. Several outfits offer guided charter trips.

Wickaninnish Inn

P.O. Box 250
Osprey Lane at Chesterman Beach
Tofino, B.C., Canada V0R 2Z0
250-725-3100
800-333-4604
Fax: 250-725-3110
wick@island.net

> **A luxury resort on an island shore**

Manager: Charles McDiarmid. **Accommodations:** 46 rooms. **Rates:** (Cd) Winter, $140–$180; spring, $170–$210; summer, $240–$280; October, $180–$220; additional person $20; packages available. **Minimum stay:** None. **Payment:** Major credit cards. **Children:** Welcome. **Pets:** Allowed. **Smoking:** Not allowed. **Open:** Year-round.

➤ **In Tofino you can see the work of Native artist Roy Henry Vickers at the Eagle Aerie Gallery. The Himwitsa Gallery sells silver jewelry and local handcrafts.**

On the far west coast of Vancouver Island, where old-growth forest still stands, the Wickaninnish opened in 1996 as a top-quality inn and restaurant. Some thirty years ago, a Tofino physician, Howard McDiarmid, was instrumental in the creation of the Pacific Rim National Park Reserve and recognized the need for lodgings. His family joined with other Tofino residents to make his vision a reality, and they have succeeded in making the inn one of the best of its kind. Named for the most powerful Native chief during the arrival of Europeans in the late 1700s, the three-story weathered cedar building was designed to blend with the natural surroundings.

Wickaninnish is filled with the work of local craftspeople. The double front door is carved with ravens with abalone shell eyes; the coffee table in the lobby was formed from driftwood, glass, and a fishing float. However, it's not the table that first catches your eye. Every visitor is drawn irresistibly to the big windows overlooking the rocky cliff and water. It's a spectacular vista, with the churning surf below and the ocean stretching to the horizon.

All guest rooms have private balconies, fireplaces, water views, TV, and a king- or queen-size bed. There's a microwave, refrigerator, and coffeemaker, and in the bath an oversize tub, with aromatherapy bath salts provided. About half the rooms have a view of the ocean from a soaker tub. The designers paid meticulous attention to detail, using natural woods, wrought iron, slate, and calm colors. There's plenty of good lighting, and on the bedside table a small bowl of lavender adds a gentle scent. Pets are pampered, too, with treats, a water bowl, and extra towels for cleanup after beach walks.

The Pointe Restaurant draws visitors from far afield, eager to taste the innovative cuisine of chef Rodney Butters. The restaurant, serving three meals a day, showcases fresh coastal seafood, Vancouver Island produce, and Pacific Northwest wines. Diners can feast in this glass-enclosed room while they watch the waves smash against jagged rocks.

A path leads down to the sandy beach. Frank Island lies offshore, and when the tide is low, you can walk to it. You can also fly kites, go sea kayaking, scuba dive, and hike in the rain forest. Winter is as busy as summer, with guests arriving to see exciting storms with 30-foot waves. Yellow slickers hang in the closets so you can walk the beach in inclement weather. In spring, 21,000 gray whales head from Baja, California, for the Bering Sea — the longest annual migration of any mammal. Whale-watching expeditions are available.

An easy way to get to Wickaninnish is to fly from Vancouver via North Vancouver Air. The inn provides a shuttle service from the airfield.

Vancouver

The Albion Guest House

592 West 19th Avenue
Vancouver, B.C., Canada V5Z 1W6
604-873-2287
Fax 604-879-5682

| An inviting B&B in a residential area |

Innkeepers: Lisa and Richard Koroscil. **Accommodations:** 4 rooms (2 with private bath). **Rates:** (Cd) Summer, $115–$155; winter, $75–$135 single or double; $15 additional person. **Included:** Full breakfast. **Minimum stay:** 2 nights on weekends. **Payment:** Major credit cards. **Children:** Welcome. **Pets:** Not allowed. **Smoking:** Not allowed. **Open:** Year-round.

➤ **The Albion is close to several good restaurants. Tomato Café, Le Crocodil, and Allegro are favorites.**

In a residential neighborhood south of the downtown core, this traditional 1906 Vancouver home opened as a bed-and-breakfast in 1992. It has received rave reviews ever since. The Koroscils, who took over in 1997, are continuing the pattern of hospitality. They go out of their way for guests, providing afternoon aperitifs, a fruit bowl in the dining room, homemade cookies, and tea. They lend bicycles, recommend nearby restaurants, book reservations, and keep an updated list of things to see and do. They're attentive, yet respectful of guests' privacy.

Artistic flair is evident throughout the inn, from the hand-painted grapevines on the living room's peach walls to the homemade cinnamon twists served for breakfast. Morning treats might also include yogurt with fruit, soufflés, or French toast.

Each of the upstairs rooms has a different atmosphere. The large Rose Room, in one corner, has a puffy white duvet on a queen-size bed. At the front of the house is the Deck Room, with a romantic green wrought-iron bedstead and a private balcony under a pine tree. Country Inn features a white feather bedcover and soft sheepskin on the rocking chair. Garden Suite, the largest, has its own entrance, a television, a wrought-iron queen-size bed, and a soaking tub for two. Rooms have clock radios and fresh flowers.

Tinkling wind chimes in the front garden emphasize the peaceful ambience. Behind the house, pots of flowers lend color to the patio and a hot tub adds another relaxing touch. Though it's quiet here, the inn is just a block from busy Cambie Street, where you'll find shops, cafés, and a movie theater.

Columbia Cottage

205 West 14th Avenue
Vancouver, B.C., Canada V5Y 1X2
604-874-5327
Fax: 604-879-4547

A 1920s home of charm and grace

Innkeeper: Susan Sulzberger. **Accommodations:** 4 rooms, 1 suite (all with private bath). **Rates:** (Cd) Summer, $125–$155; winter, $95–$135; suite, $135–$155; $20 additional person. **Included:** Full breakfast. **Minimum stay:** None. **Payment:** MasterCard, Visa. **Children:** Over age 12 welcome. **Pets:** Not allowed. **Smoking:** Not allowed. **Open:** Year-round.

➤ **Vancouver has gorgeous public gardens, such as Queen Elizabeth Park, VanDusen Garden, and the classic Chinese garden in Dr. Sun Yat-Sen Park.**

This pretty cottage on a residential corner is a quiet, relaxing retreat. Classical music plays softly in the living room, which is decorated with Oriental art.

There are two rooms on the ground floor, one flooded with morning sun and the other overlooking the garden and fish pond. Two rooms are upstairs, one with a view of the hawthorn tree and Japanese maple in front. On the landing there's a desk with a phone guests may use and a sideboard with tea and coffee. The studio suite has a private entrance off the garden and a full kitchen. Watercolors of Vancouver scenes hang on the walls.

A substantial but diet-conscious breakfast is served, as well as treats for later in the day, which may include evening sherry, cookies, nuts, and chocolates. The thoughtful innkeeper also has suggestions for restaurants, Vancouver attractions, and shopping.

False Creek Bed & Breakfast

1124 Ironwork Passage
Vancouver, B.C., Canada V6H 3P1
604-734-3369

| **Residential charm near Granville Island** |

Innkeeper: Beryl Wilson. **Accommodations:** 1 room (private bath). **Rates:** (Cd) $70 double. **Included:** Expanded Continental breakfast. **Minimum stay:** 2 nights. **Payment:** Cash or check. **Children:** Not appropriate. **Pets:** Not allowed. **Smoking:** Allowed in living room only. **Open:** Year-round.

➤ **In summer, Bridges Seafood Restaurant, with outdoor seating, is popular for lunch or dinner. Isadora's is a good family restaurant with a wide-ranging menu.**

This cozy private home, which opened to guests in 1983, is in one of Vancouver's most appealing inner-city neighborhoods, the False Creek area. The townhouse has a direct view of the busy inlet, which churns with activity on weekends when all the boats come out to play. And you are just across the inlet from the Expo '86 World's Fair site and downtown Vancouver beyond it, a short drive or aqua-bus ride away.

A five-minute walk takes you to Granville Island, where you can shop, eat in waterfront restaurants, attend the theater, and stroll the piers. The Public Market on the island (a misnomer; Granville is a peninsula, not an island — but False Creek isn't a creek, either) can take up an afternoon on its own.

Best of all, Beryl is your hostess. Outgoing, frank, friendly, with a wry sense of humor, she came to Canada from England years ago and has made Vancouver her home. She publishes and edits a small local newspaper, *The Creek.* She knows a great deal about the community and is happy to share what she knows, but don't expect to be pampered. Beryl assumes you can take care of yourself — and may ask you to put Pixie, the cat, out when you go.

Your room has shelves of books, magazines, and tourist information. Beryl serves fruit and muffins in the morning, unless you request bacon and eggs or another breakfast dish. She'll probably join you with a cup of coffee and tell a few tales of Vancouver and False Creek and its denizens.

There's a small, flower-filled courtyard in back of the house, a pleasant place to sit with a cup of tea or glass of wine in the afternoon. The deck in front, overlooking False Creek, is another relaxing spot.

False Creek Bed & Breakfast is best if you're traveling alone or as a twosome; it's for the person who wants the atmosphere of home while staying close to the city.

Four Seasons Hotel

791 West Georgia Street
Vancouver, B.C., Canada V6C 2T4
604-689-9333
800-332-3442
Fax: 604-684-4555

A modern hotel in the heart of the city

Manager: Ruy Paes-Braga. **Accommodations:** 385 rooms and suites. **Rates:** (Cd) $345–$2,250; weekend and seasonal discounts available. **Minimum stay:** None. **Payment:** Major credit cards. **Children:** Under 18, free with a parent. **Pets:** Allowed. **Smoking:** Nonsmoking floors. **Open:** Year-round.

➤   **As in other Four Seasons hotels, children receive special treatment, such as toys, menus, and little bathrobes just like their parents'.**

Typical in the Four Seasons collection of lodgings, this pace-setting Vancouver hostelry maintains a consistently high quality. Built in 1976 and renovated several times since then, it's one of the best in a city of fine hotels.

The hotel combines contemporary style with old-fashioned opulence, Oriental detail, and open-walled outdoorsiness. You might expect the combination to result in disastrous clutter, but at Four Seasons it blends harmoniously.

In the Garden Terrace, at one end of the sophisticated lobby, you can enjoy a buffet breakfast in a green and white retreat, under a handwoven tapestry depicting life in the Northwest Territories. This urban atrium of greenery also offers drinks, light meals, desserts, and a Sunday brunch served on special occasions. Pastries here approach the legendary. Try amaretto chocolate quiche or hazelnut silk pie — a wicked blend of ground hazelnuts, semi-sweet chocolate, mocha liqueur, and coffee.

For breakfast, lunch, or dinner in a different atmosphere, cross the lobby to the Chartwell, a British-flavored restaurant named for Winston Churchill's summer home. Walls of dark walnut, parquet floors, Constable-style paintings, and a green marble fireplace create the look of a gentlemen's club. The menu features fine — and expensive — regional cuisine.

The Four Seasons has received numerous awards and much acclaim for its devotion to service. A few of its amenities are valet parking, 24-hour room service, same-day laundry and valet, shoeshine, and evening turndown. Your room will have a bar, remote control TV with Spectravision, telephones, a hair dryer, bathrobes, and air conditioning.

The guest rooms are like residential apartments, attractively furnished with quiet good taste. If you need extra space, 45 deluxe north-facing rooms are available; they're actually two rooms, divided by French doors, with a dining table that's useful for private dinners.

Suites have one, two, or three bedrooms with king-size beds. Most expensive is the split-level suite, which has a large living and dining area with bar, floor-to-ceiling windows, and a bedroom upstairs.

The health club has saunas, indoor and outdoor whirlpool tubs, and a swimming pool cleverly designed to be both indoors and out. There's a sunning area with pools and falls above Pacific Centre (a 300-store shopping complex) and a Japanese garden beside it.

The Georgian Court Hotel

773 Beatty Street
Vancouver, B.C., Canada V6B 2M4
604-682-5555
800-663-1155
Fax: 604-682-8830

| **Urban lodgings in a convenient location** |

Manager: Zul Somani. **Accommodations:** 178 rooms and suites. **Rates:** (Cd) Summer, $150–$275 single or double; other seasons, $110–$150. **Minimum stay:** None. **Payment:** Major credit cards. **Children:** Under 18, free with a parent. **Pets:** Allowed ($20 fee). **Smoking:** Nonsmoking rooms available. **Open:** Year-round.

➤ **Vancouver's restaurants offer French, Indian, Italian, Thai, Chinese, and Greek cuisine; also available are African, Spanish, and Native spots.**

When you want to be near B.C. Place Stadium and a few blocks removed from downtown, the Georgian Court is the place to stay. It's across the street from the covered stadium, where convention and trade shows as well as sporting events are held. With the Canadian Broadcasting Corporation offices and studios nearby, the hotel is a convenient location for media representatives and entertainers.

Small by major hotel standards, the Georgian Court provides good value and appeals mainly to traveling businesspeople. The 20 small suites are clearly designed for transacting business in a discreet and unobtrusive setting. The walls are as gray as Vancouver's skies in winter; there are 3 telephones, 2 televisions, and a stocked mini-bar. In one corner suite the curved window looks out on busy Cambie Street Bridge over False Creek. However, the bedroom, which can be closed off from the sitting area, has no windows and can feel cramped.

The decor is similar throughout the hotel, with mahogany furniture and stylish colors of steel blue, gray, or rose. Outside, it's all brass and brick, arched windows and green marble, creating an impressive façade.

In the renowned William Tell Restaurant, classical music drifts through the ivory-tinted room and silver gleams in candlelight. Continental dishes are made from local, organically grown ingredients. Veal with morel sauce is a specialty; others are a salmon fillet with sorrel and air-dried Swiss beef. Dessert demands a choice: hot passion fruit soufflé, perhaps, or chocolate fondue or meringue glacé au chocolat. If you're feeling less decadent, you might choose a bowl of fresh cherries.

Beatty Street Bar and Grill is the hotel's casual restaurant, offering reasonably priced bistro dining until midnight. The Georgian Court takes great pride in its obliging staff and responsive room service.

Hotel Vancouver

900 West Georgia Street
Vancouver, B.C., Canada V6C 2W6
604-684-3131
800-441-1414
Fax: 604-662-1929

> **A historic landmark in the heart of the city**

General Manager: Ian Powell. **Accommodations:** 550 rooms and suites. **Rates:** (Cd) May–November: rooms, $170–$370 single; $195–$395 double; $25 additional person; suites, $490–$2,580; less in off-season. **Minimum stay:** None. **Payment:** Major credit cards. **Children:** Under 18, free with a parent. **Pets:** Allowed. **Smoking:** Nonsmoking rooms available. **Open:** Year-round.

➤ **Griffin's is a brasserie with arched windows, black and white tile, and a black granite buffet. Fine cuisine is served in 900 West.**

The grande dame of Vancouver hotels, once the most elegant landmark in the city, still occupies an important position both in the geographical center of town and in the hearts of longtime B.C.

travelers. Extensive renovation has changed the Vancouver to a more light, open place with playful touches.

You can't miss it: it's the 17-story French Renaissance building with the green copper roof and the gargoyles, right across the street from the Vancouver Art Gallery, close to the shops on Robson-strasse, and within ten blocks of B.C. Place Stadium. Convenience and excellent convention facilities make the Vancouver a favorite in the business world. Royalty is fond of the hotel because kings and queens have been staying here for years — since 1939, in fact, when King George VI and Queen Elizabeth attended the opening ceremonies.

Nowadays you'll find the latest in posh hotel amenities in the guest rooms: fresh flowers, chocolates, mini-bars, Spectravision movies, individual climate control. Each suite has a different character. Morningside is contemporary, with marble floors, glass and brass and pastels, and wraparound windows. Courtyard has a French feel, with impressionistic floral designs on the drapes and down comforters, a blue chaise, and French doors to the sitting room. Royal Suite, with four bedrooms, is the hotel's most expensive accommodation. The cost of standard rooms is determined by the size of the room and the view.

Varying services are offered. Entreé Gold guests have the use of the ninth floor, with its private boardroom, lounge, and honor bar. They receive private check-in and check-out, complimentary breakfast and afternoon canapés, international newspapers, and the most personal service.

A health club on the second floor has fitness facilities and a 50-foot swimming pool. There are saunas, a whirlpool tub, and a wading pool.

Laburnum Cottage

1388 Terrace Avenue
North Vancouver, B.C.
Canada V7R 1B4
604-988-4877
Fax: 604-988-4877

**A romantic B&B in
residential North
Vancouver**

Innkeeper: Delphine Masterton. **Accommodations:** 4 rooms in house, 2 cottages. **Rates:** (Cd) $150–$250 single or double, less in winter, $25 additional person. **Included:** Full breakfast. **Minimum stay:** None. **Payment:** MasterCard, Visa. **Children:** Welcome. **Pets:** Allowed by arrangement. **Smoking:** Not allowed. **Open:** Year-round.

➤ **Laburnum is near a pitch-and-putt course and tennis courts and is 5 minutes from Grouse Mountain, known for its skiing and panoramic views.**

If you like the notion of crossing a curved bridge to a wisteria-covered cottage set in a garden of lawns, ferns, lilies, and roses, visit the Summer House at Laburnum Cottage. It's thoroughly charming and could hardly be more romantic.

The Summer House was once a teatime retreat. Delphine Masterton turned it into a delightful getaway with a tiny kitchen, a fireplace, and a brass bed. The cottage is furnished with antique chairs, a TV, an Oriental rug, and a soaking tub in the bath.

Delphine's deceased husband Alex gardened as a hobby and created a showplace setting in this quiet neighborhood in North Vancouver, with a fountain and stream and stone-edged flower beds.

The guest rooms in the house are comfortably furnished. Grandest is the room on the main floor, with a brass bed, moiré silk drapes, antique chairs, and a French country armoire. The Queen Anne Suite, upstairs, is a corner room with a queen-size brass bed, mirrored armoire, and French moiré silk wallpaper. It also contains an antique French bed.

Delphine is a travel agent as well as an innkeeper, and the house is full of memorabilia from her travels. When you arrive at Laburnum, you'll promptly be offered tea or lemonade, and in the morning a generous breakfast. It might include orange juice, bacon or sausage, French toast, blueberry pancakes, frittatas, crêpes, fried tomatoes, or "friendship muffins" with pineapple, citron, or applesauce.

Also available is the Cottage, a separate apartment that has a loft and sleeps four to five. It has a kitchen, TV, stereo, soaking tub, and gas fireplace.

Metropolitan Hotel

645 Howe Street
Vancouver, B.C., Canada V6C 2Y9
604-687-1122
800-667-2300
Fax: 604-689-7044
reservations@metropolitan.com

An urban hotel with serene elegance

Manager: Brian Young. **Accommodations:** 197 rooms, 18 suites. **Rates:** (Cd) Rooms: $205–$255 single, $225–$275 double. Suites: $315–$800. Corporate rates available. **Minimum stay:** None. **Payment:** Major credit cards. **Children:** Under age 18, free with a parent. **Pets:** Allowed. **Smoking:** Nonsmoking rooms available. **Open:** Year-round.

➤ **Well worth a visit is the Museum of Anthropology at the University of British Columbia; it's one of Canada's finest museums.**

A sense of harmony prevails throughout this elegant urban hotel, perhaps because when it was first constructed, in 1984, a Feng Shui master assisted in its design. Feng Shui is the Chinese art of arranging an environment in accord with nature to achieve a beneficial flow of positive energy. The hotel was the Mandarin Oriental then, and a number of its artifacts remain. An example is the golden Chinese temple carving in the lobby, a screen placed according to Feng Shui principles. Black stone lions flank the entrance, and a 12-panel Coromandel screen hangs at the top of the main staircase.

Set in the heart of the downtown business and financial district, close to the convention center, World Trade Center, Queen Elizabeth Theatre, and numerous shops and restaurants, the Metropolitan caters to a variety of visitors. Business guests like the well-equipped Business Centre and seven meeting rooms. Vancouver residents come for Michael Noble's superb cuisine. The award-winning chef runs Diva, serving three meals a day and after-theater meals until 1:00 A.M. The contemporary, international dishes emphasize regional foods such as alder-smoked duck breast with chanterelle spaetzle and dried Okanagan cherries, grilled venison medallions in toasted hazelnut sauce, and swordfish with risotto and red wine sauce. The blackberry sorbet is outstanding.

The guest rooms all have small balconies; those on the 18th floor enjoy large terraces and city views. The furnishings and decorative details are of the highest quality, and there are many extra touches — automatic lights in the cabinets, eiderdown bedcovers, bedside lighting control, free shoeshine (no mirrors outside the bath is inconvenient, however). Twelve studio suites can be connected to create parlor suites. The most suitable room for a family would be a suite with a sofa bed, or two adjoining rooms. Children are welcome, and there's no charge in the restaurant for a child under age 7. In-room dining is available. Guests enjoy same-day laundry and dry-cleaning services, a morning newspaper at the door, and a health club with a swimming pool beside a high, curved wall of windows. A concierge is on duty 24 hours a day.

Not the least of the Metropolitan's charms is its friendly, efficient staff. You will be treated with the best of care.

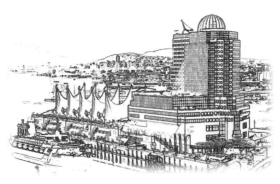

Pan Pacific Hotel

300-999 Canada Place
Vancouver, B.C., Canada V6C 3B5
604-662-8111
800-663-1515 in Canada
800-937-1515 in U.S.
Fax: 604-685-8690

A contemporary hotel next to the convention center

General Manager: Susan Gomez. **Accommodations:** 506 rooms, 39 suites. **Rates:** (Cd) Rooms in summer: $380–$430 single, $410–$460 double. Winter: $330–$380 single, $350–$400 double. Suites, $480-$900. Corporate and weekend rates available. **Minimum stay:** None. **Payment:** Major credit cards. **Chil-

dren: Under 18, free with parents. **Pets:** Allowed. **Smoking:** Nonsmoking rooms available. **Open:** Year-round.

➤ **The hotel's East-West connection is shown in a striking metal sculpture, *Pacific Rim,* a stylized outline of Pacific shores with major cities labeled; a stream winds through to the atrium's waterfall.**

Vancouver's one-of-a-kind convention center, a multifaceted building with a roof resembling five white sails, marks the site of the Pan Pacific, built in 1986 for the World's Fair. On the harbor and yet close to downtown, it overlooks Burrard Inlet and has wonderful views of the freighters, cruise ships, ferries, and pleasure boats that constantly ply the waters. Cruise ships dock just around the corner from the hotel's front door. Across the inlet, on the north, are hills with some of Canada's costliest real estate.

As you enter the hotel you face an eight-story atrium with a 20-foot waterfall in the center. The lobby, restaurants, and shops are on the floors above, in the center court and mezzanine, with guest rooms soaring to the 23rd floor.

The two top floors are devoted to five deluxe suites with stunning views. Here you'll find a grand piano, a bar, a full kitchen, fine modern art, a big canopied bed, a marble bathroom, and a whirlpool tub. When an important meeting or special occasion demands the utmost in contemporary luxury, a penthouse suite would do the job nicely. The other guest rooms, while less opulent, are attractive and well designed for comfort. Each has a view of the bay, harbor, or city.

Light is important in this climate, so the Pan Pacific is filled with color, high ceilings, and entire walls of windows that bring the outdoors in. An Oriental motif appears in such touches as bamboo-design bedcovers, understated decor, and Japanese No masks on the walls of the lounge.

Pan Pacific has three restaurants. Five Sails, overlooking the convention center and harbor, offers fresh, imaginative seafood, as well as Continental cuisine. Salmon, the local delicacy, is prepared in various ways — on gingered vegetables with sesame seeds, for example, or poached and served with thyme blossoms and lemon sauce. Café Pacifica is a more casual dining spot, and Misaki Japanese Restaurant, with private tatami rooms, serves authentic Japanese fare. Aromaz is a coffee bar on the entrance level.

The hotel's shops sell everything from canned salmon to lingerie, but the Pan Pacific is so close to Vancouver's sophisticated downtown area that you'll want to explore its restaurants and stores. Historic Gastown is easily accessible. If sightseeing doesn't keep you in shape, try the health club at the hotel. Guests may use the paddleball court, running track, weight room, and swimming pool.

Park Royal Hotel

540 Clyde Avenue
West Vancouver, B.C., Canada V7T 2J7
604-926-5511
Fax: 604-926-6082

A westside hotel on a riverbank

Manager: Mario Corsi. **Accommodations:** 30 rooms. **Rates:** (Cd) Summer, $148–$288; winter, $95–$115; $10 additional person. **Minimum stay:** None. **Payment:** Major credit cards. **Children:** Welcome. **Pets:** Not allowed. **Smoking:** Allowed. **Open:** Year-round.

➤ **North Vancouver has a number of good restaurants, including Salmon House on the Hill and Chesa's. Two of the best are the Corsi and the Café Roma.**

In typically Canadian style, the Park Royal borrows from other traditions and adds regional touches to create a unique and appealing atmosphere. Though it's a city hotel, it is removed from downtown Vancouver and set in lovely gardens that make this an oasis in the midst of a busy shopping district. Vines overhanging mullioned windows, beamed ceilings, tapestries, and paneled walls are reminiscent of an English country inn.

The guest rooms mix English traditional (stately gray velvet armchairs, Oriental carpets) with Northwest rustic (bulky pine furniture). Somewhat crowded, the rooms are nevertheless comfortable and the bathrooms well fitted. The windows on the garden side overlook a lush, curving lawn and beds of flowers and herbs along the rim of a bluff above the rushing Capilano River. The dining room on the main floor edges the gardens.

There's a lively, friendly pub belowstairs where you're welcome to sit by the fire and join in a singalong. A pianist entertains nightly in this dark-paneled room.

The exuberant innkeeper, Mario Corsi, is usually on hand to oversee the hotel's operation and greet guests personally. The Italian-born Mario has lived in Vancouver for many years and knows North and West Van well. He'll point out the nearby jogging path along the river and remind you that the ski slopes of Grouse Mountain, Cypress, and Seymour are only 10 minutes away. In the other direction, downtown is a 10-minute drive across Lion's Gate Bridge from the Park Royal.

The Sutton Place Hotel

845 Burrard Street
Vancouver, B.C., Canada V6Z 2K6
604-682-5511
800-961-7555
Fax: 604-682-5513
res@vcr.suttonplace.com

An urban high-rise in a cosmopolitan city

General Manager: Patricia Clairmont. **Accommodations:** 397 rooms and suites. **Rates:** (Cd) Rooms: $240–$415 double, $20 additional person; suites: $290–$545. **Minimum stay:** None. **Payment:** Major credit cards. **Children:** Welcome. **Pets:** Not allowed. **Smoking:** Nonsmoking rooms available. **Open:** Year-round.

➤ **A whimsical touch is the Chocoholic Bar in Fleuri Restaurant, where an imposing array of chocolate in many forms is offered in a popular buffet three times a week.**

Sutton Place considers itself to be "Vancouver's premier business hotel" and strives to keep that reputation by providing numerous services to corporate clients. These services include early morning coffee and muffins, a Continental breakfast in a private dining room, several international newspapers and televised news, week-day limousine service in the downtown area, shoeshine, overnight dry cleaning, 24-hour room service, and express check-out. Location is another asset; the hotel is a block away from the Robson Square Conference Centre and the major shopping, arts, and entertainment districts.

Formerly Le Meridien Hotel, it's now part of the Sutton Place Grande Hotels Group. Set back from the street, behind a curving drive and porte cochere, is an inviting lobby that is both elegant and intimate. On the lobby level are two restaurants. The Fleuri Restaurant features, in addition to a standard menu, theme buffets and a notable Sunday brunch. Gerard Lounge is like a British club, with paneled walls, tapestries, leather chairs, and a fireplace. Le Club, adjacent to the Fleuri, is used for receptions and other special events.

On the second level is the Versailles Ballroom, which has crystal chandeliers and peach-toned silk walls. There are several meeting rooms, each named for a French wine chateau. In the hotel's adjoining apartment complex, La Grande Residence, there's a complete fitness and beauty center with weight-training equipment, a swimming pool, steam room, and sauna.

Massage, facials, and manicures are available at Le Spa. The pool is pleasantly set up with skylights and greenery but getting there is somewhat awkward; you have to negotiate various hallways, doors, and stairs.

All the rooms have mini-bars, umbrellas, and bathrobes. A typical one-bedroom suite, richly furnished in traditional fashion but cheerful in peach and white, has a partial view of the city skyline. Good reading lamps, often lacking in standard hotels, are well located. The marble baths are roomy but not palatial. There's nothing overstated or pretentious here, just solid quality and excellent service.

Waterfront Centre Hotel

900 Canada Place Way
Vancouver, B.C., Canada V6C 3L5
604-691-1991
800-441-1414 (reservations only)
Fax: 604-691-1999

A contemporary hotel near the harbor

Manager: Michael Kaile. **Accommodations:** 489 rooms and suites. **Rates:** (Cd) Rooms, $240–$460; suites, $465–$600; rates vary seasonally. **Minimum stay:** None. **Payment:** Major credit cards. **Children:** Under age 18, free. **Pets:** Allowed. **Smoking:** Nonsmoking floors. **Open:** Year-round.

➤ **Stanley Park has a 9-kilometer path along the shore, beaches, a lagoon, a cricket pitch, and colorful totem poles.**

One of Vancouver's foremost luxury hotels, Waterfront Centre links the downtown core to the waterfront. It's an easy walk to the financial district and office buildings, and it's connected to the Trade and Convention Centre and cruise ship terminal. The 23-story hotel and its adjacent 22-story office tower are linked by public terraced gardens and fountains and share a concourse level filled with retail shops.

The open, contemporary lobby of glass, brass, and marble showcases Canadian art. Off the lobby is a bar where complimentary hors d'oeuvres are served and a pianist plays jazz tunes in the evenings. Adjacent to the bar is Heron's restaurant, with a menu that focuses on Canadian cuisine. The executive chef, Daryle Ryo Nagata, takes pride in the freshness of the herbs he uses. The rosemary, basil, marjoram, and other herbs couldn't be fresher; they're grown in a 2,100-square-foot garden on the third-floor terrace. The chef makes use of the herbs in dishes such as mushroom salad with lemon thyme vinaigrette, dungeness crab cakes with garlic chive sauce, and peach cobbler with bee pollen and stevia crust. Between July and April, those who attend the City Chef's Herbal Dinners receive a guided tour of the herb garden, a seminar and demonstration in herbal use, a cocktail reception, and a four-course dinner.

Most of the guest rooms have harbor views, east or west of the convention center across the street (the best views are on the west side). During the cruise season, from May to October, you can watch cruise ships from your room. Recent renovations have spruced up the spacious rooms with vibrant yellow and green tones, dark wood furniture, and pink marble baths. The most impressive rooms are the waterfront suites.

The hotel is a favorite of business travelers for its convenient location, top-quality service, and many amenities, from paper clips in the desk drawer to a business center with work stations, computers, and copy machines. There's a fitness center on the third floor with a grand view and doors that open to an outdoor pool and terrace, and the fragrant herb garden.

Wedgewood Hotel

845 Hornby Street
Vancouver, B.C., Canada V6Z 1V1
604-689-7777
800-663-0666
Fax: 604-668-3074
Telex: 04-55234

An elegant little hotel in the heart of downtown

Proprietor: Eleni Skalbania. **Accommodations:** 93 rooms and suites. **Rates:** (Cd) Summer, $200–$520; less in winter; corporate rates and packages available. **Minimum stay:** None. **Payment:** Major credit cards. **Children:** Under 14, free with a parent. **Pets:** Not allowed. **Smoking:** Nonsmoking rooms available. **Open:** Year-round.

➤ **The Wedgewood offers a honeymoon package of champagne, breakfast in bed, and a Wedgwood dish. Weekend escape packages include a 5-course dinner, 2 nights' lodging, brunch, and parking.**

Like a fine piece of Wedgwood china, the Wedgewood Hotel bespeaks quiet quality. That's the way the owner wants it, and that is why she chose the name (adding an *e*). To Eleni Skalbania, who brought from her native Greece a willingness to work and a talent for business, the Wedgewood must be as noted for its commitment to perfection as is the English china manufacturer.

A small downtown hotel in the European style, it has made highly personalized service its trademark. A morning newspaper, shoeshine, 24-hour room service, and a box of chocolates are complimentary to all guests; those in the Corporate Membership Programme have the use of a business center, pre-registration, and twice-daily maid service.

Entering the hotel under a Palladian arch over white, paned-glass double doors, you see a marble fireplace with a mantel holding a single piece of antique Wedgwood china. On the right of this small lobby is Bacchus Ristorante, a high-toned Italian restaurant with a country flavor. Soft seating, Persian carpets, bleached-wood paneling, and deep green and paprika colors fill the bar area. The lounge features live music six nights a week.

The rooms carry an Old World theme, with deep colors of burgundy, mauve, and steel blue, traditional furniture, and dark, rich tapestries. Most rooms have king- or queen-size beds. In this busy part of town, close to Robson Square, the art museum, and law courts, there's a certain amount of traffic noise, but once the doors are closed, the atmosphere is soothing and quiet. The suites have sitting rooms divided from the bed and bath area by beveled glass doors. The king-size bed has a canopy in the penthouse suite, which also has a marble fireplace, a wet bar, and a garden terrace.

The hotel has a compact but well-equipped exercise room.

The West End Guest House

1362 Haro Street
Vancouver, B.C., Canada V6E 1G2
604-681-2889
Fax: 604-688-8812

> A quiet, hospitable B&B
> close to Vancouver

Innkeeper: Evan Penner. **Accommodations:** 8 rooms. **Rates:** (Cd) $150–$210 single or double, $15 additional person; rates vary seasonally. **Included:** Full breakfast. **Minimum stay:** 2 nights winter weekends. **Payment:** Major credit cards. **Children:** Not appropriate. **Pets:** Not allowed. **Smoking:** Not allowed. **Open:** Year-round.

> ➤ **Stanley Park has acres of lawn, garden and forest, beaches, an aquarium, a playground, and tennis courts. Its Teahouse Restaurant is one of the prettiest in the city.**

In the heart of Vancouver, near Robson Square, the shops of cosmopolitan Robson Street, and woodsy Stanley Park, is a bright pink and white Victorian bed-and-breakfast inn. Built in 1906 as the home of the Edwards family — early photographers in the region — it was completely renovated in 1985.

Every room in this top-notch inn has period furniture, potted plants, TV, and robes. You'll find homemade chocolates and a welcome note on your bed. Most rooms are on the second floor, and two are under an angled ceiling with skylights on the third floor.

The smallest and least expensive room, number 7, is best for one person. It has a double bed tucked against a corner window — cozy, but not cramped. The largest is the honeymoon room, which has a brass bed with an ivory quilt and feather mattress, a red velvet chaise longue, and a desk at the bay window.

The substantial breakfast, served in the dining room, includes a cereal buffet, fresh fruit, and a hot entrée such as banana pecan waffles or crêpes with an apple and sausage filling. Iced tea is offered on summer afternoons, and in the evening, a tray of sherry and pâté is set out in the parlor or on the deck.

There's a flower-bedecked second-story balcony at the back of the house, overlooking the Queen Anne cherry tree in the small yard. Free, off-street parking is available.

Victoria

Abigail's Hotel

906 McClure Street
Victoria, B.C., Canada V8V 3E7
250-388-5363
800-561-6565
Fax: 250-388-7787
innkeeper@abigailshotel.com

> **A romantic Tudor inn in a quiet neighborhood**

Innkeeper: Daniel Behune. **Accommodations:** 22 rooms and suites. **Rates:** (Cd) $145–$289 double, $30 additional person. **Included:** Full breakfast. **Minimum stay:** None. **Payment:** All major credit cards. **Children:** Over age 10 welcome. **Pets:** Not allowed. **Smoking:** Not allowed. **Open:** Year-round.

➤ **Dining well is easy in Victoria. Try Camille's for imaginative West Coast cooking, Pagliacci's for Italian food, and for classic French cuisine, Chez Daniel or La Ville d'Is.**

This classic stucco Tudor mansion has been updated into a small, European-style hotel close to the Inner Harbour and yet in a quiet area.

With a recent change in ownership, Abigail's now has a less floral style and more warm jewel tones in the fabrics and furnishings. Most of the guest rooms have queen- or king-size beds; some hold two double beds. The amenities vary. Some have wood-burning fireplaces, Jacuzzi tubs, and canopy beds. All are tastefully furnished and have fresh flowers and good reading lamps. Rooms on the third floor have refrigerators.

The latest change at Abigail's is the opening of the Coach House, with six luxurious suites. Furnished in a turn-of the-century, English arts and crafts style, the suites have four-poster beds, fireplaces, and views of the Olympic Mountains and Inner Harbour.

The rooms are comfortable, but Abigail's takes most pride in its personal service. It starts with a glass of champagne at check-in, along with the innkeeper's offer to help plan sightseeing or make dinner reservations.

You may not need dinner after a day at Abigail's, however. From 8:00 to 9:30 A.M., breakfast is served in a sunny English country room with bare floors and glimpses of the kitchen. Fresh orange juice, cinnamon buns, and eggs Florentine or quiche make up a typical breakfast. Abigail's kitchen will also pack a summer picnic for your excursion around Victoria — and the innkeeper will have a few suggestions on where to take it. At 11:00, pastries and coffee are set out in the cozy library, where a fire burns in the stone fireplace on cool days. Later in the day, cookies and tea are offered, and at 5:00 P.M. it's sherry and hors d'oeuvres.

The hotel is a few blocks from Inner Harbour, the Parliament Buildings, the outstanding Royal B.C. Museum, and the antiques shops on Fort Street.

The Beaconsfield Inn

998 Humboldt Street
Victoria, B.C., Canada V8V 2Z8
250-384-4044
Fax: 250-384-4052
beaconsfield@islandnet.com

**An Edwardian inn with
Canadian flavor**

Innkeepers: Judy and Con Sollid. **Accommodations:** 9 rooms and suites. **Rates:** (Cd) $145–$350 single or double, $65 additional person. **Minimum stay:** None. **Included:** Full breakfast. **Payment:** MasterCard, Visa. **Children:** Not appropriate. **Pets:** Not allowed. **Smoking:** Not allowed. **Open:** Year-round.

➤ **The Royal B.C. Museum has creatively designed exhibits on regional history and geography. Check the gift shop for a wide range of books.**

Edwardian homes were substantial, dignified, and solid, built to last for generations, and the mansion R. P. Rithet built for his daughter Gertrude in 1904 was no exception. Gertrude married and lived in the house for many years; when she died in 1945, it fell into disrepair. By 1984, extensive reconstruction was required to restore the house to its original grandeur.

On a residential street a few blocks from Inner Harbour, where the ferries dock and much of Victoria's tourist action takes place, the Beaconsfield takes you to another world. Etched glass doors at the entrance lead you into a sun room filled with greenery and light from skylights and stained glass windows. Dark mahogany is the prevailing mode of the entry hall and library, and continues up the carpeted stairway.

In the clublike library, black leather couches face a red tile fireplace and three walls are laden with books. You might spend a few moments here at the inlaid chess table or perusing restaurant menus before an evening out. A silver tea is offered in the afternoon, and sherry and hors d'oeuvres are served in the evening.

Upstairs, the Verandah Room, originally Gertrude's sewing room, now has a partially canopied queen-size bed and a Jacuzzi. Duchess Room, in warm apricot, has a fireplace and half-canopy bed. The Attic Room is largest, filling the entire third floor. This retreat is a mix of old and new: skylights and a Jacuzzi tub, a stained glass window, red ceramic tile fireplace, and a four-poster canopy bed. From the window alcove you have a view of the Olympic Mountains.

Belowstairs are the Gatekeeper's Suite and the Garden Suite, which has a wood-burning fireplace, jetted tub, and French doors that open to a private patio.

Beaconsfield breakfasts are exceptional. Tea and coffee are set out at 7:30 A.M. in the library; later you're served a series of courses in the sun room or dining room. The rhubarb tart is especially good.

If you liked *Upstairs, Downstairs,* you'll appreciate the Beaconsfield, where the people are mannerly and the service is outstanding.

The Bedford Regency Hotel

1140 Government Street
Victoria, B.C., Canada V8W 1Y2
250-384-6835
800-665-6500
Fax: 250-386-8930

A small luxury hotel in the heart of town

Manager: Shannon Lee. **Accommodations:** 40 rooms. **Rates:** (Cd) Summer, $150–$215; winter, $95–$150 double; $25 additional person. **Included:** Full breakfast. **Minimum stay:** None. **Payment:** Major credit cards. **Children:** Under age 6, free. **Pets:** Not allowed. **Smoking:** Nonsmoking rooms available. **Open:** Year-round.

➤ **Nearby is Murchie's, a must for tea-lovers. You can buy coffee blends, china, and glassware, as well as Murchie's famous tea.**

A few years ago, The Bedford was a moldering period piece in the heart of Victoria's downtown shopping area. Renovated by the same company that restored Abigail's Hotel and the Beaconsfield

Inn, it opened in 1987 as a sleek but still very personal urban hotel. From the busy street, you enter a tiled lobby of soft mauve and rose. Octagonal pillars are decorated with plaster ram heads.

Overlooking the lobby is the mezzanine, where breakfast is served in the Red Currant. The Garrick's Head Pub, with a separate entrance downstairs, features pub fare. Its Old World atmosphere is enhanced by wood floors, paned windows, a brick fireplace, and a tartan decor.

The ten guest rooms on each floor all have queen-size beds; many boast fireplaces, Jacuzzis, and stocked mini-bars. Deep, rich colors and Laura Ashley designs add to the sense of luxury. Wingback chairs invite relaxation; plants and books adorn the mantels. There are hair dryers and thick, oversize towels in the tiled baths. Coffee and a newspaper are brought to your door each morning.

Wide window seats at the arched windows are vantage points for viewing the harbor and city, as well as the flowers, changed seasonally, that overflow window boxes. From the street below, you may hear an accordion tune or the sound of a bagpipe. The best views, which extend over the harbor area, are from the top floor.

The Empress

721 Government Street
Victoria, B.C., Canada V8W 1W5
250-384-8111
800-441-1414
Fax: 250-381-4334

A grand hotel facing the Inner Harbour

Manager: Ian Barbour. **Accommodations:** 488 rooms and suites. **Rates:** (Cd) $245–$450 single or double, $25 additional person; suites $405–$1,700; rates vary seasonally. **Minimum stay:** None. **Payment:** Major credit cards. **Children:** 18 and under, free with a parent. **Pets:** Allowed (cannot be left unattended). **Smoking:** Nonsmoking rooms available. **Open:** Year-round.

➤ **The Empress Dining Room has been transformed in recent years, moving to the realm of fine regional cuisine, artistically presented.**

This venerable, ivy-covered hotel on the harbor gracefully combines the traditional with the contemporary. Viewed from the water, the Empress looks much the same as when she was built in 1908, her cupolas, peaked gables, and steeply pitched slate roofs defying architectural typing. The changes show at the entrance, which is now off to one side, and in the back, at the Greater Victoria Conference Centre. Open and airy, filled with greenery, fountains, and Native art, the Centre attracts strollers as well as conference participants. Its assembly halls and meeting rooms can hold 1,600 people.

The hotel's reception area is a light, bright space with stairs curving up to a mezzanine that leads to the old lobby, where throngs gather every summer afternoon for an elaborate tea.

Cucumber sandwiches and crumpets are served amid soaring columns and portraits of the British royal family. Tea is also served in the Palm Court, in filtered sun under a high stained glass dome.

If you wish something stronger, you might step into the Bengal Lounge and order a drink while you survey the safari-like surroundings and a menu that features a different curry special daily. The former Library Bar is now a first-rate gallery of Native art.

Change makes little difference to the Empress; she continues to face the busy harbor with imperturbable dignity. The hotel, originally built by the Canadian Pacific Railway, is at the hub of this tourist-oriented city of double-decker buses and flower baskets.

The pace slows in winter, and in this mild climate it's a pleasant — and less expensive — time to visit. Christmas at the Empress is celebrated in a traditional English style, with a holiday package that buys four days of festivities, from an Imperial Dinner to a Boar's Head Ceremony, musical entertainment, and afternoon tea. The two-day New Year's Package focuses on the Scottish Hogmanay celebration, with a dinner and dance, Scottish dancers and piper, brunch, music, and entertainment.

Heritage House

3808 Heritage Lane
Victoria, B.C., Canada V8Z 1N3
250-479-0892

A home with a history on Vancouver Island

Innkeepers: Sandra and Larry Gray. **Accommodations:** 5 rooms (share 3 baths). **Rates:** (Cd) $75 single, $95–$100 double, $35 additional person. **Included:** Full breakfast. **Minimum stay:** 2 nights. **Payment:** MasterCard, Visa. **Children:** Not appropriate. **Pets:** Not allowed. **Smoking:** Not allowed. **Open:** Year-round.

➤ **Two excellent dining houses in the area are Deep Cove Chalet, known for its cuisine and scenic location, and Romeo's, serving Italian food.**

The Victoria suburb of Saanich is a quiet, countrified area. In 1910 it was even more peaceful, a likely location for a home to retire to. So Captain Walker, a sea captain who sailed between Russia and Japan, had a western stick-style home built for him and his daughters, who kept house for him. Later the house was owned by a Danish count; now the Grays are restoring it to reflect its original style.

Heritage House has a generous appearance, with a low, broad roof extending over the front verandah. Recent development of the surrounding area detracts from the country atmosphere, but the house still has its tree-shaded gardens and tall Douglas firs. The Grays, familiar with house restoration, have returned a bit of elegance to their B&B, furnishing it with period antiques. Three of the guest rooms have annexes that can sleep a third person.

Breakfast is served at a Chippendale table in the formal dining room. In the evenings, guests sit by the green marble fireplace in the living room and nibble on the inexhaustible supply of cookies.

The friendly innkeepers are good sources of information on nearby restaurants, walks, and jogging paths. One interesting spot for dinner is 4-Mile House. The white stucco Tudor-style restaurant was built in 1853 and is the fourth-oldest building in Victoria. Built as a roadhouse, where travelers heading from Victoria to the beach could rest their horses, it's now a restaurant that is close to a park and the beach, a short drive away.

Holland House Inn

595 Michigan Street
Victoria, B.C., Canada V8V 1S7
250-384-6644

A comfortable inn in the heart of the city

Innkeepers: Harry and Margaret Brock. **Accommodations:** 10 rooms. **Rates:** (Cd) $125–$225 single or double, $25 additional person. **Included:** Full breakfast. **Minimum stay:** None. **Payment:** Major credit cards. **Children:** Welcome. **Pets:** Not allowed. **Smoking:** On balconies only. **Open:** Year-round.

➤ **Do visit the Art Gallery of Greater Victoria. In the old Rocklands district, the mansion has a 10,000-piece permanent collection and changing exhibitions.**

This stucco inn, behind a small garden of Japanese maple trees, impatiens, and begonia, is light and bright with skylights, pale wood, and indirect lighting. The lounge on the main floor is a comfortable gathering place, with upholstered chairs, a polished granite fireplace, and a parquet floor.

There are two guest rooms on the main floor, one of them wheelchair-accessible. The others, up on the second and third floors, feature balconies, down duvets and pillows, telephones, and TV. Two have fireplaces, with wood supplied. Several contain antiques and four-poster beds, and all are furnished in an individual style. One has a theme of roses, another magnolias, another is all in blue.

Breakfast, served in the sunny atrium off the lounge, changes regularly, but might include French toast with a fig compote, zucchini fritatta, or scrambled eggs hollandaise, in addition to fruit, granola, and yogurt.

The inn is well-located, with Inner Harbour a few blocks to the north and Beacon Hill Park just around the corner. In the 154-acre park, you can see one of the world's tallest totem poles (127 feet), a rose garden, a wildfowl sanctuary and zoo, and a century-old cricket pitch. Gardens in the park bloom all year.

Laurel Point Inn

680 Montreal Street
Victoria, B.C., Canada V8V 1Z8
250-386-8721
800-663-7667
Fax: 250-386-9547

A busy, friendly hotel at the edge of the harbor

Proprietor: Arti Arsens. **Accommodations:** 202 rooms. **Rates:** (Cd) Summer, $185–$650 single or double; winter, $125–$450; $15 additional person. **Minimum stay:** None. **Payment:** Major credit cards. **Children:** Under 12, free with a parent. **Pets:** Small pets allowed in certain rooms, by arrangement. **Smoking:** Nonsmoking rooms available. **Open:** Year-round.

➤ **Between the hotel and the water is an area with lawns, trees, and a path that winds along the bluff to the Parliament Buildings, the Royal B.C. Museum, and downtown.**

At Laurel Point, you get more than typical B.C. hospitality. The employees here are invariably friendly, outgoing, and helpful. If you stop for lunch and say you're in a hurry, the prompt service becomes more so. If you're arranging for a tour bus or need sightseeing advice, the front desk will help.

The brick hotel zigzags four stories high above the entrance to Inner Harbour and has a prime view of the channel and the busy marina. Built in 1979, it does not have the quaint charm of many of Victoria's older hostelries, but its modern verve has its own appeal.

The guest rooms, some of them adjoining, have comfortable furnishings, plenty of space, and great views of the harbor's comings and goings. All rooms have two beds or a king-size bed. A six-story wing added in recent years holds the most luxurious accommodations, spacious suites with down comforters, small refrigerators, and pink marble baths. The Panorama suites hold Jacuzzi tubs and have broad water views.

Café Laurel, the hotel's restaurant, serves three meals daily and a popular Sunday brunch. The best tables are in the outer area, where windows look toward the bay and the Empress hotel. Across the hall, Cook's Landing is a lounge with harbor views where you can enjoy nightly entertainment and complimentary hors d'oeuvres.

Laurel Point has a swimming pool and a skylighted lounge overlooking a reflecting pond and gardens. Free parking helps to ease the blow of a stiff 17% tax the government adds to the room rate. For an inexpensive and interesting tour of the area, try a Harbour Ferry tour.

Mulberry Manor

611 Foul Bay Road
Victoria, B.C., Canada V8S 1H2
250-370-1918
Fax: 250-370-1968

A gracious manor home in a residential district

Innkeepers: Susan and Tony Temple. **Accommodations:** 4 rooms. **Rates:** (Cd) $120–$195. **Included:** Full breakfast. **Minimum stay:** 2 nights weekends and holidays. **Payment:** MasterCard, Visa. **Children:** Welcome by arrangement. **Pets:** Not allowed. **Smoking:** Not allowed. **Open:** Year-round.

➤ **Mulberry Manor is close to Oak Bay, where you can stroll the path along the bluff above the water and admire some of Victoria's prettiest gardens.**

This lovely haven is in one of Victoria's finest neighborhoods, a few minutes' drive from Inner Harbour but far removed from its tourist bustle. Built in 1926, it is one of the last great homes designed by the renowned B.C. architect, Samuel Maclure. The Tudor house rests on a landscaped acre behind stone walls and surrounded by trees. There are ponds, a birdbath, flower beds, and a greenhouse tucked away in back. Both Susan and Tony Temple are fond of gardening and in warm weather invite guests to enjoy breakfast outdoors.

When the weather is cool, breakfast is served in the red-walled dining room. The table is set with fine china, silver, crystal, and linens, for, Susan says, "I spent 25 years saving these things, and I like to use them." Early risers are greeted with coffee and croissants; breakfast includes fruit, cereals, cinnamon buns, homemade berry jams and lemon curd, and a different entrée, such as smoked salmon crêpes or frittata, daily.

Later in the day, you can relax with tea by the fireplace in the calm, warm living room, or in the den, which has a TV and fireplace. There's a conservatory-like billiard room in the back that overlooks the garden; light streams through the leaded glass windows and French doors.

Each of the upstairs rooms is furnished with an eye to comfort. "I try to think about what guests really want," says Susan, who supplies extra pillows and blankets, padded hangers, hair dryers, and luggage racks.

Country Room is the smallest, with twin beds and a view of the garden from the window seat. Its bath is a few steps away. Rosewood Room has a four-poster bed, casement windows, and one of the original tile bathrooms. Gilded cherubs cavort in the spacious Angel Room, which has a private balcony. Jasmine Suite, in blue and yellow, is the largest room and has a balcony and a brass and white king-size iron bed. A separate sitting room with a daybed and fireplace makes the suite a good choice for a party of three.

Oak Bay Beach Hotel

1175 Beach Drive
Victoria, B.C., Canada V8S 2N2
250-598-4556
800-668-7758
Fax 250-598-6180

**A British-style inn
overlooking the water**

Proprietor: Kevin Walker. **Accommodations:** 50 rooms and suites. **Rates:** (Cd) Rooms, $114–$214 double; $25 additional person; suites, $174–$399. **Included:** Continental breakfast. **Minimum stay:** None. **Payment:** Major credit cards. **Children:** Welcome (cribs available). **Pets:** Not allowed. **Smoking:** Nonsmoking rooms available. **Open:** Year-round.

➤ **The Snug, the hotel's cozy pub, is a jolly place for all ages — the sort of spot where, long ago, the vicar would stop in for a sherry or the bobby for a pint.**

In the lobby of this half-timbered Tudor hotel, canaries sing in their cages, tea is served in the afternoons, chestnuts are roasted by the fire at Christmas, and a carved wooden postbox accepts the mail. You might be in the English countryside; but you look out on Haro Strait and the San Juan Islands. This is England, Canadian style.

The Oak Bay Beach Hotel, built in 1927, is the epitome of Victoria's penchant for things British. It stands proudly among the fashionable homes and magnificent gardens of the Oak Bay district, a reminder of the region's genteel heritage. The hotel's beautifully landscaped garden at the edge of the sea is lovely and worth a stop on a tour of Victoria.

To sustain the British mood, sign the guest register and step into another country, another century. Your dark-beamed room is likely to be furnished with English, mostly Victorian, antiques, and the TV will be hidden behind a cupboard door. Some rooms have window seats, some have balconies overlooking the garden and sea. Recent refurbishments have lightened the decor, now in shades of pink, mauve, and blue.

Long, narrow Georgian Suite, with an adjoining library (without books) has sitting areas and a balcony overlooking the sea. The Queen Anne Room boasts an ornately carved cherrywood four-poster bed. Henry VIII is the honeymoon suite — the irony of the room's name may be intended. Its king-size bed, covered with a white Nottingham lace spread and canopy, is an imposing four-poster brass antique that reaches to the ceiling. Dark tables and chests contrast with white walls and, in the alcove, a window looks toward the sea.

Several rooms have been remodeled to enlarge the bathrooms and add bay windows. You'll have to do without air conditioning, but the windows open to sea breezes. Request a seaside room for preferred views; some rooms on the street side overlook a parking lot.

With the Romantic Adventure package (available May–October), you'll receive two nights in a suite, champagne, wine glasses, chocolate truffles, breakfast in your room, and a candlelit dinner.

Piano music and voices mingle pleasantly over quiet dinners in the hotel's restaurant. The Continental menu has a Canadian touch, featuring B.C. salmon and lamb, but it's most noted for roast prime rib with Yorkshire pudding. A traditional high tea is offered in the afternoons, and all the favorites are served: crumpets, scones, Devonshire cream, fruit trifle, and pastries. On pleasant days, you may take your tea on the terrace overlooking the gardens and sea.

If you'd like to view Victoria from the sea, the hotel's 45-foot yacht, *Pride of Victoria,* offers whale-watching and sunset dinner cruises.

Ocean Pointe Resort

45 Songhees Road
Victoria, B.C., Canada V9A 6T3
250-360-2999
800-667-4677
Fax: 250-360-1041
ocean-pointe@pinc.com

A contemporary resort on Inner Harbour

General Manager: F. Ulrich "Rick" Stolle. **Accommodations:** 250 rooms and suites. **Rates:** (Cd) Summer, $209–$279; winter, $164–$229 single or double; $25 additional person. **Minimum stay:** None. **Payment:** Major credit cards. **Children:** Welcome. **Pets:** Not allowed. **Smoking:** Nonsmoking floors available. **Open:** Year-round

➤ **Seacoast Expeditions offers whale-watching trips off Vancouver Island. In summer, small passenger ferries provide an easy way to get to various attractions.**

Victoria's splashy, sophisticated resort is anything but Victorian in style and spirit. The modern, 8-story hotel, facing Inner Harbour, boasts an up-to-date spa (algae body wraps, aromatherapy, scalp treatments, Stairmasters, racquetball), a staff physiotherapist, a complete business center, and low-sodium West Coast cuisine, among other features unknown in Queen Victoria's reign.

Every guest room has a mini-bar and most have commanding views of the harbor, an ever-changing scene of sailboats and ferries, with the Parliament Buildings on the opposite shore. Some rooms overlook the "working harbor," less scenic but interesting with boat and Johnson Street Bridge activity. The resort is within easy walking distance of downtown.

The varied rooms include 2-story lofts, junior suites, dormer rooms, and senior suites, with dining areas, kitchenettes, and light, contemporary furnishings. Rooms with the best views are on the higher floors.

The Boardwalk is the hotel's informal restaurant. At the buffet counter you can concoct a salad, choose a pasta, or build a sandwich. Across the hall is the Brasserie, a cozy, private space with black furniture and a steak and seafood menu. The Victorian restaurant, with a domed ceiling, polished silver, and an antique wine cabinet, has a more formal atmosphere and offers fine regional cuisine, artistically presented. It's known as one of the city's best restaurants.

The focus at Ocean Pointe is its waterfront vantage point. Meals are served on the expansive harborside terrace by the Boardwalk and the public spaces all take advantage of the dramatic view.

The resort was only a dream in 1984, when Rick and Kathryn Stolle saw the property and decided to build. It took 8 years to raise the financial backing and design and construct the hotel.

Ocean Pointe opened in 1992 and is widely admired for its solid quality, European hospitality (Rick had extensive hotel experience in Germany), and host of amenities. Now owned by a Japanese firm, it's still operated by Stolle Services, Ltd.

Prior House

620 St. Charles
Victoria, B.C., Canada V8S 3N7
250-592-8847
Fax: 250-592-8223
innkeeper@priorhouse.com

> Edwardian grandeur and a
> friendly welcome

Innkeepers: Candis and Ted Cooperrider. **Accommodations:** 6 rooms. **Rates:** (Cd) $115–$265 single or double, $25 additional person; off-season discounts available. **Included:** Full breakfast, afternoon tea. **Minimum stay:** 2 nights in July and August and on holidays. **Payment:** MasterCard, Visa. **Children:** Age 9 and older, welcome. **Pets:** Not allowed. **Smoking:** Outdoors only. **Open:** Year-round.

➤   **You'll find British imports and Native crafts on Government Street, the marketplace at Victoria Eaton Centre, and Bastion and Market Squares. Don't miss Munro's Books, a great bookstore.**

In 1912, a 23-room home was built for Edward Gawler Prior, the king's representative in British Columbia. A typical grand Edwardian mansion, it had rich oak paneling, stained glass windows, and carved stone terraces overlooking a garden. The lieutenant governor's home, still in a prestigious district of the city, now welcomes travelers eager to savor the splendors of a bygone era.

Every afternoon, tea and scones are served in the parlor, which is furnished with antiques, while guests browse among books on local history and decide where to dine. In the morning, everyone eats together in the dining room, where Candis serves fresh fruit, muffins, eggs, and toast. You can also choose to eat in your room.

The guests' quarters, also with antique furniture, are decorated with muted colors and floral fabrics. Some rooms enjoy views through the treetops of the Strait of Juan de Fuca and the Olympic Mountains. The smallest room is Boudoir, in pink and aqua; it has a fireplace, TV, and a clawfoot bathtub across the hall. The Garden Suite, with a private outside entrance, is where families with children stay.

The spacious Windsor Suite occupies the third floor (expect to climb narrow, steep stairs). It holds a refrigerator, TV, queen-size bed, and antique vanity. French doors open to a balcony with a broad view. The generous bath has a large marble Jacuzzi under a skylight.

The most expensive accommodation is the luxurious Lieutenant Governor's Suite, where you'll find an 1880s bed canopied in lace, a cozy fireplace, and a view of the Olympics through the trees. The large marble bath has such elegant touches as crystal chandeliers and gold swan fixtures. The refrigerator is stocked with champagne and soft drinks.

Phone jacks are in every room, and the downtown area is only minutes away, but Prior House is not geared to the business traveler. It's a peaceful, relaxing inn of high quality in a lovely neighborhood — a nice base for exploring the city.

Swans Hotel

506 Pandora Avenue
Victoria, B.C., Canada V8W 1N6
250-361-3310
800-668-7926
Fax: 250-361-3491

A suites hotel near the Johnson Street bridge

General Manager: Janine Ceglarz. **Accommodations:** 29 suites. **Rates:** (Cd) Summer, $145–$185; winter, $79–$139 single or double; $15 additional person. **Minimum stay:** None. **Payment:** Major credit cards. **Children:** Welcome. **Pets:** Not allowed. **Smoking:** Nonsmoking rooms available. **Open:** Year-round.

➤ **Victoria has many innovative art and cultural events, such as Symphony Splash in the summer and the TerrifVic Dixieland Jazz Party, one of the largest festivals of its kind in North America.**

An ugly duckling has turned into a swan in downtown Victoria. Once a rundown warehouse, granary, and feed store, it's now a sophisticated hotel with flower boxes at every window and tastefully furnished split-level suites. Also on the property are a lively pub, a café, a beer and wine store, and the brewery that makes Buckerfield's beer. (Tours are offered daily.)

The pub and the Fowl Fish Café, with their cozy atmosphere of oak and brick, fresh flowers, and original art, are popular with Victorians who like bright, contemporary surroundings. A block from the Johnson Street bridge on the north side, the complex is a few minutes walk from the city's major galleries, theaters, and shopping.

The spacious suites have full kitchens, separate dining areas, and living rooms, and hold up to six people.

The Victoria Regent Hotel

1234 Wharf Street
Victoria, B.C., Canada V8W 3H9
250-386-2211
800-663-7472
Fax: 250-386-2622

Contemporary condos on the harbor

Manager: Earl Wilde. **Accommodations:** 44 rooms and suites. **Rates:** (Cd) Summer, $159–$699; winter, $109–$599; $20 additional person. **Included:** Continental breakfast. **Minimum stay:** None. **Payment:** Major credit cards. **Children:** Under age 16, free in room with a parent. **Pets:** Not allowed. **Smoking:** Nonsmoking rooms available. **Open:** Year-round.

➤ **A short walk away is Bastion Square, the site of the original Fort Victoria, which now has shops, restaurants, and the Maritime Museum.**

Everything a seasoned traveler wants is provided at the Regent: comfortable beds, good reading lamps, lots of hangers in large closets, desks, convenient phones, coffeemakers, and quiet.

Parking is underground and secured. A morning newspaper is brought to your door. The decor is clean and uncluttered.

The bonus here is the stunning view. Half of the condominiums overlook Inner Harbour; these are the preferred rooms. From high, wide windows or your balcony you can watch the ferries and seaplanes, seagulls, and little harbor taxis scooting over the water. On clear days you can see snow-capped mountains in the distance.

Suites have one, two, or three bedrooms and equipped kitchens. Executive suites are like luxury apartments, with fireplaces, Jacuzzis, and dens. Standard rooms, the least expensive, have king-size beds and no water view.

Breakfast is served in Water's Edge Café, a small restaurant on the ground floor. It's right on the harbor, but if you're staying in a room with a view, ask to have breakfast brought to your room so you can savor every moment.

Whistler

Chateau Whistler Resort

4599 Chateau Boulevard
Whistler, B.C., Canada V0N 1B4
604-938-8000
800-441-1414
Fax: 604-938-2020

A grand lodge in the mountains

General manager: David Roberts. **Accommodations:** 563 rooms and suites. **Rates:** (Cd) Rooms, $175–$325 single or double; suites, $275–$1,000; rates vary according to season and room availability. **Minimum stay:** None. **Payment:** Major credit cards. **Children:** Under age 18, free with a parent. **Pets:** Small pets allowed. **Smoking:** Nonsmoking rooms available. **Open:** Year-round.

➤ **Events here include the World Cup Downhill race in March, the Great Snow, Earth, and Water Race in June, a country and blues music festival in July, the Vancouver Symphony in August, and jazz in September.**

The largest château-style hotel to be built in Canada in the past 100 years stands at the base of Blackcomb Mountain outside the alpine village of Whistler. Blackcomb's high-speed lifts, which provide year-round access to ski slopes, are a few yards from the doors of the imposing stone structure that is part of the chain of Canadian Pacific Hotels and Resorts.

Though the exterior has the timeless appearance of a grand château, the luxuries inside are strictly contemporary. Rooms contain individual climate control, television, and mini-bars, and some have two-line telephones with teleconferencing ability.

The recreation center has an indoor/outdoor pool, whirlpool tubs, saunas and steam rooms, and an exercise room. There are three tennis courts and an 18-hole golf course. The facilities receive plenty of use, but skiing remains the major draw. Within minutes a chair lift will take you to the longest vertical runs in North America. In summer you can ride to the top and hike the high meadows or ride a mountain bike all the way back.

Après-ski relaxation is available in La Fiesta, a casual, lively restaurant offering Mexican food and Spanish tapas. If you're still feeling energetic after a day outdoors, you can dance here until the wee hours. The Mallard Bar is a smaller, tranquil retreat featuring a light menu, specialty coffees, and extraordinary desserts. Cocktails are served by the large fireplace in the bar, which has a wildlife theme created by Canadian folk artists. Three meals a day are prepared in The Wildflower Restaurant, under the direction of its executive chef, Glen Monk. He specializes in West Coast cuisine with an Asian flair.

The hotel has underground and surface parking, valet and secretarial services, and a variety of retail stores. Only 75 miles from Vancouver on the scenic Sea to Sky Highway, it draws the convention trade but is equally appealing to tourists, honeymooners, and families.

Crystal Lodge

P. O. Box 280
Whistler, B.C., Canada V0N 1B0
604-932-2221
800-667-3363 in western states
604-688-6260 in Vancouver
Fax: 604-932-2635

A friendly hotel in the heart of the village

General Manager: John Douglas. **Accommodations:** 97 rooms and 41 suites. **Rates:** (Cd) $125–$275 double, $25 additional person. Off-season discounts and golf and ski packages available. **Minimum stay:** None. **Payment:** Major credit cards. **Children:** Age 2–12, $10 in winter; age 2 and under, free. **Pets:** Not allowed. **Smoking:** Nonsmoking rooms available. **Open:** Year-round.

➤ **Whistler has been rated the #1 ski resort in North America and is Canada's busiest winter tourist destination. It has some 10,000 hotel rooms.**

Crystal Lodge began as the Nancy Greene Lodge, built by the Olympic ski champion and her husband, Al Raine, in 1984. The five-story hotel stands in the heart of the alpine village. Arched windows, bright awnings, and window boxes full of flowers in summer soften the lines of the steel and concrete hotel and add to its European flavor. On one side, there's a heated swimming pool and whirlpool tub, a delight to every sore-muscled skier.

Inside, The Crystal Lounge is on one side of the carpeted lobby; on the other is the Spaghetti Factory, a busy family-focused restaurant with reasonable prices. The hotel also has a Japanese restaurant, Irori.

In the lobby, an evening fire burns in the stone fireplace and a television and VCR are at hand. Movies are available at a nearby video store. There are shops outside on the village street level of the lodge, selling sports clothes, ski equipment, and gifts.

Guest accommodations are roomy and comfortable, light in tone and furnished with TVs, phones, extra hooks and shelves, and pleasing colors. Some have kitchenettes, and laundry facilities are available for guests' use. Best are the balcony rooms, which face west, overlooking the swimming pool and mountain-rimmed valley. The honeymoon and VIP suites have marble kitchens and Jacuzzi tubs.

Although skiing is Whistler's claim to fame, with numerous lifts and miles of groomed runs and trails, it's not the only recreation offered. In summer you can fish, boat, windsurf, or swim in five lakes or play golf. There are three courses within five minutes of the lodge. You can hike to alpine meadows, go horseback riding, or try whitewater rafting. And if skiing is all you want, you can do that year-round on Blackcomb.

The Delta Whistler Resort

4050 Whistler Way
P.O. Box 550
Whistler, B.C., Canada V0N 1B0
604-932-1982
800-268-1133
Fax: 604-932-7332

> **A complete family resort in the mountains**

Manager: Hank Stackhouse. **Accommodations:** 292 rooms and suites. **Rates:** (Cd) Rooms, $335–$400; suites, $470–$1,200; special rates and packages available. **Minimum stay:** None. **Payment:** Major credit cards. **Children:** Under 18, free with a parent. **Pets:** Allowed if caged in room. **Smoking:** Nonsmoking rooms available. **Open:** Year-round.

▶ **Whistler is also appealing in spring and summer. Lush forests, glacier-crowned peaks, blue lakes, and flowery meadows draw hikers, bicyclists, and sightseers.**

Whistler Village is a resort community that exists mainly for skiing, though it's rapidly expanding into a year-round destination. When the snow falls, skiers by the hundreds take the winding 75-mile road from Vancouver to the slopes of Blackcomb and Whistler, headed for the mountains' 10,000 vertical feet of skiing and 180 marked and groomed runs. Whistler has an average annual snowfall of 450 inches.

Of the many lodges in the village, Delta is among the biggest, with extensive facilities. Anything you want in a winter resort you'll find here, from ski rentals to indoor and outdoor whirlpool hot tubs. There are laundry facilities, an exercise room, and a heated outdoor swimming pool. You can play tennis on covered courts, go heli-skiing, take a sleigh ride, or sink into one of the soft red chairs by the brass fireplace in the lobby and watch the colorful crowd go by.

The inn also has two restaurants. Whistler Garden serves fine Chinese cuisine, and Evergreen is a bistro-style eatery featuring West Coast cuisine. Youngsters like the children's menu and treasure chest of toys; their parents appreciate the fact that meals are free to visitors under age 6.

Such details, along with a wide range of activities, help make Delta a good family choice. Guest rooms vary, but all are furnished with practicality and an eye to maximizing space. Most have two double beds or two queen-size beds, mini-bars, phones, and television. Many contain fireplaces and Jacuzzi tubs. Some suites include saunas, balconies, and full kitchens, a boon to those who prefer not to eat every meal out.

Delta's location, 50 yards from ski lifts and 5 minutes from miles of groomed cross-country ski trails, is ideal; you can ski from your door. Popular with groups, the large inn is capable of handling crowds and has several meeting facilities and a staff that's skilled at helping to plan activities. You can expect a certain amount of noise at a place this busy, especially if you're in a room at the front of the hotel.

Several children's programs are offered at Whistler. Beginners have a slope to themselves where they'll find easy-loading chairlifts, several gentle runs, and a ski school.

Durlacher Hof

7055 Nesters Road, Box 1125
Whistler, B.C., Canada V0N 1B0
604-932-1924
Fax 604-938-1980
durlacherhof@bcsympatico.ca

A European-style chalet home

Innkeepers: Erika and Peter Durlacher. **Accommodations:** 8 rooms. **Rates:** (Cd) Summer, $110–$170 double; winter, $140–$255; ski packages available. **Included:** Full breakfast. **Minimum stay:** 2 nights on weekends. **Payment:** MasterCard, Visa. **Children:** Age 6 and older, welcome. **Pets:** Not allowed. **Smoking:** Not allowed. **Open:** Year-round.

➤ **Highway 99 from Vancouver to Whistler can be narrow and steep but is well maintained. Don't miss Shannon Falls Provincial Park and Brandywine Falls and their spectacular cascades of water.**

At the Durlachers' Austrian-Canadian inn, guests are welcomed as if they were cousins from the old country. When you arrive you take off your shoes, pull on the slippers provided, and enter a house where the hospitality is warm and genuine and the accommodations superlative.

Peter Durlacher grew up in Austria. Traces of his background are evident throughout the clean, light chalet home. Most interesting is the *kachelofen,* an ingenious heating system whereby a woodstove in the foyer warms the wall behind it and the parlor on the other side. The parlor is a comfortable place to relax after a day of skiing on the slopes of Blackcomb or Whistler. Another relaxing spot is the whirlpool tub on the deck.

Guests gather for a bountiful breakfast in the dining area beside the parlor. Erika prepares Kaiser Smoren pancakes, an Austrian delicacy baked with raisins and smothered in currant preserves. Fruit muesli, homemade breads, ham and cheese, fresh berries, and eggs Benedict are a few other breakfast examples. Three or four times a week in winter, the Durlachers prepare dinners, at extra cost, that feature Austrian dishes such as Wiener schnitzel or pork loin. Fondue and raclette are favorites with their visitors.

The one guest room on the main floor is wheelchair-accessible. Others, up the carpeted stairs, are furnished in custom-made pine and decorated in hunter green and rich jewel tones, Ralph Lauren style. The beds are queen-size or twins. In the sitting room of the honeymoon suite you'll find a bottle of chilled champagne, fresh flowers, and a tray of cheese and crackers. The suite has a whirlpool tub and private deck.

The main thing that sets Durlacher Hof apart is the ebullient charm of the hosts. They often join guests on the slopes and will invite you to join in afternoon tea, organize activities, recommend dining spots, or leave you alone if you wish.

Idaho

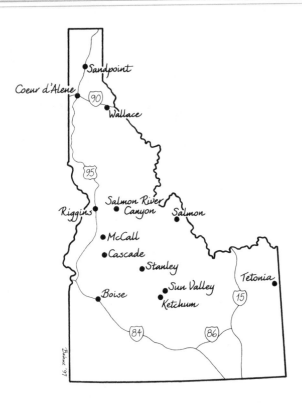

Best Intimate City Stops

Boise
Idanha Hotel, 116
Coeur d'Alene
The Blackwell House, 120

Best Country Inns and B&Bs

Ketchum
Knob Hill Inn, 124
The River Street Inn, 125
McCall
Hotel McCall, 126
Sun Valley
Idaho Country Inn, 140

Best Resorts

Coeur d'Alene
The Coeur d'Alene Resort, 121
McCall
Shore Lodge, 128
Sandpoint
Schweitzer Mountain Resort, 133
Sun Valley
Elkhorn Resort and Golf Club, 138
Sun Valley Lodge, 141

Best Romantic Getaways

Ketchum
Knob Hill Inn, 124

Best Wilderness Retreats

Cascade
Wapiti Meadow Ranch, 118

Idaho is wilderness country. Forty percent of the 53-million-acre state is covered by trees, 16,000 miles of rivers and streams gouge canyons and roar through valleys, and 200 mountain peaks rise 8,000 feet or higher. The deepest gorge in North America, Hell's Canyon, splits the state from neighboring Oregon. From the Snake River on the west through the big waters of the northern panhandle to the Bitterroot Range at the Montana border, Idaho is rugged.

This topography was millions of years in the making. Upthrust mountain masses that were under vast seas when the world was young, immense lava flows, and centuries of ice age glaciation have formed a landscape of surpassing splendor, a place to walk with care and awe.

The largest federal wilderness area in the lower 48 states is the 2.4-million-acre Frank Church–River of No Return Wilderness. It is bordered on the north by another 3.7 million acres of roadless terrain, the Selway-Bitterroot and Gospel Hump wilderness areas, and the Sawtooth Wilderness lies to the south.

South of the Sawtooths, those jagged fangs that bite the sky above the valley where the **Salmon River** begins, lie **Ketchum** and **Sun Valley.** In contrast to their primitive surroundings, these resort areas offer luxurious accommodations, fine dining, chic shopping, and superb skiing.

Boise, Idaho's capital, stands at the edge of a desert, an arid plain stretching in three directions, with a green and mountainous landscape at its northern door. Residents view their city as a place with a touch of elegance, a lot of hospitality, and an attitude that welcomes the new while preserving the old. Boise has a top-quality performing arts center and excellent museums.

The Snake River Birds of Prey Area, the greatest nesting site of eagles, hawks, and prairie falcons in North America, lies 30 miles south of Boise. To see the protected raptors, arm yourself with binoculars and join a group floating the Snake River. You can also tour the World Center for Birds of Prey, a million-dollar research facility near the Boise Airport.

Four hundred miles north, as the raptor flies, up in panhandle country, are pristine lakes, ski slopes, and forested hiking trails. **Coeur d'Alene** and **Sandpoint** have attractive resorts that draw crowds looking for outdoor recreation and comfortable lodgings.

Northern Idaho is historic mining country. The village of **Wallace** bills itself as the Silver Capital of the World. Here you can tour a silver mine or a railroad museum, watch an old-time melodrama, and buy silver bullion and jewelry.

Several airlines serve Idaho, with Boise the main hub. In the Northwest, Horizon Air (800-547-9308) offers getaway packages that include airfare and hotel accommodations.

For more information, write or call the Boise Convention and Visitors Bureau, P.O. Box 2106, Boise, Idaho 83701 (800-635-5240).

Boise

Idanha Hotel

928 Main Street
Boise, ID 83702
208-342-3611
800-714-7346
Fax: 208-383-9690

A turn-of-the-century hotel in the capital

Manager: Denny Goodman. **Accommodations:** 44 rooms and suites. **Rates:** $50–$121 single or double, $6 additional person. **Included:** Continental breakfast. **Minimum stay:** None. **Payment:** Major credit cards. **Children:** Welcome. **Pets:** Dogs allowed. **Smoking:** Nonsmoking rooms available. **Open:** Year-round.

➤ **Boise's capitol, topped by a 250-pound bronze and copper eagle, contains unusual statuary and is well worth a tour.**

The 6-story Idanha was the tallest building in Idaho when it was put up in 1901 and was considered the utmost in luxury. However, by 1979, the historic hotel seemed outdated and unusable and was scheduled for demolition. Then a group of people who loved the old brick building joined forces, bought the Boise landmark, and restored it to its original status of quiet prestige. Now it's a place of style and individuality with more than a touch of quaint charm. The Idanha had the state's first electric elevator, which is still running. Other reminders of a former day are the brass handrails and polished woods on the staircase, the red velvet settees, old brass bedsteads, tower rooms, clawfoot bathtubs, and gold-flocked wallpaper.

Within the gray walls of the lobby is a small lounge, divided from the entryway by a plant-laden ledge. The hotel's restaurant, Peter Schott's, is Boise's nod to elegance. In a setting of subdued colors, classical music, white linens, fresh flowers, and candlelight, diners enjoy fine cuisine. Try the Brie soup, a specialty, or the flavorful house salad, crunchy with cashews. The veal is served with chanterelles and the tender lamb noisettes are cooked to order.

Each guest room has a TV and phone and a few of the hotel's original furnishings and paintings. The biggest rooms are the tower and bay window rooms on the lower floors. The higher you go, the smaller the rooms. Guests receive a free daily newspaper and, on request, free airport taxi service.

No self-respecting hotel with a past is complete without its ghost, and the Idanha, which aims to please, has one. It seems that a long-ago guest who died tragically visits the fourth floor on occasion, for some people say one of the rooms has an eerie feeling, as if it's being watched. Whether you sense a ghost or not, you are certain to feel the spirit of another era.

Cascade

Wapiti Meadow Ranch

HC 72
Cascade, ID 83611
208-633-3217
Fax: 208-633-3219
wapitimr@aol.com

A wilderness ranch with civilized comforts

Proprietor: Diana Swift. **Accommodations:** 4 cabins. **Rates:** May–November, $1,000–$,1320 per person per week; November–May, $100 per person per day. **Included:** All meals and activities except rafting and guided fly-fishing. **Minimum stay:** 3 nights. **Payment:** Cash or check. **Children:** Welcome, but ranch is adult-oriented. **Pets:** Not allowed. **Smoking:** Allowed but discouraged. **Open:** Year-round.

➤ **This fly-fishing ranch is endorsed by Orvis, with guides and instruction available. Fishing waters include the Middle and South forks of the Salmon River.**

In a secluded mountain valley in the pristine wilderness of southwestern Idaho, one of the first dude ranches in the Northwest opened in the 1920s. Clark and Beulah Cox and their son, Lafe, built a log and stone lodge, hauling the massive lodgepole pine logs to the site with teams of draft horses. Later, Lafe and Emma Cox ran the ranch for 40 years.

Now Wapiti Meadow is owned by Diana Swift, a horsewoman drawn west from Virginia by the lure of Idaho's back country. She's created a resort ranch that visitors rave about.

The astute innkeeper combines rugged adventure with such civilized touches as fresh flowers, chilled wine, a cheese platter, and a fruit basket in your cabin. The one- and two-bedroom carpeted cabins are light, airy, clean, and inviting. Each cabin has a woodstove on a stone hearth (plus electric heat), a game or dining table set by the picture window, and a kitchenette with a coffeemaker and a refrigerator containing soft drinks.

Meals range from homemade sweet rolls and egg-sausage dishes at breakfast to wine-sauced chicken and occasional barbecues for dinner. Dessert might be a flaky, homemade chocolate eclair. Meals are served in the main lodge, the heart of the ranch. Any notions of leathery beef from the chuck wagon will be quickly dispelled when you join the other guests at a single long table in the dining room. Fine china, crystal, and silver set an elegant mood.

Diana says that first-time visitors are often amazed to see antique furniture from Virginia in this atmosphere of homespun warmth. She's mixed curios and heirlooms with rustic mountain country pieces to charming effect. In the living room, guests enjoy after-dinner coffee and board games around the big stone fireplace.

A wide porch stretching the length of the lodge is a favorite gathering place. It overlooks the pastures and the high, wooded ridge across the creek. Deer and elk are often spotted ambling through the meadows.

Numerous pack and float trips are available, as well as executive retreats and individually planned adventures in backpacking, backcountry fishing, and camping. You can go horseback riding, pan for gold, visit old mining sites, or photograph wildflowers.

This is one of the few remote Idaho ranches accessible by car. You can also arrange a flight to the small airfield nearby.

Coeur D'Alene

The Blackwell House

820 Sherman Avenue
Coeur d'Alene, ID 83814
208-664-0656
800-899-0656
Fax: 208-664-0656

A stately, turn-of-the-century home

Innkeeper: Kathleen Sims. **Accommodations:** 8 rooms (6 suites with private baths; 2 share 1 bath). **Rates:** $75–$125 double. **Included:** Full breakfast. **Minimum stay:** None. **Payment:** Major credit cards. **Children:** Age 12 and over, welcome. **Pets:** Not allowed. **Smoking:** Restricted. **Open:** Year-round

➤ **Lake Coeur d'Alene, the St. Joe River, old mines, and ghost towns make this region a playground and an education in frontier history**

From the time this house was built in 1904 by F. A. Blackwell as a wedding gift for his son Russell and Pauline Kelly Blackwell, it has been considered Coeur d'Alene's most elegant home. It stands in stately splendor on the corner of 8th and Sherman, the town's main street, with white wicker chairs and swing beckoning visitors to the verandah.

Inside, the sense of gracious tradition continues with wingback chairs, a deep burgundy couch, a marble fireplace, and lace-curtained windows in the living room. Beyond is the formal dining room, and then the sun room, where breakfasts of French toast, apple pancakes, and omelets are served. It's a natural step from here to the back lawn, which runs the length of the street. With its gazebo and flower gardens, this is a popular site for weddings and parties. Kathleen will also prepare dinners for groups of six or more.

The suites on the second floor have a turn-of-the-century look, subtly updated. The largest and most elaborate is the Blackwell Suite, a romantic mauve and rose setting for honeymooners. Its white wicker couch and chair have heart-shaped backs, the queen-size bed is a four-poster with lace pillows, and as a final playful touch, there's a bride and groom pair of large white bears.

The rooms on the third floor, in the former servants' quarters, have been redone with private baths. The small Maid's Room is simple, with a white cover on the double bed, a rocker, and lace curtains at low windows. The Play Room, once a nursery, has two double beds and lots of space. Families and groups often take the entire third floor, which also has a sitting area with wingback chairs and a rolltop desk.

Kathleen, a lifelong resident of the Inland Empire, as the Spokane–Coeur d'Alene region is called, can suggest enough activities and sightseeing to fill anyone's vacation.

The Coeur d'Alene Resort

115 South 2nd Street
Coeur d'Alene, ID 83814
208-765-4000
800-688-5253
Fax: 208-664-7279

A lakeside resort for golf and water recreation

Manager: William Reagan. **Accommodations:** 338 rooms and suites, plus 10 condominiums. **Rates:** Rooms, $79–$329; suites, $350–$2,500; condos, $200–$379; rates vary seasonally. **Minimum stay:** None. **Payment:** Major credit cards. **Children:** Under age 18, free. **Pets:** Not allowed. **Smoking:** Nonsmoking rooms available. **Open:** Year-round.

➤ **Within 75 miles of town are 1,500 miles of rivers and streams and 112 lakes. Silver Mountain, 35 miles east, offers bike trails, chairlift rides, and day and night skiing.**

Since it opened in 1986, this resort has become one of Idaho's major successes and earned numerous awards. It's a busy place, but not chaotic, thanks to good organization and a well-trained, friendly staff.

You'll find almost every resort comfort here on the northern shore of Lake Coeur d'Alene. There are indoor and outdoor swimming pools, a bowling alley, a highly rated 18-hole golf course, an exercise rooms, a racquetball court, two whirlpool baths, a sauna, and steam and weight rooms.

The lake offers all kinds of water sports: you can swim, fish, water ski, sail, or take a cruise or a seaplane ride. Four excursion boats carry parties of 65 to 400. Smaller boats zip golfers to the lakeside course, where a shuttle boat takes putters to the famous floating green on the 14th hole.

To get your bearings and appreciate the resort's distinctive, peaked-roof architecture, stroll "the world's longest floating boardwalk" (3,300 feet), which circles the boat-filled marina. Then walk down the long, shop-lined lobby of the resort and take note of Whispers Lounge, a quiet bar overlooking the lake. Another bar offers Top 40 entertainment and a big-screen TV.

Unless you rent a condo, your room will be in the Park Wing or the preferred 18-story Lake Tower. The spacious tower rooms have king-size beds, refrigerators, and fine views of the lake and marina. In the nine honeymoon suites, the beds are surrounded by mirrors (including one on the ceiling). Watercolors of abstract seascapes reflect the room's colors of cool blue, gray, and ivory. There are lake views, a Swedish fireplace in the sunken living area, a coffee table that pops up into a dining table, three telephones, a 33-channel TV, and a large whirlpool tub. Baths are on the small side, and climbing into the step-up tub demands agility.

The resort's main restaurant, Beverly's, on the 7th floor, is noted for its Northwest wine collection and Continental cuisine. On the main floor, the more casual Dockside also offers views of the lake. It's next to the Shore Lounge, one of the resort's three bars.

When you're looking for adventure, take a whitewater rafting trip through Hell's Canyon. A reliable, top-quality rafting outfitter is River Odysseys West, P.O. Box 579, Coeur d'Alene, Idaho 83814.

Ketchum

Heidelberg Inn

P.O. Box 5704
Ketchum, ID 83340
208-726-5361
800-284-4863
Fax: 208-726-2084

> **A budget-minded motel
> with extra conveniences.**

Resident Managers: Mary and Wayne Salman. **Accommodations:** 30 rooms.
Rates: $60–$125 single or double (rates vary seasonally), $8 additional person.
Included: Continental breakfast. **Minimum stay:** None. **Payment:** Major credit
cards. **Children:** Under age 13, free (cribs available). **Pets:** Allowed ($5).
Smoking: Nonsmoking rooms available. **Open:** Year-round.

➤ **Across the road is Warm Springs Ranch Inn, which is well known in
the area for its good food. Trout and homemade cobbler are specialties.**

One of the better values in the expensive Sun Valley area, the Heidelberg Inn offers 450-square-foot guest rooms, several with kitchenettes and fireplaces. They all have king-size or one or two queen-
size beds. Each room has a small refrigerator, a crushed velvet
swivel rocker, cable TV and a VCR, and an open closet in the van-
ity-dressing area. Coffee is provided and a Continental breakfast is
delivered to your door. One room has a marble-base fireplace made
of lava rock. Only a few units have tubs; most feature showers
with built-in seats.

Further touches make the Heidelberg even more attractive: picnic and barbecue facilities on the nicely kept grounds, a small outdoor swimming pool with a slide, a laundry room, and a sauna and
hot tub. In the renovated lobby, you can rent movies or browse
through brochures on the area.

Conveniently located along Warm Springs Road between Sun
Valley and the Warm Springs Ski Area, the two-story motel is a
mile from downtown Ketchum. A free bus shuttles skiers to all
lifts in the area.

Knob Hill Inn

P.O. Box 800
960 North Main St.
Ketchum, ID 83340
208-726-8010
800-526-8010
Fax: 208-726-2712
knobhillinn@sunvalley.net

A luxurious inn near Sun Valley ski lifts

Owners: Joe and Sandy Koenig. **Accommodations:** 24 rooms and suites. **Rates:** Summer, $160–$300 single or double; winter, $175–$350; $25 additional person. **Included:** Continental breakfast. **Minimum stay:** Varies seasonally. **Payment:** Major credit cards. **Children:** Welcome. **Pets:** Not allowed. **Smoking:** Not allowed. **Open:** Year-round.

➤ **There are four 18-hole golf courses nearby.**

The Knob Hill Inn, which lies at the heart of this famous resort area, is a country inn with a European flavor and wondrous views of Bald Mountain and the Sawtooth and Boulder ranges. A member of the prestigious Relais & Chateaux, the inn ranks high among the small luxury hotels of the Northwest.

Each spacious room is tastefully decorated in bright, cheerful colors and has a king-size or twin beds, cable TV, a wet bar, a dressing room, a marble bathroom with tub and separate shower, and glass doors that open to a balcony with a view of the mountains. Some rooms have fireplaces. Even the pool house, where there is a lap pool, Jacuzzi, and sauna, overlooks Bald Mountain and Griffin Butte.

Curved arches, soft colors, and pots of greenery make the restaurant a pleasant dining spot. There's also a European-style bakery.

Activities in the area are plentiful in all seasons. In summer, you can play golf or tennis, hike, ride horses or bicycles, and take rafting trips. In winter, skiers come from around the world to ski the mountain slopes. A public bus stops in front of the inn and goes to the ski lifts and shopping areas of Sun Valley, Ketchum, and Elkhorn.

The River Street Inn

100 Rivers Street West
Ketchum, ID
Mailing address:
P.O. Box 182,
Sun Valley, ID 83353
208-726-3611
800-954-8885, ext. 1020
Fax: 208-726-2439

> **A gracious B&B near Sun Valley**

Innkeepers: Scott and Amy Smith. **Accommodations:** 8 rooms. **Rates:** $130–$185 single or double; off-season, $89; $25 additional person. **Included:** Full breakfast. **Minimum stay:** None. **Payment:** Major credit cards. **Children:** Welcome. **Pets:** Accepted with notice. **Smoking:** Not allowed in rooms. **Open:** Year-round.

➤ **Evergreen Restaurant has a bistro menu and excellent wine list. Warm Springs Ranch serves good western food and has a deck over a creek. Salvatore's is known for its Italian dishes and Ketchum Grill for an imaginative menu.**

The mailing address is Sun Valley, but this bed-and-breakfast inn is on Trail Creek in Ketchum, the bustling little town a few miles from the Sun Valley resort area. In fact, Ketchum is a resort community in its own right, with vacation homes spread over the hills, motels filled with skiers, and restaurants busy every night. It's still a neighborly place, though, as it was when Hemingway lived here.

In summer, pansies sprout from whiskey barrels on the deck of the inn, and the cottonwoods and aspens that are bare in winter bend green over the creek. Inside, sun fills the rooms in all seasons, for there are big windows everywhere. The eight investors who put up the inn in 1985 decided against an antique look or rustic effect, and the result is a gracious white home of indeterminate age.

From an enclosed porch you enter the living room, where a fire burns in the brick fireplace all winter long. A couple of couches face the fire; brass racks beside them are filled with magazines and books.

On the creek side of the room, guests are served breakfast at a long table by the deck. Fresh fruit, juice, and muffins or coffee cake are always a part of the meal, along with a main dish such as pancakes, waffles, sausages, or omelets. Apple-stuffed danish is a house specialty. The innkeepers offer tea or lemonade and cookies in the afternoons and après-ski wine or beer.

There are six rooms upstairs and three on the ground floor. All are crisply clean, furnished luxuriously, and decorated with a sure, professional taste. They have phones, TV, refrigerators, and Japanese soaking tubs. Bathrooms have oversize glass showers.

The Bridal Suite features a dark, curved headboard on the king-size bed, a fan window near the 15-foot ceiling, and a bay with windows overlooking the creek and mountains.

McCall

Hotel McCall

1101 North Third St.
P.O. Box 1778
McCall, ID 83638
208-634-8105
Fax: 208-634-8755

A renovated hotel near Payette Lake

Owner: Dr. John Carey. **Manager:** Ginny Ackley. **Accommodations:** 22 rooms and suites (16 with private bath, 6 share 2 baths). **Rates:** $50–$195 single or double, $10 additional person. **Included:** Expanded Continental breakfast. **Minimum stay:** 2 nights during Winter Carnival. **Payment:** Major credit cards. **Children:** Under age 10, free. **Pets:** Not allowed. **Smoking:** Outdoors only. **Open:** Year-round.

➤ **McCall, once an active logging town, today offers year-round resort recreation, including excellent alpine and nordic skiing. The Winter Carnival takes place the last two weeks in January.**

This friendly inn in a mountain village in western Idaho has a country atmosphere. It's the second Hotel McCall; the original burned and this one was built in 1939. In 1988, the three-story stucco hotel was returned to the 1930s style of its heyday, with the addition of such modern features as private baths, TV, and phones. The rooms are small but comfortable, with duvets covering the beds. Soft pastels predominate.

Best are the three suites, with views of Payette Lake, sitting areas, and king-size beds. The rooms on the basement level have queen-size or twin beds and share baths down the hall. Robes are provided. There are ski racks in the downstairs hall and a game room with board games and a big-screen TV and VCR.

In the afternoon, complimentary tea and Idaho wine, and usually a snack such as the chef's spicy salsa with chips, are served on the garden patio or sun deck. A buffet breakfast of muffins, cereals, and fruit is offered in the dining room. Other extras include morning coffee on each floor and a newspaper delivered to your door.

Across the street from the hotel is the city park, with a lakeside beach, lawns, and benches.

Shore Lodge

501 West Lake Street.
McCall, ID 83638
208-634-2244
800-657-6464
Fax: 208-634-7504

> **A year-round resort at the edge of a lake**

Manager: Bill Johnson. **Accommodations:** 116 units. **Rates:** Rooms, $59–$89 single or double; $10 additional person; suites, $149; off-season discounts available. **Minimum stay:** None. **Payment:** Major credit cards. **Children:** Under age 12, free. **Pets:** Not allowed. **Smoking:** Nonsmoking rooms available. **Open:** Year-round.

➤ **Idaho is part of a national wildlife watching program. For camera safaris and wilderness adventures, contact the Idaho Outfitters and Guides Association (208-342-1919).**

Renowned for its location on the shores of Payette Lake, Shore Lodge is a popular Idaho convention site about 100 miles north of Boise. The lake and surrounding forest provide opportunities for recreation in summer; winter offers skiers abundant dry powder at Brundage Mountain ski area nearby.

The lodge began as a small resort in the 1940s and since then has expanded along 800 feet of lakefront property. A $3 million renovation, completed in 1990, brought the rooms up to date and changed the public spaces. Now the lobby, in peeled logs and stone, is decorated in rich dark colors, tartans, and natural wood. Antlers form the light fixtures and fox-hunting prints hang on the walls. The effect is that of an English country manor combined with a hunting lodge of the West — an odd juxtaposition, but not unpleasing.

A restaurant overlooks the lake, and in the adjacent library–conversation area music is sometimes performed on the grand piano.

The guest rooms have various configurations, from studio size to deluxe lakeside suites. The baths have double sinks, and the suites contain refrigerators and cable television. Preferable (and most expensive) are ground-floor suites, which have kitchens and open onto Payette Lake, and second-floor rooms, with balconies that overlook the water.

The lake can also be enjoyed from a long boardwalk and from the flower-filled terrace or coffee shop. Shore Lodge has several sun decks, two outdoor swimming pools, a weight room, a racquetball court, and two tennis courts.

Riggins

The Lodge at Riggins Hot Springs

P.O. Box 1247
Riggins, ID 83549
208-628-3785
Fax: 208-628-3725

> **A wilderness retreat by the Salmon River**

Manager: Tony Bradbury. **Accommodations:** 10 rooms. **Rates:** $140–$320 single, $250–$320 double; entire lodge, $2,750 for up to 22 people; discounts December–May. **Included:** Dinner and breakfast; 3 meals for multi-night stays. **Minimum stay:** None. **Payment:** MasterCard, Visa. **Children:** Not appropriate. **Pets:** Well-behaved outdoor dogs allowed. **Smoking:** Allowed. **Open:** Year-round.

➤ **Exodus, a company associated with the lodge, offers spring and fall steelhead fishing, rafting, chukar hunting, and theme trips such as natural history and wine tasting.**

Few wilderness retreats offer the serenity and creature comforts of this outstanding lodge, 10 miles east of Riggins in west-central Idaho. You drive for 10 miles on a dirt road along the Salmon River and cross a suspension bridge to get to the 155-acre property.

Long before any bridges or roads, generations of Native Americans gathered here to enjoy and feel healed by the hot mineral springs. Later, miners, cowboys, and packers came to ease their pains. Today's guests soak in a large pool fed by the hot springs and receive fine hospitality as well. The lodge, formerly a business and family retreat, opened in 1991 after it was bought and redecorated by the Bradbury family. Their respect for Native American traditions is evident throughout the lodge in books and displays of their impressive collection of artifacts.

There's a touch of the Old West in the living room, where guests sit by the stone fireplace in the evening and drink complimentary wine and nibble on appetizers. Meals are usually taken at one table in the dining area; if there are few guests, the congenial innkeepers will join the group. The food, far above standard, is served buffet-style. Dinner entrées might be grilled pork with cranberry chutney, roast lamb with huckleberry sauce, or grilled salmon. Local huckleberries and
elderberries are often used.

Upstairs, each cozy room has pine paneling and a colorful Pendleton blanket. Two have private balconies overlooking the sweep of lawn and the river. They all have good reading lamps, firm beds, and air conditioning (which can be noisy). One sizable room, the White Pine Suite, is on the third floor; it has two queen-size beds and a sofa bed. In recent years, the lodge has expanded with three more rooms in a new building overlooking the pond. Each room has two queen-size beds.

The lodge is popular for weddings and groups up to 22 people. A bunkroom can be used as extra sleeping space if necessary. Other features include a conference center by the pool, satellite TV, a game room, a sauna, and a stocked trout pond.

Salmon

Twin Peaks Ranch

P.O. Box 774
Salmon, ID 83467
208-894-2290
800-659-4899 outside Idaho
Fax: 208-894-2429

**An old-fashioned dude
ranch in the mountains**

Operations Manager: Eleanor Wisner. **Accommodations:** 11 cabins. **Rates:** $1,250–$1,450 per adult per week, $1,000–$1,150 age 10 and under; deluxe suite, $2,200–$2,500. **Included:** All meals and activities. **Minimum stay:** 7 nights preferred in summer. **Payment:** MasterCard, Visa. **Children:** Over age 7, welcome. **Pets:** Not allowed. **Smoking:** Discouraged. **Open:** April to November

➤ **Outdoor adventure trips available include guided fishing trips, white-water rafting, scenic river floats, and overnight pack trips up to 8,700 feet in elevation.**

One of America's first authentic dude ranches, Twin Peaks retains its Old West character. The original ranch house, homesteaded at the turn of the century, the apple orchard, and the hand-hewn barn stand as if time passed them by. Many guests return year after year to the spectacular mountain location at 5,200 feet overlooking the Salmon River Gorge. Here you may see Rocky Mountain elk, big horn sheep, antelope, black bear, golden eagles, and great blue heron. The Shoshone and Blackfoot Indians lived in this area, 18 miles south of Salmon, and the Lewis and Clark Trail is nearby.

Fishing for salmon and steelhead, hiking, volleyball, rafting, camping for the kids, horseshoes, and swimming in the heated pool are among the many activities. Riding is the big favorite. You can learn in the rodeo arena and follow a wrangler on scenic trails along the river, through open range, and into the mountains. Pack trips can be arranged.

The ranch can accommodate 52 people in cabins with one to three rooms. They're all carpeted and have twin or queen-size beds and furnishings of lodgepole pine. Daily maid service is provided. The standard cabins are comfortable but rustic and do not have sitting rooms or porches. The newer and larger deluxe cabins have three bedrooms, whirlpool tubs, and spectacular views. A deluxe suite has two bedrooms, two baths, a kitchen, and laundry facilities.

Meals are served family style, with eight guests at each round table in the dining room of the knotty pine lodge. Steaks, chili, prime rib, chicken, and fish are typical of the hearty dinner entrées. Breakfast and dinner rides are included during the week.

Twin Peaks is centrally located, west of Yellowstone National Park, south of Glacier National Park, and north of Sun Valley. You can drive to the ranch or fly to an airport that is a 3-hour drive away. A van will pick you up at no charge.

Salmon River Canyon

Shepp Ranch

P.O. Box 5446
Boise, ID 83705
208-343-7729

A riverside ranch in the wilderness

Managers: Lynn and Mike Demerse. **Accommodations:** 6 cabins. **Rates:** $200 per person per day, $900 per person for 5 days, $800 per person with 3 or more in cabin, $140 ages 8–12; group discounts and packages available. **Included:** All meals, activities, and jetboat transportation. **Minimum stay:** None. **Payment:** No credit cards. **Children:** Over age 8, welcome. **Pets:** Not allowed. **Smoking:** Not allowed. **Open:** March through November.

➤ **There's a weekly steak barbecue, often a softball game, and music and stories by the campfire. There are no phones and no TV here. Mail arrives weekly by plane.**

In the roadless wilderness of the Nez Perce National Forest, Shepp Ranch lies on the banks of Crooked Creek and the Salmon River, surrounded by pine forests and rugged mountains. It's 43 miles upriver from Riggins and 15 miles from the nearest road; access is by plane or jetboat. But whatever it takes to get here is worth the trouble.

Charlie Shepp homesteaded the ranch at the turn of the century and lived here until his death in 1936. He is buried behind the main house. Charlie farmed and built a two-story house while his partner, Pete Klinkhammer, worked the mines and ran a trap line. After they were gone, the 100-acre property changed hands several times until it finally became a center for wilderness vacations.

Two of the log cabins, each with two rooms, are on a grassy bluff above the confluence of the river and the creek. In East-West Cabin, East has a double bed and two bunks; West has a double, four bunks, a couch, and a fireplace. A good night's sleep is virtually guaranteed when there's no sound but the rush of the river to disturb you.

North-South Cabin is similar but has been remodeled in knotty pine and has an adjoining door between the two rooms, convenient for families and groups. Filer and Shepp cabins are on the slope near the main house and are more modern. Each has a separate bedroom with a sofa bed, a refrigerator, and a shower and tub. These cabins cost an extra $20.

Most visitors spend little time in their rooms; there is too much to do outdoors. In summer, rafting and kayaking on the Salmon, horseback and mule riding, fishing, jetboating, volleyball, horseshoes, archery, hiking, and swimming are a few of the activities. Hunting is offered in the spring and fall.

On horseback you can ride trails up steep ridges to gain panoramic views of the valley and river; on the boats you can jet to deep, clear fishing and swimming holes. Pick raspberries or peas in the large garden, watch for wildlife, relax in a lawn chair, or curl up with a book in the library of the main house. Friendships form quickly. You'll be introduced in the dining room, where everyone gathers when the dinner bell rings, and get acquainted while platters of food are passed. Meals are abundant and appetizing, with produce from the garden, ham from ranch pigs, milk from the cow, and bread made daily.

The five-day, Monday to Saturday package is the most popular. It gives you enough time to enjoy the experience and decide to book a room for the next year, which is just what many guests do.

Sandpoint

Schweitzer Mountain Resort

P.O. Box 815
Sandpoint, ID 83864
208-265-0257
800-831-8810
Fax: 208-263-7961

A mountain resort for skiers, hikers, and music-lovers

Hotel manager: Dee Wolfe. **Accommodations:** 82 rooms and suites. **Rates:** $59–$150 single or double, $10 additional person; rates vary seasonally. **Included:** Continental breakfast. **Minimum stay:** 3 nights on holiday weekends, 5 nights over winter holidays. **Payment:** Major credit cards. **Children:** Under 12, free. **Pets:** Not allowed. **Smoking:** Nonsmoking rooms available. **Open:** Year-round.

➤ **In the summer you can play golf, hike, and ride horses and mountain bikes. The chairlift will take you up the mountain on weekends for panoramic views.**

High above Lake Pend Oreille, in northern Idaho, Schweitzer Mountain Resort offers 2,350 acres of ski slopes, descending from Schweitzer Mountain's 6,400-foot summit. Skiers from around the world come for the 55 runs over dry powder snow. They also find stunning scenery, six chairlifts (including a high-speed quad), night skiing, cross-country trails, terrain suitable for all abilities, and luxurious accommodations.

The core of Schweitzer's 10-year, $100 million expansion plan is Green Gables Lodge, in a pedestrian village. The four-story, European-style hotel, built in 1990 of native stone and white pine, captures spectacular vistas of Lake Pend Oreille and the rugged Selkirk Mountains.

Snow from the steep, gabled roof is contained above covered walkways and in plaza-level planters that also provide landscape interest in summer. Indoors, it's a lively, come-as-you-are atmosphere, with visitors traipsing through in ski togs, jeans, gowns, and furs. Pine wainscoting and colors of deep plum and forest green in the lounge and Jean's Northwest Bar and Grill add to the mountain lodge ambience.

From the lobby, past the stone fireplace with a carved mantelpiece, you ascend a wide staircase or take the elevators to the guest rooms. Some of the well-appointed rooms feature efficiency kitchens with microwave ovens, refrigerators, toasters, and coffeemakers. (You can buy groceries at the General Store.) They all have TV with HBO. A standard room may be combined with a kitchen room to form a suite.

Conveniences include laundry facilities, a heated boot room and ski storage area, underground parking, an outdoor heated pool, and two Jacuzzi tubs on the second-floor, glassed-in deck. If you wish to check out early, ski all day, and then leave for home, dressing rooms with showers are available.

Schweitzer practically guarantees good skiing. If the skiing or snow conditions don't meet your expectations, return your lift ticket within an hour of purchase and pick up a snow check for another day. Children 6 and under ski free. Other features for children are the Enchanted Forest, where kids can play in the snow, and Kinder Kamp, offering daycare and skiing classes for children up to age twelve.

Near Green Gables is the day lodge, which has an espresso bar and deli and a pizza café.

Stanley

Gunter's Salmon River Cabins

Box 91, Scenic Highway 75
Stanley, ID 83278
208-774-2290

Log cabins on the Salmon River

Proprietors: Jerry and Nancy Gunter. **Accommodations:** 15 cabins. **Rates:** $65–$105 per cabin. **Minimum stay:** None. **Payment:** All major credit cards. **Children:** Welcome. **Pets:** Allowed ($4). **Smoking:** Allowed. **Open:** April through October.

➤ **There's a ghost town at nearby Yankee Fork, along with a mining museum and a huge gold dredge that is still intact.**

If sitting on the front porch admiring the Sawtooth Mountains while casting a fishing line into the roaring Salmon River sounds like your idea of an ideal vacation, Gunter's (formerly McGowan's) is the resort for you. While only the cabins closest to the river offer fishing from the front porch, the magnificent scenery and many recreational options make this an excellent spot for anyone looking for outdoor adventure. Visitors come for the trout fishing, hunting, hiking, rafting, horseback riding, hot springs, and cross-country skiing.

The log cabins have been renovated and now contain hand-hewn log beds. Your cabin might have a sliding glass door, a TV, a bath with shower, and a queen-size or two double beds, as well as a fully equipped kitchen. Early reservations are recommended.

There's a café across the street from the resort, and the town of Stanley, which has an airstrip, car rental agency, stores, and good restaurants, is only a mile away.

Idaho Rocky Mountain Ranch

HC64, Box 9934
Stanley, ID 83278
208-774-3544

| A 1930s log lodge in mountain scenery |

Managers: Jeana and Bill Leavell. **Accommodations:** 4 lodge rooms, 17 cabins. **Rates:** $87 per person; discounts for longer stays. **Included:** Full breakfast, dinner, tax. **Minimum stay:** 3 nights. **Payment:** MasterCard, Visa. **Children:** Welcome. **Pets:** Not allowed (horses accepted with advance notice, $3). **Smoking:** Outdoors only. **Open:** June to mid-September.

➤ **This is the heart of the Sawtooth National Recreation Area, where mountain trails lead to remote alpine lakes and rivers pound through canyons.**

In 1929, a Frigidaire distributor from New York decided to build a private guest ranch on a slope facing the rugged Sawtooth Mountains. It took sixty men six months, but once the ranch was completed it never changed. From the day in 1930 when Winston Paul invited his first guests until now, updated wiring and plumbing and a few kitchen improvements are the only differences.

The big log lodge with a wide verandah stands on 1,000 acres above the road to Stanley, headquarters for outfitters who run whitewater expeditions down the Middle Fork and Salmon rivers. At Idaho Rocky Mountain Ranch you're within easy distance of Redfish, the largest lake in the Sawtooths, and miles of hiking and riding trails. You can swim in a pool heated by a geothermal spring or prop your feet on the porch rail and watch the day go by. Inside, the mountain lodge atmosphere is enhanced by a stone fireplace and game trophies on walls of pine.

Meals are served in the big dining room, where twisted branches form the light fixtures and Paul's china is still used. The hearty food concentrates on Idaho products, with beef the overriding favorite, though there may be a special of wild game or fowl. Breakfast and dinner are open to the public, and picnic lunches are available for guests.

The entrances to the guest rooms in the lodge are designed to look like rustic cabins, with peaked roofs and overhangs and wrought-iron hinges that were made in a foundry on the premises. All the furniture was made from indigenous materials, from the bent-willow pulls on the dressers to the rush backs of the rocking chairs. The showers are lined with stone.

The cabins, mostly duplexes, are scattered over the hillside. Number 17 and number 18 are the largest units. Number 11, separate and secluded, is considered the honeymoon cabin. Swings hang from the pine trees outside, perhaps reminding newlyweds to return again with their family. There are two winter cabins; one can hold eight people. The other is a three-bedroom, two-bath house with a full kitchen.

Wound-up city folk quickly learn the joys of doing nothing at this relaxing place. The one telephone is a pay phone stuck against the porch wall, there's no TV, and you won't see a newspaper unless someone brings one from town, 9 miles away.

Redfish Lake Lodge

P. O. Box 9
Stanley, ID 83278
208-774-3536
208-774-3326 in winter

A rustic lakeside resort in the Sawtooth range

Manager: Jack See. **Accommodations:** 10 lodge rooms (with shared baths), 9 motel rooms, 15 cabins. **Rates:** Lodge rooms, $49–$53; motel rooms, $81–$117 (up to 4 people); cabins, $98–$140 (up to 8); midweek discounts in spring and fall. **Minimum stay:** 2 nights on weekends, 3 nights on holidays. **Payment:** MasterCard, Visa. **Children:** Under age 3, free. **Pets:** Not allowed. **Smoking:** Allowed. **Open:** Memorial Day through September.

➤ **In July, there's the Sawtooth Mountain Mamas Arts and Crafts Fair in Stanley, including old-time fiddling, a barbecue, and a pancake breakfast.**

About 60 miles north of Sun Valley and 7 miles south of Stanley, this lodge offers splendid views from the forested shores of Redfish Lake. Two miles of private paved road take you from Highway 75 to the two-story wooden lodge, a general store, and a boat launch.

The lodge has a restaurant and lounge with an informal, log cabin atmosphere. The second-floor guest rooms have double or queen-size log frame beds, paneled and log walls, and wash basins. The fourplex motel units, some more rustic than others, contain two double beds or one or two queen-size beds.

Scattered about in the forest along the lake are cabins with two or more rooms. Six rustic cabins have a fireplace, two double beds, and one twin. The deluxe cabins have Franklin fireplaces and sleep up to six people. Most luxurious is the three-bedroom lakeside cabin, which has a queen-size, two double, and two twin beds as well as housekeeping facilities.

Boating is the focus of activity at Redfish, with an array of fishing boats, canoes, and paddleboats standing ready. Guided pontoon boat tours of Redfish Lake and Salmon River raft day trips are available.

If you enjoy both horseback riding and fishing, you can combine them in an overnight mountain lake fishing trip. The fish you catch will be hickory smoked by the staff if you request it. Another popular horseback trip is the alpine ride to the Sawtooth Wilderness divide.

Mountain bikes, hiking trails, volleyball, and horseshoe pits round out the activities at the lodge. There is no charge for pickups at the Stanley airstrip, 6 miles north of Redfish.

Sun Valley

Elkhorn Resort and Golf Club

P.O. Box 6009
Sun Valley, ID 83354
208-622-4511
800-355-4676
Fax: 208-622-3261

A ski lodge and summer resort in Sun Valley Village

Manager: John Korpi. **Accommodations:** 125 rooms, 7 suites, and 70 condominiums. **Rates:** Rooms, $79–$139 single or double; $10 additional person; suites, $205–$325; condos, $159–$219, up to 8 people. **Minimum stay:** None. **Payment:** Major credit cards. **Children:** Under 17, free. **Pets:** Not allowed. **Smoking:** Nonsmoking rooms available. **Open:** Year-round.

➤ **On the plaza are Tequila Joe's, with a Mexican menu; the Country Kitchen, for breakfast all day long; and Jesse's, a steak and seafood house.**

At Elkhorn Resort, the emphasis is on recreational diversity. With the largest and one of the most sophisticated automated snowmaking systems in the world, prime skiing conditions are guaranteed in Sun Valley from Thanksgiving to spring. However, this resort offers vacations year-round. It has one of the best 18-hole golf courses in the nation as well as fly-fishing, bicycling, hiking, swimming in an Olympic-size pool, rafting on the Salmon River, horseback riding, and soaring, among other choices. If you're even more adventurous, try bungee jumping from a hot air balloon. There are also 18 tennis courts (tennis is complimentary; lessons and rentals are available).

The heart of the resort is the lodge and plaza, an open area surrounded by shops and restaurants. The music festivals and events held here, including a series of free, open-air concerts in the summer, are acclaimed for their high quality. The resort has a casual atmosphere and a youthful, friendly staff.

The lobby of the lodge has dark, natural woods and a brick fireplace. On one side is the Atrium Lounge, where entertainment is presented regularly. The guest rooms and suites are comfortably furnished and have ample closet and drawer space and individual touches, such as potted plants and prints of wildlife or landscapes.

A typical one-bedroom suite, in soft gray and tan, has a tiled gas fireplace in the corner, a full kitchen, a king-size bed in the separate bedroom, and a view of the golf course and sage-covered hills beyond. The bath, divided into three sections, contains two washbasins and a deep whirlpool tub.

This resort is fun for all ages; and when the grownups want some time alone, childcare is available.

The Idaho Country Inn

P.O. Box 2355
Sun Valley, ID 83353
208-726-1019
Fax: 208-726-5718

> **An Idaho-theme home in a residential area**

Innkeepers: Julie and Terry Heneghan. **Accommodations:** 11 rooms. **Rates:** $125–$185 single or double; off-season discounts available. **Included:** Full breakfast. **Minimum stay:** 2 nights on weekends. **Payment:** Major credit cards. **Children:** Welcome. **Pets:** Not allowed. **Smoking:** Not allowed. **Open:** Year-round.

➤ **Nearby are Craters of the Moon National Monument, which has cindercones, caves, and lava; the Old West mining town of Hailey; and Sawtooth National Recreation Area.**

The best of Idaho is honored in the Idaho Country Inn, set in a residential hillside neighborhood a half-mile from both Sun Valley and Ketchum. Indigenous trees and river rock went into the construction of the inn, which opened in 1990. Idaho Mudworks supplied the hand-painted sinks, tile, and dishes. Regional furniture makers used willow and other native materials, and artists from Sun Valley created many decorative works. Even Idaho's famous potatoes get into the act at breakfast.

The guest rooms reflect the history of Idaho and Ketchum with a variety of themes. The Wagon Days Room, with a king-size log bed with wagon wheel headboard, depicts early mining days. Baldy Room illustrates the winter activities around Mount Baldy, while Angler's Room, with its hand-tied flies and antique rods, focuses on the area's world-famed fishing. Cowboys are recognized in the Rodeo Room and river rafting in the Whitewater Room.

All rooms have queen- or king-size beds, private baths, direct-dial phones, TV, and refrigerators. The balconies offer sweeping views of Baldy, Griffin Butte, and downtown Ketchum. While children are welcome, the inn is geared to adults and accommodates no more than two people to a room. Some rooms have adjoining doors.

The full breakfast, served family-style in the sun room, features those famous potatoes, eggs Sun Valley, apple-walnut pancakes, eggs Benedict, muffins, and other treats.

Terry and Julie keep their library well stocked and a fire burning on the hearth in winter, a welcome sight after a day of skiing or sightseeing. Well versed in the history and activities of the area, the energetic innkeepers are happy to share their knowledge. They'll recommend restaurants and tell you where to golf, shop, hike, and ski. Terry, a longtime fly-fishing guide, might give you a few tips on Sun Valley fishing.

Sun Valley Lodge

1 Sun Valley Road
Sun Valley, ID 83353
208-622-4111
800-786-8259
Fax: 208-622-2030

A world-famous ski resort in a mountain valley

Manager: Wally Huffman. **Accommodations:** 146 rooms in lodge, 57 apartments. **Rates:** Rooms, $109–$169; suites, $209–$299; condos, $209–$309; cottages, $500–$1,000; rates vary seasonally, many packages available. **Minimum stay:** None. **Payment:** Major credit cards. **Children:** Welcome. **Pets:** Not allowed. **Smoking:** Nonsmoking rooms available. **Open:** Year-round

➤ **Most years, ski season runs from November to May; there are 17 chair lifts and 80 runs. State-of-the-art snow machines keep the slopes skiable.**

This venerable resort, made famous by celebrity visitors, superb skiing, an array of comforts, magnificent scenery, and ice-skating movies, caters to the Hollywood crowd and average tourists with equal aplomb, providing the kind of atmosphere we expect from a resort with a major reputation. But Sun Valley Lodge is not pretentious or formal; the staff is friendly and the atmosphere casual.

The entire massive Sun Valley development might never have occurred if Averill Harriman, chairman of the board of the Union Pacific Railroad in 1935, had not been trying to attract more train passengers. The result was that a ski resort was built in the faded mining town of Ketchum, which offered snow and sunshine 300 days a year.

The lodge was ingeniously constructed of concrete that was poured into rough pine molds so that the building would look as if it were timber. Completed in 1936, the lodge opened to great fanfare and quickly became the place to see and be seen as well as to ski. Since then it has become a year-round complex that offers something for everyone, from ice-skating shows to tea and petits-fours in the afternoon.

In the summer you can play golf at an 18-hole course, rent a bicycle, go bowling or riding, take a river float trip on the Salmon River, swim, ice skate, or attend the opera. You can try soaring, volleyball, windsurfing, or skeet shooting. Play tennis on one of 18 courts in the valley and shop the traffic-free, Tyrolean-style village where the fragrance wafting from the Chocolate Foundry is enough to draw crowds.

If you are bringing the family, ask about the special programs for children. Skating, tennis, riding, and games are organized for every age group, and screened babysitters are available.

Winter is Sun Valley's main season, with skiers enjoying the slopes of Dollar Mountain and Baldy. After a day of skiing, dog-sledding, or sleigh riding under cloudless skies, stop in Duchin Lounge, off the elegant oak lobby, before heading to the lodge dining room. Here you encounter tradition in the grand manner. The maitre d' leads the way with agreeable urbanity down marble stairs to tables set with white linen and white and gold china. Jacket and tie are suggested. You'll dine under crystal chandeliers reflected in many mirrors and view Bald Mountain through a curving wall of windows, while a trio plays in the background. The menu includes filet mignon, rack of lamb, duckling with raspberry sauce and Grand Marnier, and broiled lobster tails. A special trout dish is offered nightly.

Gretchen's Café, named for gold medal Olympic skier Gretchen Fraser, is more casual, a good spot for breakfast. Marble bathrooms, Chinese carpeting with Idaho wildflower designs, a refurbished foyer, and swans in the pond at the entrance are reminiscent of the decades when Hollywood stars and East Coast socialites arrived in their furs. The guest rooms do not have quite the luxury of the lobby and public rooms, but they compare well to any above-standard hotel rooms, with queen-size beds and nicely furnished sitting areas. If you're in a Hemingway mood, Number 206 is where the author finished *For Whom The Bell Tolls.*

Tetonia

Teton Ridge Ranch

200 Valley View Road
Tetonia, ID 83452
208-456-2650
Fax: 208-456-2218
ATilt@aol.com

A luxurious retreat in a mountain valley

Manager: Skip and Chris Tilt. **Accommodations:** 5 suites and an apartment. **Rates:** $250–$475 double; rates vary seasonally. **Included:** All meals and ranch activities. **Minimum stay:** 1 week, July–August. **Payment:** Cash or check. **Children:** Welcome. **Pets:** Allowed by prior arrangement. **Smoking:** Allowed. **Open:** Late May to November, December to April.

➤ **Outside activities include tours of Yellowstone and Grand Teton and the art and music festivals of Jackson. Or book a glider ride with Grand Valley Aviation, at the Driggs airport.**

This small, luxurious hideaway is more like a country estate than a typical dude ranch. The 10,000-square-foot lodge, built of lodgepole pine in 1984, has a two-story living room with a bar, two stone fireplaces, and a balcony overlooking the Tetons. There's a library on the main floor, and the dining room holds 30. But there's no question that this is a wilderness site. The ranch stands on 4,000 acres of a mountain valley on the west side of the Teton Range in Idaho. Its eastern border is the Targhee Forest in Wyoming, hard by Grand Teton and Yellowstone national parks.

The suites have woodstoves, Jacuzzis, and steam showers. Three contain king-size beds, one has two doubles, and the fifth, twin beds. Each room has a balcony that faces the mountains. The less expensive apartment includes a fireplace, queen-size bed, and kitchenette; it has no Jacuzzi or steam.

Ranch food is abundant and hearty. Lunch is usually homemade soup and salad; dinners present a different menu each night, always featuring homemade baked goods and vegetables from the garden. Wine is served; guests bring their own liquor.

This exclusive and intimate mountain retreat (only 14 guests at a time) provides an opportunity to experience all kinds of outdoor activity and to enjoy contemplative serenity. There's no extra charge for riding, and wranglers can take guests out at any time. Longer pack trips, lasting two to five days, are known for their gorgeous scenery, wildlife, and good fishing.

There are 14 miles of hiking trails on the ranch, plus many more in the Targhee Forest. You'll find fly-fishing on the nearby Teton River and several streams with native cutthroat. Further afield, such famed blue ribbon waters as the Snake and Henry's Fork are close enough for day trips. In the early fall, hunters come for grouse and pheasant, while cross-country skiers arrive with the snows. The staff grooms ski trails that begin at the lodge's back door. Downhill skiers head for the powder slopes at Grand Targhee Resort.

Wallace

The Jameson

304 Sixth Street
Wallace, ID 83873
208-556-1554

An Old West hotel in eastern Idaho

Director of operations: Rick Schaeffer. **Accommodations:** 6 rooms (3 shared baths). **Rates:** $57.50. **Included:** Continental breakfast. **Minimum stay:** None. **Payment:** MasterCard, Visa. **Children:** Welcome. **Pets:** Allowed by prior arrangement. **Smoking:** Not allowed. **Open:** Thursday through Sunday, June through September.

➤ **Silver continues to hold an important position in the region. To learn its history, take the Sierra Silver Mine Tour offered several times daily in summer.**

It was silver that put the little town of Wallace, Idaho, on the map a hundred years ago. History is helping to keep it there.

When you step onto the streets of Wallace, you take a leap back in time. On one street you'll see a château-style railroad depot (now a museum), on another an old-time theater featuring popcorn and live melodrama, and on yet another there's a red brick hotel with a saloon and dining establishment on the ground floor. The hotel is the Jameson, built in 1908 as an oasis in the frontier and restored in recent years.

The saloon is all black-polished woods and brass, and the servers dress in period clothing. Oriental carpets and carved woodwork lend an old-time atmosphere to the dining room next door, where you may order chicken, steaks, seafood, hamburgers, and pasta at reasonable prices. Dinners include the salad bar, a baked Idaho potato, and fresh bread.

Upstairs is a banquet room; the guest rooms line a high-ceilinged narrow hall another flight up. Rooms are small, furnished with antique beds, armoires, and dressers; it's easy to imagine this as the genteel frontier hotel it was. The windows overlook the quiet streets of Wallace, which hasn't changed much in the intervening years. Clean, white tile bathrooms are at the end of a hall decorated with framed *Vogue* covers and advertisements.

Breakfast is served in a small sitting area by the landing. There's a phone in the parlor.

Wallace today has about 1,400 residents and a friendly, small-town atmosphere. In the Idaho panhandle, 13 miles from the Montana border, it's still a mining town and a financial and administrative center for mining companies.

Oregon

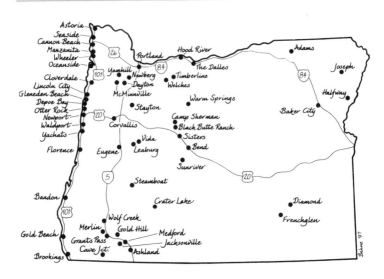

Best Intimate City Stops

Eugene
Campbell House, 215
Portland
Governor Hotel, 266
Heron Haus, 269
Hotel Vintage Plaza, 270
The Lion and The Rose, 271
Portland's White House, 274

Best Grand City Hotels

Portland
The Benson Hotel, 263
The Heathman Hotel, 267
RiverPlace Hotel, 275

Best Country Inns and B&Bs

Ashland
Chanticleer Inn, 161
Country Willows, 162
Grape Vine Inn, 166
The Iris Inn, 168
Winchester Country Inn, 175
Wolfe Manor Inn, 177
The Woods House, 178
Bend
Lara House, 186
Cloverdale
The Hudson House, 203
Corvallis
Hanson Country Inn, 207
Diamond
McCoy Creek Inn, 213
Florence
Johnson House, 216
Frenchglen
Frenchglen Hotel, 220

Best Family Favorites

Best Inns by the Sea

Best on a Budget

Yachats
The See Vue, 304

Best Resorts

Black Butte Ranch
Black Butte Ranch, 190
Gleneden Beach
Salishan Lodge, 221
Gold Beach
Tu Tú Tun Lodge, 226
Grants Pass
Paradise Ranch Resort, 225
Sunriver
Sunriver Resort, 286
Warm Springs
Kah-Nee-Ta, 295
Welches
The Resort at the Mountain, 297
Yamhill
Flying M Ranch, 307

Best Romantic Hideaways

Ashland
Antique Rose Inn, 159
Fox House Inn, 164
Peerless Hotel, 171
Romeo Inn, 172
Cannon Beach
Turk's Lodging in the Trees, 200
Cloverdale
Sandlake Country Inn, 205
Florence
Moonset, 218
Leaburg
Marjon Bed & Breakfast Inn, 241
Manzanita
The Inn at Manzanita, 245
Medford
Under the Greenwood Tree, 249

Neahkahnie
Ayers' Cottage, 254

Best Wilderness Retreats

Adams
Baker's Bar M Ranch, 157
Ashland
Mt. Ashland Inn, 170
Brookings
Chetco River Inn, 192
Camp Sherman
House on the Metolius, 194
Crater Lake
Crater Lake Lodge, 209
Gold Beach
Paradise Bar Lodge, 225
Joseph
Bed, Bread and Trail Inn, 240
Merlin
Morrison's Rogue River Lodge, 251
Steamboat
Steamboat Inn, 284
Vida
The Wayfarer Resort, 292

Best Wine Region Inns

Dayton
Wine Country Farm, 210
McMinnville
Steiger Haus, 247

With flat-topped buttes and rocky spires on the east, sandy beaches and surf-pounded headlands on the west, and green forests and valleys in between, Oregon dazzles with scenic splendor. The Cascade Range is the spine of the state, its snow-topped peaks dividing the lush, green, rainy west from the dry east, where ponderosa pine needles glisten in 300 days a year of sunshine, sagebrush grows over miles of open plain, and undergrowth in the red volcanic soil is sparse.

The southeastern quarter of Oregon is Great Basin country, an intermountain plateau of starkly sculpted beauty that was a sea 200 million years ago. Settlements, like **Frenchglen,** are few and small. In the state's far northeastern corner, the rugged Wallowa Mountains cluster near the Idaho border and Hell's Canyon. **Joseph** on the north and **Halfway** on the south are gateways into the wilderness area.

Native Americans had lived here and cared for the land and water for some 11,000 years before the 19th-century settlers arrived, following the Oregon Trail to this green and fertile Eden on the Pacific. Some of the pioneers floated down the Columbia River, rafting from **The Dalles,** past today's **Hood River,** to the Willamette Valley.

At the end of the trail they cut timber, established farms, and built towns such as **Portland,** now the state's largest city; **Salem,** Oregon's capital; **Corvallis;** and **Eugene.**

Portland is a major shipping port and a city of considerable charm. It has lovely parks, a world-renowned zoo, restored historic buildings and innovative new ones, a vital downtown core, and cultural offerings that include opera, symphony, theater, and dance. Portland also has professional sports teams and is a noted jazz center, with several clubs and annual jazz events.

Oregon's 400 miles of shoreline are open to the public by law, so the coast is one long park punctuated by sandy beaches, offshore seastacks, and rocky headlands, all carved by a ceaseless surf. **Astoria,** the northernmost town, is the oldest permanent U.S. settlement in the West. Nearby is Fort Clatsop, a replica of the fort built by Lewis and Clark to serve as the expedition's winter quarters in 1805–1806.

To the south lies **Seaside,** a lively resort town and convention center with a 2-mile beachside promenade. Farther down the coast is **Cannon Beach,** known for its art galleries, shops, and restaurants. Curving south around Neahkahnie Mountain, you come to **Manzanita.** Its low-key atmosphere is very different from the bustle of the resort area of **Lincoln City.**

Florence marks the point where the forested hills change to high, shifting slopes of sand — the Oregon Dunes National Recreation Area. Farther south are the port city of Coos Bay; **Bandon,** with a renovated historic district; **Gold Beach,** at the mouth of the Rogue River; and finally sunny **Brookings,** where azaleas and lilies grow in profusion.

Many visitors come to Oregon for the attractions of the Rogue River Valley. **Merlin** and **Grants Pass** are headquarters for raft trips on the fabled Rogue; **Jacksonville** is a quaint frontier town; **Ash-**

land is the home of the widely acclaimed Oregon Shakespeare Festival.

Central Oregon is known for its outdoor recreation. Powder-dry snow on the Cascades draws skiers in winter, while summer visitors come to **Bend** and **Sunriver** to bake in the sun, play golf, fish, hike on the trails, and explore craters and lava tubes left by once-active volcanoes.

For more information on Oregon, call 800-547-7842 (from outside Oregon) or 800-233-3306 (in Oregon) or write to the Economic Development Department, Tourism Division, 595 Cottage St. N.E., Salem, OR 97310.

Adams

Baker's Bar M Ranch

Route 1
Adams, OR 97810
541-566-3381

An old-fashioned
wilderness lodge for
families

Innkeepers: Hope and Gene Baker. **Accommodations:** 8 lodge rooms (3 shared baths), 4 apartments, 2 cabins. **Rates:** $850 per adult per week, $650 ages 9–15, $500 ages 8 and under. **Included:** All meals and ranch activities except campout. **Minimum stay:** 6 nights in summer, 2 days in May and September. **Payment:** Cash or check. **Children:** Age 6 and older, welcome. **Pets:** Not allowed ("We supply them"). **Smoking:** Outdoors only. **Open:** April through September.

➤ **The closest sizable city is Pendleton, famed for the Pendleton Round-Up in September, with parades, a pageant, a cowboy breakfast, and a tepee camp.**

In the remote country east of Pendleton, a two-story stagecoach stop was built of hand-hewn logs in 1864. Today that weathered gray building is the Ranch House at Baker's Bar M, one of the most appealing guest ranches in the West.

Gene Baker's parents bought the old place in 1938; now Gene and Hope and two of their sons welcome guests to the Ranch House, the Homestead (an old but serviceable building sectioned into rooms), and Brookside and Lakeside (two-bedroom cabins).

During your stay, you can ride horseback, swim in a hot springs pool, play volleyball and basketball in a big log barn, square dance, go birding, look for muskrat and beaver in the lake, and hike through the ranch's 2,500 acres.

The clear mountain air sharpens appetites, so the communal dining tables hold plenty of food served family style. A platter of roast beef, great bowls of green beans and coleslaw, baskets of whole-wheat rolls baked by Gene, and pitchers of milk are a typical evening meal, topped off with strawberry shortcake. You can bring your own wine or beer and store it in the cooler.

The rooms are simple, with no knickknacks or fancy soaps. In the lodge, you'll have a good bed, an open closet, a dresser, a mirror, and a chair of rawhide and twigs. Expect to sleep soundly and be wakened by birdsong or the clanging bell that announces meals.

Over a breakfast of cereals, eggs, and muffins with jam made from the Bakers' raspberries, guests talk horses with the wranglers and plan their day. Most people ride daily, led by a wrangler, and one night might have a campout. However, no one is obligated to do anything, and you might spend your time on the verandah, reading a mystery. There are plenty of fiction, conservation, and wilderness books on the living room shelves in the Ranch House.

Also in the living room is a stone fireplace with several couches and armchairs. The light fixtures are wagon wheels, a sliced log creates a bench, and antlers hold curtain rods. In the quiet of the late evening, when the only sounds are crickets and perhaps a few strains of the piano from the next room, you can relax by the fire and chat with Gene and Hope about life on a ranch that seems like a page from yesteryear. By the time you leave, you'll "feel like family," as Hope says.

Ashland

Antique Rose Inn

90 Gresham Street
Ashland, OR 97520
541-482-6285
888-282-6285

> **A grand Queen Anne home
> in a quiet neighborhood**

Innkeeper: Kathy Buffington. **Accommodations:** 3 rooms and cottage. **Rates:** $104–$159 single or double, $30 additional person. **Included:** Full breakfast. **Minimum stay:** 2 nights on weekends and holidays. **Payment:** MasterCard, Visa. **Children:** Over age 10, welcome. **Pets:** Not allowed. **Smoking:** Outdoors only. **Open:** Year-round.

➤ **The Antique Rose Inn won the Distinguished Preservation Award in 1996.**

This 3-story Queen Anne home was built in 1888 as a "catalogue house," shipped by railcar from Philadelphia. Henry Carter, a prominent businessman and banker, paid $4,000 for his family's dream home — one of the first in the area to have electric lights. The elegant home has 37 windows, nine of them stained glass.

Now Kathy Buffington maintains the home with loving care, filling the rooms with Victorian memorabilia. The guest rooms have four-poster beds, down comforters, and flowers. The Rose Room, which overlooks a magnolia tree and the hills around Ashland, has a carved fireplace, a balcony, and a king-size bed. The Lace Room, a Victorian dream, holds an oak bed covered with creamy lace and has a sitting room with a view of the gazebo and fountain in the garden. The Mahogany Room, the only one on the main floor, is a library room with paneled walls, an ornate bed, and wedding photographs of people who have lived in the house.

A few steps away from the main house is the Rose Cottage, with two bedrooms, a fireplace in the living room, a kitchen, and a porch with a sauna. Flowers hang in baskets at the entrance to the romantic cottage, which can sleep up to 6 people.

Breakfast is an elaborate event, served in the dining room with lace and silver. The personable innkeeper keeps a plate of cookies on the sideboard and offers complimentary wine in the evening.

The B&B is on a quiet street three blocks from the Shakespeare Festival theaters and close to many shops, galleries, and restaurants.

Arden Forest Inn

261 W. Hersey
Ashland, OR 97520
541-488-1496
800-460-3912
Fax: 541-488-4071

An updated farmhouse in residential Ashland

Innkeepers: Corbet Unmack and William Saiia. **Accommodations:** 4 rooms, 1 suite. **Rates:** $60–$115 double, $10–$15 less for single; $30 additional person; $20 ages 5–18, $15 under age 5. **Included:** Full breakfast. **Minimum stay:** None. **Payment:** MasterCard, Visa. **Children:** Welcome. **Pets:** Not allowed. **Smoking:** Not allowed. **Open:** Year-round.

➤ **Cucina Biazzi, a few blocks from downtown, offers good food and patio dining.**

In a quiet neighborhood that is an easy walk from the Oregon Shakespeare Festival, Arden Forest is one of the few bed-and-breakfast inns that caters to families. The turn-of-the-century farmhouse has been turned into a light, airy, comfortable lodging that appeals to both adults and children.

There's one guest room on the main floor of the house and a two-bedroom suite with a queen-size bed and twin beds. The three carriage house rooms have private entrances. All the rooms, combining contemporary furnishings with antique reproductions, are decorated with fine taste and style.

A hearty breakfast, such as yogurt with granola, baked frittata, and scones, is served at one table in the main house. The sociable hosts, strong backers of the Oregon Shakespeare Festival, encourage discussions of Ashland's lively theater scene. They are continually adding improvements to the inn; it's air-conditioned now, they've put in a kitchen for guests' use in the Carriage House, and the garden is becoming a showplace. Wind chimes, gargoyles, paths through colorful blooms, and a little stream make this an inviting place to relax.

Chanticleer Inn

120 Gresham Street
Ashland, OR 97520
541-482-1919
800-898-1950
Fax: 541-482-1919

A quiet B&B with French country inn style

Innkeeper: Pebby Kuan. **Accommodations:** 6 rooms. **Rates:** Summer, $125–$160; winter, $69–$85; spring, $95–$125; $25 additional person. **Included:** Full breakfast. **Minimum stay:** 2 nights weekends. **Payment:** Major credit cards. **Children:** Over age 10, welcome. **Pets:** Not allowed. **Smoking:** Not allowed. **Open:** Year-round.

➤ **Before dinner (Chateaulin, Monet, and Winchester Inn are good restaurant choices), browse through the gifts, such as aprons and spiced honey, at the Chanticleer.**

This gray Craftsman bungalow was remodeled as a European-style guest house in 1981 and has been popular with travelers to southern Oregon ever since. The new owner has wisely made few changes, other than adding her own artwork, since taking over the award-winning inn.

Though Chanticleer is in town on a residential hillside, just a few blocks from Main Street and the Oregon Shakespeare Festival plaza and theaters, the ambience is that of a French country inn. It's filled with flowers, puffy comforters, lace curtains, antique brass beds, and armoires, all in a light and airy environment.

The lower-level rooms have private entrances off the terraced brick patio, while those upstairs overlook the valley or lawn and gardens. The beds are queen-size or twins. All have air conditioning, telephones, alarm clocks, and a summery combination of white and colorful pastels.

The services here include turndown service and mints on pillows, shampoo and bubbles in the bath, complimentary beverages, sherry by the fireplace, and a full cookie jar. If you're attending the plays, you'll appreciate the complete set of Shakespeare in every room, along with copies of other plays being presented.

The morning meal is taken in a small sunny nook unless you've requested breakfast in bed. You'll be served homemade granola, fruit, and an inventive hot dish such as spinach-steamed eggs or French toast with almonds and berry sauce.

Country Willows

1313 Clay Street
Ashland, OR 97520
541-488-1590

A restored hillside farmhouse

Innkeepers: Dan Durant and David Newton. **Accommodations:** 9 rooms. **Rates:** $90–$185 double, $5 less for single, $30 additional person, 20% less November to April. **Included:** Full breakfast. **Minimum stay:** None. **Payment:** MasterCard, Visa. **Children:** Age 12 and older, welcome. **Pets:** Not allowed. **Smoking:** Outdoors only. **Open:** Year-round.

▶ **Winter events include the Fall Performing Arts Festival, Come Home for the Holidays and Festival of Lights, and a Taste of Ashland: Winter Food, Art, and Wine Festival.**

At the south end of Ashland, 10 miles north of the California border, a maple-lined road winds up a hill to a stylish inn surrounded by flower beds and a wide lawn with willow trees. Behind it sprawl green pastures where horses graze, and beyond them are rolling, oak-covered hills. This is Country Willows, a peaceful retreat on five acres of farmland about eight minutes from downtown Ashland and the Oregon Shakespeare Festival.

It's a blue frame home wrapped by a verandah covered with wisteria vines and hung with flower baskets. Guests can relax on the verandah, which overlooks the lawn and hills, in the living room, or by the stone fireplace in the den, with TV, movies, books, and games. In the sun room, where breakfast is served at tables set for the number in your party, the talented hosts might present an elaborate egg dish, a Mexican casserole, or French toast with strawberry butter. With advance notice, they're happy to accommodate special diets.

The guest rooms are air-conditioned and furnished with flair. Four are in the main house: Almond Room, the smallest; Oak Room, a corner spot with mountain views; Cedar Room, a large corner space; and Willow, which has a king-size four-poster canopy bed and a twin.

Out in the trim white and blue barn, behind the swimming pool and garden, are two suites. Hayloft has reminders of its barn origins, with straw colors and a queen-size bed in a loft. The large, open Sunrise Suite is the inn's most expensive room. Of whitewashed pine, it has a private deck, a gas fireplace, a microwave and refrigerator, and a big old-fashioned tub for two by a bay window.

On the other side of the heated pool and hot tub is the private Cottage, which has one large room with a white iron queen-size bed, a kitchenette, and a woodstove. A twin bed nestles into an alcove. A few steps away is a duck pond; the inn has ducks, geese, and goats.

Dan and David are adept at making guests feel at home. They provide all kinds of extra touches, such as a filled cookie jar, robes, books, puzzles, bicycles, a hammock under the willow trees, instant hot water for tea or coffee, and good suggestions for restaurants and points of interest. They encourage visitors to come in winter, when the rates are lower and cross-country and downhill skiing are available.

Fox House Inn

269 B Street
Ashland, OR 97520
541-488-1055
800-488-1055
Fax: 541-482-6940

An exquisite, romantic B&B

Innkeepers: Jim and Jacquelyn Sims. **Accommodations:** 1 room, 1 suite. **Rates:** $95–$145, rates vary seasonally. **Included:** Full breakfast. **Minimum stay:** 2 nights in summer. **Payment:** Cash or check. **Children:** Age 10 and older, welcome. **Pets:** Not allowed. **Smoking:** Outdoors only. **Open:** Year-round.

➤ **The Shakespeare Festival sells out far in advance, but there's a chance of buying unclaimed tickets before a performance. SRO tickets are usually available.**

Many nicely restored homes in Ashland are open to bed-and-breakfast guests, but few offer the romantic ambience, privacy, and quality of Fox House Inn.

The pale blue Victorian home with white trim was built in the late 1800s for a freight and transport merchant who was elected to the Ashland City Council in 1903. Jim Sims also served on the City Council — 75 years later. The Simses' work on the house was recognized in 1989 with Ashland's award for outstanding historic restoration. "But we didn't restore it," Jim says. "We renewed it" — referring to their careful attention to authenticity and detail, which shows in the polished woods, oak floors, stained glass, and antique furnishings.

If you choose Annabel's Suite, you'll have the entire second floor of the house. It includes a bedroom and separate dressing area, a sitting room with TV and stereo, and a bathroom with a shower and clawfoot tub. An ivory satin and lace comforter covers the queen-size canopy bed. Adding to the opulent tone are Persian carpets, antique rockers, and Impressionist reproductions on the walls.

On the main floor, removed from both the suite and the owners' quarters, the smaller Garden Room has a half-canopy bed, a TV, and a stereo as well as its own entrance and an enclosed garden under walnut and maple trees. A tall cedar fence encircles lilacs, camellias, and ferns; a path leads to a white table and chairs and an outdoor hot tub.

Breakfast, artfully presented on china, silver, and crystal, is lavish at Fox House. Jackie Sims likes to prepare "what you'd never do for yourself," such as granola parfait, fruit crêpes, and egg custard pancakes with cinnamon and whipped cream, all garnished with edible flowers.

To celebrate special occasions, the Simses will pamper you with extra treats. All guests receive turndown service, which includes room freshening, clean towels, candies beside the bed, and dimmed lighting.

The inn is 3 blocks from the Oregon Shakespeare Festival theaters.

Grape Vine Inn

486 Siskiyou Boulevard
Ashland, OR 97520
541-482-7944
800-500-VINE
Fax: 541-482-7944

A traditional home with contemporary flair

Innkeeper: Shirley Grega. **Accommodations:** 3 rooms. **Rates:** Summer, $95–$115; spring and winter, $80–$100; $25 additional person. **Included:** Full breakfast. **Minimum stay:** 2 nights on weekends. **Payment:** MasterCard, Visa. **Children:** Over age 12, welcome. **Pets:** Not allowed. **Smoking:** Outdoors only. **Open:** Year-round.

➤ **North of Ashland, visitors can buy fruit and produce, gifts, and deli foods at Harry and David's Country Store, the home of the Fruit-of-the-Month Club and a line of mail-order fancy foods.**

This Dutch Colonial home is a bed-and-breakfast with a difference. Surrounded by lawn and flowers, it is set back from the traffic on a busy thoroughfare a few blocks from the Oregon Shakespeare Festival. The innkeeper, formerly a graphic designer in California, has used her skill to create a charming retreat at the inn. You'll see the grapevine motif, done with a deft touch, in all the nooks and corners.

When you arrive, Shirley offers wine and snacks and shows you to your room. Two are upstairs, and a separate room, Grape Ivy, has a private entrance off the garden and is done in cool green and white, with willow furniture, a gas fireplace, and a little kitchen. Outside, past the grape arbor, is a fenced yard with a gazebo, where guests often enjoy breakfast. Shirley prepares breakfasts that have a bit of dash. You might have blue cornmeal pancakes with pineapple salsa, an herbed frittata, or a tortilla dish, along with papaya-pecan scones, fruit, and juice.

Later, after a day of sightseeing, you can relax in the garden or on the wraparound front porch with a glass of southern Oregon wine.

Off-street parking is available.

Green Springs Box R Ranch

16799 Highway 66
Ashland, OR 97520
541-482-1873

A working ranch in the southern Cascades

Owners: Don and Jean Rowlette. **Accommodations:** 3 log houses. **Rates:** $110–$150, up to 15 persons. **Payment:** Cash or check. **Minimum stay:** Prefer 2 nights or more. **Children:** Welcome. **Pets:** Allowed "if they don't chase the chickens." **Smoking:** Outdoors only. **Open:** Year-round.

➤ **One popular activity is square dancing. If a group of guests requests it, callers will come in to teach the dances.**

The Box R, as locals call it, is a ranch that sprawls across 1,000 acres in the southern Oregon Cascades. The whole area is rich in history. The main ranch house was originally a stagecoach stop on the Applegate Trail; in the meadow you can still see wheel ruts. Sometimes visitors find arrowheads, for it was once an Indian hunting ground.

Now the big white house, a 30-minute drive from Ashland, is the ranch's headquarters. Across the lawn is an elaborate pine museum, filled with pioneer and Indian artifacts and surrounded by meticulously restored carriages.

The road that winds through the ranch, past the shelter where the covered wagons are stored, takes you to the hillside guest-houses. Aspen and Shasta, which hold up to 8 people, each have two bedrooms, one bath, and a loft with pads — bring your own sleeping bags. All linens are furnished, and the modern kitchens have electric ranges, refrigerator/freezers, dishes, and utensils (bring your own groceries). The open, carpeted living rooms have natural rock fireplaces.

The largest house, Lakeview, has two bedrooms, two baths, and two sleeping lofts. It's a good choice for groups of up to 15 people or two families sharing an outdoor vacation. The big, carpeted common room, with couches and a stone fireplace, is an inviting space for conversation and games. All three log houses have views of the pine woods and fields.

There's a lot to do at the Green Springs Box R, where city kids can experience a taste of life in the country. The ranch has horses, goats, pigs, sheep, geese, a donkey, and a llama. You can feed the chickens, gather eggs, fish in stocked ponds, hike on nearby trails, and bird-watch. Wagon and sleigh rides are available with advance reservations. Some visitors like to help the wranglers with simple ranch chores or just watch the action.

Young children may ride ponies in the corral or swing on the playhorses that hang in the apple trees. There's no riding unless you bring your own horse.

The Iris Inn

59 Manzanita Street
Ashland, OR 97520
541-488-2286
800-460-7650
Fax: 541-488-3709
IrisInnBB@col.com

**A Victorian B&B in a
residential area**

Innkeeper: Vicki Lam. **Accommodations:** 5 rooms (all with private bath). **Rates:** $50–$90 single, $60–$105 double, $20 additional person. **Included:** Full breakfast. **Minimum stay:** None. **Payment:** Major credit cards. **Children:** Over age 7, welcome by prior arrangement. **Pets:** Not allowed (will arrange for boarding at kennel). **Smoking:** Outdoors only. **Open:** Year-round.

➤ **In addition to the Shakespeare Festival, Ashland is also the home of Southern Oregon State College. Further, it has more B&Bs per capita than any city in the U.S.**

Iris Inn is one of the nicest of Ashland's many bed-and-breakfast inns. Within walking distance of the Festival's theater complex, the gray 1905 Victorian stands on a residential street behind a low picket fence and tidy lawn edged with flowers. The inn's name becomes clear when you see the distinctive front door — purple iris centers its stained glass window. Indoors, the theme continues, with paintings and plates and needlework displaying the colorful flower.

Rocking chairs and a flowered couch by the bay window in the living room invite you to relax over lemonade, iced tea, or a glass of wine, available every afternoon. On display are Vicki's interesting bell collection and items found during the home's restoration: hand-forged nails, horseshoes, a pair of spectacles.

A breakfast menu typically includes raspberries and cream, fresh cranberry bread, and asparagus crêpes with cheese sauce. If you're on a special diet, let Vicki know and she'll accommodate you.

You'll find queen-size beds and period furniture in the guest rooms, which have individual color schemes and accents. One bath has a tub, the rest showers. The Parlor, on the main floor, is furnished in wicker and oak. Rose Room, with white iron and brass beds, can sleep four people; raspberry walls and roses on the quilt give this largest room its name. The Jade and Blue rooms have white iron beds and a floral motif. Vista Room, once a sleeping porch, overlooks the garden, the valley, and Mount Grizzly. It has a twin and a double bed.

Cream sherry is set out in the evening for sipping after the theater, your bedcovers are turned down, and mints rest on the pillows. If you want a wake-up call, an iron, or suggestions on things to do, Vicki is happy to oblige.

Mt. Ashland Inn

550 Mt. Ashland Ski Road
Ashland, OR 97520
541-482-8707
800-830-8707
Fax: 541-482-8707

A secluded lodge on Mount Ashland

Innkeepers: Laurel and Chuck Biegert. **Accommodations:** 5 rooms. **Rates:** Summer, $95–$180; winter, $76–$180 double; $5 less single; $30 additional person. **Included:** Full breakfast. **Minimum stay:** 2 nights on summer weekends and holidays. **Payment:** Major credit cards. **Children:** Age 10 and older, welcome. **Pets:** Not allowed. **Smoking:** Not allowed. **Open:** Year-round.

➤ **The Pacific Crest Trail cuts through the inn's land and goes on through pine and madrone groves and over meadows with wild larkspur, lupine, and beargrass.**

Most of Ashland's B&Bs are in the heart of town, close to the Festival theaters. But one of the best, Mt. Ashland Inn, is 16 miles away, on the slopes of the mountain.

This inn is extraordinary. Designed and built by an architect, the 5,000-square-foot log lodge stands on 40 acres. A stone fireplace dominates the living room and light filters through stained glass windows. Games and books fill the bookcase. From the wraparound deck, you can see past tall pines to rugged green hills and the distant valley floor, with Mount Shasta looming above it at 14,162 feet.

The guest rooms, in a stylish country decor, are furnished with antiques. The largest is the Mt. McLoughlin Room, with a king-size bed and a day bed. Its windows frame Mount McLoughlin on the east and Mount Shasta on the south. Sky Lake Suite occupies the entire fourth floor and has a king-size bed, microwave and refrigerator, and river rock fireplace. In the bath, a waterfall fills the jetted tub.

Breakfast is a three-course meal that guests rave about. Cantaloupe soup with kiwi, lemon thyme soufflé, Swedish potato sausage, and focaccia bread with homemade preserves are a few of the dishes served. You'll probably have dinner in a restaurant if you're attending the Festival, or you can picnic in Ashland's Lithia Park.

Mt. Ashland Inn is cozy on a wintry evening when the snow is falling and a fire blazes on the hearth. It's especially welcome if you've spent the day skiing. Lifts and downhill slopes are just 3 miles away, and the Biegerts have snowshoes and skis available. From the doorstep, you can follow cross-country trails right into town. Later, you can relax in the outdoor spa and sauna.

The Peerless Hotel

243 Fourth Street
Ashland, OR 97520
541-488-1082
800-460-8758
Fax: 541-482-1012

A small hotel restored with style

Innkeeper: Crissy Barnett. **Accommodations:** 6 rooms and suites. **Rates:** February 20–April 30, $89–$140; May–November, $135–$175; November–February 19, $65–$125 double; $30 additional person. **Included:** Full breakfast. **Minimum stay:** None. **Payment:** Major credit cards. **Children:** Over age 14, welcome. **Pets:** Not allowed. **Smoking:** Outdoors only. **Open:** Year-round.

➤ **You can swim and fish at Emigrant Lake and Howard Prairie Reservoir, hike in the Rogue River National Forest, ski on Mount Ashland, and play golf at Oak Knoll Golf Course.**

In 1900, this two-story red brick building was constructed as a boarding house for railroad workers. Ninety-four years later, it opened as a stylish little hotel with a great deal of charm. A brick fireplace with a green flagstone hearth is the focal point of the lobby. Beside it, railroad memorabilia are on display: lanterns, dishware, locks, photos, and, a real relic, dining car chimes.

The new owners have retained the original floor plan and the long narrow halls and high ceilings. They kept the fir flooring and left some of the exposed brick. The rooms have some antique furnishings, but the updated decor includes queen-size beds, skylights, gas fireplaces, DMS (digital music express), honor bars, phones, and air conditioning. Room service is provided by the café next door.

One of the most delightful features of the guest rooms is the stenciling and painting done by a local artist. The walls are festooned with flowers, birds, vines, and a jungle with a monkey peering from a tree. None of this is overdone; it merely adds to the distinctive quality of the hotel. Romantics will like the suite with two clawfoot tubs, side by side under a skylight, in the bath.

Breakfast is served in a sitting room near the back of the hotel. From there, French doors open into a flowery courtyard with wrought-iron chairs and a fountain.

The Peerless Hotel is in Ashland's historic Railroad District, an area that is rapidly growing as a tourist draw, with cafés, bakeries, art galleries, and interesting small shops.

Romeo Inn

295 Idaho Street
Ashland, OR 97520
541-488-0884
800-915-8899
Fax: 541-488-0817

**A gracious B&B in
residential Ashland**

Innkeepers: Deane and Don Politis. **Accommodations:** 6 rooms. **Rates:** Summer, $130–$180; winter, $95–$150 double; $30 additional person. **Included:** Full breakfast. **Minimum stay:** 2 nights in summer and on weekends, March–October. **Payment:** MasterCard, Visa. **Children:** Age 12 and older, welcome. **Pets:** Not allowed. **Smoking:** Outdoors only. **Open:** Year-round.

➤ **Be sure to visit the new Pacific Northwest Museum of Natural History, which uses sound, light, smell, and interactive videos in displaying northwestern ecosystems.**

A lovely bed-and-breakfast home, Romeo Inn has had a following for years. Its quiet luxury, tasteful furnishings, and hospitable innkeepers make it a great favorite in this town crammed with B&Bs.

The most romantic room is the Stratford Suite, an apartment on a knoll behind the inn. A peach marble fireplace stands in one corner, visible from every corner. A king-size bed stands under a cathedral ceiling. Peach is the dominant color, appearing with blue and violet in the wallpaper, in the off-white walls, and in the carpet.

From the two-person whirlpool tub you can view the stars through the skylight or watch the flickering fire. If you're on your honeymoon, you'll get a small bottle of champagne and chocolates by your bed. Outside, a rope swing and a hammock hang from tall pine trees, a birdbath and fountain (called First Love) stand in the garden of dahlias, snapdragons, and roses, and a swimming pool and spa lie at the foot of the slope.

The other guest rooms are in the house, a light gray Cape Cod from the early 1930s. They are all air-conditioned, with king-size beds and generous closet space. The two on the main floor, Canterbury and Windsor, have private entrances and sleep three people. Upstairs, Bristol is in flowery white and rose; a rocker sits by the window seat overlooking the huge ponderosa pines at the front of the house. All the rooms have robes and phones.

In a nook overlooking the pool and patio, the innkeepers serve breakfast, such as spinach crêpes, chili potatoes, or wild mushroom frittata. They're accompanied by plenty of coffee and conversation.

Waterside Inn

70 Water Street
Ashland, OR 97520
541-482-3315

| **Luxury suites overlooking a creek** |

Innkeeper: Ann Clouse. **Accommodations:** 6 rooms. **Rates:** $150–$240 double, $50 additional person. **Included:** Expanded Continental breakfast. **Minimum stay:** 3 nights on weekends. **Payment:** Major credit cards. **Children:** Over age 12, welcome. **Pets:** Not allowed. **Smoking:** Outdoors only. **Open:** Year-round.

▶ **The Oregon Shakespeare Festival is one of the oldest (1935) and largest professional regional theater companies in the U.S. It runs from mid-February through October.**

One of the finest lodgings in southern Oregon was a chicken slaughter house a century ago, but you'd never know it now. Good taste and sophistication characterize this two-story inn on a quiet side street. Each room overlooks pretty Lithia Creek — where ducks and trout swim — and most have decks under the trees. They've all been furnished with care by Ann Clouse, a former set designer in the film industry.

The eclectic decor includes art and antiques from Asia, Mexico, and the American Southwest, most of it collected during Ann and Bob Clouse's travels. The rooms can hold up to five people. Taos Room, the largest, has two bedrooms and a loft with a futon. Matsu (which means pine tree) has complete wheelchair access. On the second floor, Devon Room is bright with oil paintings done by local artists in the Waterside's gorgeous garden. Devon has a four-poster queen-size bed, a divided bath, and a full kitchen in yellow and blue.

Across the hall is the smallest room, Martinique. This studio is fresh and light in white and yellow, with skylights in the bathroom and a deck above the garden. Groups often take both upstairs rooms.

All the rooms have kitchens, private phones, a TV, CD players, individual thermostats, and irons and ironing boards. The Clouses even provide a kit of medical supplies.

On rainy days, breakfast is brought to your room; when the weather allows, it's served in the garden by the creek. Yogurt, croissants, a plate of ham and cheese and pâté, and pastries, artistically presented, are possible choices. The rooms are supplied with beverages. There is a restaurant and bar on the premises.

The Waterside, within walking distance of the downtown and theaters, offers privacy and a restful retreat. There are few places more pleasant than its rose arbor or pond, where water trickles musically from a bamboo spout.

The Winchester Country Inn

35 South 2nd Street
Ashland, OR 97520
541-488-1113
800-972-4991
Fax: 541-488-4604
AshlandInn@aol.com

A Victorian inn with modern luxury

Innkeepers: Michael and Laurie Gibbs. **Accommodations:** 18 rooms and suites. **Rates:** $95–$180 double, $5 less single, $30 additional person; rates vary seasonally. **Included:** Full breakfast. **Minimum stay:** None. **Payment:** Major credit cards. **Children:** Welcome. **Pets:** Not allowed. **Smoking:** Not allowed. **Open:** Year-round.

➤ **In addition to seeing plays, you can take a backstage tour, try on a king's crown at the costume exhibit, and attend concerts and lectures.**

Two blocks south of the renowned Shakespearean theater, this century-old home offers top-quality lodging, gracious hospitality, and fine dining. The inn has been expanded in recent years and now includes two more buildings with suites.

The main house, a stately Queen Anne, stands on a residential corner, its rose garden and terraced yard a backdrop to the patio where guests may dine. A white gazebo, the site of many weddings, adds a final touch of Victoriana to the setting. The house was built in 1887 for the Roper family, who also owned the land now occupied by the Oregon Shakespeare Festival. Later it became a hospital and then an apartment complex.

Major restoration created a handsome inn that looks like a period piece in mint condition. Inside, ivory and pewter blue prevail in the hall and small sitting room, which has a phone, newspapers, and magazines. Tall ceilings, lace curtains, and needlepoint-covered chairs accentuate the classic decor.

The Winchester's restaurant, elegant without being too formal, serves several enticing entrées and offers outdoor dining. Try the fresh salmon fillets, duck à la bigarade, or Teng Dah beef, a French Vietnamese dish. Sunday brunch also features the unusual, with a menu including Bismarck pancakes and eggs with artichoke hearts and spinach. The Winchester offers an after-theater bistro menu as well.

"Country luxury" could define the atmosphere of the guest rooms, which are accented with antiques. Laurie Gibbs says, "We tried to create the feel of the old style while adding the comforts of the new." Of the seven rooms in the main house, three have their own entrances. The Patio Room, with an antique clawfoot tub and a queen-size bed, opens upon a private patio. The upstairs rooms have queen-size beds and views of the gardens or the hills of Ashland.

In the Larkspur Cottage, next door, you can stay on the upper level in the Belvedere, which has a fireplace, bay window, and two-person Jacuzzi, or downstairs in the Courtyard Suite. On the other side of the main house, the Carriage House has two comfortable suites

You'll be offered a choice of three entrées for breakfast, served on the patio or in the dining room — spinach-mushroom omelets and almond French toast are examples, accompanied by croissants, pecan rolls, and apple and walnut breads.

On holidays, the festivities at Winchester Inn include Thanksgiving and Mother's Day celebrations and a Dickens feast at Christmas. The inn also sponsors Murder Mystery Weekends and wine-tasting dinners.

Wolfe Manor Inn

586 B Street
Ashland, OR 97520
541-488-3676
800-801-3676
Fax: 541-488-4567

A gracious home in the historic Railroad District

Innkeepers: Sybil and Ron Maddox. **Accommodations:** 5 rooms. **Rates:** Summer, $109–$139; winter, $79–$99; $25 additional person. **Included:** Full breakfast. **Minimum stay:** 2 nights on weekends, 3 nights on holiday weekends. **Payment:** Major credit cards. **Children:** Over age 12, welcome. **Pets:** Not allowed. **Smoking:** Not allowed. **Open:** Year-round.

➤ **Crater Lake National Park, Oregon Caves National Monument, and several wineries, with tasting rooms open all year, are a short drive away.**

In the early 20th century, Ashland was the dinner stop for Southern Pacific's passenger trains. Meals were served in the large hotel next to the depot owned by Julius P. Wolfe. Wolfe's successful business allowed him to buy property in 1909 and build a two-story Craftsman home with a roofline matching his Railroad Hotel's.

The hotel is gone now, but the home remains, restored and open to visitors, in a pleasant neighborhood within walking distance of downtown and the Shakespeare Festival. The innkeepers, who once owned a B&B in the Napa Valley, encourage guests to socialize in the living room over a complimentary glass of port or sherry, and they foster conversation at the breakfast table.

Breakfast is served at one long table in the dining area. The meal varies, but you can count on homemade baked goods and hot and cold cereals.

The guest rooms, most with queen-size beds, have some antiques, down comforters and pillows, plenty of lighting, and individual themes. The largest room, and the most expensive, is Lynette's Lair, which has a four-poster bed, a roomy closet, and old-fashioned lamps. Throughout the inn you'll see African artifacts and photos of Sybil's family taken when she was a youth in Kenya.

The Woods House

333 North Main
Ashland, OR 97520
541-488-1598
800-435-8260
Fax: 541-482-8027
woodshouse@mind.net

> An inviting B&B with an
> outstanding garden

Innkeepers: Françoise and Lester Roddy. **Accommodations:** 6 rooms. **Rates:** $75–$120, $5 less for single, $35 additional person. **Included:** Full breakfast. **Minimum stay:** None. **Payment:** MasterCard, Visa. **Children:** Age 12 and older, welcome. **Pets:** Not allowed. **Smoking:** Not allowed. **Open:** Year-round.

➤ **You can tour the historic town, follow Woodland Trail in Lithia Park, visit the Old West village of Jacksonville, and raft or fish on the Rogue River.**

This unpretentious Craftsman home is a good example of the B&Bs that have proliferated in Ashland in recent years. Increasing numbers of visitors to the Oregon Shakespeare Festival are finding that the town is full of roomy old homes offering gracious hospitality.

The Roddys run one of the most pleasant, with immaculate rooms furnished with antiques, tasty breakfasts, and — the best feature — a large and lovely garden with an old grape arbor, a birdbath, lattices entwined with honeysuckle, 85 rose bushes, and beds of herbs, vegetables, and berries. Indoors, watercolors of flowers continue the garden theme.

Breakfast is a major event, with guests raving over the cook's prize-winning orange-chocolate scones, asparagus-cheese pie with tomatoes and herbs, cheese blintzes with raspberries, and oatmeal-blueberry pancakes.

The guest rooms — two downstairs, two up, and two in the Carriage House in back — have been dressed up with coronet canopies above the beds and comforters. Françoise collects linens and old laces, which add a romantic touch.

Woods House is on Ashland's busy main street, so if traffic sounds bother you, request a room at the back. The separate Carriage House provides private, air-conditioned hideaways with beds canopied with light muslin. Hair dryers are provided, and phones are available.

The living room of the Woods House is a quiet place to sip a cup of coffee before breakfast, listen to music, and browse through the shelves of classics by the tile fireplace. The trim tan and beige inn was named for the Woods family, who lived in the house for forty years; third- and fourth-generation members of the family remain in the area.

Astoria

Franklin Street Station

1140 Franklin Street
Astoria, OR 97103
503-325-4314
800-448-1098

A Victorian home near city attractions

Innkeeper: Renee Caldwell. **Accommodations:** 5 rooms . **Rates:** Summer, $73–$120; winter, $68–$110 double; $5 less for singles; $10 additional person. **Included:** Full breakfast. **Minimum stay:** None. **Payment:** MasterCard, Visa. **Children:** Welcome. **Pets:** Not allowed. **Smoking:** Not allowed. **Open:** Year-round.

➤ **In June, Astoria holds a Scandinavian Festival, featuring folk dancing, crafts, food, dances around a flowered midsummer pole, and bonfires.**

This tidy home, which dates from the early 1900s, offers more than tastefully decorated guest rooms and sumptuous breakfasts. It provides a carefully nurtured atmosphere of home. The remodeled house is furnished with antique reproductions and modern amenities, creating a setting of plush comfort. Wall-to-wall rose carpeting, white wicker, and light curtains in the guest rooms add to the warm, bright decor.

The smallest is the Fisher Room, done in blue and rose, with a white iron and brass bedstead, a glass-topped table, and blue Austrian curtains. Astor Suite is the pink-walled bridal suite, where guests are pampered with satin sheets, breakfast in bed, and bouquets of flowers. Columbia Room has a view of the Columbia River from the deck. All of the rooms have queen-size beds.

Downstairs in the bright basement is Pacific Room, a two-room suite with a private entrance. Lewis & Clark Room, on the main floor, also has a private entrance.

The latest addition is the Captain's Quarters, a suite occupying the entire third floor. It has a fireplace in the living room, cherry-wood furniture, a TV and stereo, a wet bar, and a sweeping view of downtown and the river.

In the dining room, a gas log burns in a green tile fireplace that once burned coal. The mantel and carved pillars are reminders of the builder's interest in woods; Ferdinand Fisher was a shipbuilder who constructed the home for his son, Earl.

Breakfast is served in the dining room at two seatings, 8:30 and 9:30. A few of Renee's specialties are homemade cinnamon rolls, baked egg dishes, sausage, and Belgian waffles with pecans and cream. You can help yourself to beverages any time during the day.

The cream-colored house trimmed in colonial blue and burgundy is 3 blocks from downtown Astoria and within easy walking distance of the Columbia River Maritime Museum and Flavel House, a sea captain's mansion built is 1883.

Rosebriar Hotel

636-14th Street
Astoria, OR 97103
503-325-7427
800-487-0224
Fax: 503-325-6937

**A classic inn overlooking
the Columbia River**

Innkeepers: Steve and Claudia Tuchman. **Accommodations:** 11 rooms. **Rates:** Summer, $65–$139; winter, $49–$109 single or double; $10 additional person. **Included:** Full breakfast. **Minimum stay:** None. **Payment:** Major credit cards. **Children:** Welcome (cribs available). **Pets:** Not allowed. **Smoking:** Not allowed. **Open:** Year-round.

➤ **Visit Coxcomb Hill for sweeping views of the town. Astoria Column, at the top of the hill, has a circular staircase that leads up to a higher bird's-eye view.**

Astoria, at the mouth of the Columbia River in Oregon's northwestern corner, was the site of the first permanent European-American settlement in Oregon country. In 1811, John Jacob Astor's Pacific Fur Company established a fort, and the town quickly grew to become a major seaport. Sea captains and merchants began building elaborate homes, many of which remain, making Astoria a showcase of historic landmarks.

This big white frame Classic Revival home was built on a hill above town in 1902 by Frank Patton, a banker, who wanted to rival his neighbor's house. Years later, it served as a Catholic convent. Now it's Rosebriar, a small hotel with charm and personality.

Rosebriar stands on a half acre of landscaped grounds, surrounded by colorful trees like cinnamon viburnum, scarlet oak, copper beech, and cedar. A flower garden adjoins the walk to the pillared front entrance.

The inn has changed considerable in recent years, though the owners have maintained its period flavor. Now there are phones, TVs, and baths in all the tasteful, traditionally furnished rooms. Some have views of Astoria and the Columbia River; others glimpse flowering trees and the ornate, historic Flavel House

The one ground-floor room is a suite with a private entrance, a queen-size bed, and a sofa bed in the sitting room. Across the hall is a conference room, with stained glass in the windows (it was once the convent's chapel) and leaded glass French doors opening to a courtyard. The versatile space is often used for weddings, meetings, and parties. On the other side of the courtyard is a new and separate suite, the Carriage House, which has a kitchen and sitting and sleeping area in one large room. The tall stained glass windows in this restful, gray-green room came from Scotland.

A full breakfast — granola, fruit, French toast, baked pears — is served in the dining room at tables for two or four. The Rosebriar's environmentally aware proprietors make it a point to use recycled and natural materials throughout the hotel, and they patronize local firms. Every day they serve tea in the lobby-parlor, an inviting room with a fireplace, the original carved fir woodwork, Ionic pillars, and, in a curved bay, windows that overlook Astoria.

Baker City

Geiser Grand Hotel

1996 Main Street
Baker City, OR 97814
541-523-1889
Fax: 541-523-7723

| **A luxurious hotel in eastern Oregon** |

Proprietors: Barbara and Dwight Sidway. **Accommodations:** 30 rooms. **Rates:** $85–$159. **Included:** Full breakfast. **Minimum stay:** None. **Payment:** Major credit cards. **Children:** Under age 8, free. **Pets:** Dogs allowed. **Smoking:** Non-smoking rooms available. **Open:** Year-round.

➤ **In gold rush days, Baker City was known as "the queen of the mines." Miners, prospectors, ranchers, rustlers, and con men swarmed in to seek their fortune.**

The Geiser Grand was known as the finest hotel between Portland and Salt Lake City during Baker's frontier gold-mining days. The Geiser family built it in 1889 to show the wealth they had obtained from the Bonanza gold mine, and they spared no expense. Their Italian Renaissance Revival hotel had ornate balustrades and chandeliers, 70 rooms, and French menus. White-gloved waiters served lobster and blue point oysters.

With the passage of time and the Depression, the place fell into disrepair; but now it has been returned to its former glory (with larger rooms and modern comforts). A three-year, $6 million restoration has brought back the 19th-century splendor in every detail. There are a hundred crystal chandeliers, silk damask draperies, marble tables, gilt chairs, and windows 10 feet high. There's a grand staircase and a cupola with an illuminated clock. A balustrade of wrought iron and mahogany edges a mezzanine where ladies of an earlier day would take tea. The Palm Court is capped by a stained glass ceiling, the largest in the Pacific Northwest.

When the Sidwells decided the Geiser Grand should be saved from the wrecking ball and given an authentic restoration, they knew what they were doing. They have been renovating historic buildings, including the Biltmore Hotel in Coral Gables and the Freedom Tower in Miami, since the early 1980s. Their idea was not to create a museum but a functioning hotel of comfort and beauty; and so there are queen- and king-size beds in the rooms, VCRs and videos, a library with books and games, a fax and copying service, and meeting rooms that hold up to 300 people. The restaurant is open for three meals a day and includes a children's menu.

Dogs are more than welcome; they receive biscuit treats on a doily every evening. Genteel hospitality is alive and well on the frontier.

Bandon

The Inn at Face Rock

3225 Beach Loop Road
Bandon, OR 97411
541-347-9441
800-638-3092

A southern Oregon resort by the ocean

Owner: Jim Barggren. **Accommodations:** 55 rooms and suites. **Rates:** Summer, $79–$129 double; $10 additional person; winter, $59–$109. **Minimum stay:** None. **Payment:** Major credit cards. **Children:** Welcome. **Pets:** Allowed ($10). **Smoking:** Nonsmoking rooms available. **Open:** Year-round.

➤ **At this picturesque spot you can beachcomb, watch the waves spray against rugged rock formations, and visit the 1896 Coquille Lighthouse.**

On the southern Oregon coast, few resorts offer lodging, a restaurant and lounge, and an adjacent golf course. Even fewer offer the serene and sophisticated ambience of Face Rock. The inn has come under new management in recent years, and some ambitious improvements have been made.

The resort is not directly on the beach along Bandon's scenic loop road, but it has splendid ocean views from its high vantage point. The restaurant takes full advantage of them, with wall-filling windows that curve up to form a portion of the ceiling, allowing light to stream in on white linen, coral walls, and cane and chrome chairs. The lounge is an intimate spot, with a console piano, a TV, and a small bar, nice for a before-dinner cocktail or a late cappuccino.

All of the suites have ocean views. They also have fireplaces (laid with logs), phones, and kitchens. Several of the newer suites, simple but with a contemporary luxury, have an Oriental touch in the porcelain lamps, wall prints, and pale plum carpeting.

All the rooms have TV, and you can rent a VCR. Laundry facilities are available. The upper suites and one room with a king-size bed offer handicap access.

Meeting rooms can hold up to 70 people. Golfers enjoy the 9-hole course, where an often-brisk wind provides extra challenge. Riding stables are nearby.

Face Rock is a few miles outside Bandon, a peaceful town known for its cranberry products (try the chocolate-covered cranberries at Cranberry Sweets in Old Town). The town also has several offbeat shops, galleries, and cafés.

If you are visiting in summer, someone will be sure to invite you back for a stay in November. By advertising the pleasures of storm-watching on the coast, Bandon has made winter an asset. At Christmastime, the town sparkles with thousands of lights.

Bend

The Inn of the Seventh Mountain

18575 S.W. Century Drive
Bend, OR 97702
541-382-8711
800-452-6810
Fax: 541-382-3517

A resort for all ages near the central Cascades

General Manager: Ron Botts. **Accommodations:** 248 rooms. **Rates:** $59–$299, 1 to 10 people; rates vary seasonally; group rates and packages available. **Minimum stay:** 2 nights in summer and on holidays, 4 nights over Christmas. **Payment:** Major credit cards. **Children:** Welcome. **Pets:** Not allowed. **Smoking:** Nonsmoking rooms available. **Open:** Year-round.

➤ **Winter sports include skating and snowmobiling. Or take a horse-drawn sleigh to a Mongolian yurt (heated) and feast by candlelight on barbecued ribs or chicken.**

Just about any outdoor recreation you could hope to find in a resort is available at this inn, which is west of Bend in the Deschutes National Forest and 160 miles southeast of Portland. The Inn of the Seventh Mountain is close to Mount Bachelor, which offers some of Oregon's best powder skiing, numerous chair lifts, and 500 acres of downhill runs. For cross-country skiers, groomed trails wind through the forest. Lessons, tours, and rentals are available at the resort, as well as special ski packages.

During the summer, the resort is just as busy. There are five tennis courts, two pools, including one with a long slide, and three hot tubs (the heated pools are open in winter as well). The ice rink becomes a roller skating rink. Whitewater rafting on the Deschutes River, horseback riding, and mountain bikes are available, and there's a championship 18-hole golf course.

There are two main restaurants: Poppy Seed Café, a casual spot overlooking the swimming pool and landscaped grounds, and Josiah's, near the ice rink, which specializes in fresh Northwest cuisine. Live entertainment is offered in the lounge section of the dinner house. Groceries and deli foods are available at Mountain Market and Deli, in the pool area.

The guest rooms, in rough-hewn cedar buildings that form an arc around the grounds, are available in three types: bedrooms, fireside units, and condominiums. An economy bedroom is a good buy for one person or couple planning to spend a lot of time outdoors. It has all the basics — it's carpeted and has a TV, phone, a comfortable bed, and a good reading lamp, all in a small but adequate space. Other choices are fireside studios, loft units, and apartments with one, two, or three bedrooms. The larger accommodations have well-equipped kitchens, fireplaces, and private balconies. The condominiums are decorated tastefully, most keeping above the resort's minimum standards.

You'll find conventions here — this is a popular place for groups to gather. The friendly staff is eager to help each visitor find something enjoyable to do.

Lara House

640 N.W. Congress
Bend, OR 97701
541-388-4064
800-766-4064
Fax: 541-388-4064

A tranquil home by a city park

Innkeepers: Doug and Bobbye Boger. **Accommodations:** 6 rooms. **Rates:** $65–$100 single, $75–$110 double, $10 additional person. **Included:** Full breakfast. **Minimum stay:** None. **Payment:** Major credit cards. **Children:** Not appropriate. **Pets:** Not allowed. **Smoking:** Outdoors only. **Open:** Year-round.

➤ **The Pine Tavern Restaurant is Bend's oldest (1919) and still has the best view, overlooking Mirror Pond. Specialties are fresh trout, prime rib, and scones with honey butter.**

Drake Park, an 11-acre greenbelt along Mirror Pond and the Deschutes River as it curves through Bend, is one of the most appealing city parks in Oregon. Its shade trees and grassy slopes make it ideal for picnics, while winding paths offer pleasant strolls by the river. The park is full of — indeed, almost overrun by — ducks, Canadian honkers, and swans that visitors feed and pamper.

Just across the street, Lara House stands on a corner of tall fir trees and green lawn, a white and gray frame home that dates from 1910, when it was built for a Bend merchant, A.M. Lara. Now it's owned by an energetic couple who like to make guests feel at home. The Bogers will invite you to read by the fire or watch TV in the living room, soak in the outdoor hot tub, and enjoy cider and homemade treats in the sun room, where the "goody table" is kept.

From there you can step out to a terraced deck that overlooks the broad lawn and flower gardens. It's a relaxing spot to drink coffee and read the paper on a sunny morning; breakfast is served here or in the dining room. The Bogers prepare unusual dishes — chile egg puff, fruit parfaits, and almond pudding among them.

The guest room on the main floor, with a king-size bed, opens to the front deck. The other rooms are upstairs, each on a corner and furnished with taste and an eye for comfort. All have queen-size beds, and each has a distinctive feature such as a porch, a fireplace, or, in the bridal suite, lace and antiques. The closets are spacious (though short on pegs), and bathrooms are immaculate.

Shevlin Room, which gets the afternoon light, is decorated in taupe and cream. Cascade Room has a four-poster wrought-iron bed, and Drake Room features a clawfoot tub with shower. A suite with a double bed and a sitting area with a futon occupies the third floor.

In addition to Drake Park, Bend has a number of interesting attractions. You can tour the High Desert Museum, a fascinating display of wildlife; watch the headwaters of the Metolius River emerge from an underground spring; hike Black Butte to see the panorama of central Oregon at your feet; ride horseback on mountain trails; and, in winter, ski on the powdery slopes of Mount Bachelor.

Mill Inn

642 Northwest Colorado
Bend, OR 97701
541-389-9198

| **A small inn in central Oregon that welcomes families** |

Innkeepers: Carol and Ev Stiles. **Accommodations:** 9 rooms (5 with private bath). **Rates:** $37–$60 double, $15 per person in bunkroom. **Included:** Full breakfast. **Minimum stay:** None. **Payment:** Major credit cards. **Children:** Welcome. **Pets:** Not allowed. **Smoking:** Outdoors only. **Open:** Year-round.

➤ **Bend's annual festivals draw crowds to events such as the Pole, Pedal, Paddle Race in May and the Cascade Festival of Music in Drake Park.**

Casual, comfortable, clean, and affordable, the Mill Inn has gained an enthusiastic following since it opened in 1991. The Stileses offer warm, unpretentious hospitality and lodging that is close to all of central Oregon's recreation.

The inn is six blocks south of downtown Bend, and 20 minutes from the slopes of Mount Bachelor. Most visitors come for the many outdoor activities, such as whitewater rafting, fishing, biking, hiking, and golfing. The inn has a ski waxing area and storage space for skis and bikes.

Most of the simply but imaginatively furnished guest rooms line the hall on the second floor. Each has a theme decor, such as the golfing motif in Duffers, one of the smaller rooms. Next to it is Bartlett, named for the person who first built the inn as a boarding house for millworkers. These rooms adjoin, a useful feature for families. Cribs are available.

The Locker Room, favored by ski groups and singles, has four bunk beds and uses a shared bath. An all-you-can-eat breakfast of bacon and eggs or pancakes (the menu varies) is served whenever you request in the cheery dining room. Most tables are set for four.

Next to the dining area is a conversation corner with a couch, soft chairs, books, games, and a TV and VCR. Outside on the deck is a hot tub, where skiers (and others) like to relax at the end of an active day.

Rock Springs Guest Ranch

64201 Tyler Road
Bend, OR 97701
541-382-1957

A top-quality horse ranch for the whole family

Innkeepers: The Gill family. **Manager:** John Gill. **Accommodations:** 26 rooms. **Rates:** $1,450–$1,575 per adult per week, $1,065 ages 6–16, $865 ages 3–5; lower rates on holidays. **Included:** All meals, riding, and ranch activities. **Minimum stay:** 1 week, except holidays; shorter stays permitted when space allows. **Payment:** Major credit cards. **Children:** Infants free. **Pets:** Not allowed. **Smoking:** Allowed. **Open:** Late June to early September and major holidays.

➤ **The High Desert Museum has copies of dwellings in the Great Basin region, stream and pond habitats, a wildlife observation pavilion, and more.**

This is summer camp with style, designed for the entire family and as good as it gets. At the Gills' classic guest ranch in a valley 10 miles northwest of Bend, everything you could want in a horse ranch vacation is offered, from riding the range to soaking in a spa built against boulders, from barbecued steaks to hayrides.

Riding is the main interest. The ranch has a string of 65 horses, and guests may go out daily on rides led by wranglers. Children under 6 may not go on the trails but can ride with a lead in the pastures. It's a good idea to bring a babysitter if you have a young child; the ranch charges $200 for the sitter's room and board.

Counselors run a program for children from 5 to 12. Arts and crafts, a talent show, sports events, and a hayride and campout are part of the fun, as well as the swimming pool, lighted tennis and volleyball courts, and indoor game room with a piano and table tennis.

Meals are served communally, in substantial quantities, in the big, open dining room. For breakfast you might have waffles, pancakes, or French toast with bacon or sausage, homemade cinnamon rolls, and scrambled eggs. Lunch is a buffet of salads, fresh vegetables and fruit, soup, and sandwiches.

At dinner you can choose a hearty or light meal. Ratatouille is popular, as is Cajun cookery. Sirloin steaks and chicken are grilled on barbecue night, and when the kids are off on their big hayride and campout, it's Gourmet Night for the adults. Beverages are available all day; beer and wine may be purchased at the bar next to the lounge.

The lounge is like a large living room in an old-fashioned lodge, with walls paneled in warm woods, plants at the windows, dark leather couches, and a stone fireplace with a blaze crackling on cool evenings. Upstairs are the game room and a balcony with a TV, books, and poker and pool tables.

Each unit in the seven guest houses can sleep up to nine people; adjoining rooms can be opened or closed for varied sizes of families and conference groups. Most have brick fireplaces, with wood supplied, and kitchens. Indirect lighting emphasizes the warm tones of knotty pine walls and earth hues in the furnishings. All the guest units have decks; a ponderosa pine grows through the center of one. Daily maid service is provided. "This is a place to meet and make good friends," says John Gill, the president of the organization and a nephew of the ranch's founder, Donna Gill. "We like to have people come here and enjoy the ranch and horses and each other's company."

Black Butte Ranch

P.O. Box 8000
Black Butte Ranch, OR 97759
541-595-6211
800-452-7455
Fax: 541-595-2077

A fine year-round resort in the central Cascades

General Manager: Michael Justin. **Accommodations:** 120 condominiums and homes. **Rates:** Condos, $85–$178 (2–6 people); homes $126–$294; rates vary seasonally. **Minimum stay:** 2 nights in home; July and August: 2 nights in condos, 6 nights in homes. **Payment:** Major credit cards. **Children:** Welcome. **Pets:** Not allowed. **Smoking:** Nonsmoking rooms available. **Open:** Year-round.

➤ **Mount Bachelor's slopes beckon the downhill skier; Nordic trails provide cross-country skiing. Closer is Hoodoo Bowl, with weekday and family specials.**

When you want a resort that's thoughtfully designed with all the comforts and quiet good taste in a setting of supreme beauty, you need look no further that Black Butte Ranch. This condominium development, set on 1,800 acres in the high Cascades of sunny central Oregon, is one of the state's finest.

This is not a resort with disco action and boisterous play; it's a classy getaway where there is no untoward noise. But it's not stuffy; Black Butte is merely well behaved.

It is located on a plain of grassy meadows and ponderosa pine forests 31 miles northwest of Bend, an easy 3-hour drive from Portland. Mount Jefferson, Mount Washington, the three Sisters, and Mount Bachelor, a skier's heaven, ring the resort like a snowy diadem.

Black Butte, a pine-covered volcanic cinder cone, rises from the valley floor, its trail to the top inviting hikers to climb to a panoramic summit view. Black Butte Ranch offers myriad recreational pursuits: there are two meticulously maintained 18-hole golf courses, 19 tennis courts, 4 outdoor swimming pools (1 covered), and 16 miles of bicycle and jogging trails on the property, which is surrounded by Deschutes National Forest land. The stables have horses for hire; some riders bring their own.

The main lodge has a multi-tiered restaurant with floor-to-ceiling windows that overlook lawns, a lake, and the mountains rising behind the dark forest. Earth tones and natural woods create a warm environment in which to enjoy the view and a lunch or dinner of prime rib, poached salmon, and homemade rolls and soups. Upstairs, the tree-level lounge, which also has admirable views, is a pleasant and quiet spot for relaxing by the stone fireplace.

The nicely appointed gray cedar condominiums and homes are individually owned. In one condo you may find a king-size brass bed and soft, leathery chairs. The black fireplace is stacked with wood. Fiber artwork hangs under a high, slanted ceiling. Sliding glass doors lead to a deck that faces a wide green meadow and the omnipresent mountains. A phone, clock, and TV are assumed furnishings, along with coffee and tea on a tray.

When you wish to go beyond the resort, you can go into the national forest for hiking, fishing, boating, and riding. The ranch is 8 miles west of Sisters, a town with an Old West theme, where you can browse in the shops or attend a rodeo.

Brookings

The Chetco River Inn

21202 High Prairie Road
Brookings, OR 97415
541-469-8128
800-327-2688

A secluded lodge in the wilderness

Innkeeper: Sandra Brugger. **Accommodations:** 4 rooms (3 with private bath). **Rates:** $95 double. **Included:** Full breakfast. **Minimum stay:** None. **Payment:** MasterCard, Visa. **Children:** Welcome. **Pets:** Not allowed. **Smoking:** Restricted. **Open:** Year-round except Thanksgiving and Christmas.

➤ **Here you can play croquet or darts, fish from the riverbank, swim, go bird-watching, and hike along the beautiful Chetco River.**

Travel 16 miles up the Chetco River from Brookings, on the southern Oregon coast, and you'll come to this outstanding small inn. Bordered on three sides by the river, it stands on 35 acres of private forest. You notice every chuckle of the river, every frog croak and bird's cry, in this secluded hideaway far from cities and traffic.

The lodge was built of cedar and oak in 1987 on property that once held a settler's cabin. Only the rock chimney remains, along with a gnarled apple tree that draws the occasional bear when the fruit is ripe. Wildlife abounds: you'll see deer at the salt block, elk, newts, alligator lizards, squirrels, and green tree frogs. Daffodils and wood anemones bloom beneath tall oak, myrtle, and pine trees.

Indoors, the large, open common room has a black and green marble floor, leather chairs, and a woodstove backed by stonework. Snowshoes, a trophy fish, and a bear rug hanging from the loft are reminders of the rugged world beyond the front porch.

The guest rooms line the hall off the loft. Only three are used unless a group takes the lodge; the fourth contains twin brass beds and is the only one without its own bath.. Each room is slightly different. You might have a queen-size wicker bed and a river view or a room with Oriental decor and a brass dual king. Another room has a dual king with a jewel-tone velvet quilt and a window overlooking a large, glossy-leafed myrtle tree.

The inn has several energy sources (propane, battery, solar, and generator), so that the lamps can always be lighted. One of the pleasures here is the extraordinary food — far from typical backwoods fare — prepared by Sandra, an expert cook. With advance notice, she'll present a dinner that might start with smoked sturgeon and move on to savory mushroom soup, artichoke salad, and stuffed game hen with an apricot glaze. Homemade ice cream and brownies are a typical dessert. Another night, the menu could be barbecued steak, lasagna, fresh crab, or halibut. The cost for this banquet is $20 a person.

Holmes Sea Cove

17350 Holmes Drive
Brookings, OR 97415
541-469-3025

| A B&B on an oceanside cliff |

Innkeepers: Jack and Lorene Holmes. **Accommodations:** 3 rooms. **Rates:** $80–$95 double; $15 additional person; single, $5 less; discounts for longer stays. **Included:** Continental breakfast. **Minimum stay:** None. **Payment:** MasterCard, Visa. **Children:** Welcome by arrangement. **Pets:** Not allowed (dog on premises). **Smoking:** Not allowed. **Open:** Year-round.

➤ **The mild climate makes the area a gardener's paradise. The azalea has its own festival, and Brookings is the world's major producer of Easter lily bulbs.**

Two of the guest rooms in this home on a hill — 2 miles north of Brookings and high above the sea — are on the daylight-basement level. They have queen-size beds and a few extras such as mini-refrigerators, cupboards for storing snacks, and rods for hanging wet clothing. Sliding glass doors lead to a vine-covered terrace and garden. These accommodations are pleasant and comfortable but lack the grand view of the third room. Once a separate cottage, the third room is now connected to the main house and has a queen-size bed, a refrigerator, TV, and comfortable, traditional couches and chairs. A deck surrounds the house, taking advantage of the wondrous view.

Picture windows face west, where offshore seastacks stand like natural sculptures in the swirling, spraying waves. Whitecaps and boats are dots on the water, and clouds piling on the horizon turn pink and gold in the sunset. On the ground, bright yellow scotch-broom (a nuisance, but beautiful in spring) blooms along with the masses of colorful flowers in the garden.

Jack and Lorene, superb gardeners who constantly terrace and plant, have created a hillside park of trees, rhododendrons, daisies, dahlias, foxglove, and dozens of other plants. A flagstone path in the garden winds to a gazebo and down the terraced hill, along a creek, to the sandy white beach below.

In the evening, you will be asked to choose your breakfast from a menu. The next morning, there will be a tray at your door; juices, fruit cup, toast, and a basket of breads are all available.

Camp Sherman

House on the Metolius

FS Road 1420
P.O. Box 100
Camp Sherman, OR 97730
541-595-6620

A quiet riverside resort in central Oregon

Managers: Mark and Tony Foster. **Accommodations:** 7 rooms. **Rates:** $110–$170, 2–4 people. **Minimum stay:** 2 nights. **Payment:** MasterCard, Visa. **Children:** Not appropriate. **Pets:** Not allowed. **Smoking:** Discouraged (high fire danger in forest). **Open:** March–December.

➤ **In central Oregon, the peaks of the Cascades are an impressive back-drop: 10,497-foot Mount Jefferson, Mount Washington, the Three Sisters, and Three-Fingered Jack.**

From the House on the Metolius, you can see all the central Cascades. The resort is on the banks of the river in the ponderosa pine forests near the community of Camp Sherman, long a favored vacation spot for Oregonians who live on the damp, western side of the Cascades. Fly-fishers are especially fond of the area, for the Metolius has been described as "the picture of a perfect trout stream."

Fishing on the upper Metolius isn't as good as it used to be, they say, but the lower portion and the McKenzie and Deschutes rivers are nearby, and the fishing's fine.

This is barbless hook country, catch-and-release only for the native trout. Hatchery trout may be kept. A visit to House on the Metolius is a tradition for many people. The 200-acre resort, which has been owned by the same family since the 1930s, opened to guests in 1948 and immediately became popular. The cottages are scattered among the pines and meticulous lawns on a cliff above the river. Several face a slope that descends to a marshy meadow where cattle browse near the Cascade foothills. Mount Jefferson rises in white perfection on the horizon.

Some units are attached; two are separate cabins. Numbers 1 and 2, the original duplexes, are quaint and charming, with calico quilts and a 1930s atmosphere. Each has a small fireplace, and rattan chairs stand by the hearth. The smallish windows have great views of Mount Jefferson, meadows dotted with yellow balsamroot and yarrow at the bottom of the slope, and the rushing river. Both units have kitchenettes and share a patio with a barbecue.

All the rooms have fireplaces — fires are neatly laid and wood is supplied — and king-size beds that easily divide to become twins. Small kitchens have microwave ovens and coffeemakers.

Although fishing is still very popular, House on the Metolius now emphasizes its appeal as a peaceful, scenic spot for hiking, cross-country skiing, and relaxation. The sense of quiet seclusion is carefully maintained. There's a security gate, and even grass mowing is done only on certain days, to maintain the peace and quiet. As you sit on a lawn chair, taking in the majestic mountain, the flowered meadows, and the willow-edged river, the only sounds you hear are whispering pine trees and water tumbling through the canyon.

Cannon Beach

The Argonauta Inn

P.O. Box 3188
West Second Street
Cannon Beach, OR 97110
503-436-2601
800-822-2468

Cottages in the heart of an ocean resort town

Managers: Valerie and Frank Swedenborg. **Accommodations:** 3 rooms and 2 cottages. **Rates:** $85–$295, 2–11 people. **Minimum stay:** 2 nights on weekends, 3 nights on holidays, 1 week in cottages in summer. **Payment:** MasterCard, Visa. **Children:** Welcome. **Pets:** Not allowed. **Smoking:** Not allowed. **Open:** Year-round.

➤ **Cannon Beach, known for its galleries, theater, boutiques, and souvenir shops, is an easy 1½-hour drive from Portland.**

The Argonauta is not a traditional inn but a cluster of pretty cottages that house two to eleven people. The cottages are surrounded by lawns and flowers on the corner of Second and Larch Streets in this artists' community and seaside resort. Cannon Beach is quite popular with Oregonians, so make your reservations early. Haystack Rock, a monolith on the edge of the surf that is a wildlife refuge, is the distinctive feature of the broad sandy beach that borders the town; strollers are irresistibly drawn to its craggy edges and tidepools.

A few yards north of Haystack, on a low bluff above the sandy beach, are the Argonauta homes. The oldest is Town House, a 1906 Victorian cottage that is probably one of the town's earliest dwellings. It does have an Old World flavor in the stone fireplace, prints on the walls, and antique and wicker furnishings. It has been updated, however, with two bathrooms and two cable TVs. The house has two bedrooms, one with a queen-size bed, the other with a twin and a double bed.

The smallest rooms are the upper and lower suites of Lighthouse. Both have queen-size beds, Franklin fireplaces, lighthouse artwork, and nautical decor. Each holds two adults. Chart Room is a two-room suite decorated with Winslow Homer prints, maps, and sailing charts. The separate bedroom has a queen-size bed. The suite can hold three people.

The best is Beach House, a big blue home that can hold up to eleven people (though six or eight would be more comfortable); it's ideal for a family or for two or three couples traveling together. Just a few steps from the beach, the house has wide views from a protected sun deck, a living area with a river rock fireplace, three bedrooms, and two baths. Beach House is the only lodging with an ocean view.

Antiques fill the large, pine-floored home. Old oak mantelpieces form headboards in two bedrooms. The third bedroom, in rough-sawn cedar, has a skylight and a queen-size bed.

All the cottages have a TV and a fireplace as well as a full kitchen except the lower suite in the Lighthouse, which has a refrigerator only.

Cannon Beach's attractions range from splendid sunsets and wave-dashed seastacks (offshore rock formations) to a world-famous sand castle contest and a two-week Christmas celebration that includes lamplighting, carol singing, and a Christmas play.

Hallmark Resort

1400 South Hemlock
Cannon Beach, OR 97110
503-436-4566
888-448-4449
Fax: 503-436-0324

A full-service resort **overlooking the beach**

Manager: Lin Kee. **Accommodations:** 128 rooms, 14 suites, 4 houses. **Rates:** Summer, $99–$425 (up to 11 people); winter, $59–$320. **Minimum stay:** 2 nights on weekends. **Payment:** Major credit cards. **Children:** Welcome. **Pets:** Allowed in designated areas ($8). **Smoking:** Nonsmoking rooms available. **Open:** Year-round.

➤ **Exploring the tidal pools by Haystack Rock, you may see an interpreter, who will explain the intertidal environment. Guides, binoculars, and spotting scopes are provided.**

Just a flight of wooden steps above the sandy white beach, this contemporary cedar shake resort has one of the best views on the northern Oregon coast. It looks right at Haystack Rock and the Needles, offshore formations that loom from the surf and cast long shadows across the sand.

The three-story resort spreads along the edge of a bluff. Its design is not quite consistent with the generally smaller scale of Cannon Beach, but it is tasteful for a place of this size. Of course, the ocean-front rooms are preferable for their fine view. They have queen- or king-size beds, fireplaces, refrigerators (some have kitchens), and balconies.

All the rooms have TVs, telephones, and gas fireplaces. Some feature tiled spas. Coffee and a morning newspaper are provided. There's no room service, but a concierge can arrange fishing charters and dinner reservations.

The resort has an indoor swimming pool, whirlpool, and sauna area that is beautifully done in blue and white tile, with windows looking out to the beach. There is also an exercise room as well as a children's wading pool. Guests in the four beachfront houses, which hold up to eleven people, have pool house privileges.

Down the hill and across the road is one of the region's good, casual restaurants, Dooger's, justifiably famed for its clam chowder. The best dinner spot in town is Café de la Mer. Lazy Susan Café serves satisfying breakfasts, and Osburn's Market is the place to fill your picnic basket.

If you're at the Hallmark on Sandcastle Day, you will be right above the action. The annual contest, the town's major community event, draws close to 1,000 participants and up to 35,000 spectators.

Stephanie Inn

2740 S. Pacific
P.O. Box 219
Cannon Beach, OR 97110
503-436-2221
800-633-3466
Fax: 503-436-9711

A stylish inn beside the sea

General manager: Sharon Major. **Accommodations:** 46 rooms and suites. **Rates:** $139–$389 single or double, $25 additional person. **Included:** Continental breakfast. **Minimum stay:** 2 nights on weekends and holidays. **Payment:** Major credit cards. **Children:** Age 12 and older, welcome. **Pets:** Not allowed. **Smoking:** Not allowed. **Open:** Year-round.

➤ **North of Cannon Beach, Ecola State Park has grassy headlands with picnic tables and panoramic overlooks. There are trails down to the beach.**

In addition to its motels and cottages and the occasional B&B, Cannon Beach needed an inn like this, a sophisticated small hotel with casual beachside charm. Opened in 1993, Stephanie Inn is built of cedar and stone; it has wood beams and columns and a river rock fireplace in the lobby. Everything about this place is soothing, despite the tourist bustle, from the piped-in classical music to the calm colors and potted plants. A typical oceanfront room has a four-poster bed, a wingback chair and couch, and a small terrace by the lawn above the beach. Every room has a whirlpool tub, fireplace, and VCR.

Complimentary wine is provided in the evening in the library and chart room. This comfortable sitting area off the lobby has a fireplace, piano, bookshelves, and view of the beach and Haystack Rock. There's a jar of candy on the table and binoculars on the windowsill.

The restaurant upstairs is a pretty, intimate space with a romantic atmosphere, though it doesn't face the ocean. There are two dinner seatings in the summer and on weekends, with two entrées offered each night. In the morning, a breakfast buffet, which includes fresh pastries, is set out in the dining room.

The inn offers several packages that include champagne (or sparkling cider), balloons, scented bath crystals, chocolate truffles, and other special treats.

Turk's Lodging in the Trees

P.O. Box 482
Cannon Beach, OR 97110
503-436-1809
800-547-6100 (reservations only)

A contemporary home over the ocean

Proprietors: Bob and Carole Turk. **Accommodations:** 2-bedroom house, cottage with 1 bedroom and a studio. **Rates:** House, $199–$339, up to 6 people; cottage, $169–$199, up to 4 people; studio, $99–$119. **Included:** First day, Continental breakfast in house only. **Minimum stay:** 3 nights in summer, 2 nights on weekends. **Payment:** MasterCard, Visa. **Children:** Over age 12, welcome. **Pets:** Not allowed. **Smoking:** Outdoors only. **Open:** Year-round.

➤ **On December weekends, Cannon Beach holds a Dickens Festival, with Victorian decorations, costumed singers, lamplighting, gift-filled shops, and *A Christmas Carol*.**

This secluded aerie was built by hand on a forested hillside high above the ocean near Cannon Beach and is across the highway from Arcadia State Park. Guests have the exclusive use of the 1,850-square-foot home.

Built of rough-hewn fir and spruce, the main house has 24-foot ceilings of Canadian pine, finely crafted pine cabinets, and fireplaces made from 10 tons of river rock. You can watch the hearth in one fireplace from the king-size bed in the main sleeping area. Full-length windows flood the rooms with light and command a sweeping view of the Pacific. Both the stone shower and the blue tile whirlpool bath, also with a view, are big enough for two. The loft holds a queen-size bed and futons, allowing the house to hold six people.

The Garden Room, two steps down from the cheerful, well-equipped kitchen, is a sitting area with white wicker furniture, plants, and skylights. On the wide wraparound deck is a jutting ledge with a garden swing — a perfect vantage point for watching the sun set over the ocean.

Also on the 60-acre wooded property is a cottage with two accommodations. The upper level has a king-size bed in the bedroom and a trundle bed in the living area; the lower level is a studio with a queen-size bed. The studio has a kitchen and an ocean view.

Cave Junction

Oregon Caves Chateau

P.O. Box 128
Cave Junction, OR 97523
541-592-3400

A 1930s lodge near marble caves

General manager: Mike Romick. **Accommodations:** 22 rooms. **Rates:** $69–$89 double, $10 additional person. **Included:** Continental breakfast on May 1 to May 15 and September 15 to October 19. **Minimum stay:** None. **Payment:** MasterCard, Visa. **Children:** Under age 6, free. **Pets:** Not allowed. **Smoking:** Allowed. **Open:** March to December.

➤ **During tours through corridors and chambers you will learn about the remarkable calcite formations, the poet Joaquin Miller's "Marble Halls of Oregon."**

In the far southwestern corner of Oregon, a narrow, winding road (Oregon 46) leads from Cave Junction to Oregon Caves National Monument. Here Elijah Davidson, hunting deer in the Siskiyou Mountains in 1874, followed a bear and discovered the Oregon Caves.

Davidson's dog, Bruno, had chased a bear into a mossy hole in the mountainside, and the hunter went after him. Lighting his way with matches, Davidson crept down a narrow passageway that led deep into the mountain until all his matches were gone and he was suddenly in total darkness. By groping along an underground stream, he found his way out and returned home to tell his tale.

In 1909, the caves came under federal jurisdiction and are now run by the National Park Service. Oregon Caves Chateau operates under a contract with the Park Service.

The Chateau, which dates from 1934, is a handsome six-story cedar structure built against the hillside in a deep canyon. The lobby has a grand piano and an impressive fireplace made of the local marble, but its biggest attraction is the view of the Illinois Valley. Windows frame green vistas of trees and canyon; this is isolated, remote country.

The dining room has picture windows, too, and to bring the omnipresent wilderness even closer, a stream flows through the room. The restaurant is open for dinner only, serving steak, seafood, and chicken. During the day, the coffee shop offers sandwiches and salads. A light breakfast is set out in the lobby for guests.

Some guest rooms in the lodge overlook a pond and falls, others the canyon — and some have the less desirable view of the driveway. Request a room facing the canyon to enjoy crimson sunsets and trees tipped with gold in the evening light.

Many of the furnishings were made for the hotel, some in 1930s style, with fruit designs painted on wooden bedsteads. The beds are doubles or twins. On the top floor, oddly configured, narrow rooms stand under steeply pitched ceilings. With no air conditioning, these become warm in the afternoons, but evenings cool quickly at 4,000 feet.

Visitors are advised to wear shoes with nonslip soles and to take a jacket on cave tours; the temperature is always about 40 degrees cooler inside the mountain. People with heart or breathing problems or who might have difficulty negotiating the many stairs and low, narrow passageways should not take the tour. Children under age 6 or shorter than 42 inches are not permitted in the caves.

Cloverdale

The Hudson House

37700 Highway 101 South
Cloverdale, OR 97112
503-392-3533

| **A historic country home near the coast** |

Innkeepers: Richard and Judy Shinton. **Accommodations:** 4 rooms. **Rates:** Summer, $70–$85; winter, $60–$75. **Included:** Full breakfast. **Minimum stay:** None. **Payment:** MasterCard, Visa. **Children:** Not appropriate. **Pets:** Not allowed. **Smoking:** Outdoors only. **Open:** Year-round.

➤ **It's a short distance to Pacific City, home of the flat-bottom dory, where you can go crabbing, fish in the surf, or take a deep-sea fishing charter.**

The Hudson family came west from Tennessee in the late 19th century, settling in the Cloverdale area, about 25 miles south of Tillamook, near the Oregon coast. Their dairy prospered, and the Hudsons became prominent members of the community. In 1906 they built a large family home where they lived for many years until one son, Clyde, was the only one left. A photographer, Clyde lived to be 98.

Set on 4 acres among pasturelands and forested hills 3 miles east of Pacific City, the home is now a historic landmark. Rhododendrons and purple azaleas color the landscaped lawns behind a curving white fence, and a verandah provides space to admire them and the carved wooden fisherman who guards the gate. Indoors, a crystal chandelier in the dining room and stained glass frames around the windows add to the period quality.

The Shintons have named the guest rooms after their grandmothers and furnished them with heirlooms. Mary Esther, Matilda, Pearl, and Laura are memorable presences in this home. Their jewelry and combs are displayed, and their photographs hang on the walls. Mary Esther's oak piano stands in the ground-floor suite with her name. The rest of the rooms are upstairs. Pearl Room has a brass bed and a bath across the hall. Robes are provided.

For breakfast, the Shintons serve the special granola, "Wholly Cow," developed by the previous owners, along with a main dish such as eggs Florentine, mushroom quiche, crab strata, or ginger waffles with lemon sauce. They provide tea and cookies in the afternoons. For other meals, try the Riverhouse in Pacific City, known for its seafood and generous sandwiches, or Fisher's.

Sandlake Country Inn

8505 Galloway Road
Cloverdale, OR 97112
503-965-6745
Fax: 503-965-7425

> **A historic farmhouse turned luxury B&B**

Innkeepers: Femke and David Durham. **Accommodations:** 2 rooms, 1 suite, 1 cottage. **Rates:** $90–$135 double, singles $5 less, $20 additional person. **Included:** Full breakfast. **Minimum stay:** 2 nights on weekends. **Payment:** Major credit cards. **Children:** Not appropriate. **Pets:** Not allowed. **Smoking:** Outdoors only. **Open:** Year-round.

➤ **There's easy access to Three Capes Scenic Loop, the beach, and activities such as clamming and crabbing, bird-watching, salmon fishing, riding, and hiking.**

Deep in the rural, wooded countryside south of Tillamook, about a mile from the ocean, the Durhams welcome guests to their century-old home. Built of heavy bridge timbers salvaged from a shipwreck off Cape Lookout, the beautifully restored farmhouse is on the Oregon Historic Registry. (The address is Cloverdale, but the location is Sandlake.)

In the living room, a braided rug lies before the fireplace. The floors are of warm, mellow fir. Comfortable chairs face windows that overlook 2 acres of garden and forest. Rhododendrons bloom in profusion, and a 65-year-old hedge of red and pink roses borders the lawn.

The motif here is roses. In the room called Rose Garden — an airy, first-floor room — paper roses climb a trellis, and the scent of roses wafts in from the garden. A light net canopy surrounds the king-size bed. The Starlight Suite, occupying the entire upper floor, has a queen-size bed with partial canopy and a see-through fireplace between the bedroom and sitting room. There's a TV room with a VCR; vintage movies are available. In the bathroom sits the home's original clawfoot tub, now with a shower.

The newest room is Timbers, which has a private entrance, a green marble fireplace, and a Jacuzzi for two. It has a woodsy atmosphere, with exposed bridge timbers and Ralph Lauren paisley and plaid fabrics.

The most private and spacious quarters are in the cottage by the brook. Here the atmosphere is designed for a romantic twosome. There's a gas fireplace, *Casablanca* lies next to the VCR, and popcorn is available for the microwave. Heart-shaped cookies lie on the pillow, and around the corner is a Jacuzzi for two. In the morning, breakfast is brought to your door in a basket.

In the main house, breakfast is brought to your room on a tray — fruit, a hot entrée, and pastries. When you return from a day of exploring, you might enjoy a "togetherness basket." For an additional charge, Femke will prepare a picnic basket that includes smoked salmon, a warm baguette, clam chowder, sparkling cider, salad, and chocolate truffles.

Corvallis

The Hanson Country Inn

795 Southwest Hanson Street
Corvallis, OR 97333
541-752-2919

> **A country estate close to
> Oregon State University**

Innkeeper: Pat Covey. **Accommodations:** 4 rooms and cottage. **Rates:** $65–$75 single or double, $10 additional person, cottage $125. **Included:** Full breakfast. **Minimum stay:** None. **Payment:** Major credit cards. **Children:** Welcome by arrangement. **Pets:** Not allowed. **Smoking:** Not allowed. **Open:** Year-round.

➤   **The Corvallis Fall Festival is a major event. Entertainment and a wine garden are popular, but the main feature is a large display of arts and crafts.**

The drive that ascends the hill to Pat Covey's B&B passes an apple and cherry orchard and fields where sheep graze. Chickens bustle to greet you, and you feel that you're deep in the countryside. Yet you're only a short walk from Oregon's second-largest university, Oregon State, and a 5-minute drive from downtown. The inn stands in isolated splendor on the hill, surrounded by 5 acres of tree-dotted fields. It was built as a private home in 1928 by Jess Hanson, who developed champion leghorns and was highly successful at breeding hens that lay eggs in record numbers. His favorite prize-winning hen still stands, stuffed, in the foyer of the inn.

After Hanson's death, the house stood empty for 13 years. With impeccable taste and style, Pat Covey has brought it to life again, filling the rooms with antiques, fine English linen, fresh flowers, and music.

One upstairs guest room is a suite in mauve, gray, and green, with a four-poster bed covered by a white duvet. There's a cozy sitting room and a spacious bath with green tiles and a pedestal sink that evoke the period when the house was built.

Room 4 has a queen-size four-poster, a small TV and clock radio, and a white wicker rocker tucked into an alcove. The spacious corner room boasts two closets and a standing wardrobe and seven windows that overlook an oak grove. There are no desks in the rooms, but Pat has provided a quiet writing area at the end of the hall.

Downstairs in the living room, reflected firelight dances on prism chandeliers set off by peach walls and dark woodwork. A baby grand piano stands in one corner, and beyond it is a book-lined nook with a good reading chair. Guests are free to browse through the books, puzzles, and games provided in this little library.

A wall of windows in the sun room faces the garden, where weddings are often held. It's an ideal location, with a stretch of lawn, rose beds, and brick paths leading to a pergola. Tucked under the trees behind the house is a two-bedroom cottage with a kitchen and sun porch.

Pat serves breakfast at round tables in the dining room. You might be offered juice, yogurt and fruit, and French toast with raspberry sauce. It's all to be savored while you admire the view of the big firs in front, the gnarled trees in the orchard, and the mist-shrouded hills beyond. In the afternoons, Pat provides cookies with tea and coffee.

Crater Lake

Crater Lake Lodge

Winter address:
Crater Lake Company
Crater Lake National Park
1211 Avenue C
White City, OR 97503
541-830-8700
Fax: 541-830-8514
Summer address:
400 Rim Village Drive
P.O. Box 128
Crater Lake, OR 97604
541-594-2255
Fax: 541-594-2622

> **A handsome lodge in Crater Lake National Park**

Manager: George Winsley. **Accommodations:** 71 rooms. **Rates:** $99–$188, up to 4 people; $15 additional person. **Minimum stay:** None. **Payment:** MasterCard, Visa. **Children:** Under age 13, free with a parent. **Pets:** Not allowed. **Smoking:** Not allowed. **Open:** Mid-May to mid-October.

➤ **Narrated boat tours allow close-up views of the lake.**

The most beautiful lake in the world lies 1,000 feet below the rim of the crater where this national park lodge stands. Crater Lake, which fills the crater of a volcano that erupted 6,800 years ago, has an indigo hue that is breathtaking. It's surrounded by steep rock walls, revealing the geological history of the volcano, Mount Mazama.

The original lodge was built in 1915; when it was redone, at a cost of $15 million, only the stone and timber exterior remained. The rest of the lodge, which opened in 1995, was new. The designers kept the classic interior however. Mission-style oak furniture, stone fireplaces (now with gas flames rather than wood-burning), and unpeeled ponderosa pine logs are in the Great Hall. In some guest rooms, dainty flowered wallpaper contrasts oddly with the rest of the lodge's atmosphere, but otherwise the woodsy, old-fashioned atmosphere has been carefully maintained. The sturdy furnishings are of natural wood, and some baths contain clawfoot tubs. The rooms have queen-size beds and desks, but no phones. Pay phones are next to the lobby. The dining room is open only to guests; you can make reservations on the day of your arrival either in person or over the phone.

The designers of the lodge wisely kept nature as the focus, and so the main feature is the stunning view from lakeside rooms, the dining room, and the terrace. As you might expect, rooms on the lake side book months in advance.

There's a gift shop and café at nearby Rim Village. A paved pathway on the edge of the cliff above the lake leads to overlooks that allow for fine views of the water below. There are numerous hiking trails; however, hiking and climbing are not allowed inside the caldera rim except on Cleetwood Trail, which is the route to a dock and boat tours. Rim Drive encircles the lake but is closed by snow from mid-October to early July.

Dayton

Wine Country Farm

6855 Breyman Orchards Road
Dayton, OR 97114
503-864-3446
800-261-3446

> **A hilltop estate in the heart of the wine country**

Innkeeper: Joan Davenport. **Accommodations:** 6 rooms, 1 suite. **Rates:** $75–$115. **Included:** Full breakfast. **Minimum stay:** None. **Payment:** MasterCard, Visa. **Children:** Age 12 and older, welcome. **Pets:** Not allowed. **Smoking:** Not allowed. **Open:** Year-round.

➤ **Sokol Blosser Winery is open daily for tasting. With a view of Mount Hood, it's a pleasant setting for a picnic.**

The views don't get much better than this. From the deck of the white stucco farmhouse you can see over vineyards planted in Chardonnay, Muller Thurgau, Riesling, and Pinot Noir grapes to the valley below and, in the distance, the capital city of Salem. Mount Hood and the central Cascades rise sharply on the horizon. In addition, Wine Country Farm offers several unusual features. Each of the upstairs guest rooms is a corner room. The smallest room has a double bed and a window seat with a view of the valley on the south; it's next to a larger room with a king-size bed. One spacious room has a queen-size white iron bed, a fireplace, a large closet, and a bentwood rocker; the fourth room holds easy chairs and a king-size bed. The main floor rooms have fireplaces, and one has a spectacular valley view.

A suite, in a separate building, is above the wine-tasting room. A good choice for a family or anyone wanting extra privacy, it has a sitting area with a sofa bed and a bedroom with a queen-size bed. Guests here can use the kitchen downstairs in the tasting room. The wine is from the estate's own grapes.

Guests can make themselves at home in the family room, which has books and videos, and by the fireplace in the more formal living room. Breakfast is served outdoors, in the dining room, or, if it's a special occasion, in your own room. This innkeeper aims to please, offering wine and snacks in the afternoon and equipment for croquet, horseshoes, and volleyball. For a romantic adventure, ask about the horse and cart rides. For an extra charge, Joan will provide a picnic with wine and take you on a half-hour or hour jaunt to a picturesque spot in an oak grove or the vineyards. She'll pick you up later. Or you can ride in the cart, as peacocks and chickens scurry, to nearby Sokol Blosser Vineyards for wine tasting.

With its 120-year-old hand-pegged barn, flower gardens, animals, and sweeping view, this inn is exceptional, a fine base for visiting the northern Willamette Valley wineries.

Depoe Bay

Channel House

P.O. Box 56
35 Ellingson Street
Depoe Bay, OR 97341
541-765-2140
800-447-2140
Fax: 541-765-2191

A romantic inn on an oceanside cliff

Proprietor: Vicki L. Mix. **Accommodations:** 12 rooms. **Rates:** $75–$225 single or double, $30 additional person. **Included:** Expanded Continental breakfast. **Minimum stay:** None. **Payment:** Major credit cards. **Children:** Not appropriate. **Pets:** Not allowed. **Smoking:** Not allowed. **Open:** Year-round.

➤ **In September, you can enjoy the annual Indian salmon bake. In May there's the Blessing of the Fleet, when flowers and wreaths are scattered on the water.**

Channel House stands close to the southern edge of a narrow channel, the entrance to the world's smallest harbor (6 acres), Depoe Bay. Summer or winter, there's no more exhilarating a view than pounding, spraying waves against basaltic rock, of the tricky maneuverings of the commercial and pleasure boats in the passage, and of the Pacific Ocean stretching to a gold and red horizon at sunset.

Several of the rooms at the Channel House — especially the new ones, which are ideal honeymoon suites — have been designed to take full advantage of the vistas. Suite Salt Air, facing the ocean, has a king-size bed, a slate-backed woodstove, a tape deck, and a refrigerator and stove in one compact unit. It also boasts a whirlpool on its own protected deck.

Ten rooms have oceanfront views; ten have outdoor whirlpools. Two have full kitchens. The smallest room is Crow's Nest, a snug spot with scarcely enough space for a double bed, but it has a romantic appeal of its own. Binoculars hang on the wall, as they do in all the rooms with a view.

A nautical motif prevails at Channel House, with pictures of sailing ships and seascapes. Breakfast is served at tables for two in a room overlooking the ocean. For other meals, Tidal Raves is highly recommended.

Diamond

McCoy Creek Inn

HC 72 Box 11
Diamond, OR 97722
541-493-2131

An old-fashioned cattle ranch with warm hospitality

Innkeepers: Shirley Thompson, Gretchen Nichols, David Thompson. **Accommodations:** 4 rooms and a bunkhouse. **Rates:** $75. **Minimum stay:** None. **Included:** Full breakfast. **Payment:** MasterCard, Visa. **Children:** Welcome. **Pets:** Not allowed. **Smoking:** Not allowed. **Open:** April to November.

➤ **Nearby are the lava beds of Diamond Craters; the Kiger Mustang lookout, where you might spot wild horses; and imposing Steens Mountain.**

You have to drive 5 miles on a bumpy, unpaved road to get to McCoy Creek Inn, and that's after a 7-hour journey from Portland. But it's well worth the effort. This bed-and-breakfast home in Oregon's southeastern corner is an excellent retreat where you can enjoy natural beauty in quiet surroundings and share a bit of Oregon history.

The inn, on the banks of McCoy Creek, is a working cattle ranch that has been in the same family for five generations. The descendants of Charles Frazier, who built the ranch about 1914, still live here and now invite guests to their remodeled home. Gleaming fir floors and woodwork, a stone fireplace, antique furniture, and an enclosed front porch overlooking the lawns and creek make this an appealing spot that retains its old-fashioned atmosphere.

Shirley Thompson and her son and daughter share the innkeeping responsibilities. They have a wheelchair-accessible room on the ground floor and two rooms upstairs, each furnished with antiques and decorated with tasteful restraint. One has a scrolled bedstead in white iron, a daybed, a walk-in closet, and a balcony. The other, in green and burgundy, contains a handsome four-poster and has a big deck that overlooks the creek, lawns, and the high, rocky ridge. At night you can watch the stars and listen to the frogs.

The bunkhouse, out by the apple orchard, is nice for a family; it has a double bed, a daybed with a trundle, and a separate bedroom with two twin beds. The house is carpeted and has white walls, ruffled Priscilla curtains, and a modern blue and white bath — quite a change from its life as a shelter for ranch hands.

The easygoing, friendly innkeepers serve a bountiful breakfast, and by reservation, a multicourse dinner as good as you'll find in many top restaurants. A typical meal includes hot fresh bread, a tureen of mushroom soup, a green salad with strawberries and honey-poppyseed dressing, banana-kiwi sorbet, and glazed Cornish game hen stuffed with wild rice. Dessert might be homemade berry pie with whipped cream.

Children love to wade in the creek and watch the ducks, lambs, chickens, and turkeys. Peacocks stroll through the grounds under the watchful eye of Rascal, the lovable dog. Hundreds of birds fly among the trees and reeds, as McCoy is close to Malheur National Wildlife Refuge. Yellow-headed blackbirds, heron, ibis, cranes, magpies, and many others fill the air with flashes of color and song. Malheur Lake is a major stop for migratory birds.

Eugene

The Campbell House

252 Pearl Street
Eugene, OR 97401
541-343-1119
800-264-2519
Fax: 541-343-2258

> **A small, European-style inn
> in a historic district**

Proprietors: Myra and Roger Plant. **Accommodations:** 12 rooms. **Rates:** $75–$275 single or double, $15 additional person, corporate rates available. **Minimum stay:** 2 nights on some weekends. **Included:** Full breakfast. **Payment:** Major credit cards. **Children:** Welcome. **Pets:** Not allowed. **Smoking:** Outdoors only. **Open:** Year-round.

➤ **Café Zenon, one of Eugene's better restaurants, offers ethnic cuisines in an atmosphere of controlled hubbub. In good weather, you can eat outside.**

This attractive and sophisticated inn was built in 1892 for Idaho Campbell, the daughter of a pioneer, gold miner, and timber owner.

At that time Eugene had 3,000 people, a lumber mill, and a new university. Now the population is more than 115,000, and the University of Oregon is respected nationally.

Campbell House, completely renovated in 1993, stands on a landscaped acre on the east side of Skinner's Butte. It's within walking distance of downtown restaurants, the Hult Center, and the 5th Street Public Market. Behind green double doors is a small lobby (Oregon products such as hazelnuts and boysenberry syrup are sold at the desk) and a living room with couches grouped by the fireplace. The dining room has tables set for four; breakfast is served here and in the game room. The game room is a welcome spot on a rainy day, with a piano and dozens of books, games, and videos.

Expense has not been spared in restoring and furnishing Campbell House. Each room is tasteful with a touch of elegance, with a hidden TV and VCR, an honor bar, individual heat controls, and a phone. Some rooms have gas fireplaces, four-poster beds, and semi-private entrances. The first-floor rooms and meeting rooms provide wheelchair access. A few rooms are quite small, and space for hanging clothes is minimal, but the overall effect is delightful. This is an unusually fine inn with a pleasant and restful atmosphere.

Florence

Johnson House

P.O. Box 1892
216 Maple Street
Florence, OR 97439
541-997-8000
800-768-9488

A Victorian B&B in a central coast town

Innkeepers: Jayne and Ron Fraese. **Accommodations:** 5 rooms (2 with private bath) and cottage. **Rates:** $85–$115 single, $95–$125 double. **Included:** Full breakfast. **Minimum stay:** None. **Payment:** MasterCard, Visa. **Children:** Welcome by arrangement. **Pets:** Not allowed. **Smoking:** Outdoors only. **Open:** Year-round.

➤ **Climb to the top of the 150-foot heap of sand above Cleawox Lake in Honeyman State Park for a wide view of the dunes and the distant ocean.**

If your grandmother lived with worn but treasured heirlooms and always welcomed you with a cup of tea and a room prepared, you might be in the Johnson House. You would sleep under a puffy down comforter between cotton sheets, Grandma's lacy fan would be displayed in a gilded frame, and her ivory hand mirror placed just so on the dressing table. She'd have antimacassars on the chairs (to prevent stains from macassar, a men's hair oil).

It's all here, and you are definitely at home — albeit a home from a bygone day — when you stay in Milo and Cora Johnson's old place. They lived here for 60 years after Dr. Kennedy used it as his home and clinic. The doctor built the two-story white frame house in 1892, long before Florence was a major tourist destination midway down the Oregon coast.

Now the house is on the National Register of Historic Places and belongs to the Fraeses, an active, enthusiastic couple with many interests. Johnson House stands on the corner of a residential street, within walking distance from Florence's Old Town on the riverfront. The green porch with white wicker chairs and red geraniums is an inviting spot to sit and watch nothing happen, which is mostly the case in this quiet town.

Ron and Jayne maintain an authentic turn-of-the-century atmosphere in Johnson House without being slaves to it. They've furnished it with antiques, including their collection of Persian and Chinese carpets, but you'll also find modern baths, shelves of books old and new, and original prints from many periods, collected by the Fraeses when they were in the business in San Francisco.

Behind the house, on the other side of a garden of roses and lavender, is Rose Cottage. This romantic, private retreat has a queen-size bed and in the corner, behind a screen, is a clawfoot tub. Outside, roses cover a trellis by the front porch. Breakfast is delivered on a tray.

In the main house, guests gather in the dining room for breakfast, which features orange juice and fruit, perhaps Jayne's special soufflé or crêpes, and muffins.

Ron and Jayne will suggest ideas for exploring the area, such as walking on the dunes — mountains of sand that undulate down the coast for more than 40 miles, punctuated occasionally by forest islands and freshwater pools. You can go fishing in the ocean, the Siuslaw River, or one of 17 nearby lakes. Browse in Old Town on

Bay Street, where several buildings have been restored and a lively district of shops and restaurants thrives.

Moonset

c/o Johnson House
P. O. Box 1892
Florence, OR 97439
541-997-8000

A romantic cottage on the coast

Proprietors: Jayne and Ron Fraese. **Accommodations:** 1 cottage. **Rates:** $195 double. **Minimum stay:** 2 nights. **Payment:** MasterCard, Visa. **Children:** Not appropriate. **Pets:** Not allowed. **Smoking:** Allowed. **Open:** Year-round.

➤ **You may wish to browse in the shops in Old Town on the riverfront in Florence, or fish for salmon, blueback, and steelhead on the Siuslaw River.**

No signs will direct you to this unique cottage on the south-central Oregon coast, north of Florence. It stands high on an open, sloping meadow that faces west toward a panoramic sea vista. The octagonal, weathered cedar house is on an acre of meadow a quarter mile above Highway 101, and up a gravel drive lined with pink rhododendrons. At the top of the spiral stairs that lead to the living quarters are six large windows with sweeping views of the seascape. You can see Lily Lake, a meadow where elk congregate, and the low dunes and wetlands as they meet the shore.

The cottage's clear cedar ceiling reaches to a beveled point, centered by a sunflower burst design; from it a white light fixture hangs over a Herman Miller table and rattan chairs. An enameled cast-iron wood stove, an antique Persian rug, and chairs with soft down cushions complete the furnishings. A few steps down, you're in the kitchen; up the ladder, you're in the loft, where you can snuggle against lamb's wool and down on the king-size bed.

The house is full of books, and if you're honeymooning, you will find wine and flowers when you arrive. There's a VCR and movies, and a deck with a spa and sauna.

Moonset is less than a mile from Baker Beach and close to C&M Stables, where you can rent horses for canters along the shore. And there are miles of wind-sculpted sand dunes, Sea Lion Caves, and picturesque Heceta Head lighthouse. But if you choose to remain secluded in your private hideaway, it's understandable. There are few more appealing places in which to settle in and relax.

Ocean Haven

94770 Highway 101
Florence, OR 97439
541-547-3583
Fax: 541-547-3583

> **A cottage and family rooms by the beach**

Owner: Christie DeMoll. **Accommodations:** 7 rooms, 1 cottage (5 with private bath). **Rates:** $35–$85 double, $10 additional person. **Minimum stay:** None. **Payment:** MasterCard, Visa. **Children:** Welcome. **Pets:** Not allowed. **Smoking:** Outdoors only. **Open:** Year-round.

➤ **Both Yachats and Florence have good restaurants — try the Windward Inn, Lovejoy's, or La Serre. If you plan to cook, bring your own groceries or use the small store 1½ miles from Ocean Haven.**

Ocean Haven, formerly the popular Gull Haven Lodge, offers a rare find: a honeymooners' delight that is affordable. For $50 a night, you get Shag's Nest, a compact cottage on a grassy plateau above the beach on the south-central Oregon coast. It has three walls of double-glazed windows that look over the sea to the horizon, a brick fireplace, queen-size bed, a rustic deck, and geraniums on the windowsill. There's a refrigerator and a microwave oven.

A path leads down the hill to the beach, a prime area for beach-combing and agate-hunting, and a likely spot to find the prized Japanese fishing floats that occasionally wash ashore. Drawbacks are that Shag's Nest is quite small and must share a bathroom with two lodge rooms. But it's a sweet place for a happy twosome.

The other units at Ocean Haven are closer to the highway in a two-story apartment building. They're clean, comfortable, and have recently been modernized, with the old character retained. Most have equipped kitchens. Least expensive are Lavender Room and Garden Room. They share a bath and are small but cheerful and cozy, and they have ocean and garden views.

The gay-friendly lodge is 18 miles north of Florence and 8 miles south of Yachats, two prime tourist destinations. Sea Lion Caves, where you can get a close look at wild Steller sea lions, is 7 miles away, and you are 5 miles from Cape Perpetua and Devil's Churn, two landmarks on this dramatic and rugged coast.

Frenchglen

Frenchglen Hotel

Frenchglen, OR 97736
541-493-2825

**A historic hotel in
southeastern Oregon**

Innkeeper: John Ross. **Accommodations:** 8 rooms (2 shared baths). **Rates:**
$48–$50 per room. **Minimum stay:** None. **Payment:** MasterCard, Visa. **Children:**
Welcome. **Pets:** Not allowed. **Smoking:** Allowed on porch. **Open:** Mid-March
to mid-November.

➤ **Steens Mountain is a huge basalt block, formed by a major earth fault,
that stands 9,600 feet high — southeastern Oregon's most imposing landmark.**

Tucked in the upper corner of Oregon's southeastern pocket, on the
edge of the Malheur National Wildlife Refuge, this historic little
white frame hotel offers charms to soothe frazzled nerves.

Late spring is a good time to visit, for summer's deep heat and
mosquitoes are not yet in evidence. Nesting activity is intense as
breeding birds descend on the refuge, the high desert air is clean,
and the night skies are filled with stars the city dweller never sees.
The silence is broken only by frog croaks, birdsong, and cottonwoods hissing in the breeze.

To get there, pack your binoculars, bird book, and camera, and
look carefully at a road map. Frenchglen is the small smudge with
lots of empty space around it on Highway 205, about 350 miles
from Portland.

On your way to the hotel, stop at Malheur Refuge headquarters
for information on bird-watching spots and a self-guided auto tour
map that's invaluable for observing this unique valley. Some 260
species of migrating birds have been sighted on the refuge; among
them are sandhill cranes, cinnamon teal ducks, snowy egrets, and
horned owls. You can see human evidence, too, in the petroglyphs
and campgrounds of ancient cultures and in the cabins and settlers'
graves that dot the valley.

You'll also see the influence of Pete French, a 19th-century cattle
baron. At the P-Ranch, once his headquarters, his round barn still
stands among willows, sagebrush, and juniper. The village of
Frenchglen bears his name and that of his financial backer and fa-

ther-in-law, Hugh Glenn (though French's wife never saw the 132,000-acre empire; she refused to leave San Francisco).

Only eight people live in Frenchglen. One runs the state-owned hotel, which dates from 1916. It's a casual, homey place, with an old-fashioned screened-in porch, where you can sit and watch thunderstorms sweep over Steens Mountain and Gun-notch Pass.

The guest rooms are small but adequate; most have one double bed, and one has a double and a twin. Colorful patchwork quilts and John Ross's handmade pine furniture add a country flavor, as do white curtains fluttering at windows that open to desert air, the sounds of birds, and occasional plaintive harmonica notes from the porch below. Room 2 has the most space and will hold three people. The hotel has no cribs or rollaway beds. The innkeeper serves morning and evening meals family-style at two hand-carved dining tables. The hearty, low-cost dinners are popular with nearby ranch hands, so you will need reservations.

Gleneden Beach

Salishan Lodge

Gleneden Beach, OR 97388
541-764-2371
800-452-2300
Fax: 541-764-3510

A luxury resort that blends with its setting

Manager: John Lombardo. **Accommodations:** 205 rooms. **Rates:** $189–$269 double, $15 additional person; packages available. **Minimum stay:** None. **Payment:** Major credit cards. **Children:** Under age 12, free. **Pets:** Allowed. **Smoking:** Nonsmoking rooms available. **Open:** Year-round.

➤ **On trails through hillsides and by Siletz Bay, you'll see herons and seagulls, second-growth hemlock and spruce, and a 1,200-acre bay formed after the last ice age.**

An award-winning resort, Salishan is unique on the Oregon coast. It epitomizes the best of northwestern design, for its weathered gray buildings blend so unobtrusively with the forested surroundings, they can scarcely be glimpsed from the road. The resort occupies 700 acres above Siletz Bay, a curving tideland on the central coast 20 miles north of Newport.

Salishan was built in 1965 as a deliberate effort by John and Betty Gray of Portland to create a fine resort that would blend with the environment. Native plants, such as Oregon grape, ferns, salal, and oxalis were used in the landscaping. Covered walkways in the Japanese manner provide shelter from Northwest rains so you can walk under cover to the central lodge from the guest rooms.

Understated luxury describes Salishan, which has plush carpeting, excellent service, and attention to detail. The work of regional artists is prominently displayed. A wooden sculpture of diving porpoises stands near the stone fireplace in the lobby, a welcoming entry with soft couches, a blazing fire, and, around the corner, a library with a variety of newspapers and an informal sherry service. A recent multi-million-dollar renovation has placed even more emphasis on Oregon art and history.

The restaurant at Salishan has received numerous awards for food and wine. Etched glass panels form partitions in the multi-tiered room, and large windows frame stunning views of the bay and sea. The candle-lit atmosphere is calm, posh, and softly romantic, with white and rose napery and knowledgeable waiters in black tie. Specialties include roast rack of lamb, veal medallions, and mixed grill Oregon — medallions of chicken breast, veal, lamb, and liver. Regional ingredients are emphasized. Oregon shrimp, Columbia River caviar, Dungeness crab, rainbow trout, and wild mushrooms are on the menu, which changes with the season. The wine cellar, with 10,000 bottles, is famous on the West Coast. You can spend the better part of an evening just perusing the wine list — all 66 pages. You are welcome to tour the wine cellar as well.

Other restaurants are the Sun Room, a coffee shop overlooking the golf course, and the Cedar Tree, where Sunday champagne brunch and Friday seafood buffet are served.

The guest rooms all have balconies, fireplaces (wood is supplied), queen- or king-size beds, TV, phones with voice mail and dual ports, and floor-to-ceiling windows that overlook the sea or golf course. Nature's colors predominate in the subdued tones of green, tan, and soft white. The rooms in the North Chieftain wing overlook the bay, while those in South Chieftain view the golf course. These are semi-suites in which sitting rooms are separated from sleeping areas by louvered dividers. The Siletz Bay rooms have ocean views.

A large indoor pool, surrounded with greenery, has glass walls and a soaring ceiling. The resort has fitness equipment and indoor and outdoor tennis courts. The 18-hole golf course is an integral part of the overall design and defines the setting. In the Scottish tradition, trees and coastal vegetation around playing areas have been left in their natural state.

Gold Beach

Jot's Resort

P.O. Box J
Gold Beach, OR 97444
541-247-6676
800-367-5687 (reservations only)
Fax: 541-247-6716

A comfortable resort at the mouth of the Rogue

Manager: Sam Waller. **Accommodations:** 140 rooms. **Rates:** $85–$295 per room ($10 extra for rollaway in standard room), $10 less in May and October, $20 less November to April. **Minimum stay:** None. **Payment:** Major credit cards. **Children:** Welcome. **Pets:** Allowed by arrangement. **Smoking:** Nonsmoking units available. **Open:** Year-round.

➤ **Salmon and steelhead are the Rogue's prize catches. Coho and chinook provide the challenge from spring through fall, steelhead in the winter.**

Fishing the Rogue River is many a vacationer's dream, and Jot's Resort, on the north bank where the river meets the sea, will help make that dream a reality.

Guides are available for upriver fishing at $100 for a half-day and $125 for a full day, with tackle and bait included. Jot's has a sports shop that rents all manner of equipment, including 18-foot river sleds with or without motors. Fishing advice and stories are free.

The fabled Rogue isn't the only place to fish at Gold Beach, which is on the southern coast about 30 miles from the California border. Many smaller streams offer variety, and the Pacific Ocean is just outside the door. Jot's offers deep-sea charters for $55 per person, including bait and tackle. The resort rents crab rings, clam shovels, and boating equipment and has a marina with dock space available.

You can also swim in the outdoor and indoor pools at Jot's, play golf at the Cedar Bend course, ride horseback on the beach, beachcomb for driftwood, agates, and jade, or take a jet boat ride up the Rogue. At mealtimes, cross the highway to Jot's Rod 'n Reel, the most convenient restaurant, or try Captain's Table in Gold Beach, noted for its fresh seafood.

The resort's guest rooms, recently renovated, have the modern simplicity expected of a motel of this size and quality. Many units have fully equipped kitchens, queen-size beds, telephones, and cable TV. Sliding glass doors open to adjoining concrete balconies, which face the wide mouth of the river, the bridge to Gold Beach, and the mist-shrouded hills in the distance. Listen for the mournful call of a buoy and cries of seagulls; watch for sea lions and pelicans that regularly visit the waterfront.

On U.S. 101, a mile north of Gold Beach, the resort can be reached by air, sea, or highway. If you come by bus or plane, someone from the resort will pick you up. (Gold Beach City Airport has 3,200 feet of paved and lighted runway.) If you plan to arrive by sail or powerboat, contact the U.S. Coast Guard, Rogue River Station, for weather information.

Paradise Bar Lodge

P.O. Box 548
Gold Beach, OR 97444
541-247-6022
541-247-6504

| **A wilderness retreat on the Rogue River** |

Proprietors: Court and Dawn Boice. **Accommodations:** 13 rooms and cottages. **Rates:** Summer, with jet boat transportation, $198 per person; winter, $138 per person. **Included:** Jet boat ride, breakfast, dinner, and lunches. **Minimum stay:** None. **Payment:** MasterCard, Visa. **Children:** Ages 4–11, half-price; under 4, free. **Pets:** Not allowed. **Smoking:** Outdoors only, in designated areas. **Open:** Year-round.

➤ **From the inn you can hike part of the Rogue River Trail, visit the Boices' Rogue Museum, play volleyball or horseshoes, or watch the rafters go by.**

Paradise Bar is 57 miles up the Rogue River from Gold Beach, on the southern Oregon coast. Just beyond it lies Blossom Bar, one of the most treacherous rapids on this wild river. To a whitewater rafter paddling downriver, there are few sights more welcome than Paradise Bar Lodge perched at the edge of a bluff; it means you have crossed Blossom Bar and can tie your raft up at the pier, climb the steep steps up the cliff, and enjoy a hot drink and a rest.

From the other direction, you will probably arrive by boat from Gold Beach, for there are only three ways to reach the lodge: by foot on the Rogue River Trail, small plane, or boat. Court Boice offers several river trips. One is a 104-mile round trip in which a jet boat pilot shoots the rapids, points out the wildlife on the way, and tells the history of the Rogue as you head for Paradise Bar. When you reach the lodge, you'll stop for lunch or stay overnight. Lunch, served in the lodge's dining room or at picnic tables under the pine trees, is a buffet highlighted by orchard fruits, salads, homemade breads, and barbecued chicken. The bar is well-stocked.

Even if you're on a day trip, you'll have time to explore the grounds, which were homesteaded in 1907 and developed as a guest lodge in 1953. Overnighters have a longer wilderness experience. Typically, you'll arrive in time for lunch, spend the afternoon by the river, have a hearty country dinner, eat breakfast the next morning, and enjoy lunch before your return trip. Hikers are provided with a lunch.

Some rooms are attached to the main lodge; others are in cottages on the lodge's 80 acres. These are intended for groups and can sleep up to 14 people. Homestead Cottage, across the cow pasture–airstrip, was the original homestead and has a fireplace. Other cottages have names like Wake-Up, Solitude, Eagle's Nest, and Wooldridge (named for Glen Wooldridge, a famed early river runner).

The rooms are furnished with basic comforts. The lights go out at 10:00 P.M., since electricity, created by the lodge's own diesel-powered generator, is carefully conserved (if you use your hair dryer, you may cause a blackout). There's no telephone, though radio contact is available in case of emergency. This is a place to relax, enjoy the solitude once the day-trippers have headed back home, and experience the wilderness deep in the heart of Rogue country, home of deer and bear, osprey and eagle.

Tu Tú Tun Lodge

96550 North Bank Rogue
Gold Beach, OR 97444
541-247-6664
Fax: 541-247-0672

An inviting, top-quality lodge on the river

Innkeepers: Dirk and Laurie Van Zante. **Accommodations:** 16 rooms, 2 suites, 2 houses. **Rates:** $135–$310 double, $10 additional person; discounted rates in winter. **Minimum stay:** 2 nights, July to October. **Payment:** MasterCard, Visa. **Children:** Under age 4, free . **Pets:** Not allowed. **Smoking:** Outdoors only. **Open:** Year-round (dining room closed in winter).

➤ **After dinner you can join the group around the player piano, play pool or poker, or watch the river by starlight while you plan the next day's activities.**

This unusual resort has a lot to offer: river fishing, a heated outdoor lap pool, a 4-hole pitch-and-putt course, croquet, horseshoes, a pond where cutthroat trout are raised for later release in the river, and a dining room serving well-prepared regional foods.

All this is in the wilderness, 7 miles up the Rogue River from Gold Beach, a tourist town on the southern Oregon coast. When you come to Tu Tú Tun, you won't be going shopping or out to eat unless you take a drive back down the North Bank road. Instead, you'll be among lawns and gardens beside a rushing river. Around you are forested hills and canyons full of wildlife — beavers, otters, eagles, ospreys, and deer are seen regularly. The deer often nibble their way through the lodge's apple orchard.

Most of the guest rooms, in a separate two-story building across a walkway from the main lodge, are furnished with log or antique iron beds. Their balconies overlook the river or lawn and orchard. Fresh flowers and paintings by local artists lend charm, and the samples of fishing, logging, or mining equipment that decorate the walls are reminders of the region's economy. Some rooms have fireplaces and outdoor soaking tubs. They all have phones and queen- or king-size beds.

Two suites are upstairs in the main lodge. Like contemporary apartments, they have roomy baths and full kitchens, and their glass walls overlook the Rogue. Garden House is a separate, three-bedroom home. The resort's newest accommodation is River House, with two bedrooms, two baths, a kitchen, and a view of the river.

Three meals a day are available by reservation only, May through October. The breakfast menu often includes blueberry pancakes, eggs Francisco, and peach puff pancakes, with muffins and fruit. Lunch is a light entrée or a picnic packed earlier for those off adventuring.

Dinner is the culinary star of the day. Guests gather by the river-rock fireplace in Blossom Bar (named for one of the river's more challenging rapids) for hors d'oeuvres and conversation. Then they're seated for a 4-course grilled dinner. It might include chicken breast in champagne sauce, fresh Chinook salmon, or tenderloin roast. Guests pay $39.50 for breakfast and dinner, but in order to foster the family atmosphere, no money changes hands until checkout time.

In winter, breakfast is brought to your room and you're on your own for other meals. The innkeepers often suggest stopping enroute for dinner.

Gold Hill

Willowbrook Inn

628 Foots Creek Road
Gold Hill, OR 97525
541-582-0075
willowbr@chatlink.com

> **A restored 1905 farmhouse**

Innkeepers: JoAnn and Tom Hoeber. **Accommodations:** 2 rooms, 1 suite. **Rates:** $50–$70 double, $5 less single, $15 additional person. **Included:** Full breakfast. **Minimum stay:** None. **Payment:** MasterCard, Visa. **Children:** Age 12 and older, welcome. **Pets:** Not allowed. **Smoking:** Outdoors only. **Open:** Year-round.

➤ **At the Rogue River Rooster Crow in June, the rooster that crows the most in 30 minutes wins. There are also human contests and games, a parade, and barbecues.**

In this peaceful southern Oregon retreat, you can watch deer graze in the meadow, play badminton on the lawn, splash in the pool or the outdoor spa, and admire the fragrant herb garden where 100 species grow.

For breakfast the innkeepers serve such treats as fruit with mango yogurt, herbed eggs, apple pancakes, and blueberry corn muffins. They offer wine in the afternoons and keep a basket of menus from nearby restaurants on hand. Or you might bring a picnic to the bank of Foots Creek, which runs through the property. Most guests plan to attend the Oregon Shakespeare Festival plays in Ashland, 30 miles south, and eat dinner there.

The guest rooms have queen-size beds, garden views, and fresh flowers. They're furnished in a light, clean, country style with wicker, flowery fabrics, and sprigged wallpaper. In the sunny parlor, you can relax by the stone fireplace with a book, magazine, or game, or take a glass of lemonade out to the hammock in the willow tree and watch the roses grow over the fence.

The little town of Rogue River, which borders the famous river, is 3 miles down the road. It is headquarters for several outfitters who offer whitewater rafting trips and jet boat rides.

Grants Pass

Paradise Ranch Resort

7000 Monument Drive
Grants Pass, OR 97526
541-479-4333
Fax: 541-479-0218

A quiet country resort in southern Oregon

General Manager: Ken McRae. **Accommodations:** 15 motel rooms and 1 cottage. **Rates:** Rooms (double): $90 in summer, $70 in winter, $15 additional person. Cottage: $125 in summer, $90 in winter. **Included:** Continental breakfast. **Minimum stay:** None. **Payment:** MasterCard, Visa. **Children:** Welcome. **Pets:** Allowed but discouraged ($10). **Smoking:** Outdoors or in parlor section of restaurant. **Open:** Year-round.

➤ **For excitement, try a whitewater rafting trip on the Rogue River — guaranteed to satisfy thrill-seekers. Orange Torpedo Trips offers several guided river trips.**

A Kentucky horse ranch comes to mind as you drive past the white-fenced shady lane leading to a complex of white buildings set in a manicured landscape. You're a long way from bluegrass country though; this 310-acre resort is in southern Oregon, in the heart of the Rogue River Valley.

A fountain plays in a willow-edged pond, and almost-tame swans float on the tranquil lake, the surface broken occasionally by a leaping trout. A sweep of lawn encircles the ranch house, recreation barn, and long, low guest house. Beyond lie the swimming pool and hot tub, golf course, tennis courts, and jogging paths.

The resort, which began in 1913 as a cattle ranch, later turned into a guest ranch, with horseback riding and cattle roundups; in recent years it has become established as a resort and a popular site for weddings. There's a 3-hole golf course, visible from the glass-walled, intimate dining room.

The menu features local and seasonal foods in its chicken, lamb, veal, steak, and seafood dishes. Fresh breads and desserts are prepared daily. The wine list includes Northwest and California labels.

The comfortable guest rooms, their walls white or tastefully floral, are simply furnished with four-poster queen-size or two double beds — and no phones or TV. They are in a one-story building with breezeways leading to a verandah that overlooks the lake. The best views are on the lake side, as the others face a gravel parking lot and the big white barn where guests gather to play pool and table tennis or to visit at the bar.

The cottage can sleep four in a queen-size bed and two twins and can be rented with or without the use of a kitchen.

Halfway

Clear Creek Farm

Route 1
P.O. Box 138
Halfway, OR 97834
541-742-2238
800-742-4992

An inviting bed-and-breakfast farm in eastern Oregon

Innkeepers: Rose and Mike Curless. **Accommodations:** 7 rooms (4 have private baths in bathhouse). **Rates:** $40 single, $60 double, $30 additional person. **Included:** Full breakfast. **Minimum stay:** None. **Payment:** MasterCard, Visa. **Children:** Under age 13, $10. **Pets:** Allowed by arrangement. **Smoking:** Outdoors only. **Open:** Year-round in house, summer only in Barn and Granary.

➤ **Halfway's best restaurant is Pine Valley Lodge (open weekends only in winter). Main Street Café is good for sandwiches and espresso.**

If you like wide open spaces, you will love Clear Creek Farm, which stands on 80 acres in Oregon's far northeast corner, close to the Idaho border. Eagle Cap Wilderness and the upper Snake River and Hell's Canyon are easily accessible. The farm is about 14 miles from the river and some 30 miles from the Hell's Canyon Dam and boat launch site.

The farmhouse is a few miles from Halfway, so called because it was once the stage stop midway between the long-gone communities of Carson and Pine Town.

Lodgings here are divided between the farmhouse, the Barn, and the Granary. The rooms in the house have queen-size and twin beds. The Granary has queens and bunks. The Barn's accommodations, rustic but comfortable with a king-size and double bed and sets of bunks, are available only in the summer. Guests here use baths in an immaculate bathhouse with showers. When a group takes the entire place, they share the baths; otherwise guests are each assigned a bathroom. Laundry facilities are available.

Clear Creek Farm breakfasts provide plenty of fuel for a day spent roaming the farm, bicycling, or rafting. Sourdough biscuits, coffee cakes, fresh fruits and berries, and Dutch babies are a few of the choices. Bison sausage is a specialty. Guests are welcome to wander through the orchard and pick peaches or cherries.

Children are enchanted with the farm. There are cats, a dog, horses, a neighboring bison ranch, and ponds stocked with trout.

Hood River

Columbia Gorge Hotel

4000 West Cliff Drive
Hood River, OR 97031
541-386-5566
800-345-1921
Fax: 541-387-5414

A country inn overlooking the Columbia

General manager: Boyd Graves. **Accommodations:** 42 rooms. **Rates:** $150–$270 double, $30 additional person. **Included:** Full breakfast. **Minimum stay:** None. **Payment:** Major credit cards. **Children:** Under age 5, free. **Pets:** Allowed, if on leash while in lobby. **Smoking:** Allowed in lounge only. **Open:** Year-round.

➤ **During the Roaring Twenties, Hollywood stars and other celebrities often stayed here. Valentino especially liked it, so the lounge bears his name.**

In June, 1921, in the farming town of Hood River, 60 miles east of Portland, Simon Benson unveiled a scheme to draw tourists to the Pacific Northwest. In time a grand reception was held for the opening of the Columbia Gorge Hotel, a Spanish-style yellow stucco hotel that Benson built after spearheading the construction of a highway up the Gorge. The fact that it rained buckets that day fazed no one — the hotel was a significant landmark on the Columbia River Gorge, and everyone knew it would be successful. And so it was, for a time. With the Great Depression, the stylish inn fell on hard times, and by 1960 it had become a nursing home.

Finally, in the early 1980s, new owners took over and began restoring the hotel.

Entering the lobby, you encounter a circular tufted couch with a large vase of flowers at its center. Lace curtains hang on the glass doors leading to the Valentino Lounge, which has a marble fireplace, pink and green chairs, and tall windows overlooking of the river.

The guest rooms are furnished with a 1920s flavor, and no two are alike, though all have TVs and phones. There are some family suites with two bedrooms. The Falls Room overlooks Wah-Gwin-Gwin Falls, a 206-foot waterfall that cascades to a pool, then slides into the Columbia. In the plush Valentino Room, above the cliff and the river, there is a fireplace and a four-poster canopied bed. Personal touches include flowers in your room, a basket of toiletries, and roses alongside the mints you're given with turndown service.

The inn's jazz-age reputation has been modified a bit; now it's a homier place, like a gracious country estate offering unpretentious, friendly service. One of its major attractions is the complimentary World-famous Farm Breakfast, which includes fruits served in a pineapple boat, oatmeal, apple fritters, eggs, bacon, sausage, hashbrowns, biscuits with apple blossom honey, buttermilk pancakes — you won't need to plan lunch. Ask for a riverside table so you'll have a view.

You may wish to explore the grounds for a closer look at the falls, the bridges over the creek in the front garden, and the white lawn swing under an arbor of hanging fuchsias. The only jarring note is the roar of traffic from the freeway, a sound Valentino never heard.

Hood River Hotel

102 Oak Street
Hood River, OR 97031
541-386-1900
800-386-1859

> **A restored historic hotel in a riverside town**

Innkeeper: Pasquale Barone. **Accommodations:** 31 rooms, 9 suites. **Rates:** Rooms: $49–$89 single, $59–$99 double; suites, $89–$145. **Minimum stay:** None. **Payment:** Major credit cards. **Children:** Under 12, free with a parent. **Pets:** Allowed by arrangement. **Smoking:** Nonsmoking rooms available. **Open:** Year-round.

> ➤ **Every day you'll see brightly colored sails darting across the Columbia; gorge winds make this area one of the world's best spots for sailboarding.**

Though it's in the heart of bustling Hood River, the restored Hood River Hotel has the atmosphere of a gracious European country inn. French doors with beveled glass open to a classic lobby and adjoining bistro where visitors enjoy cappuccino or wine by the fire. A wide staircase leads to the mezzanine and guest rooms.

The inn was once the annex to the Mount Hood Hotel, an elegant 19th-century hostelry that was razed some 60 years ago. Later the brick building was closed, but in 1989 Pasquale Barone, an Italian-Canadian economist and windsurfer, bought it. While revamping the building, the enthusiastic innkeeper and his partner, Jacquie Brown, were careful to restore the hotel's historic character. Tall windows dominate the two-story lobby, the rooms have antique reproductions and paddle fans, and the original fir floors and skylights are in place. The old-fashioned brass elevator has been polished and put back to work.

A typical room contains a four-poster canopy queen-size bed, Chinese area rugs, and a cherrywood bureau. All the spacious suites have sitting rooms and kitchens. Rates depend upon the size of the room and views, which encompass the town, the refurbished railroad depot, and the Columbia and Hood rivers. Sometimes you'll hear the trains, so if you want a quiet room be sure to ask for it.

Lakecliff Estate

P.O. Box 1220
3820 Westcliff Drive
Hood River, OR 97031
541-386-7000
Fax: 541-386-1803

A historic country home with a river view

Innkeepers: Judy and Bruce Thesenga. **Accommodations:** 4 rooms (2 with private bath). **Rates:** $85–$100 single or double, $15 additional person. **Included:** Full breakfast. **Minimum stay:** None. **Payment:** Cash or check. **Children:** Welcome. **Pets:** Not allowed. **Smoking:** Not allowed. **Open:** May–September.

➤ **The inn is just west of Hood River, a town known for its orchards and for its location near some of the best windsurfing in the world.**

Perched on a basalt bluff above the Columbia River about 60 miles east of Portland, Lakecliff Estate looks like the old-fashioned summer house it was intended to be, with dark green shakes and red trim, a red roof, stone chimney, and a sun room with white wicker furniture. Built in 1908, the place was designed as a vacation home for a prominent Portland family, the Deharts. Now it's a bed-and-breakfast on the National Register of Historic Places. Flowers bloom profusely in the garden and on the deck, and the lower lawn has been leveled so guests may play croquet and other lawn games. The living room furniture is grouped around the stone fireplace (one of five in the house).

Three of the carpeted guest rooms, on the second floor, have queen-size beds; one holds twin beds that can be joined. A pine cone motif in the Garden Room, which overlooks a mass of blossoms, brings the woodland indoors. The other rooms, all tastefully furnished in varying styles, have river views and fireplaces.

In the mornings, guests get acquainted as Judy serves fresh juice, fruits of the season, and such treats as huckleberry pancakes or baked French toast with Lakecliff bacon.

Your hosts are likely to join you for coffee and conversation after the dishes are cleared. They're happy to offer suggestions for hiking on nearby Mount Hood, prime spots to watch windsurfers, or good restaurants in the area. They'll also direct you to Three Rivers Winery and the Hood River Vineyards Tasting Room, where you can sample wines.

There's a major windsurfing competition in mid-July (book lodgings early), and several companies offer windsurfing lessons. The hundreds of colorful sails tacking back and forth across the Columbia River make an irresistible subject for photography.

Jacksonville

Jacksonville Inn

175 East California Street
Jacksonville, OR 97530
541-899-1900
800-321-9344
Fax: 541-899-1373

> **A frontier hotel with
> modern comforts**

Innkeepers: Jerry and Linda Evans. **Accommodations:** 8 rooms, 3 cottages. **Rates:** Rooms: $100–$135 single, $110–$145 double, $10 additional person; cottages: $190–$235. **Included:** Full breakfast. **Minimum stay:** None. **Payment:** Major credit cards. **Children:** Welcome. **Pets:** Not allowed. **Smoking:** Allowed. **Open:** Year-round.

➤ **This is a good place to look for antiques, with many shops in the area. There are also art galleries and museums and a hands-on children's museum for all ages.**

The entire southwestern Oregon town of Jacksonville is a National Historic Landmark in recognition of the relics that remain of its pioneer past. Once it was a booming gold mining center, the county seat with a fancy courthouse, headed for bigger and better times. Beautiful homes were built, and in 1863 locally quarried sandstone went into the construction of a two-story general store.

But the boom faded. In 1883 the railroad bypassed the town in favor of Medford, and as the population dwindled, the county seat was also moved to the larger city. These blows meant that Jacksonville was left largely untouched by change and is therefore today a valuable piece of history.

The general store has become Jacksonville Inn, an important part of that history. It offers rooms with restored frontier antiques, such as brass and oak bedsteads and Boston rockers, as well as air conditioning. In the mortar of the brick walls you can see flecks of gold, and in one room there's a whimsical, unplanned touch: one brick is loose, and the curious guest who pulls it out will be cascaded with business cards and notes, left by others with the same urge. All the rooms were recently refurbished and have queen-size beds. Room 1 boasts a canopy bed and a whirlpool tub.

Reserve rooms early for mid-July to Labor Day, when the Peter Britt Music Festival draws hundreds of visitors. Or you can reserve one of the cozy cottages.

Guests eat breakfast in the inn's restaurant, which is open to the public for three meals a day. For breakfast you might have a combination of orange juice, fruit, and quiche or Belgian waffles with raspberry sauce.

The dinner menu focuses on steaks and seafood, with prime rib, veal, and chicken dishes also available; a notable chocolate mousse pie leads the dessert choices. The impressive wine list has some 1,500 domestic and imported labels.

The decor is red plush, and soft lighting casts shadows on the old brick walls. Patio dining is available. The lounge in back, which offers a bistro menu, is a pleasant stop for a nightcap.

Part of the inn holds a wine and gift shop, where you can taste wines and select merchandise of excellent quality.

Touvelle House

P.O. Box 1891
455 North Oregon Street
Jacksonville, OR 97530
541-899-8938
800-846-8422
Fax: 541-899-3992
touvelle@wave.net

A Craftsman mansion in a picturesque town.

Innkeepers: Carolee and Dennis Casey. **Accommodations:** 6 rooms **Rates:** Rooms: $85–$105 double; off-season, $75–$95. Suite: $155, up to 4 people. **In-**

cluded: Full breakfast. **Minimum stay:** None. **Payment:** Major credit cards. **Children:** Over age 12, welcome. **Pets:** Not allowed. **Smoking:** Outdoors only. **Open:** Year-round.

➤ **For fine dining, try the McCully House; for a casual, lively atmosphere go to La Fiesta, and for a good lunch, the Tea Cottage.**

A few blocks from the antiques and gift shops of Main Street, and close to the entrance to the pioneer cemetery but set apart on its own 1¹/3 acres, the Touvelle House was built in 1916 for Frank and Elizabeth Touvelle. They admired the new Craftsman style, a simpler design than the elaborate Victorian, so their house has broad, overhanging eaves, square-beamed ceilings, and a stately air.

Now it is owned by the friendly, outgoing Caseys, who are eager to make their bed-and-breakfast visitors welcome. A plate of fruit and homemade cookies is always on the table, and guests can help themselves to iced tea and raspberry lemonade. The broad verandah with white wicker chairs is a relaxing spot on a hot afternoon. Or cool off in the pool, surrounded by lilacs and honeysuckle; Touvelle House is one of the few B&Bs in the area with a pool and spa. In chilly weather, you can sit by the stone fireplace in the living room. A low-fat but filling breakfast is served in the dining room.

The Judge's Chamber is the only guest room on the main floor; decorated in moss-green and berry, it has an antique brass bed that can be converted to twins. The second- and third-floor rooms and suites have period furnishings and queen-size beds, and some have decorated fireplaces. The rooms have taste and charm, with enough special touches to create a mood yet remain uncluttered. Granny's Attic, on the third floor, is a hideaway with a playful, childhood theme; its windows overlook the tops of the oak trees in the front yard.

Touvelle House attracts a number of business guests, for it has meeting space and a den offering privacy, phones, and a fax machine (as well as TV and books). A big plus for all visitors is Carolee's kindliness. A nurse who raised nine children, she knows all about the art of hospitality.

Joseph

Bed, Bread and Trail Inn

P.O. Box 639
700 South Main
Joseph, OR 97846
541-432-9765
800-452-3781

**A comfortable B&B in a
wilderness town**

Innkeepers: Jim and Ethel Chandler. **Accommodations:** 5 rooms (3 with private bath, 2 share 1½ bath). **Rates:** $50–$60 single, $70–$80 double, $10 additional person. **Included:** Full breakfast. **Minimum stay:** None. **Payment:** MasterCard, Visa. **Children:** Age 12 and older, welcome. **Pets:** Not allowed. **Smoking:** Outdoors only. **Open:** Year-round except November.

➤ **Fishing or rafting the Minam, Grande Ronde, and Snake rivers is unforgettable. The Snake runs through North America's deepest river gorge, Hell's Canyon.**

In the Wallowa Mountains of northeastern Oregon, the "Switzerland of America," the Chandlers welcome visitors to a magnificent wilderness. In this remote region of forests and 10,000-foot peaks that tower over valleys, lakes, and rivers, you'll find beauty and recreation any time of year.

Skiing draws visitors in the winter. In the summer you can hike on wooded trails, photograph the wildflowers in alpine meadows, or boat, fish, and water-ski on deep blue Wallowa Lake. The Chandlers will refer you to experienced guides who offer rafting trips, llama treks, and horseback trips into the nearby Eagle Cap Wilderness Area, a landscape largely unchanged since Chief Joseph and the Nez Perce Indians walked its paths.

At the Wallowa County historical museum in Joseph you can learn about the early pioneers and the Nez Perce. A number of artists live nearby, and several galleries show their works. A tour of a lost wax casting foundry can be arranged.

Returning to the inn, you'll be offered a cup of coffee or tea and conversation with fellow guests in the common area on the main floor. Pleasant aromas drift in from the kitchen; Jim bakes bread nearly every day.

On the second level are five sparkling clean guest rooms, furnished country style. Two have king-size beds; twins are available. Each room contains two beds. Three boast views of the mountains, and all have window seats or soft chairs in which to relax with a book or magazine from the Chandlers' library.

Jim and Ethel are known for their generous breakfasts. Juice, fresh fruit with vanilla yogurt, and oatmeal are followed by an entrée such as German pancakes, French toast, quiche, or chile relleno casserole.

Annual events in the area include Chief Joseph Days in July, a Western Art show in April, and Mule Days and an Alpenfest in September.

Leaburg

Marjon Bed & Breakfast Inn

44975 Leaburg Dam Road
Leaburg, OR 97489
541-896-3145

A B&B in a garden by the river

Innkeeper: Margie Haas. **Accommodations:** 1 room, 1 suite. **Rates:** $95–$125 double. **Included:** Full breakfast. **Minimum stay:** None. **Payment:** No credit cards. **Children:** Not appropriate. **Pets:** Not allowed. **Smoking:** Allowed. **Open:** Year-round.

➤ **Trails, some with wheelchair access, lead to views of waterfalls along the McKenzie. Be sure to stop at Koosah Falls and Sahalie Falls.**

On the banks of the bubbling McKenzie River, 24 miles east of Eugene, Margie Haas offers elegant accommodations in an inn surrounded by flowers. Some 700 rhododendrons and 2,000 azaleas bloom in bright profusion each spring on the parklike grounds.

Inside the cedar and glass contemporary home, the hospitable innkeeper offers two romantic guest rooms. The Master Suite, furnished in white French Provincial, has a 7-by-12-foot bed and leads through wide glass doors to the patio, lawn, and river. In the spacious bath, full-length windows by a sunken tub overlook a small Oriental garden.

The Guest Room is smaller, with an Oriental motif, hand-carved teak furnishings, and a queen-size bed with a crocheted spread. Through a large picture window are views of the lawn and a gnarled 100-year-old apple tree at the entrance; in April and May, it is covered with pale pink blossoms. The bath, just across the hall, has a fishbowl shower that allows a private view of the river while bathing under the light from two crystal chandeliers.

Relax in your room or wander into the living room, where a cheerful fire may be burning in the floor-to-ceiling stone fireplace. Several of the furnishings here and in the dining room were collected during Margie's world travels.

Breakfast at Marjon is always a feast. Margie brings forth a parade of treats such as sculptured fruit, banana nut muffins, and sausage-vegetable frittata, as well as the more usual juices, jams, teas, and coffee. Your table will have special decorations befitting the time of your visit.

Lincoln City

The Hideaway Motel

810 Southwest 10th
Lincoln City, OR 97367
541-994-8874
Fax: 541-994-8874

Comfortable rooms with ocean views

Proprietor: Sharon Oldenthal. **Accommodations:** 6 rooms. **Rates:** $70–$125 double, $5 additional person; winter and midweek discounts (except holidays and spring breaks). **Minimum stay:** None. **Payment:** MasterCard, Visa. **Children:** Welcome. **Pets:** allowed ($5). **Smoking:** Nonsmoking rooms available. **Open:** Year-round.

➤ **Lincoln City is a major seaside resort area on the northern Oregon coast. A consolidation of five small towns, it sprawls for 7 miles along Highway 101.**

The Hideaway, in a central location but secluded corner, is a convenient base for exploring the area. It's on a bluff above the beach, at the end of a street west of Lincoln City's busy core, with a pond and a small park on the south. A goat trail leads from the inn to the sandy beach.

Buttercups and bright orange montbretia grow in front of the main building, which is light blue with dark blue shutters and a mansard roof. This is the largest unit, with two bedrooms, a knotty pine–paneled living room with a fireplace, a dining area by the bay window, and a kitchen with all the necessities, including a popcorn popper. Early American furniture, café curtains, an old trunk full of firewood, and shelves of books give the cottage a homey flavor. Crow's Nest, tucked under angled, low ceilings, is an attic room with a fine view, just right for a cozy twosome.

All the rooms have queen-size beds. Some have walls of knotty pine, others are painted in light pastels. Four hold fireplaces (wood is supplied), two boast private sun decks, and all have TV and VCR. Better yet, each one has a view of the broad blue Pacific, surf-washed sands, and a sky full of colorful kites. A pretty lake nearby is good for sailing, water skiing, and windsurfing; Siletz Bay, on the south, is noted for fishing and crabbing; and golfers can play at three courses. For panoramic views of the sea and coastal headlands, hike the Cascade Head Trail, 6 miles north of town.

Spyglass Inn

2510 S.W. Dune Avenue
Lincoln City, OR 97367
541-994-2785

> **Spectacular ocean views, privacy, and hospitality**

Innkeepers: Jim Murphy and Diane Disse. **Accommodations:** 3 rooms (all with private baths). **Rates:** $85–$105 (cash discount; $5 more with credit card). **Included:** Full breakfast. **Minimum stay:** None. **Payment:** MasterCard, Visa. **Children:** Over age 12, welcome. **Pets:** Not allowed. **Smoking:** Not allowed. **Open:** Year-round.

➤   **The place for fine cuisine, one of the best on the coast, is the Bay House. It has a grand view of Siletz Bay. More casual is Kyllo's.**

The Spyglass is set high on a forested hill at the south end of town, far removed from the bustle and sprawl of this resort town and a 3-minute drive from the beach. This private home offers comforts that travelers appreciate (perhaps a result of Jim Murphy's ten years in the hotel business), such as individual heat control, clock radios, robes, and good reading lamps. There is no TV; phones are available.

Beyond the black and white tile contemporary entryway is a sitting room with a red tile fireplace and eclectic art objects. Next to it is the dining area, where breakfast is served. Jim might prepare shrimp timbales, eggs in cream and butter, soufflé, or whatever you request. You can also have breakfast in your room if you like.

Each guest rooms, furnished with antiques and reproductions, has a special appeal. Ivy Room, with ivy stencils on the walls, is in white and dark green and has an antique bed. A corner room, it has a panoramic ocean view. The Blue Iris Suite features a four-poster bed with a lacy canopy, a Jacuzzi tub, and a balcony, plus an attached room with a window seat and a twin bed. Probably the best views are from Berry Room, which has berries stenciled on the wall, a white iron and brass bed, and a two-person soaking tub.

The library loft above the sitting room is ideal for settling in with a game or book in the evening or during one of the coast's frequent rainstorms. If you can tear yourself away, Jim and Diane will recommend points of interest nearby. Shopping is popular because Lincoln City has a complex of factory outlet stores and numerous antiques shops.

Manzanita

The Inn at Manzanita

P.O. Box 243
67 Laneda
Manzanita, OR 97130
503-368-6754
Fax: 503-368-5941

> Luxurious rooms in a quiet
> oceanside town

Innkeepers: Karen and David Romano. **Accommodations:** 13 rooms. **Rates:** $100–$145 single or double, midweek rates available. **Minimum stay:** 2 nights on weekends and in summer. **Payment:** MasterCard, Visa. **Children:** Not appropriate. **Pets:** Not allowed. **Smoking:** Not allowed. **Open:** Year-round.

➤ **For a bird's-eye view of the shoreline, hike to Neahkahnie Mountain's summit (1,700 feet). The trail winds through stands of cedar and fir to rocky outcroppings.**

On the northern Oregon coast, the quiet village of Manzanita is the ideal escape when you're looking for privacy, tranquil beach strolls, hidden coves, and forest walks. It is set between two state parks (Nehalem Bay and Oswald West) and shadowed by the steep slopes of Neahkahnie Mountain.

The Inn at Manzanita offers luxurious lodgings in the heart of town. The rooms have lots of glass, beamed ceilings, and pine or cedar walls. Each one has its own decor (Beachcomber, Woodsman, Whalewatcher, Starseeker), as well as a fireside spa, a wet bar with a refrigerator and coffeemaker, a TV and VCR, and a small deck. Movie rentals can be arranged.

Most of the rooms have ocean views, though some are mere glimpses through the pines and spruce. The newer units are attractive and comfortable but overlook the street. One room, the Cottage, has a kitchen.

The inn is 200 feet from a 7-mile stretch of sandy beach — perfect for strolling, beachcombing, kite-flying, castle-building, and romantic sunset walks beside the surf. It's also close to two fine restaurants: Blue Sky Café and Jarboe's.

McMinnville

Steiger Haus

360 Wilson Street
McMinnville, OR 97128
541-472-0821

A wine country inn

Innkeepers: Susan and Dale DuRette. **Accommodations:** 5 rooms. **Rates:** $70–$100 double, $15 additional person. **Included:** Full breakfast. **Minimum stay:** None. **Payment:** Major credit cards. **Children:** Over age 10, welcome. **Pets:** Not allowed in house or garden. **Smoking:** Not allowed. **Open:** Year-round.

➤ **One of the area's best restaurants is Nick's, an informal café known for superb Italian cookery. Nearby wineries offer tours and tastings.**

Steiger Haus has several qualities that make it a special bed-and-breakfast. The home has a European flavor, with its angles, decks, and terraces overlooking flower gardens and ivy-covered slopes. Nestled among gardens and trees in a residential district adjacent to a park, it's an easy walk to Linfield College and downtown shops and restaurants, and a short drive to several Willamette Valley wineries.

The owners have created a harmonious blend of old and new in the inn's furnishings. Homemade quilts cover queen-size beds, and some of the furniture is of locally carved pine. The atmosphere is reminiscent of an English country garden. On the main level is a sunny kitchen-dining area, where breakfast is served. The menu features fresh fruit and an entrée such as French toast with kiwi syrup or berry cobbler.

On the lower garden level (Zsa Zsa Gabor slept here), there's a suite and two rooms. Fireside Suite, the inn's most expensive accommodation, has a deck, a TV, and a fireplace. Upstairs, the Treetop Suite has a soaking tub and a bay window with a view into the trees. Those who prefer twin beds take the Rooftop Room. Guests on this upper level are close to a reading room filled with books and a sitting room with a TV. Susan and Dale, who've lived in McMinnville since 1970, go out of their way for their guests. They'll book restaurant reservations and help with ideas for day trips throughout northern Oregon.

Youngberg Hill Vineyard B&B

10660 Youngberg Hill Road
McMinnville, OR 97128
503-472-2727
Fax: 503-472-1313
martin@youngberghill.com

A B&B in wine country

Innkeepers: Jane and Martin Wright. **Accommodations:** 5 rooms. **Rates:** $130–$150. **Included:** Full breakfast. **Minimum stay:** 2 nights on holidays. **Payment:** Major credit cards. **Children:** Over age 10, welcome. **Pets:** Not allowed (boarding at a nearby kennel can be arranged). **Smoking:** Outdoors only. **Open:** Year-round.

➤ **A picturesque 6-mile walk leads from the farm over the hills to Yamhill Valley Vineyards, which offers tours and tastings.**

From the Wrights' hilltop home, in the heart of Yamhill County wine country, the view across the valley is beautiful. Fields of yellow mustard and purple clover contrast with the green of the vineyards in spring; beyond them are stands of dark firs and the foothills of the Cascade Range and on the far horizon the white bulk of Mount Hood. Twelve acres of the 50-acre farm are planted in Pinot Noir vines, which produce grapes for the Wrights' wine.

The house, built in 1989 and designed to take advantage of the stunning views, has a sitting room with a fireplace and a woodstove, one guest room on the ground floor, and four upstairs rooms. All are air-conditioned, furnished with antique reproductions, and have fluffy down comforters on queen- or king-size beds. There are brick fireplaces in the Garden Room and Wadenswil, which is named for a grape grown on the property.

This inn offers many extra touches such as hair dryers, an ironing board and irons, games, and alarm clocks. The 3-course breakfast, served in a light-filled dining room, includes Jane's specialty, baked goods such as ginger scones and strawberry bread. You might also have eggs Benedict or crab fondue with fruit and, when blackberries are in season, blackberry muffins.

The B&B is an ideal headquarters for exploring the Willamette Valley wineries. If you'd rather go trout fishing, the innkeepers will tell you how to get to the Nestucca River.

Medford

Under the Greenwood Tree

3045 Bellinger Lane
Medford, OR 97501
541-776-0000
grwdtre@cdsnet.net

A historic B&B home in orchard country

Innkeeper: Renate Ellam. **Accommodations:** 5 rooms. **Rates:** Summer, $125; winter, $95. **Included:** Full breakfast. **Minimum stay:** None. **Payment:** Major credit cards. **Children:** Age 13 and older, welcome. **Pets:** No small pets; horses allowed. **Smoking:** Outdoors only. **Open:** Year-round.

➤ **The buildings here date from 1861 to 1912; the earliest and most primitive is hand-hewn and hand-pegged.**

In *As You Like It*, Shakespeare mentions living "under the greenwood tree." "It means in the forest, the home of shepherds and milkmaids," Renate explains. "It was a refuge for those who wanted the gentle ways of woodland people. My inn reflects this pastoral feeling. There's a romantic quality about it." The large, square, clapboard house, surrounded by pear orchards, stands on an expanse of green lawn shaded by 300-year-old oak trees. Honeysuckle and yellow roses grow near the gazebo.

The inn is a link with southern Oregon history. County records show that the Walz familiy came to Medford by covered wagon and homesteaded on 238 acres. The Walzes ran the region's first weigh station, where farmers had their hay and grain weighed before taking it to market. Renate takes pride in maintaining the old house and 10 acres of landscaped grounds and gardens. "I like to take guests on a tour of the place, so they can see my Civil War–period farm buildings and the old weigh scale," she says. "Sharing this history is important, I think, to keeping those links with our heritage."

The guest rooms are named after four kinds of pears grown in this fertile valley. The Bartlett Room is an intimate haven of Chippendale and chintz with a sitting room furnished in white wicker. The Bosc Room has a brass and iron bedstead, white candlewick bedcovers, scalloped lace curtains, and a redwood shower.

The d'Anjou Room is elegant and indulgent, with pink roses, lace, and velvet; while the Comice Room has a four-poster canopy bed with a crewel comforter, willow twig chairs in a tiny sitting room, and a pale pink bath with brass fixtures. The Speckled Pear Room, on the main floor, has a queen-size bed and a clawfoot tub.

In the morning, you'll enjoy an abundant, three-course breakfast in the dining room at hand-carved tables. Each afternoon, Renate serves her guests an elegant tea.

Merlin

Morrison's Rogue River Lodge

8500 Galice Road
Merlin, OR 97532
541-476-3825
800-826-1963
Fax: 541-476-4953
m/rrrt@chatlink.com

A wilderness lodge on the Rogue River

Owners: B.A. and Michelle Hanten. **Accommodations:** 4 rooms in lodge, 9 cabins. **Rates:** Spring, $85 per person per day; summer, $95; fall, $130. **Included:** Breakfast and dinner in spring and summer, all meals in fall. **Minimum stay:** None. **Payment:** Major credit cards. **Children:** Welcome. **Pets:** Not allowed. **Smoking:** Allowed in some rooms. **Open:** May to mid-November.

➤ **The Hantens have owned Morrison's Rogue River Lodge since 1964 and have weathered many floods, including one when the Rogue reached a highwater mark 2 feet above the mantel.**

As you round the bend in the river where Taylor Creek meets the Rogue, 85 miles from the southern Oregon coast, Morrison's Rogue River Lodge comes into view, and that's when first-time rafters exclaim in surprise. A sweep of manicured lawn, a bright red lodge, and the glint of a swimming pool among the trees are uncommon sights in the wilderness.

Morrison's is a favorite refuge for a devoted clientele that returns year after year to fish and brag and tack pictures of steelhead catches on the dining room wall. Others, equally loyal, come to raft the river and swap scare stories and tack up pictures of their whitewater escapades. The Rogue's Gallery at Morrison's is full of photographs and memorabilia, as if it were the home of proud parents showing off the exploits of their offspring.

In the sitting room, a big stone fireplace, soft furniture, and a baby grand piano draw guests on cool evenings to play board games, read, listen to music, or chat by the crackling fire. Beyond the wide windows are picnic tables in groves of pine and redwood, two tennis courts, a putting green, and a swimming pool. Volleyball and horseshoes are more recent additions.

The main attraction is the fabled Rogue River. Guests may choose among raft trips ranging from one afternoon to four days of bouncing and floating over the Rogue's green water, catching glimpses of otter, deer, osprey, eagles, and an occasional bear.

In the fall, when the wild water lures anglers the way Hot Shot flies lure steelhead, the lodge fills with those who've waited all year for the chance to spend a few days with B.A. and his daughter Michelle. Gear and box lunches are provided on fishing excursions, and the fish you catch are frozen or smoked so that you can take them home. Or it can be cooked for breakfast.

The pine guest rooms are simple but comfortable. All the cabins — second-story duplex units on posts, in case of flooding — have air conditioning, a refrigerator, and a fireplace. Five sleep two people, and the others, four.

Dinners are served family-style to guests and to the public (for $20–$28) by reservation in the dining room or, in summer, on the two-level deck facing the river. The menu, which changes nightly, has moved from hearty, simple dishes to something more elaborate. There are always two entrées such as Navajo salmon with green chili sauce, duck with plum sauce, or grilled beef tenderloin with béarnaise sauce. You can purchase cocktails, beer, and wine.

Breakfasts feature generous helpings of bacon and eggs, pancakes, muffins, and homemade raspberry and blackberry jams.

Pine Meadow Inn

1000 Crow Road
Merlin, OR 97532
541-471-6277
800-554-0806
pmi@pinemeadowinn.com

A gracious country home in southern Oregon

Innkeepers: Nancy and Maloy Murdock. **Accommodations:** 4 rooms. **Rates:** $80–$110. **Included:** Full breakfast. **Minimum stay:** None. **Payment:** No credit cards. **Children:** Over age 7, welcome. **Pets:** Not allowed. **Smoking:** Not allowed. **Open:** Year-round.

➤ **A number of outfits offer raft and kayak trips on the Rogue River. The largest is Orange Torpedo Trips (541-479-5061), with 2-hour to 3-day trips on several rivers.**

In the dry pine country of southern Oregon, not far from the Rogue River, the Murdocks built a lovely home with the intention of opening a bed-and-breakfast. By the time they were through, they had created a haven that now offers guests a friendly welcome, privacy, and comfort in a beautiful setting. Their personal tastes are evident throughout the inn, with Maloy's photography hanging on the walls and Nancy's flowers a riot of color in the garden.

There's a pleasant living room, for relaxing over a book or the album of photos showing the inn's construction, and a dining room where breakfast is served. At a table set with gold-plated flatware, crystal, candles, and flowers, guests enjoy a healthful, fat-free meal. Homemade breads and pastries, flavored coffees, and unusual dishes such as an apple, oatmeal, and spice waffle with apricot syrup are typical of the menu, which changes regularly. Much of the fruit and produce comes from the Murdocks' large vegetable garden. From the dining room, French doors open to the lush flower and herb garden and a deck with a hot tub.

Books and magazines (and good reading lights) are in every guest room, along with several other homey touches: fresh flowers, a bowl of candies, and rose petal potpourri. If you're in the Garden Room, you'll have a view of the oak trees and koi pond. The Heather Room is the smallest and has a white iron bed. The Laurel Room has a long window seat and an antique oak bed. Willow Room, the largest, is done in cool blue and white and features a sitting area, a window seat with a view of Mount Walker, and an antique bed and dresser.

Five acres of private forest with walking paths and benches lie behind the inn. Quiet country roads allow longer walks and jogging. In the meadows that give the inn its name you'll see birds, squirrels, deer, and wildflowers. Nancy and Maloy are always available to offer ideas for sightseeing and recreation and provide restaurant suggestions (the Black Swan at Paradise Ranch Inn is a good choice), but they allow their guests plenty of privacy. Theirs is an ideal B&B to use as a base when exploring southern Oregon.

Neahkahnie

Ayers' Cottage

9350 Nehalem Rd.
Neahkahnie, OR
Mailing address:
P.O. Box 784
Manzanita, OR 97130
503-368-6782

> An enchanting cottage near the coast

Innkeepers: Sydney and Dan Ayers. **Accommodations:** 1 cottage. **Rates:** $75 first night, $55 per night thereafter. **Included:** Continental breakfast. **Minimum stay:** None. **Payment:** No credit cards. **Children:** Welcome if well supervised. **Pets:** Dogs allowed if kept in pen on property. **Smoking:** Not allowed. **Open:** Year-round.

➤ **Nearby Oswald West State Park is named for the governor who in 1912 preserved the coastal beaches for the public.**

On a sloping acre in this quiet residential community, the Ayers' have built an enchanting guest cottage several yards from their own home. Lawns and lovely gardens surround the two homes. Roses climb trellises, lavatera blooms by the driveway, and quaint birdhouses perch atop poles made of branches.

As you climb the stairs in the Tudor cottage, you hear soft music playing and scent the aroma of potpourri, and then you enter what appears to be a room from a fairy tale. Pretty teapots and flowerbud china stand on the shelves, lace curtains hang at the windows, and lace coverlets lie on the pineapple four-poster bed. In one corner, a woodstove stands on a hearth of river rock. The tiny kitchen contains a microwave oven, coffeemaker, and refrigerator. Breakfast is brought to the door in a basket.

Stenciled ivy twines around the door to the bathroom, which has a tub and shower. There is a VCR, and movies and games are tucked inside a closet. There is no ocean view, since the property is several blocks from the shore, but the windows and private deck overlook tall trees and flowers nodding over a white picket fence.

Ayers' Cottage is full of quaint charm, but guests' comfort is the top priority. Every comment in the guest book is a rave review.

In Neahkahnie, just north of Manzanita, you can walk the beach, play ball with Mary and Martha, the Ayers' dogs, hike up Neahkahnie Mountain, fly a kite, golf, and dine in excellent restaurants such as Blue Sky and Jarboe's.

Newport

Ocean House

4920 N.W. Woody Way
Newport, OR 97365
541-265-6158
541-265-7779
800-562-2632

> **A gracious B&B with a grand ocean view**

Innkeepers: Bob and Marie Garrard. **Accommodations:** 5 rooms. **Rates:** $110–$140 double, $5 less single. **Included:** Full breakfast. **Minimum stay:** 2 nights on summer weekends. **Payment:** MasterCard, Visa. **Children:** Not appropriate. **Pets:** Not allowed. **Smoking:** Outside only. **Open:** Year-round.

➤ **Yaquina Head Lighthouse is open for tours. There are stairs to the tide pools, and a manmade tide pool designed for wheelchairs.**

On a cliff above the surf at Agate Beach, this bed-and-breakfast is a dream house. It's spacious and comfortable, with a stunning view and a showpiece garden, and has innkeepers with a fine sense of hospitality.

The guest rooms all have ocean views and decks, among other several appealing features. The Windrift Room, on the main floor, has a private entrance to the front deck overlooking the garden and the sea. Michelle's Room, on the first upstairs landing, has a panoramic view, white wicker furniture, a glassed-in deck, and a large bathroom.

The other rooms, upstairs, have Jacuzzi tubs. Melody's Room has a king-size bed, a secretary, and a white wicker chair. There's a sweeping ocean view from the Overlook Room, which has a king-size bed and a fireplace. The Rainbow Room's view is angled, but it's the largest room, with a four-poster bed and double Jacuzzi.

Guests enjoy a sizable breakfast in the dining area by the plant room and admire the view from small decks along the path in the garden and on the high bluff.

Starfish Point

140 N.W. 48th Street
Newport, OR 97365
541-265-3751
Fax: 541-265-3040

A small inn of suites over the water

Owners: Niel and Kathleen Atkinson. **Accommodations:** 6 suites. **Rates:** $155–$175 double, $12 additional person. **Minimum stay:** 2 nights on weekends and some holidays. **Payment:** Major credit cards. **Children:** Welcome. **Pets:** Small dogs allowed. **Smoking:** Discouraged. **Open:** Year-round

➤ **Newport's $25 million aquarium has drawn acclaim since it opened in 1992, with sea otters, jellyfish, starfish, an aviary, a shop, and educational programs.**

Quality is the byword at Starfish Point, which offers sophisticated, contemporary lodgings on the central Oregon coast. All the units have two bedrooms and baths on two levels. They have whirlpool baths, carpeting, fireplaces, full kitchens, stereo, and TV. Some have a sunken living room and a small octagonal sitting area, the "captain's study," with magnificent views of the ocean and Yaquina Head. Blue porcelain lamps stand on rattan tables by the king-size beds. Oriental prints in blue and burgundy complement the rusty red hearth tile and white walls. The tubs are in royal blue tile.

The owners have made numerous improvements and added their own brand of enthusiastic hospitality, making Starfish Point a friendly place to visit as well as a place of understated luxury. The Atkinsons will lend crab traps, provide barbecues, and smoke the salmon you catch. They place fresh flowers in the rooms and make sure each kitchen has a blender and a popcorn popper as well as more basic tools. Local phone calls are free.

No two units are identical, but every room has a good view. Number 6 boasts a panoramic overlook from a Jacuzzi-for-two. From Starfish Point, which stands under evergreens at the edge of a cliff, a path with a rope railing provides easy access to the sheltered cove and beach below.

Agate Beach Golf Course is four blocks away. In Newport, you can stroll along the historic bayfront, where fishing boats bring in their catches and restaurants and shops cater to tourists. You might arrange for a deep-sea fishing or whale-watching trip or tour the Mark Hatfield Marine Science Center. Everyone wants to see the star of the aquarium, Keiko the orca whale.

Sylvia Beach Hotel

267 Northwest Cliff
Newport, OR 97365
541-265-5428

A unique coastal hotel for book lovers

Innkeepers: Gudrun Cable and Sally Ford. **Manager:** Ken Peyton. **Accommodations:** 20 rooms. **Rates:** $66–$146, $10 less single, $15 additional person. **Included:** Full breakfast. **Minimum stay:** 2 nights on weekends. **Payment:** Major credit cards. **Children:** Over age 12, welcome. **Pets:** Not allowed. **Smoking:** Not allowed. **Open:** Year-round

➤ **Canyon Way Bookstore and Restaurant offers Pacific Northwest cuisine, homemade bread, a good number of wines, outdoor tables, and books.**

An old-fashioned inn by the sea, filled with books and people who love conversation and reading and good food — it sounds like a literature lover's paradise. And it is. Not only does the Sylvia Beach Hotel have a third-floor library crammed with books, all its rooms are dedicated to authors and are representative of them.

In the moody Edgar Allan Poe Room, a pendulum (securely fastened) hangs over the bed while a stuffed raven poses on a bust. An impressive mural of African life hangs in the Alice B. Walker Room. The small Oscar Wilde Room has a single bed and rocker and is filled with framed wry quotations from the satirist's work ("When the gods wish to punish us they answer our prayers").

Other rooms are named for Tennessee Williams (double bed with white netting, stuffed palm tree with fabric parrot), Mark Twain (an imposing corner room with fireplace), Agatha Christie (a first-floor room containing clues to many of her mysteries), and Gertrude Stein, among others.

Goody Cable, a Portlander whose experiments always involve the combination of literature, people, and conversation (and often music, as in her offbeat café, the Rimsky-Korsakoffee House), developed the hotel's concept and enlisted the help of friends in realizing it. Each person (or team) chose an author and was assigned a room. As a result, each one is distinctive, with its own charm and character.

In spite of the whimsy, the rooms are eminently practical, with clean baths and plenty of hot water, soap, and pegs for hanging things. This is still a hotel, not a museum, and the theme is never overdone. In the bright, open lobby, guests are welcomed whether they have a literary bent or not. Coffee and tea are available all day, and mulled wine is served in the evening.

Upstairs in the library, windows overlook the beach and surf, for the hotel stands at the edge of a bluff on the shoreline. The library is cozy and inviting, with beanbag chairs in the loft. It's a fine spot for reading while the wind makes the windows creak and the surf rumbles below.

The hotel was built in 1910 as New Cliff House. Later, as Hotel Gilmore, it was a popular destination for seaside tourists. When Goody and Sally took over, there was little evidence of its former grandeur. With careful restoration, however, the four-story, dark green hotel on Nye Beach has regained its pride. The partners named their venture Sylvia Beach as a tribute to the patron of authors and literature at Shakespeare and Co., a bookstore in Paris during the 1920s and 1930s.

Meals are served at tables seating eight in the downstairs dining room. The serve-yourself breakfast consists of fruit, cereals, juices, coffee cake, and a baked dish such as vegetable or salmon quiche. The informal, sunny room is also a restaurant, Tables of Content, serving a five-course dinner every night. The food, fixed-menu and served family style, is superb. A recent dinner included half an avocado with a tangy dressing, a green salad with poppyseed dressing, poached salmon, rice with mushrooms and walnuts, and an Oregon chardonnay. A Queen of Sheba chocolate torte might be the dessert.

"I like a view but I like to sit with my back turned to it," Gertrude Stein once said. At Nye Beach, in the Sylvia Beach Hotel, she might have decided otherwise.

Oceanside

SeaRose Bed and Breakfast

P.O. Box 122
1685 Maxwell Mountain Road
Oceanside, OR 97134
503-842-6126

A B&B in a quiet coastal town

Innkeeper: Judy Gregoire. **Accommodations:** 2 rooms (private baths). **Rates:** $75–$90 double, $15 additional person. **Included:** Full breakfast. **Minimum stay:** None. **Payment:** MasterCard, Visa. **Children:** Over age 14, welcome. **Pets:** Not Allowed. **Smoking:** Not allowed. **Open:** Year-round.

➤ **The main focus is the beach, where you can hunt for agates and sand dollars. At Cape Meares, there's a restored lighthouse and the Octopus Tree.**

This home above the sea is on a loop road off Oregon's main shoreline highway, making it even more of a hideaway than most coastal lodgings. Three Capes Loop road connects three major promontories, each with a state park: Cape Meares, Cape Lookout, and Cape Kiwanda. The northernmost is Cape Meares, and Oceanside lies just south of its sheltering headland. It's a quiet community, with a curve of beach, a wildlife refuge, and a number of old-fashioned beach houses. SeaRose is one of these houses, pressed against a steep, west-facing hill. Its vertical siding rises directly from the road, but the interior has great charm, and the view reaches to the edge of the sea and sky. When you climb the stairs from the street and garage, you enter a guests' foyer, which has books, a microwave, and a refrigerator with drinks and ice cream. Coffee, tea, and popcorn are set out, and there's a phone on the table for guests.

On one side is the Nicole Room, with a double bed, a quilt in smoky blue and rose, and a reading corner. A basket holds an assortment of soaps and shampoos for use in the cedar-walled bathroom, which has a clawfoot tub. The Antoinette Room, on the other side of the foyer, has a queen-size bed, a separate entrance, and a private deck through sliding glass doors. A blue duvet, floral wallpaper, and a rocker lend flavor to the tastefully decorated room. The tidy bathroom has blue-stained pine wainscoting and an old-fashioned vanity and clawfoot tub.

Up another flight of stairs are the owner's living quarters and the guests' dining area. A colorful windsock flies on the deck outside, a fire burns in a woodstove on weekends, and through picture windows you can watch hang gliders land on the beach when a southwest wind blows.

Judy's breakfast specialties include homemade breads, seafood omelettes, and apple-blueberry pancakes. The best place for dinner is Roseanne's, overlooking the water. A casual restaurant, it is known far beyond Oceanside for its charm and excellent food. Tillamook, east of Oceanside on Highway 101, is a major cheese-producing center and has the West's largest cheese plant. Also in Tillamook is the County Pioneer Museum, with exhibits of natural history and the belongings of early settlers.

Otter Rock

The Inn at Otter Crest

P.O. Box 50
Otter Rock, OR 97369
541-765-2111
800-452-2101
Fax: 541-765-2047
reservations@ottercrest.com

| **Clifftop condos on the coast** |

General Manager: Todd Samples. **Accommodations:** 126 rooms and suites. **Rates:** Rooms, $99–$299 (up to 10 people); $10 rollaway. **Minimum stay:** 2 nights in July and August and on holiday weekends. **Payment:** Major credit cards. **Children:** Welcome . **Pets:** Not allowed. **Smoking:** A few smoking rooms available. **Open:** Year-round.

➤ **All along this craggy shore, powerful waves crash, unleashing plumes of spray that soar high into the air before turning into foam on the choppy sea.**

This clifftop condominium resort off Highway 101 occupies an enviable position on one of the most scenic promontories of Oregon's dramatic coastline. It's reached by an entry road bordered with rhododendrons and ferns. When you arrive, the van will whisk you and your luggage to one of the units, which range from studio rooms to deluxe suites.

The condos are furnished according to their individual owners' tastes, but you can count on comfortable, modern facilities. Loft suites are narrow, with high ceilings, and have two queen-size beds. All rooms have a telephone, TV, refrigerator, and a deck or balcony (some shared). If you have a fireplace, it will be laid with a pressed sawdust log when you arrive. One a day is supplied; more are available for a fee.

Eighty percent of the rooms have ocean views, but some are better than others, so if you want a panorama of the Pacific, ask for a room with an unobstructed view. You may be able to see spouting whales. The best views go to the guests who have made the earliest reservations. Probably the biggest bargain is a studio room, which has a full kitchen, a corner fireplace, and both a pull-down bed and a fold-out couch.

On Otter Crest's 40 acres there are four tennis courts; an outdoor, heated swimming pool and two Jacuzzis; basketball, volleyball, shuffleboard, and badminton; and jogging paths and hiking trails in the surrounding forest (unfortunately, a clearcut has scarred the landscape on one side). The beach is a secluded stretch of sand and rock curled with crawling surf and pocked with tide pools.

While their parents play tennis or bask in the sun, children enjoy a program of building sand castles and other activities (summer only), making Otter Crest appealing to families. The resort's restaurant is the Flying Dutchman, perched on a cliff.

Portland

The Benson Hotel

309 S.W. Broadway
Portland, OR 97205
503-228-2000
800-426-0670
Fax: 503-226-4603

A downtown hotel with a proud history

General manager: Bob Parsons. **Accommodations:** 287 rooms and suites. **Rates:** $205–$700 single or double, $25 additional person; corporate and weekend rates available. **Minimum stay:** None. **Payment:** Major credit cards. **Children:** Under 18, free with a parent. **Pets:** Small pets allowed with prior arrangement. **Smoking:** Nonsmoking rooms available. **Open:** Year-round.

➤ **A few of the many good nearby restaurants are Pazzo, Jake's, Brasserie Montmartre (with jazz), and, for a touch of old Portland, Dan and Louis Oyster Bar.**

The bronze drinking fountains on downtown Portland street corners were donated to the city by the turn-of-the-century lumber baron Simon Benson, who was also responsible for this distinguished, French baroque hotel and a number of other Oregon landmarks.

Built of brick in 1913 as the Oregon Hotel (the doors to some guest rooms still bear the distinctive OH), and later changed to the Benson, it was Portland's grandest hotel for decades. Newcomers challenged that status, but with a $20 million renovation, the Benson, now a West Coast hotel, has regained its reputation for fine quality. It's a Northwest classic, with traditional furnishings and a gracious atmosphere.

The stately, polished lobby with high arched windows is still its best feature. Chandeliers hang above Oriental carpets on marble floors, and the walls are paneled in Circassian walnut that was shipped around Cape Horn from Russia. The silver-plated mirror at the head of the stairwell dates from the 1880s, and the railing along the veined white Italian marble staircase is cast iron. A blaze crackles in the fireplace in the winter .

The guest rooms have all been updated, with new carpeting, muted gray and cream colors with touches of brass, queen- and king-size beds, and rich, mahogany-tone furniture. All the rooms have desks. The Benson Rooms, the largest, have comfortable sitting areas, similar to junior suites. A health club with fitness machines is on the seventh floor.

The oak-paneled London Grill, below the lobby, has a lighter atmosphere than in the past. Continental cuisine is served here and in the adjoining private dining room. For an even smaller party, the Wine Room is open for groups of eight to ten; here special dinners are designed around fine wines of the west.

Buffet luncheons, prepared in the London Grill, are served on weekdays in the Lobby Court. In the evenings, jazz lovers drop in for music and cocktails. Also on the street level is Piatti's, serving Italian cuisine.

The hotel's concierge is knowledgeable and helpful, ready to make reservations for dinner or tours, order flowers, have luggage repaired, and recommend local picnic spots. Haircuts, manicures, and shoeshines are available, and there's a small gift shop by the espresso bar off the lobby. The hotel has several meeting rooms and a ballroom.

Room service operates 24 hours a day; your wake-up call will be from a person rather than a computer, if you request it; and your bed linens are turned down at night. These personal touches, added to a full renovation, remind Portlanders of the days when the Benson meant the best.

Fifth Avenue Suites Hotel

506 S.W. Washington Street
Portland, OR 97205
503-222-0001
800-711-2971
Fax: 503-222-0004

**A downtown hotel known
for personal service**

Manager: Craig Thompson. **Accommodations:** 221 rooms and suites. **Rates:** $165–$250 single or double, $15 additional person. **Minimum stay:** None. **Payment:** Major credit cards. **Children:** Under 18, free. **Pets:** Small dogs allowed. **Smoking:** Nonsmoking rooms available. **Open:** Year-round.

➤ **The hotel occupies the historic Lipman Wolfe building and is one block from Pioneer Place Shopping Center.**

Built in 1912, this 10-story building was once a distinguished department store. When the Kimpton Group took over, it underwent a major renovation, and now it's one of Portland's fine hotels, especially popular with business travelers. The location is ideal, in the center of downtown and near shops and the Portland Center for the Performing Arts.

The cozy, residential ambience is apparent when you enter the lobby, which has soft lighting, leather and mahogany furnishings, and a large corner fireplace. If you arrive by car, you'll enter on the lower level, which allows you to be away from the street and weather and be led into the vestibule and check-in area.

About half of the rooms are spacious, airy suites with large windows, sunny colors, and rooms divided by sliding French doors. They have three phones and two TVs. All the suites and rooms have overstuffed chairs, writing tables, computer and dataport adapters, robes, and an array of toiletries. There's a business center with fax, copy machine, computers, and printer; 4,500 square feet of meeting rooms are also available. Guests on the 8th and 9th floors stay in Executive Level suites, which have even more convenience: in-room fax machines, two-line speaker phones, free local phone calls, coffeemakers, and desk amenities (staplers, paper clips, Post-it notes, etc.)

But Fifth Avenue Suites does not cater only to business travelers. Families with children appreciate the information on activities for kids; strollers and cribs are also provided. The fitness center has workout machines and the Aveda Spa offers body treatments. The hotel offers several extras: juice and muffins in the morning with a complimentary newspaper, and wine served each evening in the lobby.

Adjacent to the hotel is the 185-seat Red Star Tavern & Roast House, the place to go for "comfort food." Open for breakfast, lunch, and dinner, it has brick, wood-burning ovens, rotisseries, and grills.

Governor Hotel

611 S.W. 10th Avenue
Portland, OR 97205
503-224-3400
800-554-3456
Fax: 503-241-2122

A restored historic city hotel

General manager: George Forbes. **Accommodations:** 100 rooms and suites. **Rates:** Rooms, $185–$240 single or double; suites, $240–$500; weekend and special occasion packages available. **Minimum stay:** None. **Payment:** All major cards. **Children:** Under 18, free with a parent. **Pets:** Not allowed. **Smoking:** Nonsmoking rooms available. **Open:** Year-round.

➤ **If you're here during the Rose Festival in June, you'll have a prime seat for the big parade. The event also features races and other entertainment.**

This small luxury hotel with a sense of history and a lot of charm is in the heart of the downtown, close to the MAX light rail system, art galleries, business centers, and shopping.

A $15 million renovation combined the old Arts & Crafts Governor Hotel with the 1920s Italian Renaissance Princeton Building to form a modern lodging that honors tradition.

Classical music drifts through the small lobby, where a comforting blaze burns in the green tile fireplace. Potted palms, tall bookcases, polished woodwork, and leather chairs add to the Old Northwest atmosphere. On the walls, sepia murals illustrate highlights of the Lewis and Clark Expedition.

Art deco sconces light the upstairs halls. There is only one elevator, so you may have to wait at busy times. The rooms, furnished with warmth and style, have honor bars, desks, and rather small baths in period tile. For two people, a Junior Suite is the best buy; it costs the same as a double-double standard room but is larger and has a sitting area and a fireplace. Penthouse suites have balconies, and penthouse parlor suites feature fireplaces, whirlpool baths, and wet bars.

The Princeton Club, a fully equipped athletic facility, is available to guests for a fee. Business guests appreciate the hotel's multilingual staff and Executive Business Center, which offers secretarial services, and fax and computer hookups in guest rooms. There are several meeting rooms and a private dining room with its original glass dome. Jake's Grill, off the lobby, has excellent seafood. Valet parking is available.

The Heathman Hotel

S.W. Broadway at Salmon Street
Portland, OR 97205
503-241-4100
800-551-0011
Fax: 503-790-7110

An elegant downtown hotel near the Performing Arts Center

General Manager: Pierre Zreik. **Accommodations:** 151 rooms and suites. **Rates:** Rooms: $190–$210 single, $210–$230 double. Suites: $235–$775. Weekend rates and packages available. **Minimum stay:** None. **Payment:** Major credit cards. **Children:** Under age 13, free. **Pets:** Not allowed. **Smoking:** Nonsmoking rooms available.

➤ **The hotel is adjacent to the Performing Arts Center; the Portland Art Museum and the Oregon Historical Society are nearby.**

When the Heathman Hotel, built in 1927, was restored, its classical art deco exterior of terra cotta brick and sandstone was retained, but only one of the original rooms, the tea court, remains. A few steps up from the lobby, its eucalyptus-paneled walls, a curving stairway, arched windows, 18th-century oil paintings, and a grand piano create a sense of timelessness. A fireplace and an Austrian chandelier were added during the renovation. The hotel is now on the National Register of Historic Places.

The Heathman's afternoon tea ritual is an elaborate one, complete with starched linen and silver tongs. Champagne and sherry are also on the menu, along with scones and pastries. Overflow seating is at mezzanine tables with a view of the court.

Also on the mezzanine is a bar where light suppers and cocktails are served, a popular spot for theater patrons. The library here contains some 300 signed books from the authors who've stayed at the Heathman.

In the main restaurant, three tiers of tables overlook Broadway through frosted, etched glass windows in an airy setting. Coffered ceilings and marble tables hint at art deco, and Andy Warhol's prints of endangered species enliven the walls. The menu is seasonal Northwest fare, meaning plenty of fresh seafood with a nouvelle touch. Poached Northwest scallops with greens and citrus hollandaise, rack of Oregon lamb with whole-grained mustard and cracked black pepper, and Szechuan salmon with citrus beurre blanc are entrées from a recent winter menu. Lunch dishes include Oregon mussels steamed in white wine, shallots and herbs, or a steamed chicken and bok choy salad served warm with ginger vinaigrette. Gelato is made on the premises.

The guest rooms, a third of them suites named for prominent Portland families, are reached by rosewood-paneled elevators from a small, elegant lobby of marble and Burmese teak. A classic, residential atmosphere, with touches of Oriental and contemporary decor, pervades the hotel's upper levels. The rooms, where works of Northwest artists hang on the walls, were redecorated in 1997. The recently opened Grand Suite, on the ninth floor, has an understated elegance, with antiques and mahogany furnishings. The Grand Suite has two bedrooms and a Jacuzzi.

In all the rooms, television sets are concealed within cabinets, and a wide selection of complimentary movies is available to guests. In the closet you'll find thick terry-cloth robes, and in the bath, Portuguese black soap, bath gel, and other toiletries. Your bedclothes will be turned down at night, and Jaciva chocolates placed nearby.

A runner's guide to the city is included in your room packet. The hotel has a workout room, and if you'd like more extensive facilities, you may visit a nearby health club for a fee. If you prefer, rowing and exercise machines will be delivered to your door at no charge.

The Heathman offers polished service and the extra touches, such as fresh flower arrangements in public areas, that define a gracious hotel. Not only is the staff pleasant, greeting guests with smiles of welcome, it is endlessly resourceful. The concierge can handle almost any request, from car rentals to language interpreters.

Heron Haus

2545 N.W. Westover
Portland, OR 97210
503-274-1846
Fax: 503-274-1846

**A B&B mansion on a
northwest hillside**

Innkeeper: Julie Keppeler. **Accommodations:** 6 rooms. **Rates:** $95–$300 single
or double, $65 additional person. **Included:** Continental breakfast. **Minimum
stay:** None. **Payment:** Visa, MasterCard. **Children:** Age 13 and older, welcome.
Pets: Not allowed. **Smoking:** Not allowed. **Open:** Year-round.

➤ **Two of northwest Portland's many fine restaurants are Zefiro's for
Pacific Rim cuisine, and Papa Haydn's for original dishes and lavish desserts.**

This large white home, built in 1904 for a prominent local family,
looks like a sorority house at an Ivy League campus. Indeed, layers
of English ivy have, over the years, created a weathered covering
along the west side of Heron Haus. "I wanted to maintain the in-
tegrity of this lovely old house," says Julie Keppeler. "The ivy gives
a nostalgic feeling of permanence and stability."

Heron Haus caters to a sophisticated clientele that expects top
quality. Close to downtown, it's set against the northwest hills,
where the city's roots run deep. The inn is surrounded by gracious
old homes in a quiet residential district, yet within walking distance of the restaurants and boutiques that crowd one of Portland's
liveliest neighborhoods.

Each guest room in the polished, immaculate inn has a distinctive Hawaiian name, reflecting Julie's life away from her native
Northwest — twenty-four years spent in Hawaii raising four children.

The spacious rooms have sitting areas, desks, cable TV, and telephones along with an abundance of magazines and books from Julie's library. In Kulia, an intimate room on the second floor with a
queen-size bed and love seat, you may luxuriate in a raised whirlpool spa connected to the large bath. An expanse of shuttered windows views the city lights at night. Ko is a large and airy junior
suite with a garden view. Its original shower with seven spray
spouts is still in place. Manu, a suite on the third floor, offers a
secluded haven in shades of blue. It has a four-poster king-size bed

and a four-poster double bed. Mahina occupies the east end of the third floor. It has a king-size bed, a fireplace, and mountain views.

Every morning the aroma of fresh coffee wafts up the grand oak staircase, tempting guests to a breakfast of fruit and croissants and pastries from the city's finest bakeries, with fancy jams and preserves. You may be served by the fireplace in the dining room or, on sunny days, in the enclosed porch overlooking the swimming pool, the city, and Mount Hood.

Off-street parking is provided.

Hotel Vintage Plaza

422 S.W. Broadway
Portland, OR 97205
503-228-1212
800-243-0555
Fax: 503-228-3598

A small urban hotel with excellent service

General Manager: Craig Thompson. **Accommodations:** 107 rooms and suites. **Rates:** Rooms: $165 single, $185–$190 double; suites: $230–$250. **Minimum stay:** None. **Payment:** Major credit cards. **Children:** Under 16, free with a parent. **Pets:** Not allowed. **Smoking:** Nonsmoking rooms available. **Open:** Year-round.

➤ **Pazzo, off the lobby, is an upbeat restaurant with innovative Italian cuisine. Some diners like to eat in the bar area.**

When Kimco Hotels (now the Kimpton Group) purchased and began renovating the historic Wells Building in 1990, Portlanders who travel knew their city was about to gain a fine new hotel, for the San Francisco company is known for its quality accommodations in well-restored landmarks.

The Vintage Plaza, centrally located near Pioneer Square, the Center for Performing Arts, and downtown shopping, is a European-style hotel that emphasizes personal service and attention to detail. An Oregon wine theme is reflected in the decor, and the suites are named for wineries. In the nine two-story Townhouse Suites, you'll find grape cluster patterns and rich wine damask fabrics. The suites have granite-topped wet bars, a VCR, game tables, and soaking tubs with jets.

On the tenth (and top) floor are nine Starlight Rooms, with expanses of conservatory-style windows that overlook the city. The rooms have a clean, casual look, with rattan chairs and pale blue and green fabrics. Roman shades provide both privacy and partial views of the stars.

All the other rooms and suites have custom cherrywood furniture and granite and brass accessories as well as an honor bar and refrigerator. Complimentary extras are morning coffee and newspaper, shoeshines, and wine served by the dramatic marble fireplace in the lobby.

In a ten-story atrium, the lobby is a comfortable place for relaxing. It has inviting sofas, bookshelves, a piano lounge, and a picture window overlooking a wine-tasting room stocked with regional vintages.

Groups like the Vintage Plaza for its five conference rooms and full audio-visual services, while business travelers are pleased with the computer-compatible telephones and a business center that offers fax, computer, copying, and secretarial services.

The Lion and the Rose

1810 N.E. 15th Avenue
Portland, OR 97212
503-287-9245
800-955-1647
Fax 503-287-9247

A majestic Victorian home with a close-in location

Innkeeper: Kay Peffer. **Accommodations:** 6 rooms (4 with private bath). **Rates:** $95–$120 single or double, $15 additional person. **Included:** Full breakfast. **Minimum stay:** None. **Payment:** Major credit cards. **Children:** Over age 6, welcome. **Pets:** Not allowed. **Smoking:** Not allowed. **Open:** Year-round.

➤ **Northeast Broadway has become one of Portland's trendiest districts, with many lively shops and cafés.**

In 1906, Gustav Freiwald, a brewery owner and real estate speculator, built an ornate Queen Anne home in Portland's Irvington district. Architecturally intriguing, with English plasterwork oriel windows, it is now a city-designated landmark and on the National Register of Historic Places.

Stone lions flank the imposing front entrance, and roses grow profusely in the garden. Polished mahogany gleams in the dining room, where breakfast is served in the morning and tea in the afternoon, and there are two parlors furnished with antiques, one a music room with a piano and pump organ. Throughout you'll see high ceilings, gilded radiators, and leaded and beveled glass. At Christmastime, the mansion is filled with glittering trees and decorations.

The guest rooms continue the period theme. Lavonna, with a sitting area in the cupola, is probably the most popular. It has a king-size iron bed with a canopy. It shares a bath with Avandel, a quiet hideaway with a carved, high-back oak bed. Escapade, considered the honeymoon room, has a garden view and a king-size canopy bed draped in organza. Every room has a phone, clock, and desk. A balcony running the width of the house overlooks a magnolia tree and an herb garden with a fountain and gazebo; in this urban setting, it also faces a brick apartment building.

Kay Peffer goes out of her way to provide guests with every comfort. Morning coffee, afternoon dessert, robes, and soft drinks are some of the extras she offers. If you're visiting friends or relatives in Portland, you are welcome to bring them to breakfast (at extra charge) with 12 hours' notice.

Mallory Hotel

729 S.W. 15th Avenue
Portland, OR 97205
503-223-6311
800-228-8657
Fax: 503-223-0522

> A comfortable hotel on the
> edge of downtown

Manager: Linda Anderson. **Accommodations:** 143 rooms. **Rates:** $70–$110 single, $75–$120 double. **Minimum stay:** None. **Payment:** Major credit cards. **Children:** One child under age 12, free with a parent. **Pets:** Allowed ($10 fee). **Smoking:** Allowed. **Open:** Year-round.

➤ **The country's largest urban wilderness is Forest Park, in the west hills. It's next to the Hoyt Arboretum, with 214 acres of trees from around the world.**

The Mallory, built in 1912, is a popular Portland hotel and a fine bargain. A well-maintained hostelry a few blocks west of downtown proper, it is a favorite among Oregonians visiting the big city.

Behind the buff brick exterior is a bright and open lobby, a smart mix of crisp, off-white walls and dignified green wingback chairs. Columns reach to a coffered ceiling with gilt rosettes, and small crystal chandeliers are elegantly reflected in a wall of mirrors that makes the space seem twice its size.

The dining room off the lobby continues the color scheme. It's a pleasant, open space with tall windows draped in white. The Driftwood Room is a small, dark lounge on the other side of the lobby, a nice spot for a nightcap. The decor in the hotel's guest rooms is eclectic, with some rooms well-appointed and others modest. All have satellite TV, and the corner rooms have refrigerators. The big corner rooms are the best. Those on the upper floors view Mount Hood. The amenities in some rooms include a retractable clothesline in the bathtub (most rooms have both a tub and shower) and an embroidered pin cushion and sewing kit. The linen is perfectly clean and adequate, but you won't find extravagantly monogrammed towels here.

The Mallory doesn't pretend to be a luxury hotel. It provides serviceable, comfortable, and inexpensive lodgings with several extras. There is only one elevator, but you will enjoy friendly concierge and housekeeping services, soft drink and ice machines on each floor, free parking, and a newsstand that carries the *New York Times* and *Wall Street Journal*, as well as Oregon papers.

Portland's White House

1914 N.E. 22nd Avenue
Portland, OR 97212
503-287-7131
800-272-7131

A mansion in an east-side residential neighborhood

Innkeepers: Steve Holden and Lanning Blanks. **Accommodations:** 8 rooms. **Rates:** $98–$139 double, $20 additional person. **Included:** Full breakfast. **Minimum stay:** None. **Payment:** Major credit cards. **Children:** Over age 12, welcome. **Pets:** Not allowed. **Smoking:** Not allowed. **Open:** Year-round.

➤ **The Lloyd Center is a major main shopping mall on the east side, with large stores and boutiques, restaurants and cafés, and an ice rink.**

In the heart of a quiet, tree-filled neighborhood (but mere blocks from a large shopping center), stands one of Portland's most unusual homes: an ornate white mansion complete with Greek columns, a fountain, a circular driveway, and a broad verandah.

The house, built at the turn of the century by a wealthy lumber baron, recalls the stately world of a past time. The walls of the entrance are covered with landscape murals, the floors are polished oak and inlaid Honduran mahogany, and crystal chandeliers hang from the ceiling.

A wide central staircase leads to a landing where sunshine streams through the delicate pastels of antique stained glass windows. Upstairs, the rooms are furnished in a style befitting the period. A brass queen-size bed stands against one wall; lace curtains billow at oversized windows; clawfoot bathtubs are large. The Carriage House, redone with stained glass windows, has two rooms, each with a king-size bed, marble bath, and Jacuzzi.

The 1,650-square-foot basement ballroom in the main house offers plenty of space for banquets, receptions, and parties. In the gracious dining room, you will join other guests in feasting on French toast with sautéed apples, orange eggs Benedict, or, a house specialty, 12-cheese quiche. Weather permitting, you can eat outside by the fountain in the courtyard; you may also take breakfast in your room.

Every detail in this completely refurbished home, from Oriental carpets to brass doorknobs, is given loving attention. The resulting atmosphere combines an old-fashioned romantic elegance with warm hospitality.

RiverPlace Hotel

1510 Southwest Harbor Way
Portland, OR 97201
503-228-3233
800-227-1333
Fax: 503-295-6161

| A luxury hotel on the Willamette River |

General Manager: James Jones. **Accommodations:** 74 rooms, 10 condominiums. **Rates:** Rooms: $195 single, $215–$235 double; suites: $220–$700; condos: $350–$460; weekend and corporate rates available. **Included:** Continental breakfast. **Minimum stay:** None. **Payment:** Major credit cards. **Children:** Welcome. **Pets:** Not allowed. **Smoking:** Nonsmoking rooms available. **Open:** Year-round.

➤ **Tom McCall Waterfront Park, part of Portland's riverfront revival, is the scene of many festivals and community events.**

Portland's splashy waterfront hotel has been described by its builders as evoking the feel of a turn-of-the-century resort, an English manor, or a New England yacht club. The brick and wood exterior, three rooftop rotundas, window flower boxes, and the marina setting create an ambience of quiet luxury, yet the hotel has an unmistakably regional and informal flavor.

Hand-crafted rugs, oak wainscoting, tile and marble fireplaces, and sophisticated floral arrangements gracefully combine the traditional and contemporary in the public areas and guest rooms.

A doorman escorts guests into the plush, carpeted lobby. At the east end is the hotel's main restaurant, Esplanade, which features a Continental menu with fresh seafood. The Patio, open in the summer, serves meals on a terrace above the river; you may also eat outdoors on the verandah by the bar, a teak and slate lounge that is a nice spot for a light lunch or dessert.

The rooms are decorated in warm blues and yellows, their sleek lines softened by overstuffed furniture and flowers. Wet bars, whirlpool baths, and wood-burning fireplaces are some of the extras in the RiverPlace suites. They overlook the city skyline, a landscaped courtyard, or the busy Willamette River. All the rooms have movie channels, TV, and air conditioning; four have facilities for the handicapped.

You'll be served complimentary sherry when you arrive and a Continental breakfast with your preferred newspaper in the morning; plush robes hang in your closet, and fine toiletries are provided. Chocolates are placed at your bedside, and if you request a down comforter or futon, it will be supplied. The service is exemplary. Whether you need a shoeshine, a shirt pressed, or assistance with tour or travel information, you will get it with a smile.

For exercise, there are waterfront jogging paths and the River-Place Club, available for a nominal charge. It has a track, pool, weight room, and sauna and steam rooms.

RiverPlace is south of downtown, at one end of an esplanade that is reminiscent of a European riverside village, with small shops, quaint lampposts, and cobblestone walkways.

Seaside

Anderson's Boarding House

208 North Holladay Drive
Seaside, OR 97138
503-738-9055
800-995-4013

> **A relaxing home in a town by the sea**

Innkeeper: Barb Edwards. **Accommodations:** 6 rooms plus cottage (all with private bath). **Rates:** $70 single, $75–$85 double, $10 additional person; week-days in winter, 3 nights for the price of 2. **Included:** Full breakfast (except in cottage). **Minimum stay:** None. **Payment:** MasterCard, Visa. **Children:** Welcome. **Pets:** Not allowed. **Smoking:** Not allowed. **Open:** Year-round.

➤   **Near the mouth of the river you can watch for birds and wildlife — muskrats, deer, river otters, minks, elk — at Necanicum Estuary Park.**

Seaside, a bustling resort town and convention center at the beach, is on the northern coast, an easy hour-plus drive from Portland. Here at the end of the Lewis and Clark Trail, there's a wide, smooth, sandy beach, protected by rocky headlands.

A major facelift has taken place in Seaside, with civic energy pouring into an upgraded downtown, where you'll find flower-trimmed brick malls, shops, and numerous restaurants. A 2-mile promenade above the beach is perfect for bicycling, roller skating, and strolling.

A few blocks inland, on the east bank of the Necanicum River, Anderson's Boarding House provides lodging reminiscent of a Victorian summer home. The big blue house with neat white trim was built in 1898 as a family home. Later it was run as a boarding house; the proprietor, Babe Anderson, lived there from the 1920s until 1970. Finally it was remodeled and opened as a bed-and-breakfast.

Guests have their own entrance from the side porch or can enter through the living room, which is furnished with period antiques. In the dining room, lace and linen cover the table where breakfast is served. Fruits, juices, French toast, omelettes, baked egg dishes, and fruit crêpes are among the variety of dishes Barb Edwards serves. There are two refrigerators where guests can store drinks and snacks.

Most of the rooms are on the second floor. They have a light country Victorian look, with white wicker rockers and armoires and a TV. Two have views of the river, where you may see seals and herons. The doors have brass numbers dating from the inn's boarding house days, and all the beds, both queen-size and daybeds, are covered with down duvets. Beds of wood or brass and white iron are reproductions of antiques and designed for comfort.

The cottage is a private retreat with a kitchen at the edge of the river, where ducks and cranes fly by. It sleeps six, with a queen-size bed in the bedroom, a sleeping loft that children love, and a daybed with a trundle in the living room. Breakfast is not included, but the cottage has a kitchen.

Gilbert Inn

341 Beach Drive
Seaside, OR 97138
503-738-9770

**A large Victorian home a
block from the beach**

Innkeepers: Dick and Carole Rees. **Accommodations:** 9 rooms and 1 suite.
Rates: May through September, $89–$105 double; $10 additional person; October through April, $84–$100. **Included:** Full breakfast. **Minimum stay:** 2 nights on weekends, 3 nights on some holidays. **Payment:** Major credit cards. **Children:** Welcome (crib available). **Pets:** Not allowed. **Smoking:** Not allowed. **Open:** Closed in January.

➤ **Good meals include the clam chowder at Dooger's, barbecues and
seafood at the Nostalgic Café, and the entire menu at Pacific Way Bakery
in Gearhart.**

Alexander Gilbert was an adventurous entrepreneur, a Frenchman who came to Astoria (via Montreal and San Francisco) when it was a booming seaport and opened several popular saloons. In the 1890s he sold his businesses, joined a development company in Seaside, and built this three-story gabled home. He became mayor of the burgeoning town and in 1906 donated the land for the promenade by the beach.

The yellow and white Victorian home, a block from the promenade, is handy to downtown but removed from its convention bustle. You enter through a west-facing, many-windowed sun porch to a large parlor paneled in old-growth fir. A stately brick and fir fireplace stands against one wall and lace curtains hang at wide bay windows. The inn's furnishings throughout are in a flowery, country French style.

The guest rooms retain a period flavor with antiques, many of them family heirlooms, and cozy comforters. The 1880s Suite, on the ground floor, was Alexander Gilbert's original beach cabin, built before the big house. Now it's a charming hideaway with a TV and a private bath with tub and shower.

The Garret Room, on the third floor, sleeps four and has a view over nearby roofs to the sea. The romantic Turret Room, with its four-poster bed, angled walls, and wicker chairs, is popular with honeymooners. Flounced white curtains float at windows with their original wavy glass.

You'll be served a satisfying morning meal in the glassed-in breakfast room, an inviting, sunny space with pale rose walls, white wrought-iron chairs, and hanging greenery. Afterward, Carole and Dick are happy to recommend the sights around this town they know so well.

Sisters

Conklin's Guest House

69013 Camp Polk Road
Sisters, OR 97759
541-549-0123
800-549-4262
Fax: 541-549-4481

A spacious home in the central Cascades

Innkeepers: Frank and Marie Conklin. **Accommodations:** 5 rooms. **Rates:** $90–$120 June–December; $70–$100 December–June; $25–$30 per person in dorm room (minimum 3 persons). **Included:** Full breakfast. **Minimum stay:** None. **Payment:** MasterCard, Visa. **Children:** Over age 12, welcome. **Pets:** Outside pets on leash allowed. **Smoking:** Outdoors only. **Open:** Year-round.

➤ **For a taste of the frontier, go to Bronco Billy Saloon, in Hotel Sisters, where swinging doors lead to the bar and the restaurant serves barbecued ribs.**

Conklin's Guest House is everything a good bed-and-breakfast should be: a warm and inviting home, pleasant accommodations, a generous breakfast, and, most important, innkeepers who welcome you like old friends. It has become more luxurious in recent years, but the hospitality remains.

The spacious white house stands on 4 acres of land at the eastern edge of Sisters, the town that celebrates the Old West, 1990s style. Wooden boardwalks and false storefronts create a frontier mood for shops that lure tourists by the thousands. But it's the dependable sunshine and the pristine high desert setting that are most appealing. Skiing, fishing, rafting, hiking, and boating are among the favorite activities in the central Cascades.

The Conklins' large parlor has French doors that open to a solarium. An ample breakfast is served in the solarium or by the pool, where the view is of pastureland and, on the near horizon, Broken Top and the snowy peaks of the Three Sisters.

All the guest rooms have a queen-size and single bed. Two spacious rooms are on the main floor: Forget-Me-Not Room and Lattice Room, which have wheelchair access. Upstairs are two rooms, Columbine, which has an east-facing sitting room and a clawfoot tub, and Morning Glory, which has a balcony overlooking the pool, pond, and gazebo. The Heather Room is a dorm room with a queen-size bed and 5 single beds. It's popular with wedding parties and other groups.

The Conklins, long familiar with the area, will suggest activities and recommend restaurants to try. They invite guests to relax on the wraparound verandah, enjoy the swimming pool, borrow bicycles, and use the barbecue. Unassuming and gregarious, they're ideal B&B hosts.

Lake Creek Lodge

Sisters, OR 97759
541-595-6331

| An old-fashioned family resort in the woods

Manager: Diana Pepperling. **Accommodations:** 15 houses and cottages. **Rates:** $60–$255 in summer, 6% gratuity, 1–4 people; $50 additional person; rates vary seasonally; weekly and group rates available. **Included:** Dinner (summer only). **Minimum stay:** 2 nights, November to May. **Payment:** No credit cards. **Children:** Under age 2, free (bring own crib). **Pets:** Allowed in winter on leash, discouraged in summer ($8). **Smoking:** Allowed. **Open:** Year-round.

➤ **The lodge is near stables (Black Butte Ranch and Blue Lake Corrals) and is a 20-minute drive from Hoodoo Bowl, popular for winter skiing.**

Since 1935, families have been making lasting friendships at this lodge in central Oregon, near Camp Sherman and the Metolius River.

It's that kind of place: casual, relaxing, unpretentious, and secluded on its own 40 parklike acres of ponderosa pine and green lawn. Wild roses and columbine edge the paths, and clover blooms purple around the trout pond. Lake Creek, which runs from Suttle Lake to the Metolius River, flows through the property.

In summer, barrels of geraniums stand in front of the main lodge; in winter, icicles drip from the eaves. Inside, the informal sitting room with knotty pine beams has a stone fireplace and trestle tables stacked with magazines and information on what to see and do, and antlers sprout from the walls.

The rustic theme continues through the homey guest houses that bear the stamp of vacation cottages of the 1930s. Linoleum covers the kitchen floors, and country quilts cover pine beds (if you need a firm bed, ask for it). The houses have two and three bedrooms and large screened porches. The cottages, which date from the lodge's earliest days, are smaller and darker but comfortable. They have no kitchen, but there's a refrigerator on the porch — tied shut with a rope so the wily raccoons can't raid your groceries. The cabins can sleep up to seven people, and the Inn — a 3-bedroom, 2-bath house ($170) — can hold ten. Lake Creek Lodge has a sizable swimming pool, a smaller, shallow pool, tennis and paddle tennis courts, and a pond where kids under 12 can fish.

In summer, children eat dinner with their new friends in a special section of the dining room. Dinners are substantial: prime rib, roast pork, fried chicken, and turkey with all the trimmings are some of the fixed-menu meals. There are weekly weenie roasts and occasional salmon bakes. If you bring your own beer or wine, the kitchen will chill it for you. The dining room is closed in winter (except for groups), so you'll do your own cooking or drive the 12 miles to Sisters.

Lake Creek Lodge can be addictive, because you know it's not likely to change. It will always offer fishing in the Metolius, hiking on woodland trails, and the chance to watch your kids make life-long friends while you sit on the grass in a bent-twig chair reading, perhaps, Gene Stratton Porter.

Stayton

Bird and Hat

717 North Third
Stayton, OR 97383
503-769-7817

Friendly lodgings in the Willamette Valley

Innkeeper: Jacqulin Kirby. **Accommodations:** 2 rooms (shared bath). **Rates:** $55 single, $60 double, children $7.50, senior discounts available. **Included:** Full breakfast. **Minimum stay:** None. **Payment:** No credit cards. **Children:** Welcome. **Pets:** Allowed by arrangement. **Smoking:** Allowed on porches. **Open:** Year-round.

➤ **Bicycles can be rented at the Upper Echelon, a shop two doors down from the B&B.**

It's not quite the amazing bargain it was when the little attic room was open, but this B&B is still a good buy when you're exploring the Willamette Valley.

Tulip Tree Room, upstairs, overlooks an enormous old tulip maple tree. It's furnished with Victorian antiques and has a double bed. Peach Room, decorated in soft peach colors, has a view of a dogwood tree with peach-colored blooms. This room has a TV, a king-size bed, a daybed, and a private porch. An alcove, often used as a nursery, holds a crib that can be converted to a youth bed.

On the main floor is a parlor with Victorian furniture, a TV, and books. Breakfast, served in the dining room, includes fruit, juice, muffins, and an entrée that varies according to the innkeeper's mood — perhaps stuffed pancakes with fruit syrups, eggs Benedict, or poached eggs.

The house, built in 1907, stands on a corner in Stayton, a small town 20 miles east of Salem, Oregon's capital. In the heart of the valley's countryside, it's an excellent stop for bicyclists and other tourists.

Steamboat

Steamboat Inn

42705 North Umpqua Highway
Steamboat, OR 97447
541-498-2230
800-840-8825
Fax: 541-498-2411

A riverside resort with top-quality cuisine

Innkeepers: Jim and Sharon Van Loan. **Accommodations:** 8 cabins, 5 cottages, 2 suites. **Rates:** $125 double in cabins, $160 cottages, $235 suites, $20 additional adult. **Minimum stay:** None. **Payment:** Major credit cards. **Children:**

Under age 4, free. **Pets:** Not allowed. **Smoking:** Not allowed. **Open:** March–December; restaurant open May 13–October 31.

➤ **The North Umpqua River, twisting, cascading, and sometimes flowing smooth as molten green glass, defies description.**

There are several compelling reasons for making the winding 38-mile drive east along the North Umpqua River from Roseburg, in southern Oregon, to Steamboat Inn. Fishing tops the list.

Fly-fishing the North Umpqua has long been recognized as a challenge like no other. The inn where many fishers gather in their quest for steelhead is on a bluff above the river, in the center of a 32-mile stretch of white water reserved for fly-fishing. A catch-and-release policy is required for wild steelhead in this swirling, boulder-strewn stream, where pools bear names like Fighting Hole and Sawtooth. If you'd like to have a fishing guide or rent equipment, the Van Loans will arrange it; and if you want to brush up on technique before pulling on your waders, they have instructional cassettes for rent.

At sundown, after the last cast has been made, another reason for coming to Steamboat becomes apparent: the Fisherman's Dinner. Guests who have reserved a space gather for hors d'oeuvres (such as hot pesto soup and salmon cakes) and wine or sparkling cider before moving to the candle-lit dining tables, one of them a 20-foot slab of sugar pine.

A memorable feast follows. It might include a colorful arrangement of herbed cucumber with black sesame seeds, garbanzos, shredded carrot, and purple cabbage, each section of the palette topped with tangy dressings; an entrée of spicy chicken (or barbecued salmon or tenderloin); snowpeas and herbed squash; and pasta. Wine decanters are passed and conversation flows as guests become acquainted. Dessert might be nectarines with ginger and cream. Dinners cost $35 and are open to the public.

Steamboat's tradition of outstanding meals began with Frank and Jeanne Moore, who ran the inn between 1957 and 1975. Theirs was hearty country fare; Sharon has refined it, added a nouvelle touch, and created a national reputation for herself. Some of their recipes and menus appear in their popular cookbook, *Of Thyme & The River.*

Next to the main building is an inviting library and below it, on the bluff above the river, are four duplexes, all with fireplaces. Simply but comfortably furnished, they share one long deck. The five newer cottages, on a wooded slope a half mile up the road, away from the river, are small homes geared to light housekeeping.

Cedar-sided, with high vaulted ceilings, skylights, fireplaces, and natural wood walls, they have plush carpeting and contemporary furnishings throughout their two levels as well as king-size beds, twin beds in lofts, and deep soaking tubs.

Many guests come to Steamboat not to fish but to hike in the forest (a trail across the river extends 60 miles to join the Pacific Crest Trail), swim in Steamboat and Canton creeks, relax in seclusion, and admire the scenic North Umpqua.

Sunriver

Sunriver Resort

Sunriver, OR 97707
541-593-1000
800-387-2876
Fax: 541-593-5458

> **A resort and a community in the central Cascades**

Managing director: Charlie Peck. **Accommodations:** 411 rooms, suites, condos and homes. **Rates:** $99–$495; rates vary seasonally; group rates available. **Minimum stay:** 5 nights in summer and Christmas week, 3 nights on other holidays. **Payment:** Major credit cards. **Children:** Welcome. **Pets:** Not allowed. **Smoking:** Nonsmoking units available. **Open:** Year-round.

➤   **The High Desert Museum shows the natural and cultural history and wildlife of the area.**

In the early 1960s, Sunriver was an ambitious plan on paper for a resort unlike any other in the Northwest. Today it's a vital community, a major economic force in the region, and a 3,300-acre playground for vacationers who flock to dry, sunny, central Oregon.

The multimillion-dollar resort just off Highway 97, 15 miles south of Bend, is on a vast meadow that was once grazing land for cattle. The sometimes placid, sometimes roaring Deschutes River flows through the property, the air is spicy with the scent of ponderosa pine, and the Cascade mountain range stands in snowy splendor against blue sky.

About 1,600 residents live here permanently, and many more come and go throughout the year, staying in private homes or condominium units. Numerous options are available: single rooms, suites, condos, and private homes. Most units are roomy and well furnished in Northwest contemporary style. The older single rooms can feel cramped. They are situated, for the most part, in culs-de-sac reached from roads that twist and circle among the trees.

The main lodge is the heart of Sunriver — it has the check-in desk; the Owls Nest Lounge; the Meadows restaurant for fine dining; and the Merchant Trader, which combines a country store, a gift and pro shop, and casual café with indoor and outdoor seating. In the Meadows, children under age 8 eat free when they order from the children's menu. You'll find other good eating spots in the Country Village, a large complex of shops.

Sunriver is very popular with golfers, for good reason. There are three 18-hole championship courses: Woodlands, Meadows, and the new, award-winning Crosswater. Set on 600 acres of woodland and wetlands, Crosswater was designed to blend harmoniously with the natural environment. It's open only to members of the golf club and guests staying at the resort (the other two courses are open to the general public).

In addition to golf, Sunriver offers tennis on 28 outdoor and 3 indoor courts, swimming, and bicycling. Thirty miles of paved biking paths wind through the property. You can go horseback riding on wilderness trails, canoe or raft on the Deschutes, play racquetball, ice skate (in the winter), and learn about local wildlife at the Nature Center. On a clear evening, don't miss the small observatory, which has telescopes that allow a close look at stars, planets, and galaxies.

The resort is almost as busy in winter as in summer. Mount Bachelor, with numerous ski lifts and runs, is very close. Cross-country skiers can ski right from the lodge across the gentle hills of the golf course.

With 25,000 square feet of meeting space, Sunriver holds many conferences. Careful planning and an efficient staff keeps them from interfering with the individual traveler's enjoyment.

The Dalles

Williams House Inn

608 West 6th Street
The Dalles, OR 97058
541-296-2889

> **A Victorian family home on the Oregon Trail.**

Innkeepers: Barbara and Don Williams. **Accommodations:** 3 rooms (1 with private bath). **Rates:** $55–$65 single, $65–$75 double; use of hide-a-bed, $15 single, $20 double. **Included:** Full breakfast. **Minimum stay:** None. **Payment:** Major credit cards. **Children:** Welcome. **Pets:** Not allowed. **Smoking:** Outdoors only. **Open:** Year-round.

➤ **Recommended are Ole's Supper Club for prime rib in a casual atmosphere, the more formal Wasco House, and the historic Baldwin Saloon.**

In the summertime, when Bing cherries are ripe, guests at Williams House find bowls of the sweet purple fruit on the porch, in the gazebo, and throughout the house — a token of the innkeepers' hospitality and a reminder of their working cherry orchard in the area.

Cherries and other fresh fruits are served at breakfast, along with homemade granola, bran muffins, and eggs. Weather permitting (as it usually does in this dry climate east of the Cascades), Barbara brings breakfast out back to the pretty gazebo. Otherwise, it's served in the gray and red dining room on the Duncan Phyfe table.

Williams House, a gingerbread-trimmed Victorian complete with balconies, dormers, a tower, and a verandah, was built in 1899. The Williams family has owned it since 1926, maintaining it in excellent condition. The first-floor guest room, Elizabeth's Suite, has a four-poster bed, a sitting area with a sofa bed, and a ring shower in its seven-foot clawfoot tub.

Red-carpeted stairs lead to the second floor, where, from the tiny balcony off Harriett's Room, you can see the Klickitat Hills across the Columbia River in Washington. This room has a canopied four-poster double bed and a blue chaise longue. In Edward's Room, a balcony faces north. This yellow and green room has a walnut double bed and a window seat filled with colorful cushions. Every room has a TV, and telephones are available.

Though the inn's style is formal and traditional, it isn't stuffy, perhaps because it has been a family home for years and Barbara and Don are relaxed hosts. You'll see family heirlooms throughout the house as well as Barbara's collection of Oriental art.

In the parlor, built-in bookcases stand beside the green marble fireplace, and a console piano invites an old-time tune. Even traffic noise from the highway below the property does not detract from the mood.

Don, a fourth-generation resident of The Dalles, is a gold mine of information on the area and is well versed in the town's history. As Fort Dalles, it was the final stopover before the last leg of the Oregon Trail. Here immigrants aiming for the Willamette Valley got ready to float the Columbia River or take the overland route on Mount Hood.

If you're visiting in mid-July, you can participate in the annual Fort Dalles Days and Rodeo, a celebration featuring steak feeds, chili cookoffs, cowboy breakfasts, a rodeo, country western dance, and races and exhibitions.

Timberline

Timberline Lodge

Timberline, OR 97028
503-272-3311
503-231-7979 (in Portland)
800-547-1406
Fax: 503-272-3710

| A grand historic lodge on the mountain |

Area Operator: Richard Kohnstamm. **General Manager:** Gary Hohnstein. **Accommodations:** 59 rooms, 10 chalet bunk rooms with shared baths. **Rates:** $65–$170 single or double, $15 additional person. **Minimum stay:** 4 nights during Christmas holidays. **Payment:** Major credit cards. **Children:** Welcome. **Pets:** Not allowed. **Smoking:** Not allowed. **Open:** Year-round.

➤ **Popular with climbers, Mount Hood offers accessible challenge, especially from the south. At the top awaits a breathtaking view of the Cascades, foothills, and valleys.**

About 65 miles east of Portland, where the Cascade Range divides western Oregon from the dry, eastern part of the state, a majestic edifice of wood and stone stands against the south flank of 11,235-foot Mount Hood. Timberline Lodge is like the rough-hewn castle of a legendary Norse mountain king, set on Oregon's highest mountain.

Timberline was constructed during the Great Depression as a WPA project. More than 150 Northwestern artisans — carpenters, stonemasons, woodcarvers, metalworkers, painters, weavers, and furniture makers — built the enormous lodge in two years for less than a million dollars.

The architectural style, suggestive of the rugged terrain, was distinctive enough to be given a new name: Cascadian. The design, and the fact that the entire lodge was built by hand with materials taken from the forests and rocky slopes, give Timberline a unique character. Today the 3-story building is a living art museum and beloved Oregon institution as well as a mountain retreat at 6,000 feet. The front door is five feet wide, ten feet high, and weighs 1,100 pounds. The ironware alone, massive and hand-forged, weighs 400 pounds; the remainder is thick ponderosa pine.

A Portland artist, Marjorie Hoffman Smith, coordinated the interior decoration, using Indian and pioneer motifs, alpine wildflowers, and native wildlife as her sources of inspiration. Looms were constructed on the site for weaving draperies. The fabric from old army uniforms and blankets was dyed and made into bedspreads and chair coverings. Headboards were carved, rugs hooked, and furniture handmade from native fir and pine. A volunteer group has painstakingly restored and re-created most of the original furnishings and fabrics, which deteriorated or were destroyed over the years. They are displayed in the Rachael Griffin Historic Exhibition Center on the main floor.

In the second-floor lounge, six pillars tower 92 feet above the massive stone fireplace. Wrought-iron light fixtures, polished oak floors, heavy timbers, and floor-to-ceiling windows that view Mount Hood's glaciers and snowy peak help to create a warm, rustic, and inviting atmosphere. The Ram's Head Bar is a perfect spot for enjoying an aperitif while you watch the sunset glow on the mountaintop.

In the lodge's restaurant, American and Continental dinners are served by candlelight. Breakfast and lunch menus are also available. The Blue Ox Bar, downstairs, serves casual fare and imported beers.

Six ski lifts carry skiers to tree-lined runs below the lodge and on open slopes a mile above it. You can ski in your shirtsleeves on the Fourth of July on Palmer Glacier above the lodge. If you spend a midweek night in winter, you receive a discount on skiing. New Year's Eve is a dream come true for the truly dedicated skier: lifts are open until the wee hours. Skis may be rented at Wy'East Day Lodge, just across the parking lot.

In summer, hikers swarm to the trails that honeycomb the area. Walk the Timberline Trail, a 35-mile trek that encircles the mountain, or choose from dozens more that wind among mossy green forests, across snowfields, past streams and waterfalls, and through meadows that are solid purple with lupine in July.

Vida

The Wayfarer Resort

46725 Goodpasture Road
Vida, OR 97488
541-896-3613

A classic, peaceful Oregon resort on the river

Managers: Dorothy Hoffman and Scott Marble. **Accommodations:** 12 rooms and cabins. **Rates:** $70–$195 per day, $420–$1,170 per week, 1–4 people; $8 additional person. **Minimum stay:** 3 days, April 20–September 15. **Payment:** MasterCard, Visa. **Children:** Welcome (cribs available). **Pets:** Small pets allowed on leash. **Smoking:** Outdoors only. **Open:** Year-round.

➤ **The area offers fishing, rafting, bicycling, hiking, soaking in hot springs, winter skiing, and golf on the Tokatee course, considered one of the best in the West.**

This is the essence of western Oregon. Deep in the woods, 30 miles east of Eugene on the banks of the McKenzie River and Marten Creek, a complex of cabins stands on 11 acres of lawn and fruit trees. Most of the cabins are perched right at the edge of the river, their decks overlooking ferns and moss-covered alder and maple trees.

Butterflies flutter over colorful flower beds, and purple grapes and berries encircle the vegetable garden. A raft floats on the trout-stocked pond, waiting for an adventurous child. Pygmy goats wander the pasture. There are tennis courts, volleyball and badminton facilities, a playground, and guided fishing trips.

From Interstate 5, you get to this bit of paradise by taking Highway 126 east toward the Cascades, a road that travels through some of Oregon's prettiest countryside. Cross the McKenzie River via a white covered bridge, and a few miles later, after winding through cedar and spruce, firs and ferns, you reach the Wayfarer.

The secluded resort is both a peaceful place to relax and a base for active recreation. You can fish the emerald-green McKenzie

River and glacier-fed Marten Creek, hike, raft, play tennis, and golf at nearby Tokatee Golf Course.

The cabins have kitchens, queen-size or twin beds, fireplaces, barbecues, and picnic furniture on the decks above the gurgling creek. You can rent a studio duplex unit, a one- or two-bedroom cottage, The Ol' Homestead (4 bedrooms, 2 baths), or the two-bedroom Octagon, a cabin with a semicircular fireplace, wet bar, laundry facilities, and large common room suitable for meetings. Octagon is also accessible to wheelchairs.

Natural wood interiors, comfy furniture, patchwork quilts, and old-fashioned rocking chairs add to the atmosphere in the cabins, with a bowl of hazelnuts the final touch. Each unit has a TV; there's a pay phone in a gazebo on the property. There's also a laundry room for guests.

Waldport

Edgewater Cottages

3978 S.W. Pacific Coast Highway
Waldport, OR 97394
541-563-2240

A group of cottages by the ocean

Proprietor: Cathy Sorensen. **Accommodations:** 8 rooms and cottages. **Rates:** $55–$125 double; $10–$15 additional person. **Minimum stay:** 2–6 nights depending on unit and season. **Payment:** Cash or check. **Children:** Welcome. **Pets:** Allowed ($5–$10). **Smoking:** Outdoors only. **Open:** Year-round.

➤ **The Alsea Bridge Historical Information Center has historical displays on coastal transportation and the Alsea Indians.**

This cluster of weathered, cedar-sided cottages sits halfway down the Oregon coast, south of the fishing town of Waldport. The units vary widely, from studio-size Wheel House, which sleeps two and is part of a hillside fourplex, to the three-bedroom, three-bath Beachcomber, a house that can sleep 15. Beachcomber is rented to single groups only. The two-story home has a solarium, skylights, and comfortable rooms.

All of Edgewater's units have electric heat, TV, equipped kitchens, and fireplaces. Most include thoughtful extras such as corkscrews, wine glasses, and nutcrackers for cracking the crabs you'll catch or buy. Because they stand on a grassy bluff directly above a broad sandy beach that stretches from Waldport to Yachats, the cottages have fine ocean views. Pine Rest, a few feet from the edge of the bluff, is a knotty pine cabin with a king-size bed and a wind-sheltered sun deck. West Wind has two bedrooms, a red enamel wood-burning fireplace in the living room, and a sun deck.

The Edgewater is a friendly, casual spot — the kind of place where the proprietor is happy to lend a playpen, popcorn popper, or food processor. Many guests consider it a second home and return year after year.

Heather Cottage

P.O. Box 528
Waldport, OR 97394
541-563-3620

A quaint cottage with bargain rates

Owners: Jean Weakland and Patricia Montgomery. **Accommodations:** 1 cottage. **Rates:** $45 single, $55 double (one night free if staying a week). **Minimum stay:** 2 nights. **Payment:** No credit cards. **Children:** Welcome. **Pets:** Not allowed. **Smoking:** Outdoors only. **Open:** Year-round.

➤ **Next door, Gale Gallery and Glashaus Pottery features the works of numerous Oregon artists. You can watch stoneware being made in the studio.**

South of Waldport on the central coast, this quaint little gem nestles in a tangle of shore pines, holly trees, heather, and rhododendron. The white, shake-roofed cottage is reminiscent of a summer cabin of the 1940s, even to the old-fashioned radio in the living-dining room. Conceding to the 1990s, however, it has TV as well.

There's a full kitchen, with perky blue and white checked curtains at the windows and a popcorn popper on the shelf, as well as a few staples. Firewood is provided for the glass-fronted woodstove on a brick hearth in the living room (there is also electric heat). The simple white bedroom holds a queen-size bed and bookshelves.

Outside there's a picnic table, and, in front, an old-fashioned lawn swing. But you really feel you've stepped back a few decades when you see shirts flapping on the clothesline in the side yard.

Jean and Pat, both former teachers, have supplied the cottage with games, puzzles, books, and a folder full of information on the area. Beach walking, combing the agate beds, golfing at Waldport's 9-hole course, windsurfing, and fishing and crabbing are some of the activities available. There are three navigable rivers close by.

Heather Cottage, a short walk from the beach, has no ocean view. It's close to busy Highway 101, so you can hear the traffic, but separated from it by a hedge.

Warm Springs

Kah-Nee-Ta

P.O. Box K
Warm Springs, OR 97761
541-553-1112
800-554-4SUN
Fax: 541-553-1071

A Native American resort in central Oregon

Manager: Zuanne Jarrett. **Accommodations:** 139 rooms. **Rates:** Rooms, $115–$200 single or double, $14 additional person; midweek and winter discounts available; no tax charged. **Minimum stay:** 2 nights on weekends, 3 nights on holidays. **Payment:** Major credit cards. **Children:** Under age 14, free. **Pets:** No pets in lodge, dogs on leash allowed in tepees and RV area in village ($9). **Smoking:** Nonsmoking units available. **Open:** Year-round.

➤ **The Museum at Warm Springs, run by the Confederated Tribes, houses a superb collection of artifacts related to Native American history and cultures.**

When the Walla Walla and Wasco Indian tribes were forced from their homeland on the green banks of the Columbia River to the dry, sagebrush-covered terrain of central Oregon, the future looked bleak. They had left 10 million acres of fertile land for 640,000 acres of barren, rocky hills that offered no strengths on which to base an economy. In 1879, the Paiutes joined the Warm Springs tribes, and for the next sixty years the three groups eked a poor living by farming the arid land, foraging, and fishing. It was a sad and too-familiar story.

In 1939, however, the confederation took the country's offer of independence and began a steady move toward prosperity. A sawmill and plywood plant were the start of a forest products industry; and with funds received when ancient fishing grounds were covered by the construction of The Dalles Dam, Kah-Nee-Ta was built. The resort is now a major tourist draw and convention center.

The lodge stands at the crest of a hill on the southeast side of the reservation, not far from where the Warm Springs River runs into the north-flowing Deschutes River, 11 miles from the town of Warm Springs and 119 miles southeast of Portland. With the noted architect Pietro Belluschi consulting, the handsome building was designed to resemble an arrowhead, its two wings meeting at the lobby and restaurant.

The culture and heritage of the Confederated Tribes are evident throughout the lodge. A glass case displays Indian baskets, cornhusk bags, and century-old beadwork; the central lobby is dominated by a gray concrete fireplace with triangular beams that reach to the ceiling in tepee fashion; Indian art hangs on the walls. In the main restaurant, the Juniper Room, you can try Native American dishes (updated for modern palates). Prime rib, chicken teriyaki, and pork chops are on the menu, but you can also try medallions of venison with garlic-madeira sauce or (with three-hours' notice) a bird stuffed with wild rice and juniper berries and roasted in clay. Indian fry bread is served with every meal, along with huckleberry jam. Local berries flavor sauces, ice cream, and pies.

In recent years, since a major remodeling, the Juniper Room has become a choice dining spot. Pink linens, potted palms, and carpeting in stylized Indian designs brighten the interior, while large windows look out to the austere beauty of ancient hills.

The large tiled swimming pool, surrounded by shaded terraces, can be seen from the balconies of most rooms. The furnishings are those of any good, modern hotel, with a TV, a phone, and comfortable beds. Robes are provided. The Chief Suite is wonderfully roomy and has extras such as a bar, a whirlpool, and a kitchen with a Jenn-Aire grill and microwave oven.

You can play golf on an 18-hole course that winds along the banks of the Warm Springs, play tennis, fish, go whitewater rafting, or go a mile down the road to the mineral baths at the village that is another, less grand part of Kah-Nee-Ta. The lodgings here include recently updated motel rooms, RV spaces, and tepees with concrete floors (bring your own sleeping bag).

Once a week in summer, traditional Indian dancing and an alderwood salmon bake are presented. In June, Pi-ume-sha Treaty Days commemorate the Warm Springs Treaty of 1855. Parades, tournaments, and dance contests — like Teen Boys' Fancy Dance and Girls' Buckskin Graceful War Dance — are held.

Welches

The Resort at the Mountain

68010 East Fairway Avenue
Welches, OR 97067
503-622-3101
800-669-7666
Fax: 503-622-2222

A golf resort on Mount Hood

Manager: Scott Cruickshank. **Accommodations:** 157 rooms and suites. **Rates:** Summer, $99–$240 for 2 to 4 people; less in winter; group rates and packages available. **Minimum stay:** None. **Payment:** Major credit cards. **Children:** Under age 18, free with a parent. **Pets:** Not allowed. **Smoking:** Nonsmoking rooms available. **Open:** Year-round.

➤ **Mount Hood is "the mountain for all seasons." It offers skiing even in the summer on Palmer Snowfield. In winter, skiers flock to the many slopes.**

Fifty miles east of Portland, in the foothills of Mount Hood, the Resort at the Mountain occupies 365 acres of landscaped grounds and natural forest. Today's resort is far different from the campgrounds of Welches Resort back in 1888, when Samuel Welch and his son, Billy, welcomed travelers to their homesteaded land by the Salmon River.

Samuel, a Quaker from Pennsylvania, came west on the Oregon Trail in the early 1850s. He ran the Hudson's Bay Company trading post in the area, but his dream was to build a resort, and so he set up the campsites. By 1890, he had built Welches Hotel, which stands today.

Now the housing is luxurious, the recreation is varied, and the dining is Continental, but the high-country setting is much the same, with tall fir trees cloaking hillsides that slope toward Oregon's highest peak, 11,235-foot Mount Hood.

Because golf is a major attraction (you can play 27 holes on fairways that host more than 250 golfing events a year), the theme is Scottish. Antique golf clubs, historic prints, and artifacts from Scotland convey the Old World motif. In the stone and glass main lodge, which holds restaurants and meeting rooms, you will find a lobby with couches facing a stone fireplace. Down the hall is Highlands dining room, serving three meals a day and a notable Sunday brunch — a varied buffet of seafood, prime rib, lamb, fruits, salads, pastries, and unlimited champagne.

The Quiet Bar is a comfortable lounge with a green granite bar where diners can wait for a table in Highlands. The Tartans, a casual coffee shop overlooking the golf course, offers breakfast and lunch from June through October.

The lodgings vary from a single room to two-bedroom suites. Most have fireplaces and views of the golf course. A deluxe room has two queen-size beds and a mini-bar; a fireside studio suite is more luxurious, with a king-size bed, a fireplace, and a small kitchen. The suite is a good choice for a family, as it adjoins a room with two beds. The rooms have storage space for skis and golf clubs, a well as TVs, phones, and clock radios.

The Resort at the Mountain offers many activities in addition to golf and skiing. The only one not nearby is windsurfing (even that you'll find on the other side of the mountain, on the Columbia River). There is an outdoor swimming pool, whirlpools, a sauna, a weight room with bicycles, aerobics classes, and six tennis courts. You can borrow racquets for badminton or tennis. Volleyball, horseshoes, rafting on the Deschutes, and riding are easily arranged. You can fish for steelhead from May to August.

Wheeler

Wheeler on the Bay Lodge

P.O. Box 580
580 Marine
Wheeler, OR 97147
503-368-5858
800-469-3204
Fax: 503-368-4204

A trim bayside lodge on the
north coast

Proprietors: Glen and Juana Handy. **Accommodations:** 10 rooms . **Rates:** $80–$115 single or double. **Minimum stay:** 2 nights in summer and on holidays. **Payment:** MasterCard, Visa. **Children:** Welcome. **Pets:** Not Allowed. **Smoking:** Not Allowed. **Open:** Year-round.

➤ **If you come to Wheeler for the fishing and crabbing, you can launch your boat at the public launch or rent a boat and gear at either of the two main marinas.**

The hunters and fishers who used to stay at the Webfoot Motel wouldn't recognize the place. It's been transformed from basic lodging to a retreat with all the comforts. The lodge perched at the edge of Nehalem Bay is an example of the many changes taking place on the northern Oregon coast. Remodeled in 1989 and again in 1995, it is now neat and trim in gray and teal, with gabled roofs and flowers. Beside it is a 100-foot dock with moorage for guests, and kayak rentals are available.

All the rooms have queen-size beds, a refrigerator, microwave oven, and coffeemaker. Most have views of Neahkahnie Mountain, and six have whirlpool tubs. For the best bay and mountain views, book one of the three end rooms: Glory Suite, Sunset Room, and Honeymoon Room. They overlook Lazarus Island, where elk are often seen.

Wheeler is a small inland town from the ocean, nestled against a hill above Nehalem Bay. Next door to the lodge is a restaurant, Heron Café and Lounge. Across the street is Wheeler Market Place, a collection of shops selling antiques, gifts, and fabrics. Nina's is well known for its good pizza and pasta, and Treasure Café, a local favorite, serves breakfast until 3:00 P.M. and dinner in the summer months.

Wolf Creek

Wolf Creek Tavern

P.O. Box 97
Wolf Creek, OR 97497
541-866-2474

A country stage stop in southern Oregon

Innkeepers: Mike and Joi Carter. **Accommodations:** 8 rooms. **Rates:** $40 single, $55–$75 double, $15 for rollaway. **Minimum stay:** None. **Payment:** Major credit cards. **Children:** Welcome. **Pets:** Not allowed. **Smoking:** Discouraged. **Open:** Year-round.

➤ **Nearby, the ghost town of Golden has been revived as an example of an old mining town. Historic buildings include a quaint church with a graveyard.**

A hundred years ago, the overland route from Sacramento to Portland took six days by stagecoach. It was a hot and dusty (or cold and muddy) 710 miles, so inns along the way provided rest and refreshment. One of those inns was the Wolf Creek Tavern, 20 miles north of Grants Pass. The imposing, two-story stagecoach stop, built in the mid-1800s, is now owned by the state of Oregon and listed on the National Register of Historic Places, but it's still a haven for the weary traveler.

In its heyday, the inn served companies that carried freight and passengers; it took 500 horses, 28 coaches, and 30 wagons to maintain a regular schedule. Then, in 1887, the railroad came and the stagecoach rolled into history. The inn continued to operate, but over time it deteriorated until the state stepped in. By 1979, the tavern was restored, ready to open the doors of its white-pillared facade to guests once again.

The furnishings reflect the past, but the beds and baths are comfortably up to date. Five rooms have double beds, and three, twin beds. One tiny chamber is labeled as a "typical hotel room of the 1880s"; it's where Jack London stayed in 1911 and finished a story. Every room has a rocker and air conditioning, the latter a boon during southern Oregon's hot summers. Number 3, on the first floor, is wheelchair accessible, with a ramp, wide doors, handrails, and a shower seat.

Wolf Creek, a mile from I-5, is a truck stop, and the steady rumble of two-ton semis can disturb the nostalgic mood the inn attempts to create. To be assured of a quiet night's sleep, request a room away from the road.

Lunch, dinner, and breakfast in summer are offered in the restaurant. The dinner menu features fresh fish from the coast, prime rib on weekends, and a number of English specialties, such as Cornish pasties, shepherd's pie, and bangers. Cheesecakes and tortes are among the desserts.

After dinner, you can stroll on the lawn by the apple trees and roses. For yet more Victoriana, relax in the ladies' parlor, where gentility prevails among the marble-topped tables and curved-back chairs, or in the gentlemen's tap room, which still bears boot marks on the fireplace. The inn now has a gift shop selling hand-woven clothing and beaded jewelry.

Yachats

The Burd's Nest Inn

P.O. Box 261
664 Yachats River Road
Yachats, OR 97498
541-547-3683

A festive bed-and-breakfast home on the central coast

Innkeepers: Joni and Burd Bicksler. **Accommodations:** 2 rooms. **Rates:** $85–$90 double. **Included:** Full breakfast. **Minimum stay:** None. **Payment:** Master-Card, Visa. **Children:** Not appropriate. **Pets:** Not allowed. **Smoking:** Not allowed. **Open:** Year-round.

➤ **Good restaurants include La Serre, with an indoor garden setting, and the romantic Adobe Resort, which has an ocean view.**

From the rainbow of colors on its Spanish tile roof to the sequined sombreros on the dining room wall, Burd's Nest is full of delightful surprises. Reflecting its owners' personalities, the B&B is flamboyant, whimsical, lively, and welcoming — the sort of place where you are greeted as a friend and the hosts take your picture before you leave. But for all its sense of fun, guests never feel overwhelmed by attention. Joni is too savvy an innkeeper for that, making sure the guests have all the privacy they want.

The Bickslers, transplanted Californians, bought and restored the hillside stucco house in the late 1980s. It stands on 2 acres of landscaped gardens and trees within walking distance of downtown Yachats, the Yachats River, and the beach. Three creeks run through the property.

The living room shows the owners' many interests. Bent twig furniture stands by a marble fireplace with cat andirons; branches are hung with tiny birdhouses. Candles and cacti sit on the mantel. There's a spinning wheel in one corner, an antique baby carriage in another. A 48-star American flag covers a wall. It might seem like overdone clutter anywhere else; here, it's exuberance.

The guest rooms, on the second floor, have king-size beds and ocean views. Swallow's Nest has a 1930s theme, a bed in a lace-curtained alcove, and French doors leading to a shared balcony. Robin's Nest, with the same balcony, is furnished in country Spanish style; its shower is paved in Mexican tiles. Robes and hair dryers are provided.

The dining room holds more examples of an eclectic collection. A multi-colored tablecloth, wall hangings, a gold-painted stove, and a sideboard with Mexican pottery. The windows overlook camellias and a grove of tall firs. Joni prepares a baked dish for breakfast, along with muffins, fruit juice, and a treat such as baked apples with currants.

Staying at The Burd's Nest feels like a celebration, and that's how Joni and Burd, outgoing people who love life and vivid color, want you to feel. They'll suggest restaurants and activities, such as beachcombing, whale-watching, canoeing, hiking, fishing, and exploring the unhurried town of Yachats.

Sea Quest

95354 Highway 101
Yachats, OR 97498
541-547-3782
800-341-4878
seaquest@newportnet.com

> **A luxurious home facing the beach**

Innkeeper: Elaine Ireland. **Accommodations:** 5 rooms. **Rates:** $130–$170, single or double. **Included:** Full breakfast. **Minimum stay:** 2 nights on weekends, 3 nights on holiday weekends. **Payment:** MasterCard, Visa. **Children:** Not appropriate. **Pets:** Not allowed. **Smoking:** Not allowed. **Open:** Year-round.

> ➤ **The central coast is spectacular. At Cape Perpetua, walk the Trail of Restless Waters to see waves crashing against cliffs and spouting from fissures.**

On a grassy bluff facing the sand and sea, this lovely home is a good choice for anyone new to the bed-and-breakfast experience, for it offers the privacy of a hotel with the personal touch of a B&B. Each room has its own entrance, and guests have an entire floor to themselves. No one feels pressured to socialize, even at breakfast.

However, the exuberant hostess is available to visit if you wish. The Irelands occupy the second floor of the house and set out a buffet breakfast in their large, open living room. Quiche, pancakes, homemade granola, yogurt, and pastries are a few of the morning specialties that guests take to tables by the brick fireplace or out to the deck facing the beach.

Guests have their own book-filled sitting room with a TV, VCR, and games. The rooms, mostly in mauve and gray-green, have queen-size beds piled with pillows, and all but one have whirlpool tubs. Each has something unique. Twig room contains an interesting bent-twig bed, Brass room has a high brass bed and wicker couch; and Telescope room holds an impressively solid cannonball bed.

Seaquest is a few miles south of Yachats, near Tenmile Creek and the dramatic shoreline.

The See Vue

95590 Highway 101
Yachats, OR 97498
541-547-3227
Fax: 541-547-4726

A well-priced motel with personality

Innkeepers: Jean and Larry O'Hearn. **Accommodations:** 10 rooms, 1 suite. **Rates:** Summer, $42–$65 single or double; $6 additional person; winter, $35–$58. **Minimum stay:** 2 nights on weekends. **Payment:** Major credit cards. **Children:** Welcome. **Pets:** Allowed. **Smoking:** Nonsmoking rooms available. **Open:** Year-round.

➤ **Cape Perpetua was named by Captain Cook in 1778 on Saint Perpetua's Day. Markers explain facts of interest along the 4-mile trail to the summit.**

This little motel, on a bluff between Highway 101 and the ocean, offers inexpensive lodging, character, and charm. Behind its rustic-shake facade are individually decorated rooms, each with an ocean view. A lawn slopes to the edge of a bluff, where a path leads to the beach.

Rooms contain twin or double beds, some antiques, plants, books, and wine glasses. Six have kitchens and four have fireplaces.

In Salish Room you'll find a Northwest Indian motif, with murals by Judy Tallwing and a cedar carving of a blue heron. The Oriental has memorabilia of the Far East — a teapot and cups, a cricket cage, bamboo hangings. Princess and the Pea is a whimsical fantasy of wicker, musical instruments, old bronze, and a velvet headboard at the platform bed. Brass rubbings of a knight and his lady hang on the wall.

Granny's Room has a braided rug on the kitchen floor and a rocker in the bedroom, the Study is full of books, and Crow's Nest has a nautical theme and a second-story view.

The largest unit, Sea Rose Suite, has a bedroom, an alcove with a single bed, a loft, a kitchen-dining room, and a large family room with a double hide-a-bed. It's named for the sea rose agate, a stone found on the beach below.

Shamrock Lodgettes

P.O. Box 346
Yachats, OR 97498
541-547-3312
800-845-5028
Fax: 541-547-3843

A group of cabins and rooms on the ocean shore

Innkeepers: Bob and Mary Oxley. **Accommodations:** 6 cabins, 13 rooms. **Rates:** $71–$112, 2 to 4 people; $7 additional person; discounts for week-long stays. **Minimum stay:** 4 nights in cabins in summer. **Payment:** Major credit cards. **Children:** Welcome. **Pets:** Allowed in cabins if well behaved and housebroken. **Smoking:** Allowed.

➤ **Don't miss the dramatic view from Cape Perpetua, 800 feet above the shore, or Devil's Churn, a mass of restless ocean in a rock formation.**

Just south of the bridge in Yachats, 28 miles south of Newport and 25 miles north of Florence, 4 acres of parklike grounds provide a tranquil setting for these trim, rustic cabins and motel-style rooms. The oldest cabins, named for Oregon rivers (Alsea, Umpqua, Siletz, Siuslaw), date from 1952. Their thick log walls, wood floors, and stone fireplaces bespeak solidity, while updated comfort is promised by modern bathrooms, electric heat, and efficiency kitchens.

Four are one-bedroom cabins; two have two bedrooms. Siletz, the most expensive, holds up to eight people and has a broad ocean view. The newer, adjoining units have white walls, king-size beds, and views of the Yachats River or the ocean. Deluxe apartments have whirlpool tubs in the bathrooms. Fireplaces, TV, and phones are included in all the rooms.

The most recent addition is the hemlock and cedar spa, where you may relax in a sauna or tile hot tub, use the mirrored exercise room, or, by appointment, get a therapeutic massage. The lawns that slope to a low bluff above the sandy beach are kept in perfect condition and punctuated with groups of azaleas, rhododendrons, and ferns. Under the pine trees, a gray lawn swing offers a restful spot for gazing at the bay and beach while you listen to the chorus of song from scores of birds.

The Oxleys have owned the Shamrock Lodgettes since 1968. They spend time and effort on their guests' comfort; one expression of their hospitality is the newspaper placed on your doorstep each morning. Their office is full of information on the area, from tide tables to restaurant menus.

If you don't wish to cook every meal, try La Serre in Yachats, a restaurant with lots of glass and greenery. Its seafood, salads, and whole-wheat bread are excellent.

Ziggurat

95330 Highway 101
Yachats, OR 97498
541-547-3925

A terraced pyramid on the central coast

Innkeepers: Mary Lou Cavendish and Irv Tebor. **Accommodations:** 2 suites. **Rates:** $125–$140 single or double, $25 additional person. **Included:** Full breakfast. **Minimum stay:** 2 nights. **Payment:** Cash or check. **Children:** Over age 14, welcome. **Pets:** Not allowed. **Smoking:** Outdoors only. **Open:** Year-round..

➤ **The annual Smelt Fry in July is an old-fashioned celebration. Yachats also has an Arts and Crafts Fair in March and a Kite Festival in October.**

A four-story, zigzagging pyramid rises on the central Oregon coast, facing the Pacific just where Tenmile Creek runs into the ocean. It never fails to elicit comment, for Ziggurat is a unique 6,500-square-foot cedar and steel building with triangular windows and numerous decks.

The two suites, on the lower floor, have hand-crafted furniture, built-in bookcases, and a color scheme of silver and mauve.

Between the upper and lower floors are soaring white walls displaying modern art, a book-filled nook with a comfortable leather chair, and numerous windows with views of sea and sky. "It's like living in a sculpture," Irv says. Guests have the run of most of the house.

Breakfast is served at a marble table in the dining room. The meal may include oatmeal pancakes with fresh blueberries, a fruit plate, an omelet, and homemade bread.

Yamhill

Flying M Ranch

23029 Northwest Flying M Road
Yamhill, OR 97148
503-662-3222
Fax: 503-662-3202

A ranch resort in the country

Innkeepers: Barbara and Bryce Mitchell and family. **Accommodations:** 24 rooms and 8 cabins. **Rates:** Rooms: $60–$70 double; cabins (sleep up to 10): $75–$200. **Minimum stay:** None. **Payment:** Major credit cards. **Children:** Welcome. **Pets:** Allowed (must be leashed). **Smoking:** Nonsmoking rooms available. **Open:** Year-round.

➤ **Sign up for the overnight horseback ride to a log cabin on Trask Mountain; you'll be treated to a barbecue, entertainment, and breakfast before heading back.**

At the base of Trask Mountain in the Oregon Coast Range, where the North Yamhill River and Hanna Creek join, the Flying M sprawls over 600 acres on a broad meadow under fir trees, alders, and maples. The main lodge, a massive, gabled building of Douglas fir logs, stands on one bank of the curving river; the guest rooms (in the "Bunk House Motel") and cabins are on another bank several yards away. There are also more than 100 campsites.

Tennis courts and an enormous swimming pond (a block long, 200 feet wide) are on another part of the meadow, the stables are just over the fence, and a big chunk of the property is taken up by a private airstrip. A number of guests like to fly in for a meal or an overnight stay. (The ranch is a 1¼ hour drive from Portland.)

The large, high-ceilinged dining room is in a lodge with a history, though it was constructed in 1984. More than a century ago a hotel called Travelers Home stood on the grounds, a rest stop for wayfarers bound for the coast by horseback or stagecoach. The road from Yamhill to the Flying M closely follows the old stagecoach road and passes over the scene where the only stage holdup in the area occurred.

In 1922, Bryce's parents moved to the site. Bryce was born here, and he and his wife, Barbara, have lived on the property since 1957. The lodge they built was a popular rest stop until it burned down in 1983. Only the great stone fireplace remained, and the Mitchells constructed the present lodge around it. Skins and game trophies hang on the bleached-log walls of the dining room, saddles and antlers decorate the beams, and windows overlook the clear green river. Meals feature Pacific Northwest foods and a few exotic dishes such as buffalo and emu; several Oregon labels are on the wine list.

Sawtooth Lounge also has a view of the water. This is where guests gather around a bar made from a six-ton log and imbibe, listen to the music, and dance on weekends. There are meeting rooms and a gift shop, but it's the outside activity that is the big draw at the Flying M. The ranch has 45 horses, and wranglers lead daily rides into the canyon and up Trask Mountain. You can take breakfast, lunch, or overnight rides. Riders must be older than 8; for younger children there are ponies, which parents may lead on nearby trails.

The motel rooms are not large, but they have all the necessities, including one or two queen-size beds. Two have television. There is no air conditioning; however, it's cool under the trees. The better rooms are on the river side of the building. The cabins are furnished in a similar manner and decorated with a country flair. All but the Honeymoon Cabin have kitchens. The Honeymoon Cabin is very small but has a fireplace, a Jacuzzi, and a river view. Royal Hideout, by the side of the river, is the largest and sleeps ten in two bedrooms and a loft. The Wortman Cabin is the most secluded.

Washington

Best Intimate City Stops

Best Grand City Hotels

Best Country Inns and B&Bs

Best Inns and Cottages by the Sea

Seaview
   The Shelburne Inn, 445
   Sou'Wester Lodge, 446

Family Favorites

Cle Elum
   Hidden Valley Guest Ranch, 332
Leavenworth
   Haus Rohrbach, 357
Mount Baker
   The Logs at Canyon Creek, 376
Port Townsend
   Bishop Victorian Hotel, 401

Best Island Getaways

Bainbridge Island
   Bombay House, 322
Lopez Island
   Inn at Swifts Bay, 366
   MacKaye Harbor Inn, 369
Lummi Island
   West Shore Farm, 370
   The Willows Inn, 372
Orcas Island
   Chestnut Hill, 385
   Orcas Hotel, 386
   Rosario Resort, 388
   Spring Bay Inn, 389
   Turtleback Farm Inn, 390
San Juan Island
   Friday Harbor House, 417
   Hillside House Bed & Breakfast, 419
   Lonesome Cove, 420
   Olympic Lights, 421
   Roche Harbor Resort and Marina, 423
   Trumpeter Inn, 425
   Wharfside Bed & Breakfast, 427
Vashon Island
   Artist's Studio Loft B&B, 461
   Back Bay Inn, 464

Best on a Budget

Carson
Carson Hot Mineral Springs Resort, 329
Mount Rainier National Park
National Park Inn, 378
Sumas
Silver Lake Park Cabins, 457
Vashon Island
AYH Ranch Hostel, 462

Best Resorts

Blaine
The Inn at Semi-Ah-Moo, 327
Port Ludlow
Port Ludlow Resort & Conference Center, 398
Stevenson
Skamania Lodge, 456
Winthrop
Sun Mountain Lodge, 465

Best Romantic Hideaways

Greenbank
Guest House Bed & Breakfast Cottages, 344
Langley
Eagles Nest Inn, 352
The Garden Path Inn, 354
Leavenworth
Mountain Home Lodge, 358
Lopez Island
Inn at Swifts Bay, 366
Lopez Farm Cottages, 368
Olympia
Puget View Guesthouse, 383
Orcas Island
Chestnut Hill Inn, 385
Port Angeles
Domaine Madeleine, 392

San Juan Island
Westwinds Harmony Cottage, 426

Best Wilderness Retreats

Glenwood
The Flying L Ranch, 342
Mazama
Freestone Inn, 373
Mazama Country Inn, 375
Mount Rainier National Park
Paradise Inn, 379
Port Angeles
Lake Crescent Lodge, 394
Quinault
Lake Quinault Lodge, 414
Stehekin
Silver Bay Inn, 454

With a series of horn blasts, the white ferry backs from the wharf and heads across salty blue water toward the next island harbor, carrying its load of passengers and cars. The scent of creosote fades, gulls swoop and cry, and travelers swarm over the decks, exclaiming over the sharp peaks of the Olympic Mountains to the southwest, the snow-topped Cascades on the mainland to the east, and the green beauty of **Lopez Island, Orcas Island,** and **San Juan Island.**

From the islands, Puget Sound continues south, cutting deeply into the state and defining the eastern shore of the Olympic Peninsula. Much of the lush, green peninsula is occupied by the misty rain forests and snow-cloaked mountains of 1,400-square-mile Olympic National Park. On its north edge are the gateway city of **Port Angeles** and beguiling, old-fashioned **Port Townsend.**

In addition to the San Juans, Puget Sound holds **Whidbey Island** (the longest island in the U.S.), **Bainbridge Island,** and **Vashon Island,** all popular tourist destinations.

East of the sound, on the mainland, lies the most populated region of the state, with **Seattle** as its hub. It was the Alaska Gold Rush that turned Seattle into a metropolis at the turn of the century. Some $200 million in gold went through the city in a decade, and much of it stayed, creating a foundation for an international urban center. Now Seattle has industry, opera and ballet companies, museums, galleries, fine restaurants, major league sports, and the largest university in the Northwest.

The Evergreen State has three national parks, an active volcano (Mount St. Helens), 2,500 miles of shoreline, and the highest peak in the Cascade Range, **Mount Rainier** (14,410 feet). It's moist and mild in western Washington, but dry east of the Cascades. This is apple and wine country; farther east are the great grain fields. **Spokane** is the main eastern city, near the Idaho border.

Through the length of the state runs the Columbia River. Where it turns west, it forms the border of Oregon, then continues its stately flow to empty into the ocean near the Long Beach Peninsula. **Seaview** and Long Beach are old resort communities on the peninsula by Willapa Bay.

North Cascades National Park is the place to go for pure, unspoiled wilderness. It has vast avalanche slopes, pristine lakes, wildlife, and forests, bordered by small communities like **Mazama** and **Winthrop,** which cater to hikers and skiers.

For more information on Washington, write to the Washington State Tourism Development Division, 101 General Administration Building AX-13, Olympia, WA 98504 (phone: 360-586-2088, 360-586-2102, or 800-544-1800).

Anacortes

The Majestic Hotel

419 Commercial Avenue
Anacortes, WA 98221
360-293-3355
800-588-4780 (reservations only)
Fax: 360-293-5214

A contemporary hotel with Old World details

Owners: Jeff and Virginia Wetmore. **Accommodations:** 23 rooms. **Rates:** $98–$215 single or double, $15 additional person; reduced in winter. **Included:** Continental breakfast. **Minimum stay:** None. **Payment:** Major credit cards. **Children:** Under age 4, free. **Pets:** Not allowed. **Smoking:** Nonsmoking rooms available. **Open:** Year-round.

➤ **Cranberry Lake and Lake Campbell, near Anacortes, are good fishing and swimming spots. Cranberry has nine trails for hiking, biking, and riding.**

This little gem of charm and warmth is in the heart of the historic downtown district. A former logging town on Fidalgo Island, connected by bridge to Whidbey Island in Puget Sound, Anacortes is best known as the ferry terminus to the San Juan Islands. But the area has more to offer: accessible parks with forest, lakes, and mountains; five marinas with more than 2,000 moorage slips; an old-fashioned narrow-gauge steam train; and a few good restaurants. Cap Sante, a bluff at the eastern edge of the city, is a vantage point for views of the area.

The Majestic, a remodeled 1889 building that was once a store, opened in 1990 as a top-quality hotel for business travelers, honeymooners, or anyone looking for a special getaway. High ceilings and windows create a light, open lobby, enhanced by pale peach walls and faux marble columns. A curving staircase leads to the mezzanine, where a buffet of croissants and coffee is set out in the morning.

Off the lobby, through doors of stained glass, is the sophisticated dining room, where tall, many-paned windows overlook a fenced flower garden. The menu features fresh, contemporary northwestern cuisine with a Pacific Rim influence. More casual is the Salmon Run bistro, around the corner by the Rose & Crown bar. The Rose & Crown has an English theme with dark woods, a brass rail, and stained glass, part of the owners' collection of antiques.

The room comforts are up to date: Laura Ashley and Ralph Lauren fabrics and designs, coffeemakers, wet bars, and tile or marble bathrooms. No two rooms are alike, though each has a warm, comfortable atmosphere.

There are eight Majestic Suites. Those on the fourth floor have oversize soaking tubs and balconies with views of the town, the channel and boat marina, and Guemes Island. Roomy sitting areas have a TV with HBO. One suite has an Oriental motif, with red and black lacquered furnishings and carvings from a Ming Dynasty temple. The honeymoon suite, in shades of blue, is furnished in white wicker with a king-size bed.

On the second floor there's a small library with dark mahogany woodwork and bookshelves behind etched glass. To see the view from the highest indoor point in Anacortes, climb to the hotel's cupola, which rises above the atrium and its stained glass skylight.

Ashford

Alexander's Country Inn

37515 State Road 706
East Ashford, WA 98304
360-569-2300
800-654-7615
Fax: 360-569-2323

| An early-20th-century inn with country charm |

Manager: Melinda Simpson. **Accommodations:** 12 rooms. **Rates:** Summer, $89–$135; winter, $59–$75; $15 additional person. **Included:** Full breakfast. **Minimum stay:** None. **Payment:** MasterCard, Visa. **Children:** Welcome. **Pets:** Not allowed. **Smoking:** Not allowed. **Open:** Year-round.

➤ **Apart from the inn are two houses, Forest House and Chalet. Each, sleeping up to 8, has three bedrooms, a kitchen, and forest views. One has a fireplace.**

Built in 1912 as an outgrowth of Alexander Mesler's 1892 homestead, this hotel is the oldest structure in the Mount Rainier area. As the Mesler Inn, it took in summer guests for years, including Presidents Theodore Roosevelt and William Howard Taft. But as the decades passed, the inn fell slowly into disrepair.

Under new ownership in the 1970s, renovation began on the distinctive landmark, famous for its big water wheel and octagonal tower. By 1984 it was completely restored as a classic country inn.

The third-floor Tower Room suite is unusual, with a steep, narrow staircase leading to a sitting room with white wicker and an antique armoire. One suite has a king-size bed; the others have queens, many with handmade patchwork quilts. All the rooms have private baths; two are across the hall from the room.

Alexander's has a gift shop and is also a notable restaurant; many visitors to Mount Rainier wouldn't dream of passing up the restaurant's wild blackberry pie. Specialties are rainbow trout caught in the inn's own trout ponds (catch your own, if you wish), breads and desserts baked on the premises, and a list of 40 wines. In winter, the restaurant is open only on weekends except for the guests' breakfast. The old-fashioned country breakfast may include blueberry pancakes, ham and eggs, or French toast, served in the dining room by the big stone fireplace. In the evening, complimentary wine is offered in the upstairs parlor.

The southwest entrance to Mount Rainier National Park is only a mile from the inn. You are always aware of the lofty mountain; at 14,410 feet, it is the rooftop of the Northwest and can be seen for many miles. Its glaciers never melt, and the winter snowfall is prodigious. In summer, alpine meadows explode with the color of wildflowers. Hiking trails meander through ancient forest of Douglas fir, red cedar, and western hemlock. Rainier's magnificence has been praised in a thousand ways, and every one of them is right.

Bainbridge Island

The Beach Cottage

5831 Ward Avenue N.E.
Bainbridge Island, WA 98110
206-842-6081

| **Waterfront cottages on an island bay** |

Proprietors: Robert and Diane Meyer. **Accommodations:** 4 cottages. **Rates:** Summer, $115–$135; winter, $95–$115 single or double; $20 additional person. **Included:** Full breakfast. **Minimum stay:** None. **Payment:** Major credit cards. **Children:** Over age 16, welcome. **Pets:** Not allowed. **Smoking:** Outdoors only. **Open:** Year-round.

➤   **You can dock your own boat in front of the cottages, or you may borrow one to row across the bay for lunch.**

The Beach Cottage began in the early 1980s with a remodeled 80-year-old cabin on the waterfront, 4 miles from the town of Bainbridge. Since then, three more small houses have been redone as part of a complex of terraced gardens with paths and a trickling stream winding among them.

Each cottage has a private deck and a view of the marina, the Olympic Mountains, or the Seattle skyline. There's also a large, shared deck above the water, a good spot for a barbecue. If you are planning to cook, bring your own groceries (you can buy them in Bainbridge); the cottages are stocked with staples. When you arrive, you'll find breakfast ingredients in the refrigerator, the fire lit, and music playing.

Up the hill, at the top of the waterfall, is the Loft, a cottage that sleeps four people. Pilot House, with two bedrooms, also sleeps four. The Galley, with one bedroom, is directly off the main deck. The original cottage, once a fishnet shed on pilings, is the smallest, perfect for honeymooners.

All the cottages have fireplaces, queen-size beds, well-equipped kitchens, TV, and stereo.

Bombay House

8490 Northeast Beck Road
Bainbridge Island, WA 98110
206-842-3926
800-598-3926

| A country home with a water view |

Innkeepers: Bunny Cameron and Roger Kanchuk. **Accommodations:** 5 rooms (3 with private bath). **Rates:** Summer, $59–$149; less in winter. **Included:** Expanded Continental breakfast. **Minimum stay:** 2 nights on weekends. **Payment:** Major credit cards. **Children:** Age 6 and older, welcome. **Pets:** Not allowed. **Smoking:** Restricted. **Open:** Year-round.

➤ **Just a half-hour ferry ride from Seattle, Bombay House seems eons away. All you hear are birds and an occasional rooster crow.**

This bed-and-breakfast home, built in 1907 by a shipbuilder, occupies a sloping half-acre above Rich Passage, on the southwestern side of Bainbridge Island. From the shaded lawn, lush flower garden, and wide verandah, you can watch the ferries and pleasure boats sail through the passage while you sip lemonade or iced tea flavored with lemon balm out of the garden.

The house is roomy and light, with country antiques and Alaskan art collected by Bunny and Roger during their catering days in Anchorage. The guest rooms all have views of the lovely grounds or the sea. The names describe them: Red Room has boysenberry walls, Morning Room is flooded with sun against yellow walls in the morning, Crow's Nest is small and cozy. The largest is Captain's Room, formerly the master bedroom. A carved bed and futon rest on dark green carpeting, and a paddle fan keeps the room cool. Even with an old parlor stove ("Very Hot Beast"), chests, a table, and chairs, the room is not crowded. A clawfoot tub with shower is behind louvered doors.

Breakfast features homemade pastries and jams, fruit, cereal, and muffins. Hors d'oeuvres are sometimes served in the evenings. Christmas guests receive fruit baskets, and if you're celebrating an anniversary, Bunny likes to prepare a wine and cheese basket.

A tasteful, bright decor and personal touches such as fresh flowers and fluffy robes make the inn a cheerful place to be anytime of the year. In spring and summer, the garden is at its best, profuse with red rhododendron, purple wisteria, roses, California poppies, and bright blue bachelor buttons.

You are unlikely to tire of the view from the rustic stone and log gazebo under the fruit and pine trees, but if you decide to see more of the island, you'll find a couple of parks, one with great views of the Seattle skyline, some nice places to eat in the village, and peaceful country roads leading to farms and summer homes.

Bellingham

The Castle

1103 15th Street
Bellingham, WA 98225
360-676-0974

A hilltop mansion filled with antiques

Innkeepers: Larry and Glo Harriman. **Accommodations:** 3 rooms (1 with private bath). **Rates:** $45 single, $75–$95 double. **Included:** Expanded Continental breakfast. **Minimum stay:** None. **Payment:** MasterCard, Visa. **Children:** Age 12 and older, welcome. **Pets:** Not allowed. **Smoking:** Not allowed. **Open:** Year-round.

➤　**The Whatcom Museum of History and Art has regional history exhibits and northwestern art. It's in a stately building (1889) that was once the city hall.**

You will never see another bed-and-breakfast quite like The Castle, a mauve Victorian home on a hill in Bellingham's historic Fairhaven district. From the outside it looks imposing and a bit eccentric, but that's nothing compared with what you encounter inside. It will thrill you or give you nightmares, depending on your attitude toward ornate old houses.

Larry and Glo, the owners of Lar-Glo Antiques, have been dealing in antiques for many years and have furnished The Castle with a collection dating from the 16th century. A few examples are numerous dark, heavy, elaborately carved cabinets from Germany and Scandinavia; a gold dust-filled, Steuben-style French chandelier; Austrian porcelain figures; carved swan plant holders; a gilded French chandelier with art glass; William and Mary chairs; and an 18th-century French hall tree. There are early electric lamps, clocks, cupids, mannequins in period costumes, and much more. And that's just the first floor.

There are six guest rooms, but only three are occupied at a time. The Folk Art Room contains a museum-quality collection of South American, Indian, and Mexican artifacts, while beaded bags and old dolls are displayed in another. The Cupola Room is a lavish, red-carpeted suite with a queen-size bed in the cupola and the usual amazing assortment of antiques. The large bathroom has double-facing sinks, a tub with a pressed metal shield, and mullioned windows.

Up on the third floor, a huge hand-painted mural, *Spirits of Wardner's Castle,* depicts some of the home's history and people, particularly James Wardner, who built the place in 1890. Wardner was a speculator who made and lost fortunes in mining and real estate and offbeat schemes, such a as a black cat fur farm. Despite its museum atmosphere, The Castle is not gloomy. Light streams through the stained glass windows and sun porch, from which you can see Bellingham Bay and the mountains. The beds are modern, and breakfast, served by candlelight, is a healthful assortment of fruit and yogurt, rolls, granola, and cheese.

There's a gift shop on the premises.

Schnauzer Crossing

4421 Lakeway Drive
Bellingham, WA 98226
360-733-0055
800-562-2808
Fax: 360-734-2808
schnauzerX@aol.com

A modern home with a view of the lake

Innkeepers: Donna and Vermont McAllister. **Accommodations:** 2 rooms and 1 cottage (all with private bath). **Rates:** $115–$190 double, $25 additional person (child, $10). **Included:** Full breakfast. **Minimum stay:** 2 nights on weekends and holidays. **Payment:** MasterCard, Visa. **Children:** Welcome (crib and futon available). **Pets:** Not allowed. **Smoking:** Not allowed. **Open:** Year-round.

➤ **Nearby are the outdoor sculpture collection at Western Washington University, the Sehome Hill Arboretum, and Fairhaven Historical District.**

Visiting the McAllisters is like a reunion with old friends — the ones who have a home at the lake. Donna is a natural hostess with a sure sense of her guests' needs, and she goes out of her way to be sure they feel welcome. Vermont, a physician, leaves the innkeeping to Donna, but you're likely to find him deep in a discussion with visitors at the breakfast table when it's time for him to leave for the office. Both of the McAllisters, as well as their three sons, enjoy people and sharing their life on the shores of Lake Whatcom, southeast of Bellingham.

The contemporary cedar-sided home is not directly on the lake; it does have views of the water, and public access and boat launches are nearby. From the front room's big windows, which reach to a dramatic cathedral ceiling, you can see the lawns and gardens, trees, glimpses of homes on the shore, and beyond to the blue lake.

The living room is a sunny, inviting space, with rattan couches on champagne plush carpeting, orchids on the coffee table, and canaries singing in their cages. A metal sculpture of mountains and fir trees, an abstract version of the Northwest environment, hangs on one wall.

More windows angle up the walls of the dining area, where guests are served breakfast on crystal and china. On a typical morning, Donna prepares individual quiches and fresh fruit skewers, along with her special bran and blueberry Schnauzer Crossing muffins. Conversations are lively as guests discuss their plans for the day.

The commodious rooms have such welcome extras as down comforters, clock radios, flowers, candies, and such toiletries as hand creams, razors, and sewing kits. Robes hang in the closets. Queen Room, with an iris theme, overlooks Lake Whatcom, while Garden Suite views trees and greenery. Garden Suite is a good choice for a family; there is a futon in the sun room as well as a telephone, TV, brick fireplace, and separate entrance. The luxurious bath has a whirlpool tub and double-headed shower.

The cottage, one large room overlooking the lake, offers total privacy under 100-foot cedar trees. It has skylights, a Jacuzzi, a microwave, a wet bar, and a deck.

The McAllisters have two beloved schnauzers, hence the name of their B&B.

Blaine

The Inn at Semi-Ah-Moo

9565 Semi-Ah-Moo Parkway
Blaine, WA 98230
360-371-2000
800-770-7992
Fax: 360-371-5490

| **A top resort on** |
| **Washington's north border** |

Manager: Bruce Wenger. **Accommodations:** 198 rooms. **Rates:** Rooms, $189–$419; suites, $209–$499; varies seasonally. **Minimum stay:** None. **Payment:** Major credit cards. **Children:** Under age 18, free with a parent. **Pets:** Allowed ($50). **Smoking:** Nonsmoking rooms available. **Open:** Year-round.

➤ **Miles of walking, biking, and jogging paths wind through the Semi-Ah-Moo property; 5 miles of beaches invite beachcombing and bird-watching.**

This resort, on a sandspit across Drayton Harbor from downtown Blaine, is within view of Peace Arch Park, right at the Canadian border. You can see the Gulf Islands and Vancouver Island across the Strait of Georgia and, at night, the lights of White Rock, B.C.

Mile-long Semi-Ah-Moo Spit, 110 miles north of Seattle, is named for the Salish Indian tribe that lived here for 3,000 years. From the late 1800s until the 1970s, the cannery business boomed. The spit was both a major salmon packing center and a winter anchorage for the fishing vessels. Many of the old cannery buildings have been refurbished for use by the resort. The former boiler room, for example, is now the bakery.

Semi-Ah-Moo is both a condominium development and vacation lodging. The inn's design emphasizes the human scale with a pastel exterior, dormers, angles, many windows, and hallways with alcoves. There's a full spa and a 30,000-square-foot health club that is nothing short of spectacular, with indoor and outdoor tennis courts and pools, a weight room featuring the latest equipment, a padded running track, and squash and racquetball courts. There are steam rooms, sauna, hot tubs, and tanning booths. Many visitors come to Semi-Ah-Moo just for the athletic complex.

Others come for the conference facilities, while the third big draw is the golf course. The 18-hole course, designed by Arnold

Palmer, curves up the hill from a forest of hemlock, fir, and cedar, its sandtraps pure white sand and its fairways 100 percent bent-grass.

Boaters like the 300-slip marina, where yacht maintenance and haulout are available. You can fish nearby for halibut, cod, and salmon and, in spring and fall, fly-fish for sea-run cutthroat trout from the beach at Semi-Ah-Moo Park.

The guest rooms are tastefully furnished in a contemporary mood, with pine woodwork, plush chairs, sizable beds, and TVs hidden in pine wall cabinets. Most of the rooms have views of Mount Baker, and 37 have fireplaces. The bathrooms have big fluffy towels and complimentary toiletries. You can request the view you want: the water or the courtyard.

There are three dining spots: Stars offers a waterfront view and fresh seafood; Pierside specializes in pizza, pasta, and salads; and Packers Lounge serves lunch and dinner daily. Adjacent to Packers is the Oyster Bar.

Carson

Carson Hot Mineral Springs Resort

P.O. Box 370
Carson, WA 98610
509-427-8292

Simple lodgings and hot mineral baths

Innkeeper: Helen Hegawald. **Accommodations:** 9 hotel rooms (shared baths), 14 cabins, 1 suite. **Rates:** Rooms, $37.45; cabins, $53.50; suite, $107. **Minimum stay:** None. **Payment:** MasterCard, Visa. **Children:** Welcome. **Pets:** Not allowed. **Smoking:** Not allowed. **Open:** Year-round except Christmas Day.

➤ **An 18-hole golf course has been added, but the resort's casual, simple atmosphere remains unchanged.**

Nobody comes to Carson for luxurious guest rooms. You are given a plain metal bed, a dresser, a mirror, and towels. The lavatories (one for men, one for women) are down the hall, and the showers are in the mineral bath house. The cabins are similar, though they also have tables, and two have cooking facilities. The luxury at this hotel lies in its bathhouse. After a blissful soak in hot mineral water and perhaps a soothing massage, you understand why this out-of-the-way hotel on the Wind River in the Columbia River Gorge has so many devotees.

The hot springs were discovered in 1876 and quickly became a popular gathering place, with people arriving on horseback and by wagon and steamboat. The three-story hotel and a general store were built in 1897 by Isadore St. Martin, who was very proud of the quality of the mineral water on his property. (Pride proved his undoing, as he was killed during an argument about the water.) The cabins were added in the early 1920s.

The mineral water, pumped from a natural spring, pours into old-fashioned clawfoot tubs at 126 degrees and is cooled for comfortable bathing. Some people swear that the water, rich in sodium, calcium sulfate, and other minerals, has health benefits; there's no doubt that it is relaxing. By the time you've concluded your soak, sweat, and massage experience, you'll be limp but utterly refreshed and ready for a cool drink and hearty meal at the hotel restaurant.

If you stay in the suite, you can enjoy a mineral water bath in your own hot tub. The suite, which sleeps six, has two bedrooms, a sofa bed, and a kitchen.

Cashmere

Cashmere Country Inn

5801 Pioneer Avenue
Cashmere, WA 98815
509-782-4212
800-291-9144

| **A classic farmhouse in apple country** |

Innkeepers: Patti and Dale Swanson. **Accommodations:** 5 rooms. **Rates:** $75–$80. **Included:** Full breakfast. **Minimum stay:** 2 nights on weekends and holidays. **Payment:** Major credit cards. **Children:** Not appropriate. **Pets:** Not allowed. **Smoking:** Not allowed. **Open:** Year-round.

➤ **In the fall, when the apples are ripe, the innkeepers hold an Apple Cider Pressing Party.**

In the heart of Washington's apple-growing country, this 1907 farmhouse offers comfort and hospitality. Behind the white picket fence are pretty gardens and, on one side of the property, an orchard. In back are the swimming pool and hot tub. When you arrive, Patti and Dale will offer tea or lemonade and invite you to enjoy the pool, play croquet, relax by the fireplace in the living room, or, if you're ready to explore, direct you to the area's attractions (don't miss the carefully restored Pioneer Village).

The guest rooms are furnished with taste, and all have queen-size beds. Most are upstairs; only the Yellow Room is on the main floor. In the blue and white Floral Room, botanical prints hang on the wall. This is the least expensive room; the bath, which has a clawfoot tub and shower, is across the hall. There are no phones or TV in the rooms, but a phone for guests' use is downstairs. Rooms are air-conditioned and have ceiling paddle fans.

Breakfast is served in a charming, sunny nook off the kitchen or on the patio by the pool. Patti is noted for her good cooking and in fact has published a book of her best-loved recipes. A sample breakfast might be fruit, baked eggs with ham and mushrooms, country potatoes, and strawberry rhubarb muffins with cinnamon butter.

Cashmere isn't known for its great dining spots, but there are several restaurants in nearby Wenatchee. If you like Italian food, Patti suggests Visconti's.

Chelan

Whaley Mansion

415 Third Street
Chelan, WA 98816
509-682-5735
800-729-2408 in U.S.
Fax: 509-682-5385

A hospitable B&B close to Lake Chelan

Innkeepers: Mary Kay Addis and Carol Addison. **Accommodations:** 6 rooms. **Rates:** Summer and holidays, $115–$135; winter, $85–$105. **Included:** Full breakfast. **Minimum stay:** None. **Payment:** Major credit cards. **Children:** Unable to accommodate. **Pets:** Not allowed. **Smoking:** Not allowed. **Open:** Year-round.

➤ **For a good meal, the innkeepers recommend Campbell's restaurant.**

The white frame house with pink awnings stands decorously behind its lawn and flower beds, giving no hint of the treasures within. While it doesn't have its former lacy extravagance, the Whaley Mansion still has a romantic atmosphere.

The guest rooms are furnished with white iron and brass queen-size beds, white quilts with flounces, and walls of mirrors. Some overlook Lake Chelan. In the Bridal Suite, there are taffeta boudoir chairs, a silk-covered ceiling, and satin sheets on a king-size brass bed. The little library on the second floor contains books, a TV, and a selection of movies for the VCRs in every room.

Breakfast, presented with a flourish in the dining room, begins with hand-dipped chocolates, Mary Kay's specialty. ("You'd be amazed at how many people stop refusing chocolates for breakfast once they've tasted these," she says.) Then comes fruit sorbet, crumpets with homemade nectarine jam, egg-stuffed artichokes with shrimp, and flaky croissants — a typical meal.

The heart of the place is its ebullient owner, who greets guests with a hug and tells stories of the Whaleys, who lived here from 1911 to 1975. She'll sing, too — and to hear Mary Kay's rendition of "Five-Foot-Two," accompanied by player piano, is worth the price of the room. She and Carol are glad to supply information on the area, from cruising Lake Chelan to hiking in the backcountry of the North Cascades. The blue eyes twinkle behind heart-shaped glasses as she says, "We're former moms. We know how to take care of people."

Cle Elum

Hidden Valley Guest Ranch

3942 Hidden Valley Road
Cle Elum, WA 98922
509-857-2344
509-857-2322
800-526-9269
Fax: 509-857-2130

| **A family ranch with Old West flavor** |

Innkeepers: Bruce and Matt Coe. **Accommodations:** 14 cabins. **Rates:** $89–$99 per adult, $50 ages 6–12, $25 ages 3–5; discounts for longer stays. **Included:** All meals. **Minimum stay:** 2 nights on weekends and in summer. **Payment:** MasterCard, Visa. **Children:** Under age 3, free. **Pets:** Not allowed. **Smoking:** Allowed. **Open:** Year-round.

➤ **Hiking, bird-watching, and fishing in Swauk Creek are popular in the summer; in winter, skiers come for the peace and solitude of the snowy woods.**

The winding gravel road off the highway north of Cle Elum, in central Washington, goes over hill and dale, past forest and pasture, horses, deer, and meadows for 3 miles, until you come to high gateposts topped with a saddle. You have reached Hidden Valley, just outside the southern end of Wenatchee National Forest, the hilltop site of a delightful guest ranch.

At the turn of the century the property belonged to a homesteader. The apple trees he planted still bloom white and pink in spring and bear fruit in autumn, and the artesian well he dug provides "the purest, sweetest water you'll ever taste," according to Bruce Coe, whose family now owns the ranch.

Cabins of log and rough-hewn lumber are scattered through the orchard and dandelion-dotted pasture. Three are housekeeping units, useful for groups and families. All are solid, with tongue-and-groove construction, and a bit worn, as befits a western ranch. Most have sweeping views of the valley. Horseshoe pegs, wagon wheel bedsteads, branding irons, and rawhide chairs add to the Old West atmosphere, though the bathrooms are basic and modern, with showers. The bath in Hilltop Cabin is a little different, with a blue tile soaking tub and a window overlooking the valley. This cabin is the only one with a fireplace, but the others do not really miss it, as most guests prefer to gather in the recreation lounge or dining room.

In the big cedar lodge, a fire is usually burning in the hearth; there's often a pool or table tennis game or singalong in progress and always plenty of conversation. For quieter moments, seven shelves of books await readers.

Outside, stone steps lead to a swimming pool, and the cooking pit nearby is a reminder that Saturday is barbecue night. The food is plentiful — "good, hearty, American cooking," Bruce says. The day may start with ham or sausage and eggs, fruit, and beer pancakes. Dinner might be chicken, ribs, or beef roast, with produce from Yakima Valley and cheesecake or cherry cobbler for dessert. It's all serve-yourself, and coming back for second or third helpings is only good manners. Wine and beer are available.

The clang of a triangle means mealtime or riding time. Lean and lanky Matt, Bruce's brother, leads daily horseback trips into the wilderness ($25 for 1d hours). Children must be at least 6 to ride.

Concrete

Cascade Mountain Inn

3840 Pioneer Lane
Concrete-Birdsview, WA 98237
360-826-4333

**A B&B close to the
mountain wilderness**

Innkeepers: Ingrid and Gerhard Meyer. **Accommodations:** 6 rooms (all with private bath). **Rates:** $75 single, $89–$110 double, $28 additional person. **Included:** Full breakfast. **Minimum stay:** None. **Payment:** MasterCard, Visa. **Children:** Over age 12, welcome. **Pets:** Not allowed. **Smoking:** Not allowed. **Open:** Year-round.

➤   **The inn can be a jumping-off point for North Cascades National Park, Mount Baker, Ross Lake, and the North Cascades Pass ski and wilderness areas.**

When you visit this corner of Washington in the North Cascades foothills, some 2 hours north of Seattle, bring your camera and binoculars. You're almost sure to see bald eagles, especially if you come in winter, when the eagles arrive to feed on Skagit River salmon.

Ingrid and Gerhard say they never tire of watching the birds. This bit of the Northwest was their retirement choice when they left their native Germany, built this country inn, and decorated it with treasures from their world travels. The Scotland Room, which catches the morning sun, offers touches of the Highlands — a tartan comforter, heather, and prints of Scottish scenes. In a soft pink and cream setting, the German Room features eiderdown quilts and pillows brought from home and porcelain plates recounting the Grimm brothers' fairy tales.

A "Grandmother's Flower Garden" quilt on an Eastlake bed and vintage Norman Rockwell plates proved atmosphere in the American Room. From the window, you see the late afternoon sun reflected on Sauk Mountain and a meadow that is often filled with woolly sheep.

Hand-crafted artifacts from Peru fill the Peruvian Room, which has twin beds, while the large Philippine Room in the sunset corner is decorated with shells, bamboo plants, and paintings of native life. In a separate suite, the Studio has its own entrance and cozy sitting area along with a kitchenette. The story of Bremen, the Meyers' home, is illustrated in pictures and tiles.

A full breakfast is served in the breakfast room or, weather permitting, on the patio, which faces the lawn and meadow. You may arrange with Ingrid in advance for a picnic basket.

Coupeville

The Captain Whidbey Inn

2072 W. Captain Whidbey Inn Rd.
Coupeville, WA 98239
360-678-4097
800-366-4097
Fax: 360-678-4110

A historic log inn on Penn Cove

Innkeeper: John Stone. **Accommodations:** 12 lodge rooms (2 shared baths), 13 lagoon rooms, and 3 cottages. **Rates:** $85–$195 single, $95–$105 double, $15 additional person. **Included:** Full breakfast. **Minimum stay:** 2 nights on weekends, 3 nights on holidays. **Payment:** Major credit cards. **Children:** Welcome. **Pets:** Not allowed. **Smoking:** Not allowed in lodge. **Open:** Year-round.

➤ **For a leisurely sail, charter John Stone's boat, the *Cutty Sark*. John also offers six-day sailing trips around the San Juan Islands**

Accessible by both bridge and ferry, the Captain Whidbey Inn is a 90-minute drive north from Seattle, on the eastern shore of Whidbey Island. At the head of Penn Cove, it is north of Coupeville and near the center of the long, narrow island.

The rustic log inn has changed very little since it was built in 1907. Constructed of indigenous madrone, it looks as if it might be the weathered retreat of a retired sea captain. It was actually built as the centerpiece of Still's Park, a recreational complex designed by a circuit judge from Seattle, Lester Still. Small steamships brought turn-of-the-century guests to the resort; today's seafarers come in sloops and motorboats to the piers at Penn Cove.

The inn stands on a sweep of green lawn 50 feet from steps that lead down to a narrow beach. Several newer buildings are scattered over the grounds, but the original lodge bears the patina of a historic and beloved retreat. Vintage madrone logs, inside and out, have a time-worn polish. Old wine bottles hang from the ceiling in the lounge and the Chart Room, and bookshelves beckon from the landing.

From the dining room windows you can watch boats in the wide cove as you enjoy seafood and other regional foods. The house specialty is mussels. "Penn Cove is famous for its mussels," says John, "so we offer a special tribute to the mussel every January." The annual Mussel Festival features recipe and eating contests and an all-mussel dinner, among other events.

The guest rooms in the lodge are smaller than those in the newer sections and share single-sex baths. Twelve rooms have basins, however, and all are furnished with antiques and down comforters on the beds.

Nearby are cottages and the spacious, paneled Lagoon Rooms, which face Kennedy's Lagoon, in the north corner of Penn Cove. The cottages have cozy sitting rooms and fireplaces to ward off the evening chill, and most of them overlook the lagoon, the cove, and Saratoga Passage. Some can view the Cascade Mountains to the east, on the mainland.

Breakfast, served in the restaurant, features homemade rolls, fresh fruit, quiche, and trout amandine.

Deer Park

Love's

31317 North Cedar Road
Deer Park, WA 99006
509-276-6939
888-929-2999
Fax: 509-276-6939

> **A country home in eastern Washington**

Innkeepers: Bill and Leslie Love. **Accommodations:** 2 rooms (private baths). **Rates:** $75–$98 single or double. **Minimum stay:** None. **Payment:** MasterCard, Visa. **Children:** Welcome by arrangement. **Pets:** Welcome by arrangement. **Smoking:** Outdoors only. **Open:** Year-round.

➤ **Christmas is celebrated here in a big way: there's a craft show early in December, then the house displays six trees and thousands of outdoor lights.**

At first glance, this home in the countryside north of Spokane appears to be a carefully restored example of Victorian architecture, complete with a tower, wraparound porch, scalloped shingles, and fretwork. In fact, the Loves' bed-and-breakfast was built in 1986 after fire destroyed their log house. Its meticulous craftsmanship makes the reproduction extraordinary.

The gray house with mauve, plum, and white trim, stands on 5 acres of meadows, woodlands, and gardens. Artistic taste and nostalgia for Victorian romance are evident throughout, from the framed lace on the walls to the old-fashioned valentines under a glass tabletop. In the dining room, each lace-covered breakfast table for two is made from a sewing machine table. Breakfast, served on cut glass and china, might include a fruit compote with yogurt, sour cream blueberry pancakes, and ham and eggs.

Upstairs, the guest rooms have queen-size beds. Annie's Room holds family heirloom furniture and lacy curtains and pillows. The Turret Suite is beautifully decorated in English wallpaper and has a gas fireplace, a carved wooden bed, and a sitting area in the turret. The bath contains a thoughtful mix of romance and practicality: candles and bubble bath, a hair dryer and a curling iron.

There are three common rooms: a sun room, a parlor for reading and board games, and the Garden Room, which is often used for wedding receptions. It overlooks the English garden and apple trees. The charm, hospitality, and atmosphere at Love's make it popular for weddings, on the lawn or by the fireplace. The innkeepers view their home as a personal ministry but are not at all intrusive toward guests with different beliefs.

There's a lot to do in the area. You can hike, bicycle, go cross-country skiing, swim, fish, and go boating on a number of nearby lakes. In winter, when the pond near the house freezes, you can skate. For indoor entertainment, play Victorian games in the parlor or enjoy a relaxing hour in the hot tub.

Freeland

Cliff House

5440 Windmill Road
Freeland, WA 98249
360-331-1566

A contemporary home on Whidbey Island

Innkeepers: Peggy Moore and Walt O'Toole. **Accommodations:** 1 cottage, 1 house. **Rates:** House, $385 double, $485 for 2 couples; cottage, $165. **Included:** Continental breakfast. **Minimum stay:** 2 nights, except midweek in January, February, and December. **Payment:** Cash or check. **Children:** Over age 14, welcome. **Pets:** Not allowed. **Smoking:** Not allowed. **Open:** Year-round.

➤ **On a clear day, Mount Rainier and downtown Seattle are visible. Nearby, you may see whales and seals cavorting in the waves and eagles overhead.**

When you book this stunning home by the sea for a night, it's all yours. The centerpiece atrium filled with tall ferns and tropical plants, the stone fireplace, the kitchen with breakfast tucked in the refrigerator, the Indian and African artifacts, the hot tub on the deck — all are yours to enjoy. The owners are happy to visit, but the main feature here is privacy. Cliff House hides in near-total seclusion on 13 acres of Whidbey Island forestland.

Designed by Seattle architect Arne Bystrom and built in 1980, the glass and cedar shake house received the prestigious AIA award for design that year. It's easy to see why. Cliff House stands on a bluff 40 feet above the sea, facing southwest to the Olympic Mountains, its great glass walls taking full advantage of the view and light.

Poles support the inner structure, which is open to the peaked roof, and living spaces flow around the soaring, 30-foot glass atrium. Flagstones, Oriental carpets, primitive and contemporary art, and items from the owners' travels make an elegant, eclectic setting. A sunken living area has a fireplace and comfortable couch. The angular kitchen is fully equipped (but bring groceries for all meals except breakfast, which is ready for you in the refrigerator).

There are CDs, a television, and some 300 movies. An open staircase leads to a loft, where you can watch pleasure boats and freighters from the king-size feather bed.

The cottage, Seacliff, is set back among the trees. It's a charming hideaway, with roses painted around the door, a fireplace, a small kitchen, and a queen-size feather bed.

Gig Harbor

The Maritime Inn

3212 Harborview Drive
Gig Harbor, WA 98335
253-858-1818
Fax: 253-858-1817

| **A small inn near the harbor** |

Manager: Kathy Franklin. **Accommodations:** 15 rooms. **Rates:** Summer, $80–$115 single or double; $20 additional person; winter, $68–$98. **Included:** Continental breakfast. **Minimum stay:** None. **Payment:** Major credit cards. **Children:** Welcome. **Pets:** Not allowed. **Smoking:** Not allowed. **Open:** Year-round.

➤ **The inn is across the road from the public docks, where overnight moorage is available.**

This two-story hotel has some individual touches that make it a good choice if you want to be right in the heart of town and close to the picturesque harbor, where you can watch the fishing and pleasure boats, with forested hills and Mount Rainier behind them.

There's a small lobby with a fireplace and wingback chairs; beyond it is a well-lit hall leading to the guest rooms. The clean, tailored rooms hold queen-size beds and gas fireplaces with tile hearths. Some lack good reading lamps and towel hooks; otherwise they are very comfortable. There are five "specialty rooms," which have sports themes such as golf, polo, and boating.

For breakfast, you serve yourself from a tray of pastries and coffee set out on a hall table, and eat in your own room. There is plenty of parking in a large lot behind the hotel.

The Pillars Bed & Breakfast

6606 Soundview Drive
Gig Harbor, WA 98335
253-851-6644

| A stately B&B in a
waterfront town |

Innkeepers: Alma and Jim Boge. **Accommodations:** 3 rooms. **Rates:** $90 single, $120 double, $30 additional person. **Included:** Expanded Continental breakfast. **Minimum stay:** None. **Payment:** MasterCard, Visa. **Children:** Welcome by arrangement. **Pets:** Not allowed. **Smoking:** Not allowed. **Open:** Year-round.

➤　**This old fishing village has a picturesque waterfront, numerous boutiques and souvenir shops, cafés, and a good bookstore.**

Four tall, white pillars give this stately home its name. Built in 1965 as a southern-style mansion, it stands back from the road on a hillside overlooking Colvos Passage, in the far southwest curve of Puget Sound. It's a 10-minute walk from the boat harbor.

Inside, the gracious atmosphere continues with traditional furnishings, a tasteful decor, and immaculate rooms. Guests are welcome to play the piano in the living room or relax in plush chairs by the stone fireplace and watch TV or read. A cut-glass decanter of sherry rests on the coffee table.

From the foyer, where crystal chandeliers sparkle, you ascend wide stairs to the guest rooms. Each has a down-covered queen-size bed, extra pillows, a clock radio, and good reading lamps. Vashon Room boasts a sweeping view of Puget Sound and Vashon Island; Rainier Room faces the mountain and sound. The largest is Gazebo Room, a suite decorated in a soft green garden theme with white wicker and louvered shutters at windows that offer a glimpse of the gazebo in the back garden.

Alma and Jim Boge are skilled innkeepers, available to guests yet not intrusive. When you arrive, they'll greet you warmly, help carry your bags, and give you the key to the house; then you're on your own and probably won't see them again until breakfast.

Jim is a retired baker. He makes the sticky buns and other breads served with the meal. Cereal and fruit (and eggs on request) are also served. Over coffee, the Boges will recommend restaurants in town such as Marco's for Italian food and Tides Tavern, a lively spot for pizza and beer. They will invite you to swim in their indoor pool and relax in the hot tub, and they'll direct you to attractions such as Kopachuck State Park and the community summer theater.

Glenwood

The Flying L Ranch

25 Flying L Lane
Glenwood, WA 98619
509-364-3488

A wilderness ranch near Mount Adams

Innkeepers: Jacquie Perry and Jeff Berend. **Accommodations:** 6 rooms in lodge (3 with private bath), 5 rooms in guest house, 2 cabins. **Rates:** Rooms, $70–$110 double; $10 additional person; cabins, $110–$120; group and weekly rates available. **Included:** Full breakfast. **Minimum stay:** 2 nights in cabins; 2 nights on weekends, and in summer in lodge and guest house. **Payment:** Major credit cards. **Children:** Welcome. **Pets:** Allowed by arrangement. **Smoking:** Not allowed. **Open:** Year-round.

➤   **Guided mountain hikes on Mount Adams are available.**

Mount Adams, in south-central Washington, is famous for its meadows of wildflowers, huckleberry fields, and hiking and cross-country ski trails. The Flying L sits at the foot of the mountain on 160 acres of woods and fields. The ranch has welcomed visitors to the area since 1957, when the Lloyd family opened it. Now under new ownership, it still offers workshops, retreats, and summer hiking packages. Cross-country skiers can glide over 3 miles of groomed trails, while more challenging trails can be found just north of the property. Bicycles are available. There's an outdoor spa as well.

The guest rooms in the 3,000-square-foot lodge have a western theme. Two have queen-size beds, one has twin beds, and the rest are doubles. All share a common kitchen, which has been stocked with staples such as coffee, sugar, and spices.

In the two-story Guest House, the rooms are named for noted westerners, such as Will Rogers, Yakima Canutt, who trained horses for the movies, and Jackson Sundown, a Nez Perce champion saddle bronco rider. The Mount Adams Suite is a good family choice; it sleeps up to five people in cheery yellow and apricot rooms. There's a woodstove, a rattan couch covered with a bright Mexican throw, and sliding glass doors to the balcony shared with other rooms.

The cabins in the woods are geared to light housekeeping, with woodstoves, kitchens, and twin and double beds. Cooking facilities are available, or you can come to the cookhouse for a breakfast of fruit, hotcakes, bran muffins, and a baked egg casserole, while you meet the other guests and learn about the ranch's history.

Artists like the Flying L for its numerous workshops in watercolors, oils, and other media. Classes are held in the big room in the main lodge. In this room, guests like to sit by the fire and visit, play games, or browse through dozens of books on art and the West.

Greenbank

Guest House Bed and Breakfast Cottages

3366 South Highway 525
Greenbank, WA 98253
360-678-3115

| **A romantic island hideaway** |

Innkeepers: Mary Jane and Don Creger. **Accommodations:** 5 cottages, 1 log lodge, and a farmhouse suite. **Rates:** $110–$285. **Minimum stay:** 2 nights on weekends. **Included:** Full breakfast. **Payment:** Major credit cards. **Children:** Not appropriate. **Pets:** Not allowed. **Smoking:** Outdoors only. **Open:** Year-round.

➤ **Guests can use the pool, hot tub, exercise room, and picnic area and play horseshoes or badminton. All the rooms have VCRs, and movies are free.**

On Whidbey Island, north of Seattle, this inn is for people seeking solitude. A large freshwater pond — the home of waterfowl, wild-life, and musical frogs — dominates the nearly 25 acres surrounding the idyllic retreat.

You can take a suite in the farmhouse, which is furnished in 1920s style but has a TV and Jacuzzi, or one of the charming cottages. Farm Guest Cottage is a knotty pine haven with a deck for lounging or watching wildlife. Hansel and Gretel, a rustic log cabin, is set amid Douglas firs with a view of the pond through mullioned windows. A sleeping loft complete with books, warm rugs, and quilts overlooks a small living room with a woodstove.

Nestled in the trees is the Carriage House, which is small but feels spacious thanks to skylights and a picture window. A wood-stove stands on a raised hearth in one corner, ready to warm you on chilly mornings and evenings. The newest log cottages are Emma Jane–Tennessee and Kentucky Pine, both with separate bedrooms, king-size feather beds, river rock fireplaces, and skylights. The Log Lodge, at the edge of the pond, has a big stone fireplace, a loft with a sitting area, and a master bedroom with a king bed.

Breakfast makings are stashed in the kitchen of each cottage. They include fresh croissants or rolls, cereal, and eggs. You may find a large goose egg (from one of the resident geese) in your refrigerator, delicious in an omelet. Bring your own groceries for other meals; the kitchens are equipped.

Holly

Willcox House

2390 Tekiu Road
Bremerton, WA 98312
360-830-4492
800-725-9477
Fax: 360-830-0506

> **A spectacular estate on the water**

Innkeepers: Cecilia and Phillip Hughes. **Accommodations:** 5 rooms (all with private bath). **Rates:** $119–$189 single or double. **Included:** Full breakfast. **Minimum stay:** 2 nights on weekends. **Payment:** Major credit cards. **Children:** Over age 15, welcome. **Pets:** Not allowed. **Smoking:** Outdoors only. **Open:** Year-round.

➤ **Bremerton, across the peninsula from the inn, is a longtime Navy town. It has a naval museum and an old destroyer open for tours.**

On a steep bluff above Hood Canal, this grand mansion is the epitome of old-fashioned luxury. As you drive down the narrow private road under hanging moss and ferns and past a moon gatehouse, you feel you are entering a fantasy world. The effect continues when you reach a circular driveway and face the three-story, 10,000-square-foot home.

The mansion, built in 1937, was designed by noted northwestern architect Lionel Pries for Constance and Colonel Julian Willcox. It was considered the entertainment center of the region. One guest room is named for Clark Gable, among the many celebrities who came here.

Later the house was used as a boys' school and a conference center. When the Hugheses bought it in 1988, they spent 14 months restoring it. There are five marble and copper fireplaces, 13-foot ceilings, floors of oak parquet and walls of polished walnut, and cut-glass door inserts. A baby grand piano stands in one corner of the living room, and white damask sofas form a conversation area near the fireplace. The art deco motif recalls the home's origins. A few steps away is the bar and game room, with puzzles, games, pinball, and a pool table. There is no TV, but the library upstairs has leather chairs and shelves full of books — a reader's dream.

The guest rooms, bright with flowers and furnished with antiques and period pieces, have extra comforts such as hair dryers, clothes steamers, and towel warmers. The largest room is Constance's Room, with a working marble fireplace (wood is supplied), a view of Hood Canal and the Olympic Mountains, and a chaise longue. The more gentlemanly Julian's Room has deep colors, paisley wallpaper, an antique writing desk, and a valet. It even has a secret hidden room. Pierre Cardin robes hang in the closet; the bathroom has a double Jacuzzi tub. Clark Gable's Room, overlooking the cedar trees and water, is decorated in warm apricot and green.

Guests socialize over complimentary wine, cheese, and fruit in the afternoon, then go to dinner or eat at Willcox House, where a formal 4-course meal is served on Saturday nights. The rest of the week, less lavish dinners are available. Reservations are necessary.

Breakfast may feature egg puffs, omelets, or Belgian waffles with apricot brandy butter, along with fruit, muffins, and granola. Strolling on the grounds is a feast for the senses. Sweet-scented wisteria droops over the brick terrace, birds visit the lush gardens, fish swim in the pond, and a mossy waterfall tumbles into a pool. For more vigorous exercise, fish or swim in Hood Canal (not really a canal but a large inlet), or borrow the Hugheses' rowboat and use their 300-foot dock.

Kalaloch

Kalaloch Lodge

157151 Highway 101
Forks, WA 98331
360-962-2271
Fax: 360-962-3391

> **A lodge and cabins on an oceanside cliff**

Manager: Sam Claude. **Accommodations:** 60 rooms. **Rates:** Lodge, $76–$107; motel, $112–$122; cabins, $122–$187 single or double; $10 additional person. **Minimum stay:** None. **Payment:** Major credit cards. **Children:** Under age 5, free. **Pets:** Allowed in cabins ($10). **Smoking:** Allowed. **Open:** Year-round.

➤ **When hiking from beach to beach, use a tide table (free at information centers) to learn the daily highs and lows. Both require caution.**

On the west coast of the Olympic Peninsula, wilderness meets seacoast in a jumble of coves, bays, foaming breakers, and beaches piled with white driftwood. "Beach logs are the bones of the rain forest picked clean by the sea," one sign reads.

Five miles north of the Queets River, where Highway 101 parallels the coast above the Quinault Indian Reservation, Kalaloch (pronounced Klay-lock) Creek runs into the sea. Overlooking this juncture is Kalaloch Lodge, with rooms in the main lodge, motel units, or cabins. The bluff cabins can sleep up to 9 people, and log cabins can sleep up to 4 people. Most have kitchens and fireplaces; all hold refrigerators. The newest accommodations are suites in the former bar and library in the lodge.

The rooms are comfortably furnished and clean and are booked months in advance because of the setting. Vacationers in search of razor clams, surf smelt, perch, and summer sea cutthroat, as well as hikers, sightseers, and beach lovers, all swarm to Kalaloch in the summer.

Those who like the drama of ocean storms or who simply want to get away at any time of year find making reservations on short notice easier in the off-season. Once in a while winter visitors get sunshine, though you can't expect it in a region with an average rainfall of 140 inches.

Kalaloch means "lots of clams," "easy living," or "sheltered landing," depending on whom you talk to. The Indians considered it a safe spot to beach dugout canoes, there are plenty of clams (the lodge will rent you a shovel), and the living feels easy indeed when you're ensconced in the lounge, contemplating the region's wild beauty and scarlet and peach sunset.

The hexagonal restaurant takes full advantage of the western view. Open all day, it specializes in local salmon and oysters, served amid nautical decor.

La Conner

La Conner Channel Lodge

205 North First Street
La Conner, WA 98257
360-466-1500
Fax: 360-466-1525

| **A stylish hotel on the water** |

Manager: Gary Tachiyama. **Accommodations:** 40 rooms and suites. **Rates:** Rooms: $148–$207 double, $20 additional person. **Included:** Continental breakfast. **Minimum stay:** None. **Payment:** Major credit cards. **Children:** Welcome. **Pets:** Not allowed. **Smoking:** Not allowed. **Open:** Year-round.

➤ **Palmer's is a fine dining spot serving northwestern cuisine with a French flair.**

Native stone, soft gray colors, and warm, natural wood lend a soothing atmosphere to Channel Lodge, La Conner's only hotel on the waterfront. It's perched at the edge of the waterway, where you can watch the boat traffic or dock your own boat at the pier.

Rooms generally have honey-toned wood walls and a slate fireplace and are clean and simply furnished. There are large easy chairs, a queen- or king-size bed, a phone, TV, refrigerator, and coffeemaker. From the balcony, steps descend to a small patio. Some rooms have Jacuzzi tubs and views of the water. Captain's Quarters accommodates 4 people. Classical music plays while a light breakfast is served on the mezzanine level at tables with bright linens. You can also take breakfast in your room.

The lodge is a few blocks from the center of town, which has dozens of shops selling gifts, clothing, antiques, and the works of local artists. Despite its popularity with tourists, the town retains its pleasant, low-key, offbeat charm.

White Swan Guest House

1388 Moore Road
Mount Vernon, WA 98273
360-445-6805

A Victorian farmhouse in a flower garden

Innkeeper: Peter Goldfarb. **Accommodations:** 3 rooms (share 2 baths) and cottage. **Rates:** Rooms: $65 single (weekdays only), $75–$80 double; cottage: $125–$135 double; $20 additional person. **Included:** Continental breakfast. **Minimum stay:** None. **Payment:** MasterCard, Visa. **Children:** Welcome in cottage. **Pets:** Not allowed. **Smoking:** Outdoors only. **Open:** Year-round.

➤ **La Conner, in the Skagit Valley, is famous for its spring flowers and annual Tulip Festival. Mount Baker stands on the far horizon, a snow-mantled cone.**

Graceful poplar trees line the drive to this well-kept 1890s farmhouse on Fir Island, 6 miles from La Conner. Iris, lilies, peonies, and delphiniums bloom profusely behind the white picket fence, and big cottonwoods shade the grounds and the cottage in back. The impression is one of peaceful country charm, though you're greeted by exuberant (but harmless) dogs.

When Peter Goldfarb arrived in 1986, the 3-acre site was less inviting: a tumbledown house stood behind a junkyard. Today, after major restoration, it's a showpiece.

Peter has brought the flower theme indoors, for roses and other flowers appear in the vibrant decor of every room. In the yellow dining room, the polished fir floors glow, and the bay window overlooks a palette of blooms. A generous Continental breakfast is served here, often with berries from the garden.

Upstairs, past rich green walls trimmed with white, are the guest rooms. The largest has yellow walls, a king-size brass bed, and a view of the Skagit River. The Peach Room, in peach and green, has a white and brass bed and a view of Mount Baker. Most appealing is the Turret Room, which has, in addition to a pink and white bedroom with a brass bed, a quaint sitting area in the little tower. It's said that the original owner, who ran the ferry across the Skagit River, built the tower as a lookout so that he could see when his services were needed.

Peter named his inn after the flocks of swans that feed in the yard and fields. This motif is evident in the two bathrooms, which have swan-shaped soaps and figures.

The two-story cottage, a few steps from the main house, is a light, open home with tall, multi-paned windows and red oak flooring. Staples such as coffee, tea, and honey — and Peter's irresistible chocolate chip cookies — are provided in the blue and white tile kitchen. The bathroom is on the main floor, the bedroom upstairs. The cottage sleeps four comfortably but is often booked by honeymooners.

Langley

The Boat Yard Inn

P.O. Box 866
200 Wharf Street
Langley, WA 98260
360-221-5120
Fax: 360-221-5124

A waterfront inn on a working harbor

Innkeeper: Alice Urbano. **Accommodations:** 9 rooms. **Rates:** $155–$195 double, $10 additional person. **Minimum stay:** 2 nights on holiday weekends. **Payment:** Major credit cards. **Children:** Under age 12, free. **Pets:** Not allowed. **Smoking:** Not allowed. **Open:** Year-round.

➤ **The historical museum displays logging equipment, Indian tools and arrowheads, dolls, vintage clothing, maps and photos, and an early store.**

At the foot of the bluff where the town of Langley sits, facing eastward, is a small marina and working harbor. Here, near the wharves and Nichols' BoatYard and Barney's Boathouse, is the Boat Yard Inn, with corrugated metal buildings reminiscent of an old-fashioned cannery. However, these are new buildings, containing spacious, attractive, contemporary studios and lofts.

Each of the five studios has a queen-size bed on an elevated platform and a sleeper sofa in the sitting area. They feature handsome Ralph Lauren fabrics, pine furniture, and native art. Each has a tiled gas fireplace, a TV, and a small kitchen with a rangetop and microwave. Coffee, tea, and a coffeemaker are provided. There are no phones (a pay phone is available). The larger lofts are good for families. They're like the studios except for the addition of a one-bedroom loft with a queen-size bed.

There's no clutter here, just plenty of space, comfortable seating, good lighting, and a few artistic touches. The quality is high throughout. Most of the rooms, in four buildings separated by a courtyard and dune grass, have water views; some are so close that the waves lap beneath the window when the tide is in. When it's out, you can walk along the sandy beach and watch the ducks, seagulls, and herons wade beside the pier pilings.

Eagles Nest Inn

4680 Saratoga Road
Langley, WA 98260
360-221-5331
Fax: 360-221-5331

A secluded home with warm hospitality

Innkeepers: Joanne and Jerry Lechner. **Accommodations:** 4 rooms. **Rates:** $95–$115, $15 additional person. **Included:** Full breakfast. **Minimum stay:** None. **Payment:** Major credit cards. **Children:** Age 12 and older, welcome. **Pets:** Not Allowed. **Smoking:** Outdoors only. **Open:** Year-round.

➤ **Restaurants include Café Langley, serving eastern Mediterranean foods; Pizzeria, for creative pizzas and a good grilled chicken sandwich; and Raven Café, for tasty lunch fare.**

High on a hill overlooking the trees and Saratoga Passage, near Langley on Whidbey Island, this octagonal contemporary home offers a retreat from the busy world. Built of cedar, it stands on 3 acres of sloping fields and woodland.

The guest rooms are spacious and light, with wicker and brass furnishings and pastel colors. The largest is the Garden Room, which can sleep four. It has a private entrance and garden motif, but no water view. From the Saratoga Room, with its king-size brass bed, triple French doors open to a balcony with a view of the Passage and Mount Baker. Forest Room lets the outdoors in, with a large bay window and skylight. It has a king-size bed and color accents that change with the seasons. All the rooms have VCRs, and the innkeepers have more than a hundred movies you can borrow.

The Eagles Nest sits at the top of the house, a private aerie in green, peach, and white, with eight windows providing a 360-degree view and a private balcony.

The Lechners serve a country breakfast on the deck or at an oval table in the dining area near the kitchen. You might have a baked apple or pineapple boat, pecan praline French toast with wild blackberry syrup, eggs, or Belgian waffles. Beverages are always available, and the cookie jar is always full.

Robes are provided for trips to the inn's outdoor spa. There are nooks for reading and a puzzle and game table. The innkeepers provide virtually everything a guest wishing a quiet time could desire. They will suggest things to do on the island if you ask, or they'll leave you in complete peace.

Galittoire

5444 South Coles Road
Langley, WA 98260
360-221-0548
Fax: 360-221-5986
galittoire@whidbey.com

A contemporary country home on Whidbey Island

Innkeeper: Mahesh Massand. **Accommodations:** 2 suites. **Rates:** $175–$265 single or double; $50 additional person; winter discounts available. **Included:** Full breakfast. **Minimum stay:** 2 nights on weekends except December–early February. **Payment:** Major credit cards. **Children:** Welcome. **Pets:** Not allowed. **Smoking:** Outdoors only. **Open:** Year-round.

➤ **The innkeeper wants to provide "an ideal setting for physical, mental, and spiritual refreshment and revitalization."**

Exceptional in every way, Galittoire has gained a devoted following since it opened in 1991. This contemporary guesthouse sits on 10 acres of woodland and lawn a mile inland from the village of Langley, on Whidbey Island's east coast.

The innkeeper pampers guests, providing a ride at the ferry landing, drinks and hors d'oeuvres, a hot tub and weight room, some 300 movies in the entertainment room, luxurious amenities, and an outstanding breakfast. Mahesh, an expert cook, prepares such delectable items as fruit compote and thick French toast stuffed with cream cheese and topped with peach mousse. In the evening, if you're dining early, he'll let you choose dessert instead of appetizers.

The dining area faces wooded glades and a hilly, 3-acre lawn, the centerpiece of the multilevel, L-shaped home. It's a perfect setting for a wedding or a civilized game of croquet. An island of flowers and blossoming trees holds a gazebo. Guests are welcome to wander through the house, noting the stained glass flamingos and swans, the butterscotch tile floors, the wide glass walls, and Mahesh's office. He is an architect, and his organic style is evident in the design of the house.

The rose-carpeted Master Suite is on two levels. Upstairs is the bedroom, with a half bath, fresh flowers, and a king-size bed facing high windows and the lawn. When moonbeams shine in on this retreat in pale mauve and pomegranate, the effect is magical. Downstairs there's a dressing area with cedar-lined closets and beyond it an oversize tile bathroom that is a hedonist's delight. It has the sauna, weight room, and hot tub, which guests in the other suite may arrange to use.

The Garden Suite, which has a more traditional, less playful bath, is done in white, mauve, and forest colors and has sliding glass doors that open to the decks and lawn.

Guests rave about their good night's sleep here, possibly because of the excellent extra-thick mattresses. Or it may be due to the relaxing atmosphere that surrounds this unusually fine bed-and-breakfast.

The Garden Path Inn

P.O. Box 575
111 First Street
Langley, WA 98260
360-221-5121
Fax: 360-221-6050

Contemporary suites in the heart of Langley

Innkeeper: Linda Lundgren. **Accommodations:** 2 suites. **Rates:** $80–$150. **Included:** Continental breakfast. **Minimum stay:** None. **Payment:** MasterCard, Visa. **Children:** Not appropriate. **Pets:** Not allowed. **Smoking:** Not allowed. **Open:** Year-round.

➤ **Langley loves a party: Mystery Weekend in February, Artists in Action in May, Choochokam Arts Festival in July, and the Island County Fair in August.**

As you follow a brick path through a garden and pass through a wisteria-twined trellis to get to these upstairs apartments on Whidbey Island, you are prepared to be enchanted before you open the door.

Suitable for one or two people, the first suite is one large room, with the bedroom and kitchen sectioned off by walls not quite ceiling height. The effect, combined with windows and skylights, is bright and airy. The room is furnished in exquisite taste — not surprisingly, since the innkeeper is an interior designer with a shop downstairs. The walls are pale gray, the carpet dark gray. A couch covered in a pink and blue floral fabric stands under a window, and a big bowl of flowers fills the table in an alcove.

The bedroom has a queen-size bed with a telephone and white wicker chair. On the bed is a little brass tray with miniature chocolate champagne bottles. You can cook light meals in the little kitchen, which has a toaster oven. Breakfast is in the refrigerator.

The other, larger suite is equally appealing, with a contemporary theme and a view of Langley's main street and waterfront.

The Inn at Langley

P.O. Box 835
400 First Street
Langley, WA 98260
360-221-3033
Fax: 360-221-3033

**A coastal inn of
northwestern elegance**

Owners: Pam and Paul Schell. **Innkeepers:** Stephen and Sandy Nogal. **Accommodations:** 24 rooms and suites. **Rates:** Rooms, $179–$199 single or double; $35 additional person; suites $269. **Included:** Continental breakfast. **Minimum stay:** 2 nights on weekends and holidays. **Payment:** Major credit cards. **Children:** Over age 12, welcome. **Pets:** Not allowed. **Smoking:** Not allowed. **Open:** Year-round.

➤   **Whidbey Island has pebbled beaches, trails for horseback riding and bicycling, golf courses, and antiques shops and boutiques.**

This shingle and glass inn stands snug against a cliff overlooking Saratoga Passage, on the east coast of Whidbey Island. It is a place of understated elegance, with furnishings of the finest quality. Each room has a wood-burning fireplace, refrigerator, coffeemaker, and TV. Jacuzzi tubs face the fire and the sea; every room has a view of the water and a private balcony with flower boxes full of color. Otherwise the decor is muted, with an Oriental simplicity.

The heart of the Inn at Langley is the Country Kitchen, where five-course dinners are served on Friday and Saturday nights and on Sundays in the summer. In the dining area, which has an open exhibition kitchen on one side and an immense river rock fireplace on the other, guests gather at one large cherrywood table. A festive atmosphere prevails: the entertainment involves watching the chef prepare delicacies from such local ingredients as Penn Cove mussels, blackmouth salmon, salt marsh lamb, forest morels, island apples, and loganberries. Greens and the edible plants and herbs that are part of the inn's landscaping are used in the exceptional food. Many of the wines are from Northwest wineries.

Breakfast is a buffet of fruit, cereal, muffins, and juice, and morning newspapers are available in the lobby. The inn has a conference room that accommodates up to 25 people.

Guests at the Inn at Langley often take their cue from the inn's logo, a bespectacled heron reading a book, and spend their days relaxing and reading, enjoying the peace and light.

Leavenworth

Haus Rohrbach

12882 Ranger Road
Leavenworth, WA 98826
509-548-7024
800-548-4477
Fax: 509-548-5038

A chalet with mountain and meadow views

Innkeepers: Bob and Kathryn Harrild. **Accommodations:** 10 rooms (8 with private bath), 3 suites. **Rates:** $75–$160 double, $20 additional person. **Included:** Full breakfast. **Minimum stay:** None. **Payment:** Major credit cards. **Children:** Welcome in lodge rooms; over age 12 in suites. **Pets:** Not allowed. **Smoking:** Outdoors only. **Open:** Year-round.

➤ **Leavenworth is an alpine storybook community nearly midway between Seattle and Spokane. Since the 1960s, it's been a major tourist attraction.**

Haus Rohrbach is like a roomy ski lodge that is especially homey and comfortable. A common room, warmed by a woodstove, adjoins the kitchen and dining area; here you are welcome to toast your toes after a day of whitewater rafting or skiing. A pot of coffee or tea will be waiting, along with the chance to chat with Bob or Kathryn.

Many guest rooms, as well as the large common area, open onto wide balconies with flower boxes overflowing with color during the warm months. The mountain and meadow panorama spreads below as you enjoy the midday rays or an alpine sunset. The rooms have hand-crafted wood beds and chests, pine wainscoting, country wallpaper, eyelet curtains, and soft down comforters.

All the woodwork was done by Bob, including the extensive re-modeling of the original house, which was built in 1975. The new and redone suites, one a part of the house and the others separate, have a light country atmosphere. Each contains a gas fireplace, Jacuzzi, double shower, CD player, and a kitchenette with a microwave and coffeemaker.

Breakfast may consist of Kathryn's fresh cinnamon rolls, oven omelets, homemade jam, and French toast. The Harrilds also offer desserts and ice cream specialties in the evenings, for an additional charge.

Several features make this a good spot for families. High chairs are provided, there's a Coke machine on the terrace, and the playroom is a haven for youngsters, with low tables and benches, teddy bears, books, and dozens of games.

Haus Rohrbach has an outdoor swimming pool and hot tub, and you can soak in warm, watery comfort within sight of meadows filled with cattle and distant mountains green with fir and ponderosa pine.

Mountain Home Lodge

8201-9 Mountain Home Road
P.O. Box 687
Leavenworth, WA 98826
509-548-7077
800-414-2378
Fax: 509-548-5008
info@mthome.com

A small luxury inn in the mountains

Innkeepers: Kathy and Brad Schmidt. **Accommodations:** 10 lodge rooms and house. **Rates:** Summer, $90–$175, $30 additional person; winter, $185–$305, $75 additional person. **Included:** Full breakfast in summer, all meals in winter, except in house. **Minimum stay:** 2 nights, November 15–May, 2 nights on weekends and holidays in other months. **Payment:** Major credit cards. **Children:** Not appropriate unless entire lodge is booked. **Pets:** Not allowed. **Smoking:** Outdoors only. **Open:** Year-round.

➤   **For winter tours, the lodge offers guided snowmobile trips. Red Tail Canyon Farms offers an old-fashioned sleigh ride with Belgian draft horses.**

Here's a resort for those who love luxury in the wilderness. Everything is available, from a hot tub to horseshoes, a swimming pool to ski trails, and yet the ambience is that of a small inn rather than a major resort. Because the cedar lodge was built as a private home in 1983 and has few rooms, it provides an intimate setting for establishing camaraderie. The separate house, called the "Cabin," is a 5,000-square-foot log home that sleeps 8 people and offers a panoramic view. It has an equipped kitchen where you can prepare your own meals, or the innkeepers will arrange for a chef. Or you can dine in the lodge.

There is no set program of activities at Mountain Home, so you can be as busy as you choose. In the summer, lounging by the pool and admiring the view may be enough, for the scenery is magnificent. You are in the North Cascades, where dramatic peaks, forested and glaciated, stand jagged against the sky. From the lodge, which stands at the 2,000-foot level against a 2,500-foot mountain, you see the Stuart Range and Icicle Valley; on a moonlit night, the mountain ridges are shadowy ghosts, with the valley glimmering at their feet.

A few steps lead from the pool to a terrace dotted with umbrella-shaded tables and pots of petunias, and from there you enter the lodge. The dominant feature of the living room is its stone fireplace. Handsome redwood burl furniture, covered with sheepskin, is grouped around the fireplace.

Meals are served in the same room at oak tables. The elegant country cooking, featuring such delicacies as applewood smoked breast of duck with marionberry compote followed by chocolate cake with strawberries and cream, guarantees that the most ravenous skier or hiker will not leave hungry. There's no hard liquor, but beer and wine are offered, and coffee, tea, and cocoa are always available. Breakfast is another treat for calorie burners: fruit cup, eggs Lorraine, fried potatoes, sausage, hot biscuits, and cinnamon rolls ought to see you through the morning. On request, the kitchen will pack a lunch for the trail. From November 15 through March, meals are included in the room rate. In the summer, lunch is $9 and dinner $24.95.

Most of the guest rooms have queen-size beds; the deluxe Mountain View Suite, the largest room, has a king-size bed, Jacuzzi, and fireplace. The rooms are carpeted and have handmade quilts and a tasteful mixture of antique and handmade pine and maple furniture.

Summer brings fresh mountain breezes, wafting the scent of pine, to offset the heat. You can swim, play tennis or volleyball, and wander through the orchard, which provides fruit for meals.

You'll probably want to take the short drive into town to see a little Bavaria in Washington. Leavenworth has an alpine motif that is carried off well, with a definite Northwest sense of grace and good humor. Come the snow, the season gets busier. The snow cat is dusted off to transport guests back and forth, since the road to the lodge is impassable in winter. Skiers flock in to glide over the 50 kilometers of groomed trails and sled down the 1,700-foot slope. Winter rates include the use of ski equipment, sleds, toboggans, ski trails, and VCR movies. For downhill skiers, Stevens Pass and Mission Ridge provide vertical runs with a dozen lifts.

Run of the River

P.O. Box 285
9308 East Leavenworth Road
Leavenworth, WA 98826
509-548-7171
800-288-6491
Fax: 509-548-7547
rofther@rightathome.com

An inviting log home overlooking a river

Innkeepers: Monty and Karen Turner. **Accommodations:** 3 rooms, 3 suites. **Rates:** $85–$140 single, $95–$150 double. **Included:** Full breakfast. **Minimum stay:** 2 nights on weekends and holidays. **Payment:** Major credit cards. **Children:** Not appropriate. **Pets:** Not allowed. **Smoking:** Not allowed. **Open:** Year-round.

➤ **For authentic and commendable German meals, try Österreich Restaurant, and for good continental dining go to Lorraine's Edel Haus.**

Aspiring B&B owners should take lessons from Monty and Karen Turner. These hospitable innkeepers know exactly what travelers want and how to provide it. It's no surprise that their inn has won numerous awards and grateful comments from guests; it is one of the most appealing in the Northwest.

The pine log lodge lies below the confluence of the Wenatchee and Icicle rivers, in beautiful Icicle Valley. This is the setting that lured Monty and Karen from Las Vegas, where both were elementary school teachers, and led them to open a B&B. The inviting inn has the warmth of natural wood and a casual country atmosphere. There's a big, open living and dining room with a fireplace and soft couches, but most people head immediately for the broad deck and the view of the river and wooded island. Whimsical birdhouses hang above the porches and in the trees. A whirlpool tub overlooks the river.

Each of the guest rooms features hand-hewn log furniture crafted by Cole Hurst, an artist who also designed the spiral wooden staircase. Two of the upstairs rooms have river views. River Room has old fishing gear on the wall and a door to the upper deck. Roses provide the motif in Rose Suite, which has a loft, a Jacuzzi, and a deck entrance. From this vantage point you're facing Icicle Ridge and Tumwater Canyon, and through the cottonwoods you can glimpse Wedge Mountain.

You'll awake to the morning sun in the Meadows Room, on the east side. Its picture window overlooks a meadow where ducks, geese, and deer graze. In the Aspens Room you can sit on a swinging log bench and watch the river or relax by the fire in the glass-fronted woodstove.

The Pinnacles, which has a view of the Pinnacles rock formation, contains a Jacuzzi and a woodstove enclosed by river rock. The Tumwater Suite is a separate apartment with a private entrance. The country theme predominates, with a cornhusk wreath and old-fashioned scythes on the walls, a rocker, and a twig ladder leading to a loft. The suite has its own river rock hot tub and a door to the deck and the outdoor hot tub. All the rooms have small refrigerators.

Breakfast, served family-style, might include whipped blueberry yogurt, a fruit plate with strawberries from the Turners' berry patch, French toast, and a baked egg dish. Coffee, tea, and homemade cookies are available all day. Other touches that make Run of the River special include binoculars in the guest rooms, walking sticks, backpacks, bicycles, and maps for hiking or scenic drives.

This recreational wonderland is prime territory for rafting, horseback riding, bicycling, cross-country skiing, and hiking. There's an 18-hole golf course across the river from the inn.

Sleeping Lady

7375 Icicle Road
Leavenworth, WA 98826
509-548-6344
800-574-2123
Fax: 509-548-6312
sleepingla@aol.com

A mountain resort and conference center in central Washington

Manager: Werner Janssen. **Accommodations:** 49 rooms. **Rates:** Rooms: $130 single or double, $25 additional person; bunkhouse: $210 up to 5 people, $45 additional person. **Included:** Expanded Continental breakfast. **Minimum stay:** 2 nights. **Payment:** Major credit cards. **Children:** Under age 4, free. **Pets:** Not allowed. **Smoking:** Not allowed. **Open:** Year-round.

➤ **The Kairos Quartet is the center's resident music ensemble, and concerts are held every other weekend.**

Harriett Bullitt, a wealthy philanthropist from Seattle, is dedicated to protecting the natural environment. When she built this mountain resort, which opened in 1995, she was determined to make it a showcase of environmental conservation. She succeeded to a remarkable degree, creating not only attractive, comfortable lodgings and meeting rooms, but an energy-efficient system that sets a standard for other developers. Recycled materials were used in construction and native plants in the landscaping. All kitchen waste is composted, all soaps and shampoos are biodegradable. Even Sleeping Lady pencils are made from recycled aluminum and sustainable yield forest wood.

Sleeping Lady is a mountain resort and conference retreat on 67 acres beside Icicle Creek, near Leavenworth. Named for the mountain profile above it, the center is close to wooded hiking trails and cross-country ski trails (snowshoes and skis are available to rent). It's a great place for bird-watching. Most guests come to attend conferences in this serene setting; there is more than 10,000 square feet of meeting space. Leisure travelers are welcome, but may reserve rooms no more than 30 days in advance.

The rooms are in clusters of cabins set against granite boulders, in an aspen grove, around a courtyard, or beside a large pond. There are two or three rooms per cabin, and each has beamed ceilings, pine floors and furniture, white walls with natural wood trim, and lots of light. Coffeemakers and coffee are provided. In keeping with the theme of environmental awareness, the sheets are of unbleached muslin and the cotton towels are free of dyes and additives. There is plenty of drawer space, tucked under built-in beds. Aerie, considered the honeymoon room, is a separate unit with a king-size bed, refrigerator, wet bar, and jetted tub with decorative tile.

Guests walk on curving paths under Ponderosa pine trees to reach the Kingfisher dining lodge, a 130-seat hall by the river. On the slope by the entrance is a dramatic glass sculpture made by famed artist Dale Chihuly and designed as a spray of icicles. Meals are served buffet style; breakfast features homemade yogurt with berries, granola, breads, pastries, and hot cereal. Guests who are not attending a conference may eat other meals in the dining hall on weekends by advance reservation and are served first. The food, prepared by chef Damian Browne, is extraordinary. Try the wild mushroom and sherry soup or the grilled chicken breast with Chelan pears, blue cheese dressing and walnuts, and you'll be back for more. Much of the produce used comes from the one-acre organic garden. Julie Winters, the resident horticulturist, is happy to talk with visitors about gardening techniques and the wonders of vermiculture.

There's also a dance studio, a library, a sauna, a massage room, and a hillside swimming pool surrounded by faux stone. A chapel, left from the days when the property was a church camp, has been remodeled into a 200-seat performing arts theater with a grand piano and a 12-foot movie screen. Another building holds the Grotto Bar, where beer, wine, and coffee are served. Entering the bar, one of the few places with TV, is like stepping into a rock cave with a fireplace. The bar itself is made from recycled glass, and the floors came from the old Sears Building in Chicago.

The Sleeping Lady complex is virtually unique and has achieved both acclaim and success. It's also a comfortable, relaxing retreat, a base for exploring the wilderness, and a place to enjoy good music and fine food.

Long Beach

Boreas Bed & Breakfast

607 N. Boulevard
P.O. Box 1344
Long Beach, WA 98631
360-642-8069
888-642-8069
boreas@aone.com

> **A 1920s beach home on the Long Beach peninsula**

Innkeepers: Susie Goldsmith and Bill Verner. **Accommodations:** 2 rooms (share one bath) and 3 suites. **Rates:** $95–$125 single or double, $15 additional person. **Included:** Full breakfast. **Minimum stay:** 2 nights on some weekends. **Payment:** Major credit cards. **Children:** Welcome. **Pets:** Not allowed. **Smoking:** Not allowed. **Open:** Year-round.

➤ **Boreas was the Greek god of the north wind, bringing crisp, clear weather.**

If you're unfamiliar with B&Bs and fear you will be intrusive in someone's home, try Boreas. Here the guests have full run of the house and the owners live next door. There will be many opportunities to meet the other guests and trade travel tips, such as at breakfast, where you'll share a table and get acquainted while eating dishes such as frittata with artichoke hearts and peach kuchen.

The 1920s beach home of weathered shake with blue trim is a block west of Long Beach's main street, with only an expanse of sand and grasses between it and the ocean. The innkeepers' eclectic mix of art and antiques creates a casual, cozy atmosphere.

When you enter, you step into a country kitchen where family photos are stuck on the refrigerator door and a plate of brownies sits on the counter. Tea, coffee, and popcorn are always available for guests in this homey spot. There are two living areas: one is small with a fireplace, and the other is spacious with a grand piano and couches by the windows overlooking the beach and ocean.

Upstairs, the South Room, with a queen-size bed and alcove, shares a skylighted bath with the East Room, which has a king-size bed and daybed. Also on this level is the romantic North Suite, which has a queen-size bed, vaulted ceiling, skylights, and an ocean view. The Dunes Suite and the Garden Suite have private entrances and are a few steps from the enclosed gazebo and spa with 30 jets. You can have the tub to yourself if you light a candle and place it in the gazebo window — that's the signal that the spa is in use.

A short walk to the beach, Boreas is also within easy walking distance of shops and restaurants

Lopez Island

Edenwild Inn

P.O. Box 271
Lopez Island, WA 98261
360-468-3238
Fax: 360-468-4080
edenwildinn@msn.com

> **An inviting Lopez Village inn**

Innkeepers: Jamie and Lauren Stephens. **Accommodations:** 8 rooms. **Rates:** $130–$155 single or double. **Included:** Full breakfast. **Minimum stay:** None. **Payment:** MasterCard, Visa. **Children:** Welcome. **Pets:** Not allowed. **Smoking:** Outdoors only. **Open:** Year-round.

➤   **Lopez has several public parks with pebbly beaches, woodland paths, and picnic areas.**

Behind a rose-covered fence, a well-tended garden, and a pond where water lilies float, Edenwild stands like an oversized Victorian country home. This is as close as Lopez Island gets to splendor. The inn, built in 1989 on two acres, has a wraparound verandah and an arbor where meals are served in warm weather.

Indoors, the atmosphere is calm and uncluttered, with pale oak floors and a few antique furnishings. The parlor invites relaxation on couches arranged by the gray brick fireplace, piano, and book shelves. Next to it is the dining room where breakfast is served to guests as well as dinners to the public on Wednesday through Saturday.

The guest rooms, on the ground and upper floor, are accented with antiques, fresh flowers, and pastel colors. A few have fireplaces and views of San Juan Channel or Fisherman Bay. They all have queen-size beds; the largest holds both a king and queen bed and has a sitting area. A number of special touches add to Edenwild's character: individual thermostats for heat control, chocolates and coffee in each room, afternoon sherry, umbrellas to lend, and a refrigerator stocked with soft drinks.

The inn is in Lopez Village, the only town on the island, and convenient to the few shops and restaurants. Bay Café is well known for its superb food. Try Gail's for excellent light lunches and Holly B's Bakery for pastries. A local favorite, especially for its good hamburgers, is the Galley, down the road from the village.

Inn at Swifts Bay

P.O. Box 3402
Route 2
Lopez Island, WA 98261
360-468-3636
Fax: 360-468-3637

A luxury retreat on an inviting little island

Innkeepers: Carol and Timothy Ortner and Daniel Zawarski. **Accommodations:** 5 rooms (3 with private bath). **Rates:** Rooms, $85–$175 single or double; $25 additional person. **Included:** Full breakfast. **Minimum stay:** 2 nights on holiday weekends. **Payment:** Major credit cards. **Children:** Not appropriate. **Pets:** Not allowed. **Smoking:** Outdoors only. **Open:** Year-round.

➤ **The Bay Café's choices include swordfish with red pepper tapenade, scallops in Thai green curry, and pork tenderloin with peanut sauce.**

Lopez Island, one of the San Juan Islands 80 miles north of Seattle, is a pastoral retreat with a single village, farmlands, and many quiet coves and bays. Between Swifts and Shoal bays, 2 miles from the ferry landing, is a Tudor country inn that deserves every bit of the high praise lavished on it.

The hosts provide both a warm welcome and privacy, pampering and a casual atmosphere. They expect you to kick off your shoes, get comfortable, and relax in the outdoor spa or by the fire. They understand the importance of such details as desks and good reading lamps in the rooms, a refrigerator and microwave (with popcorn) for guests' use, brochures about the area, robes and slippers, and an out-of-the-ordinary breakfast. In the raised dining area, guests sit at tables for two near a bay window overlooking cedar trees and flowers, with Swifts Bay in the distance. Breakfast might be a mushroom soufflé with homegrown herbs, or crab cakes decorated with nasturtiums and pansies.

In the den, guests find a piano, movies for the VCR, and a basket of toiletries that travelers often forget to pack. A phone and fax machine are available.

The guest rooms, on the main and second floors, are individually decorated and designed for comfort. One roomy suite has a wicker couch, a rocker, a dressing area with a large closet, and a private back entrance, facing the wooded hillside. Another features skylights, sleigh beds, and an elegant black and white bathroom. Suite 5 has a private entrance and deck, a VCR, refrigerator, and a double shower in the bath. With a queen-size bed and sofa bed, it can sleep three people.

The innkeepers will recommend shops and cafés and tell you what there is to see and do. You can go kayaking, bird-watching, or bicycling (a big favorite on this flat, rural island), and shop at the Farmers Market.

Lopez Farm Cottages

Fisherman Bay Road
Lopez Island, WA 98261
360-468-3555
800-440-3556
Fax: 360-468-3558

> **Secluded cottages in a peaceful setting**

Innkeepers: John and Ann Warsen. **Accommodations:** 4 cottages. **Rates:** Summer, $125 double; winter, $110. **Included:** Continental breakfast. **Payment:** MasterCard, Visa. **Children:** Not appropriate. **Pets:** Not allowed. **Smoking:** Not allowed. **Open:** Year-round.

➤ **Ferries travel daily to Lopez from the mainland and Shaw, Orcas, and San Juan islands.**

About three miles from the Lopez Island ferry landing, these cedar-sided cottages nestle under the trees on 30 acres of farmland. They face an old orchard and grassy meadow where deer and rabbits often graze. Each white-trimmed cottage has a queen-size bed, double shower, gas fireplace, and small kitchen with a microwave oven and refrigerator. Windows on all sides let in light and views of the country scene. The cottages have identical amenities and a simple floor plan, but the decor varies with bright colors, artwork, and fresh flowers.

In keeping with their goal of providing a getaway of complete privacy, the innkeepers bring breakfast in a basket in the evening, while guests are out having dinner, and tuck a bottle of orange juice in the fridge. Muffins, fruit, coffee, and teas are provided.

The registration arrangement here is unusual. When you first arrive at this off-the-beaten-path spot, you may see no one on the premises. You'll find a sheltered kiosk with a telephone, menus from Lopez restaurants, maps, and ferry schedules. A call on the phone summons the innkeeper, who arrives within minutes and helps you settle into your cottage.

John Warsen, formerly a commercial builder in California, brought to Lopez memories of his grandparents' farm in New York, where he spent happy childhood vacations. His dream was to re-create that atmosphere on Lopez Island. His partner, Ann Warsen, dreamed of owning a bed-and-breakfast. Their combined ideas resulted in Lopez Farm Cottages, which opened in 1996. Ambitious future plans include hot tubs, barbecues, campsites, and more cottages, while retaining a quiet, pastoral setting and an ideal romantic escape.

MacKaye Harbor Inn

Route 1, Box 1940
Lopez Island, WA 98261
360-468-2253
Fax: 360-468-2393

> **A former family home, now an inn on a cove**

Innkeepers: Robin and Mike Bergstrom. **Accommodations:** 3 rooms, 2 suites, carriage house. **Rates:** Summer, $79–$175; $25 additional person; winter, $79–$155. **Included:** Full breakfast. **Minimum stay:** None. **Payment:** MasterCard, Visa. **Children:** Age 9 and older, welcome. **Pets:** Not allowed. **Smoking:** Not allowed. **Open:** Year-round.

> ➤ **Lopez Island, 40 square miles of forest, farm, and beach, is a favorite of bicyclists seeking easy roads and scenic countryside.**

MacKaye Harbor Inn is across the road from a sandy, pebbly beach in one of Lopez Island's many coves, with a grand western view of sea, sky, and islands. The blue house trimmed in white stands on 3 acres, surrounded by tree-shaded lawn and open fields. It was built in 1922 by the children in the Trolnes family as a surprise for their parents: a cabin had occupied the site, and while the elder Trolnes were visiting their native Norway, the house was constructed.

Now it is an inn that extends a friendly welcome to Lopez visitors. The most spacious room is Harbor Suite, which is furnished in antiques and has a fireplace and a waterfront view from its private deck. Also roomy is the Captain Suite, which has a queen-size brass bed with a floral quilt, a bath in oak and tile, and large windows that look out on MacKaye Harbor.

Flower Room, overlooking the dahlia garden, has flowers everywhere — carved on the armoire, twining over the wallpaper. A white antique bed from Norway is in the Blue Room. Rose Room, which sleeps three, has a mauve and rose color scheme and a view of the harbor.

All rooms have private baths; some are down the hall.

The Carriage house has a studio room with a daybed and small kitchen; the other, larger room is a complete apartment with a kitchen, garage, TV, VCR, steam room, and laundry room. It sleeps six.

An ample meal is served for breakfast — typically ham or bacon, eggs, fruit, and pastry. The rose and pale pink dining room manages to show off flounces and ribbons without becoming too dainty. The innkeepers recommend village restaurants for other meals. They have kayaks to rent and bicycles that guests may borrow.

Coffee, tea, sodas, and cookies are always available in the inn's front room, a fine place to curl up on the couch beside the fireplace and watch the sunset. Chocolate truffles await beside your bed.

Lummi Island

West Shore Farm

2781 West Shore Drive
Lummi Island, WA 98262
360-758-2600

A country home on a quiet island

Innkeepers: Polly and Carl Hanson. **Accommodations:** 2 rooms (both with private bath). **Rates:** $80 single, $90 double. **Included:** Full breakfast. **Minimum**

stay: None. **Payment:** MasterCard, Visa. **Children:** Welcome by arrangement. **Pets:** Not allowed. **Smoking:** Outdoors only. **Open:** Year-round.

➤ **At Legoe Bay, watch the Lummi Indians fish for salmon with reef nets, an ancient skill developed for pulling fish into anchored boats.**

It's only a short ferry ride across Hale passage from the mainland, but Lummi Island seems far removed from a rushing world. It's a bucolic retreat off the coast of northern Washington, just west of Bellingham.

The Hansons' bed-and-breakfast lies on a slope on the northern tip of the island, overlooking Georgia Strait. Carl and Polly designed and built their unique cedar home with assistance from their son, Eric, a craftsman, using native materials such as an Alaska yellow cedar driftwood log, which is the center pole of the octagonal structure. The rest of the house radiates from the pole.

In the sitting room on the main floor, guests like to relax by the circular Swedish fireplace and watch the seascape and bald eagles and re-tailed hawks that soar by the wide windows. Mouthwatering fragrances emanate from the kitchen around the corner as Polly prepares a substantial breakfast, which may include puff pancakes with hot blueberry sauce, fruit, and yogurt.

Lunch is available at an island coffee shop, and Polly will occasionally provide dinner at a reasonable cost. The ingredients could not be fresher: peas and blueberries from the garden, jam from nearby crabapple trees, and eggs from the Hansons' chickens. Salmon and other seafood are often provided by local fishers who trade their catch for Carl's welding work.

Guest rooms are on the ground level, reached by a spiral staircase that descends to the lower level or by a separate entrance. Both rooms have views, king-size beds, and tidy, cedar-paneled bathrooms. Eagle Room has an eagle motif and a reading corner with space for a crib. Heron Room features the bird commonly seen on the island, with heron designs on the blue quilt, pillows, and walls.

The rooms are comfortable, but the main level is most appealing, with its marvelous views, deck, fireplace, books and games, and Polly's Loft — a cozy hideaway above the living room.

Polly and Carl go out of their way to make you feel welcome. They'll pick you up at the ferry landing at no charge (or in Bellingham for a nominal fee), point out the beaches and walking paths on the island, introduce you to their English angora rabbits, and even supply hats and mittens if the weather turns chilly.

The Willows Inn

2579 West Shore Drive
Lummi Island, WA 98262
360-758-2620
willows@pacificrim.net

A country inn with romance and hospitality

Innkeepers: Victoria and Gary Flynn. **Accommodations:** 4 rooms, a cottage, and a guest house. **Rates:** $110–$145 double in high season, $95–$135 after Labor Day; $270–$290 for guest house, up to 4 people. **Included:** Full breakfast. **Minimum stay:** 2 nights on weekends in summer. **Payment:** MasterCard, Visa. **Children:** Age 14 and older, welcome. **Pets:** Not allowed. **Smoking:** Outdoors only. **Open:** Year-round.

➤ **The island has a handful of permanent residents and numerous cyclists and tourists escaping the crowds that favor the San Juan Islands.**

Everything about this country inn is appealing: glorious vistas, lush flower gardens, comfortable rooms, friendly hosts, superb food. The renovated house is an island landmark; a family resort on the Lummi coast nearly 80 years ago, it was run by Victoria Flynn's grandparents. The place was sold in the 1950s, but Victoria and Gary bought it back and have turned it into an extraordinary retreat.

The Flynns, who have lived and traveled in Scotland, know how to welcome a bed-and-breakfast guest. Bowls of flowers fill the common rooms on the main floor, robes hang in the closets, and tea and cookies are always available.

The upstairs guest rooms, Sunrise and Sunset, have king-size beds (or twins) and baths with showers. West-facing Sunset is charming in blue and white, with windows that open to the sound of wind and waves. Sunrise, in pastel peach, looks east toward apple and laburnum trees.

Cooler in summer are the ground-floor rooms: Rose, with an American Renaissance mahogany bedroom set that came west around the Horn, and Hillside, containing Eastlake furniture from Victoria's childhood.

Piece o' Cake is the enchanting honeymoon cottage on a slope behind the house and flower gardens. Decorated in crisp pink and white with wicker furniture, it has a tiny kitchen, a table for two, and a bath complete with tub toys. The double bed stands under a skylight, and a glass door leads out to the wide front deck, an ideal vantage point for sipping wine as you watch the sunset.

The guest house, Highland Home, has a Scottish motif in its two bedrooms and two baths (one with a whirlpool, the other with a double shower).

After early-morning coffee and hot Irish soda bread delivered to your door, a three-course breakfast is served in the dining room of the main house. The Willows is also known for its Saturday dinners. Multicourse dinners, featuring grilled herbed lamb, lime ginger chicken, and fresh halibut, are served by candlelight.

"We're selling romance," Victoria says. "I wanted to bring back the love and light that were here before and that I remember."

Mazama

Freestone Inn

Box 11
17798 Highway 20
Mazama, WA 98833
509-996-3906
800-639-3809

A comfortable lodge in a back-country valley

Innkeeper: John Coney. **Accommodations:** 12 rooms, 6 cabins, 2 houses. **Rates:** Spring, $85–$225; summer, $115–$280; fall, $85–$210; winter, $90–$250, single or double; $25 additional person. **Minimum stay:** Varies. **Payment:** Major credit cards. **Children:** Under 18, free. **Pets:** Not allowed. **Smoking:** Not allowed. **Open:** Year-round.

➤ **The staff at Jack's Hut will arrange whitewater rafting, horseback riding, mountain biking, hiking, fly-fishing, and mountain climbing.**

If you love the wilderness and outdoor life but are equally fond of exquisite cuisine and fine wines, Freestone is your kind of place. The secluded resort is in the Methow Valley, on Wilson Ranch, a mile west of Mazama. It takes several hours to get there from Seattle, on a road surrounded by snowcapped mountains. When the North Cascades route, Highway 20, is closed in winter, you can take Highway 2, over Stevens Pass.

The two-story pine and clapboard inn opened in 1996. A former owner of the property, Jack Wilson, built six cabins in the 1940s and guided pack trips; those rustic cabins on Early Winters Creek have been redone with decks and more windows added, and are a good choice for a family. Each has a stone fireplace, a kitchen, and a queen-size bed; one also has two twins. More cabins are under construction. Families and groups also like the lodges by Freestone Lake, which have living rooms, kitchens, and up to 3 bedrooms.

In the main inn, the guest rooms have gas fireplaces, king-size beds, and balconies or patios overlooking the lake. Two of the rooms have whirlpool tubs; you won't be roughing it, unless you feel deprived without room service.

The inn's gathering place is the Great Room, which has a 30-foot ceiling, pine beams, and wrought-iron chandeliers. The main focus here is the immense fireplace made from river rock, or freestone. Beyond it is the dining room, one of the inn's major attractions. The chef, Jeff James, uses local ingredients for the dishes on the menu, which changes seasonally. The honey-grilled pheasant breast with wild rice and cranberry risotto and blue cheese is a favorite, followed by apple tart with maple-cinnamon ice cream. California and Northwest labels dominate the wine list.

Cross-country skiing is the big draw in the Methow Valley. More than 100 miles of groomed trails web the meadows and hills. There's also ice-skating on the lake and heli-skiing. Everyone makes at least one trip to Winthrop, a town out of the old West, with false fronts, boardwalks, and old-fashioned shops and cafés.

Mazama Country Inn

HCR 74, Box B9
Mazama, WA 98833
509-996-2681
800-843-7951
Fax: 509-996-2646
mazama@methow.com

A ski resort in northeastern Washington

Innkeepers: Bill Pope and George Turner. **Accommodations:** 10 rooms in main lodge, 4 rooms in annex, 6 cabins. **Rates:** Rooms: summer, $70–$95 double, $15 additional person; winter, $150–$175, $50 additional person; cabins, $95–$170. **Included:** All meals in winter for lodge and annex guests. **Minimum stay:** 2 nights in cabins. **Payment:** MasterCard, Visa. **Children:** Welcome in summer, over age 12 welcome in winter. **Pets:** Allowed in cabins. **Smoking:** Not allowed. **Open:** Year-round.

➤   **Everything you need for Nordic skiing is near the inn: 175 kilometers of groomed trails, equipment rentals, instruction, ski passes for trails.**

Hot, dry summers and snowy winters characterize the Methow Valley, east of the Cascade Mountains in northern Washington. There's plenty of summer activity in the area, including whitewater rafting and fishing on the Methow River, mountain bike touring, windsurfing on the Pearrygin Lake, and hiking on the Pacific Crest Trail. But the best time for Mazama Country Inn is in winter, when the snow creates a Christmas card setting and cross-country skiers yearn for the double groove of a groomed trail.

The inn is about a 4-hour drive from Seattle and 14 miles north of the restored western town of Winthrop, just off Highway 20. You can stay in the cedar lodge, the annex, or the cabins, which are older lodgings of considerable size — one can sleep up to 12 people.

The lodge rooms are plain, with pine wainscoting, a wallpaper border with a ski motif in most rooms, and soft comforters. In this lodge, guests spend most of their time out in the snow or by the fire, drink in hand. They can also soak in a steamy, outdoor hot tub or sweat in the sauna. There's a small sitting area on the upper landing, with a couple of couches, a piano, and some games.

The combined living and dining areas feature huge peeled logs supporting a soaring ceiling, a stone fireplace, and windows on three sides with views of the evergreen forest. In summer, the restaurant menu offers a range of choices — crab salad, seafood pasta, lamb chops, and scallops among them. In the winter, dinner is served family style. It features entrées such as prime rib, fried chicken, and pasta dishes, with salad and dessert. You make your own lunch in winter from the sandwich fixings, cookies, and fruit that are set out.

Each room in the annex has queen-size beds and a private deck with a view of the forest or Goat Peak. Two contain twin beds as well. Families and groups like the cabins, which have kitchens and lots of space. Three sleep six, and one sleeps eight people. Goat Wall Retreat, within walking distance of the inn, is a large log cabin with a view of open meadows; Lost River cabin is 6 miles away. It has hardwood floors, braided rugs, a woodstove, TV, and a piano in the living room. Deer Run and Phoenix House are both large, well-equipped homes with laundry facilities and a TV.

Mount Baker

The Logs at Canyon Creek

9001 Mount Baker Highway
Deming, WA 98244
360-599-2711

| Rustic cabins in the woods

Proprietor: Hazel Olsen. **Accommodations:** 5 cabins. **Rates:** Summer: $75 double, $10 additional adult, $6 child; winter: $85 double; weekly rates in summer. **Minimum stay:** 2 nights, 3 nights on holiday weekends. **Payment:** No credit cards. **Children:** Welcome. **Pets:** Allowed ($4 charge). **Smoking:** Allowed. **Open:** Year-round.

➤ **At the ranger station in Glacier, 2 miles east of the Logs, pick up maps and information for exploring the Mount Baker region.**

Where Canyon Creek flows into the North Fork of the Nooksack River, 9 miles west of Mount Baker, the Logs offers lodging of rustic charm on 73 acres. Mossy paths wind through the ferns and forest to the cabins, which are widely spaced under the trees and along the babbling creek. They sleep from two to ten people and are ideal for families, for each has a fully equipped kitchen and two bedrooms with twin bunk beds. The living rooms contain double-size sofa beds. Roomy and cozy, the cabins have braided throw rugs and natural rock fireplaces. Firewood is supplied, along with bedding, linen, towels, and dishes.

Within a few steps of the cabin door, a wealth of summer recreation is available for every age. You can fish for trout in Canyon Creek and in the river, look for fossils along the creek bar, hike in Mount Baker National Forest, pick blueberries, and picnic by the creek at a table made from a slab of fir. There's a solar-heated swimming pool near the cabins and facilities for badminton, volleyball, and horseshoes. Youngsters like the swings that hang in the tall trees. In the winter, the Mount Baker Ski Area offers downhill and cross-country skiing.

Good restaurants in the area include Mountain Laurel Café and Milano's.

Mount Rainier National Park

National Park Inn

Mount Rainier Guest Services
P.O. Box 108
Ashford, WA 98304
360-569-2275

A comfortable, reasonably priced lodge

Manager: Brenda Oxender. **Accommodations:** 25 rooms (18 with private bath). **Rates:** $64–$119 single or double, $10 additional person. **Minimum stay:** None. **Payment:** MasterCard, Visa. **Children:** Under age 2, free. **Pets:** Not allowed. **Smoking:** Not allowed. **Open:** Year-round.

➤ **Mount Rainier has 27 named glaciers, the largest number in the lower 48 states. They fill deep valleys between high, rugged ridges.**

Lodgings in Mount Rainier National Park became available in 1885, when James Longmire built a cabin for his family and the occasional visitor. The Longmires homesteaded at the 2,700-foot level, near hot mineral springs that the Indians believed to have healing powers. The hot springs are still there, in a meadow across the road from today's inn, next to a half-mile trail.

National Park Inn, though not grand or luxurious, is far from rustic. Originally the annex to an earlier hotel, it was improved over the years and eventually closed for a year's remodeling. It re-opened in early 1990 with a warm and open lobby, well-furnished rooms (two with wheelchair access), an informal restaurant, and a cozy lounge reserved for overnight guests. The lounge is an ideal retreat on a chilly night, with couches by a stone fireplace. From the porch in front, there's a postcard view of the mountain's peak.

A covered walkway connects the hotel to a 1911-vintage log cabin housing the gift shop.

Nearby are an information center, a small museum, and hiking trails. Walk through old-growth forest of Douglas fir, western red cedar, and western hemlock trees that soar more than 200 feet above the mossy valley floor. For hikes through subalpine meadows of wildflowers, closer to Rainier's immense glaciers, you can continue farther into the park to Paradise. The inn offers facilities for cross-country skiers in winter. You can glide right out the door, across silent white meadows. into the woods on secluded nature trails.

Paradise Inn

Mount Rainier Guest Services
P.O. Box 108
Ashford, WA 98304
360-569-2275

A grand lodge on a majestic mountain

Manager: Pamela Newlun. **Accommodations:** 126 rooms (31 with 2 shared baths), including 12 suites. **Rates:** $68–$121, 2–6 people; suite, $127; $10 additional person. **Minimum stay:** None. **Payment:** Major credit cards. **Children:** Welcome (under age 2, free with own crib). **Pets:** Not allowed. **Smoking:** Not allowed. **Open:** Mid-May to early October.

➤ **Across from the inn, the Henry Jackson Visitors Center offers slide shows and movies about the park, a cafeteria and gift shop, and 360-degree views.**

The Indians called it Tahoma, meaning "Next to Heaven" or "Mountain of God." The white explorers named it for an English admiral. Whatever you call Mount Rainier, only one word describes it: awesome. The 14,410-foot mountain, the highest in the Cascade Range, creates its own arctic weather in a temperate zone, and its annual snowfall is among the world's weightiest. In the winter of 1971–1972, 93 feet of snow fell on Paradise Ranger Station — the most snowfall ever recorded anywhere.

On the south shoulder of this behemoth, at 5,400 feet, Paradise Inn was built in 1916 to provide visitors with food and lodging. Today the imposing Alaskan cedar lodge still welcomes pilgrims who come to marvel, explore, or climb — 1.8 million every year.

Most stay only for the day, however. If you spend the night, an entirely different experience awaits.

After you have admired the three-story, log-supported lobby with the parquet floors and stone fireplaces and huge tables, after you've eaten dinner while gazing at the eye-popping view, after a nightcap in dimly lit, paneled Glacier Lounge, you'll go up to your room. A main lodge room won't be spacious (some are quite small), but recent renovation work included new and spruced-up furnishings. There is no TV. The annex rooms are larger, most facing the rugged Tatoosh Range. You'll sleep soundly in the crisp mountain air, and if you awake at dawn and the weather is clear, you'll have an exhilarating sight: sunrise on Mount Rainier.

Slip on your shoes and jacket and hit the trail: night-dark glaciers turn pink and crimson as the mountain greets the day. At your feet, avalanche lilies and anemones dot green meadows like an earthbound Milky Way. By the time you've returned for breakfast an hour later, the sky has turned from pale gray and rose to deep cerulean and the shadowed glaciers to dazzling white. Another day has begun in Paradise.

The dining room serves breakfast, lunch, dinner, and an ample Sunday buffet brunch. Dinner entrées include salmon, poached or grilled — the best item on the menu, other than the homemade soups. The kitchen will pack a trail lunch if you ask the night before. The lobby is a sociable place, where overnighters and day guests meet on cushy couches around the fire or play a few tunes on the piano. In the evenings, park rangers give slide talks on mountain geology and history. There's a snack bar and a gift shop selling trinkets and books — which you may need if a storm sends you indoors. The weather is unpredictable on Rainier.

Ocean Park

Caswell's on the Bay

25204 Sandridge Road
P.O. Box 1390
Ocean Park, WA 98640
360-665-6535
888-553-2319
Fax: 360-665-6500

> **A gracious guest house facing Willapa Bay**

Innkeepers: Marilyn and Bob Caswell. **Accommodations:** 5 rooms. **Rates:** $95–$150 single or double, winter discounts for longer stays. **Included:** Full breakfast. **Minimum stay:** 2 nights on holidays and festival weekends. **Payment:** Visa, MasterCard. **Children:** Over age 10, welcome. **Pets:** Not allowed. **Smoking:** Outdoors only. **Open:** Year-round.

➤   **Notable restaurants include the Ark, the Shoalwater, the Sanctuary, and Cheri Walker's 42nd St. Café.**

On three acres of wooded and landscaped grounds, this B&B is one of the most relaxing places to stay on the peninsula. It looks Victorian, in yellow with white and burgundy trim, but it was built in recent years and opened as an inn in 1995. In summer, baskets of flowers hang at the covered verandah, and the gardens and gazebos invite romantic strolls. Caswell's is a popular site for weddings and family reunions.

A crystal chandelier hangs in the foyer; beyond is the open, light living room and wide view of the bay. Guests have the run of the house, as the owners' living quarters are in a separate section. You're welcome to help yourself to tea, coffee, and cookies in the kitchen and store your drinks and snacks in the refrigerator. The Caswells, friendly, organized, and eager to please, serve afternoon tea in the sun room and breakfast in the dining room at one table. This is ideal for guests who like to meet other travelers. Breakfast might include fruit, quiche, sausage, and Bob's specialty, baked oysters.

The guest rooms, off a loft above wide, open stairs, are furnished with fine antiques and have queen-size beds with lacy pillows. The Turret Room also has a twin bed. Victorian Rose, the least expensive, is pretty in rose with white wicker and carved walnut furniture. Shoalwater Room has a 3-piece walnut set and velvet settee in deep purple as well as reproductions of Tiffany lamps. In the spacious Terrace Room, seven windows overlook the bay and garden, and glass doors open to a private balcony. French antiques furnish the large room, which, like the others, has a TV, ivory carpeting, and flowers.

The Caswells have a wealth of information on the area and are happy to recommend shops, restaurants, and art galleries. Be sure to stop in at Shoalwater Gallery, just down the road, where Marie Powell shows her pastel paintings.

Klipsan Beach Cottages

22617 Pacific Highway
Ocean Park, WA 98640
360-665-4888

Beachside cottages in the southwest corner of the state

Managers: Mary and Dennis Caldwell. **Accommodations:** 10 cottages. **Rates:** Summer: $80–$150, 2-6 people; winter: $70–$105. **Minimum stay:** 2 nights on weekends. **Payment:** MasterCard, Visa. **Children:** Welcome. **Pets:** Not allowed. **Smoking:** Outdoors only. **Open:** Year-round.

➤ **When the oyster industry faded in 1854, Oysterville did, too, leaving homes and a church. Unchanged, the village is now a National Historic District.**

Eight of these cedar cabins on the Long Beach Peninsula are quintessential Northwest. In a row facing seaward, they overlook salal and scrubby pine and dunes with paths to the beach. Now weathered and gray, with white brick chimneys, and moss on the roofs, the cabins date from the 1940s and have the rustic charm of vacation homes of the period.

They've been updated since then, with reasonably modern bathrooms, fully equipped kitchens, carpeting, and west-facing decks. All have TV, a microwave, and a woodstove or fireplace. Firewood is provided. Several cabins have queen-size beds; most have doubles.

The other two cabins are actually houses that, with three bedrooms, can sleep up to eight people. One has a large kitchen, a deck, a fireplace, and an ocean view. It's tucked in the woods, away from the dunes, but the walk to the beach is a short one. The second, a two-story building on the north side, is removed from the rest and has a fireplace and a path leading from the deck to the dunes and beach.

The cabins have no phones, but there's a pay phone by the covered outdoor cooking and picnic area.

Long Beach Peninsula is a stretch of land at Washington's southwesternmost corner. A regional vacation spot for generations, it is filled with old-fashioned summer homes. It is said that this peninsula has the longest beach in North America — 28 miles of uninterrupted sand waiting for strollers, kites, and sand castles.

Olympia

Puget View Guesthouse

7924-61st Avenue N.E.
Olympia, WA 98516
360-459-1676

A private cottage facing Puget Sound

Innkeepers: Barbara and Dick Yunker. **Accommodations:** 1 cottage. **Rates:** Summer and all weekends, $89 double; off-season rates available. **Included:** Continental breakfast. **Minimum stay:** None. **Payment:** MasterCard, Visa. **Children:** Welcome. **Pets:** Small pets allowed by arrangement. **Smoking:** Allowed. **Open:** Year-round.

➤ **Olympia is a short drive from the cottage; the capitol is well worth a tour. The State Capitol Museum contains a fine collection of Native American artifacts.**

If you're looking for a romantic beachfront cottage in a classic Northwest setting, Puget View Guesthouse may be the answer. It sits on a cliff on an acre of land next to the forest of Tolmie State Park, on the southern shore of Puget Sound and facing Long Branch Peninsula and the Olympic Range.

The Yunkers' guest house is across the lawn from their own log home. Rhododendrons bloom beside the cedar shake cottage, and red geraniums provide spots of color on the deck. With a queen-size bed and a sofa bed, the house can sleep four. The decor is simple: pale lavender walls, a couple of posters, painted wood floors, braided throw rugs, and white curtains on windows that look out to the Sound.

There is no kitchen, but a microwave oven and burner are provided, along with a barbecue and a bar refrigerator. The Yunkers will recommend nearby restaurants, and in the mornings Barbara crosses the yard with a tray holding what she terms a dressed-up Continental breakfast — fruit, juice, coffee or tea, and breads. If you take the Romantic Retreat package, you'll also receive sparkling cider when you arrive, breakfast served with crystal, silver, fresh flowers, and linens, a keepsake candle, and a souvenir gift.

Dick and Barbara know the area well and are excellent sources of information on what to see on nearby islands, at Mount Rainier, in Seattle, and on the Olympic Peninsula. You can rent boats, scuba dive in the underwater park offshore, go kayaking or canoeing in the protected waters, or explore the state park. On winter days, you may prefer to curl up with a book and a cup of tea in your cottage, where you'll hear little but the lap of the sea at the bottom of the cliff.

Orcas Island

Chestnut Hill Inn

P.O. Box 213
Orcas Island, WA 98280
360-376-5157
Fax: 360-376-5283
chestnut@pacificrim.net

| **A romantic island sanctuary** |

Innkeepers: Marilyn and Dan Loewke. **Accommodations:** 5 rooms. **Rates:** $105–$195. **Included:** Full breakfast. **Minimum stay:** None. **Payment:** Major credit cards. **Children:** Not appropriate. **Pets:** Not allowed. **Smoking:** Not allowed. **Open:** Year-round.

➤ **Orcas is an island of artists. Explore the byways and you'll find studios selling pottery, weavings, paintings, and sculpture.**

The Pacific Northwest has no lack of romantic retreats, but few can compare with Chestnut Hill. This hilltop inn provides every comfort, along with a peaceful setting and innkeepers who go out of their way to make guests feel welcome.

Among the comforts are four-poster feather beds with fine cotton sheets and piles of pillows, fireplaces in each room, cozy robes and slippers, extravagant breakfasts, complimentary champagne and sparkling juice, and wine and cheese on winter afternoons.

The Victorian-style home looks like a country home of the 19th century, complete with wraparound verandah and gazebo, but it was built in 1970 for a woman who wanted a reminder of the home she had known in Minnesota. She had a quaint chapel built beside an old pear orchard, which still stands on land that is part of the San Juan Conservation Trust.

The Loewkes bought the 16-acre hideaway and opened their bed-and-breakfast in 1995, after months of renovation. The rooms in the main house are named and decorated for their views of the barn and pasture, the large pond, and the chapel. On the ground floor, separated from the main house and with their own entrances, are the serene, flowery Garden Room and the large and luxurious Chestnut Suite. The suite contains a custom-designed pine entertainment center with TV, VCR, and stereo, a cozy sitting area with fireplace, wet bar, and refrigerator stocked with snacks and drinks. With a fluffy canopied featherbed, piles of pillows, and a Jacuzzi in the slate and glass block bathroom, it's a romantic's dream. These rooms don't have the expansive views of the upstairs rooms, but their appeal more than makes up for it.

Marilyn serves multicourse breakfasts at tables for two in the dining room. In addition to fresh fruit, juice, and cereals, breakfast might include apricot French toast, an artichoke frittata, or a crab and leek omelette. Dinners, offered from November through April and served at candle-lit tables, are examples of Marilyn's cooking talent with dishes such as peppercorn-crusted salmon and halibut with ginger-scallion butter. There are usually four entrée choices, with prices from $19.50 to $21.50. In the summer she'll make up a picnic basket to take on your island outings. Don't expect peanut butter sandwiches in these elegant hampers. You're more likely to have crudités with basil aioli and pan-fried oyster panini.

Like many guests, you might choose to take your picnic no further than the pond at the bottom of the hill. There you can row to a tiny island and enjoy your feast in the shade of a weeping willow tree. For longer jaunts, the innkeepers have bicycles to lend.

During Christmas week, the inn offers a "Christmas in the Chapel" package. Guests can walk down the slope to the festively decorated, candle-lit chapel for musical concerts.

Orcas Hotel

P.O. Box 155
Orcas, WA 98280
360-376-4300
888-ORCASWA
Fax: 360-376-4399

A Victorian hotel overlooking the ferry landing

Manager: Craig Sanders. **Accommodations:** 12 rooms (2 with private bath). **Rates:** Summer: $65–$160 single, $69–$170 double; $15 additional person; discounts available in winter. **Included:** Full breakfast in summer. **Minimum stay:** None. **Payment:** Major credit cards. **Children:** Not appropriate. **Pets:** Not allowed. **Smoking:** Not allowed. **Open:** Year-round.

➤ **Eastsound has several good restaurants and shops. The village of Olga has an excellent casual spot — Café Olga, open only for breakfast and lunch.**

If you come to Orcas Island, one of the most heavily used islands in the San Juans, you won't miss this hotel on a hill across the road from the ferry landing. It's a striking sight, a three-story gray and white Victorian with red roof and porch. Even if you don't stay here, the pleasant café is a good place to stop for an espresso and sticky buns while you wait for the ferry.

You may learn a bit of history, too, about early residents such as Octavia Van Moorhem, who sold fried chicken and fruit pies to visitors when the hotel was built at the turn of the century. Her husband, Constant, established the flower beds that are being restored to their colorful glory. The hotel itself, which was restored in 1985, is now on the National Register of Historic Places.

The main restaurant, which seats up to 40 and is one of the few eating establishments on the island with wheelchair access, has a view of the ferry landing, a stone fireplace, botanic prints, and an antique plate collection. Fresh fish from island waters, "the luck of the catch," is a specialty. The restaurant is closed in winter, but the café continues to serve light meals.

Upstairs, the neat and trim guest rooms contain antique furnishings and patchwork quilts stitched by island quilters. One room has twin beds; all others have brass queen-size beds. Honeymooners prefer Blue Heron and Killebrew Lake rooms, with their feather beds, balconies, and private baths with whirlpool tubs.

Orcas Island has recreation to suit almost every interest: bicycling, sailing, kayaking, canoeing, golf, and horseback riding. The bicycle shop down the road from the hotel will deliver rental bikes. You can charter a boat, fish, picnic, tour other islands, and walk on dozens of hiking and nature trails. At 2,405 feet, Mount Constitution is the highest point in the San Juans and has a view you'll never forget: islands sprawling below like green jewels across the sea and mainland mountains looming on the horizon.

Rosario Resort

One Rosario Way
Eastsound, WA 98245
360-376-2222
800-562-8820
Fax: 360-376-3680

An island estate on a beautiful bay

Manager: Christopher French. **Accommodations:** 130 rooms. **Rates:** Summer and all weekends, $95–$210 single or double; $10 additional person; winter (midweek), $63–$140. **Minimum stay:** None. **Payment:** Major credit cards. **Children:** Under age 12, free with a parent ($5 for crib). **Pets:** Not allowed. **Smoking:** Allowed. **Open:** Year-round.

➤   **From the summit of Mount Constitution, you can see a spectacular panorama: the San Juan Islands, the Olympic Mountains, Vancouver Island, and the Cascades.**

Orcas Island, in the center of the San Juan archipelago in Washington's northwest corner, is a popular spot for mainlanders seeking evergreen forests, secluded inlets, and sun-splashed beaches. It was here that Robert Moran, a shipbuilder and former mayor of Seattle, decided in 1905 to retire at age 49 and, presumably, end his days, for he had been told he was too ill to live long.

On a site near Cascade Bay, on the west side of the island's east arm, he built a 54-room mansion as a legacy for his family. The first two stories were solid concrete, and six tons of copper sheeting formed the roof. He called the Mediterranean-style villa Rosario, after the strait between the San Juans and the mainland.

Honduran mahogany, teak, and brass went into the home of this master shipbuilder. Moran put in a tile swimming pool, a bowling alley, and a music room with a green tile fireplace and an enormous pipe organ. He lived to the age of 86.

Today, the estate is a resort that sprawls along the shoreline and hillside above the bay, offering a variety of activities and comforts. There are tennis courts, a marina, three swimming pools, a sauna and whirlpool, a fitness program, and fishing and cruising charters. Organ concerts and historic talks are presented regularly in the Music Room.

Recent remodeling has considerably improved the rooms, which are not in the mansion, but in separate buildings spread over the nicely landscaped grounds. Most rooms are now on a par with good hotel rooms. They have king-size beds or two queen-size beds, phones, TV, coffeemakers, and refrigerators. Some are directly above the water and others are against the hill, with sweeping views of the bay. Not all have water views.

The bright yellow, tiered dining room in the mansion has grand views from every table. The resort's other restaurant, the more casual Cascade Bay Café, near the marina, is open seasonally.

Moran State Park and Mount Constitution are close to Rosario. You can walk or drive (or bicycle, if you're among the intrepid) to the top of the mountain, the highest point in the San Juan Islands.

Spring Bay Inn

P.O. Box 97
Olga, WA 98279
360-376-5531
Fax: 360-376-2193

A B&B inn on a secluded cove

Innkeepers: Carl Burger and Sandy Playa. **Accommodations:** 5 rooms. **Rates:** $160–$215, $20 additional person. **Included:** Full breakfast. **Minimum stay:** None. **Payment:** MasterCard, Visa. **Children:** Welcome. **Pets:** Not allowed. **Smoking:** Outdoors only. **Open:** Year-round.

➤ **Spring Bay Inn's packages include day-long kayak trips, fishing charters, environmental education programs, and weddings.**

At the end of a dirt road riddled with potholes, this large, two-story inn overlooks a private bay off Orcas Island's east arm. It's a place for travelers looking for something special — the setting, accommodations, and hospitality are extraordinary.

First thing in the morning, coffee and muffins are set out for early risers. Then, at eight or so, those who want a bit of adventure climb into kayaks (after a safety lesson) for two hours of close-to-shore ocean paddling, led by a guide. By 10:30, appetites are ready for brunch back at the inn. Carl and Sandy serve hearty, healthy meals that might include granola waffles, low-fat sausage, muffins, and various juices.

For the rest of the day, guests explore other parts of the island, follow the trails of the 57-acre property or the neighboring forest, or relax on the verandah, enjoying the view of trees and water. The handsome golden retriever, Carson Down-Goodboy, may keep you company. Another relaxing spot is the bayside outdoor spa.

The rooms are large, light, and airy, with high ceilings. The inn has eight stone fireplaces and an open common room with shelves full of field guides and information on points of interest. Every guest room has a high, narrow Rumford fireplace, a bay view, a refrigerator, and a king- or queen-size bed with a handmade quilt; two have private balconies. If you reserve Ocean or Driftwood Room, you'll have a grand view of the trees, beach, and water from the bathtub.

The good-humored, friendly innkeepers, who are retired park rangers, will share their knowledge of the area and direct you to trails, beaches, and other island attractions. They'll recommend restaurants and make reservations; or you can bring your own picnic and grill dinner on the barbecue.

Turtleback Farm Inn

P.O. Box 650
Route 1
Eastsound, WA 98245
360-376-4914
800-376-4914
Fax: 360-376-5329

A classic, gracious farmhouse turned country inn

Innkeepers: Susan and Bill Fletcher. **Accommodations:** 11 rooms. **Rates:** $80–$210. **Included:** Full breakfast. **Minimum stay:** 2 nights during May 1–October 31. **Payment:** Major credit cards. **Children:** Welcome by arrangement. **Pets:** Not allowed. **Smoking:** Outdoors only. **Open:** Year-round.

➤ **Restaurants include Bilbo's, for southwestern ambience and a courtyard; Christina's, for innovative cuisine and a water view; and La Famiglia, for Italian food.**

Offering an island sanctuary for discriminating travelers, Bill and Susan Fletcher enjoy welcoming guests to their renovated farmhouse and their new Orchard House at the base of Turtleback

Mountain, about 8 miles from the Orcas Island ferry landing. Their charming country retreat is one of the West's most romantic inns; it has a special magic, with a warm ambience and 8 acres of meadows, ponds, and wildflowers.

The Fletchers moved to the San Juan Islands from the San Francisco area several years ago. "We fell in love with this old farm and decided that it had to be rescued from the brambles," Bill says. The house had been used for storing hay and required major remodeling. The Fletchers removed the blackberry vines, added two wings and a wide deck on the southwest side, painted, and decorated.

Polished floors gleam in the guest rooms, which are furnished with a blend of antique and contemporary pieces. Comforters, filled with hand-carded wool, have been made by island craftswomen. The atmosphere is one of peace, quiet, and privacy. The two-story Orchard House, which resembles a Shaker-style barn, is set in the midst of an apple and pear orchard. Its four rooms are named after the types of apples that grow here. Each room has a king-size bed, a gas fireplace, a clawfoot soaking tub, and a large shower.

You'll have a sumptuous breakfast at Turtleback — fresh eggs, granola, fruit, and homemade pastries served in the airy dining room or on the deck. If you're staying in the Orchard House in the summer, breakfast will be delivered to your room.

On Orcas you can sail, canoe, kayak, hike, fish, and beachcomb in pebbly coves. Walk along the beach at Obstruction Pass and you're likely to hear the hoarse barking of sea lions and maybe see the back of a sleek orca whale.

After dinner in Eastsound (Bilbo's and Christina's are good choices), you'll return to the inn to find sherry and a crackling fire in the living room, along with convivial company.

Port Angeles

Domaine Madeleine

146 Wildflower Lane
(off Finn Hill Road)
Port Angeles, WA 98362
360-457-4174
Fax: 360-457-3037
domm@olympen.com

An exquisite hideaway on the peninsula

Innkeepers: John and Madeleine Lanham Chambers. **Accommodations:** 5 rooms. **Rates:** $135–$165 double, $25 additional person. **Minimum stay:** 2 nights on weekends and holidays, April 15–October 15. **Payment:** Major credit cards. **Children:** Age 12 and older, welcome. **Pets:** Not allowed. **Smoking:** Outdoors only. **Open:** Year-round.

➤ **The cozy Honeymoon Cottage has a solarium with a mountain view, a fireplace, a sitting area, and a Jacuzzi.**

Setting, atmosphere, and hospitality combine to make this one of the most romantic places to stay in the Northwest. Eight miles east of Port Angeles, on a bluff overlooking the Strait of Juan de Fuca, Domaine Madeleine is surrounded by 5 acres of woodland, lawns, and gardens. John, a botanist, tends 55 types of rhododendrons and a Northwest version of Monet's garden. He's happy to take guests on nature walks, pointing out trilliums and mushrooms. Lavender — some 350 bushes of it — blooms in fragrant profusion along the lane from Finn Road to the house.

The energetic Madeleine brings her French background to the stylish inn, flipping omelets, chatting with guests, and setting an elegant breakfast table. The menu changes daily. On a typical morning the Chamberses might serve fresh French bread, a seafood mélange, crème caramel, and an artistically arranged fruit plate. There are always lemon muffins and, of course, madeleines.

Oriental antiques furnish the white-walled living room, which has a 14-foot-high basalt fireplace and a television and VCR. Guests are welcome to play the harpsichord, made by John, that stands in one corner. The most compelling feature is the big window, which frames a spectacular view of Vancouver Island, the Canadian mainland, and the Cascades.

On the main floor, the Monet Room has a water lilies theme and a private entrance from the garden. A fireplace and a mirrored Jacuzzi for two add to the romantic atmosphere. Renoir Room has no tub, but there's a shower big enough for two. Renoir's French doors open to the living room that is used exclusively by this room's guests in the evening.

The Ming Room, upstairs, is a quiet retreat with a 30-foot balcony, a king-size bed, and a Jacuzzi. You'll find binoculars in the cabinet, along with a stereo and a selection of operas and classical music. There's also a refrigerator, microwave oven, and coffeemaker. In a separate building, the Rendezvous Room has become a favorite with guests looking for privacy and luxury in a warm, intimate setting. From the king-size bed you have a view of the water and passing ships, and you can watch the fire in the fireplace from the oversized Jacuzzi. There's a nook with a refrigerator, microwave, and coffeemaker; breakfast is brought to your room.

Flowers, fruit, chocolates, robes, and hair dryers are part of the pampering John and Madeleine offer. They've even placed French perfumes in the baths. Domaine Madeleine is close to Olympic National Park, Dungeness National Wildlife Refuge, and Port Townsend. Courtesy transportation to the Victoria ferry and Port Angeles Airport is provided.

Lake Crescent Lodge

HC 62, P.O. Box 11
Port Angeles, WA 98362
360-928-3211

| **A classic lodge overlooking the lake** |

Manager: Britt Steele. **Accommodations:** 52 rooms (shared baths) and cottages. **Rates:** $65–$138 single or double, $10 additional person. **Minimum stay:** None. **Payment:** Major credit cards. **Children:** Welcome in cottages and motel units. **Pets:** Allowed in cottages ($10). **Smoking:** Allowed. **Open:** Lodge, late April to October; fireplace cottages, year-round.

➤ **Lake Crescent looks inviting on a hot day, and the hardy can swim in its cold waters. You can also rent a rowboat and fish for Beardslee trout.**

Clear and blue as a Scottish loch, Lake Crescent lies at the northern edge of Olympic National Park, rimmed by fir, cedar, and spruce trees, with Storm King Mountain and Pyramid Peak rising from its shores. On the south side of the lake, this fir and cedar lodge was built in 1915, one of several lakeside lodges of which only two remain.

Owned by the National Park Service, Lake Crescent Lodge is run by concessionaires and has cottage and motel units as well as lodge rooms. Although the facilities have been updated and expanded over the years, the older cottages maintain their exterior rustic appearance and charm, with roofs extending over porches and trellises with blooming flowers. Inside, you'll find comfortable motel-style furnishings, modern tile baths, and windows that overlook the lake. Most cottages and motel rooms have two double beds; some have queen- or king-size beds. Four cottages have fireplaces, refrigerators, and coffeemakers.

Least expensive are the five lodge rooms sharing two baths down the hall, one for men, one for women. The bedrooms, each with a washbasin, are modestly furnished and best suited for travelers who are alone or in couples. No closets or pegs are provided, the walls are thin, and the floors creak. But casement windows open to lovely views of the lake, with bright red rowboats rocking at the edge of the shore.

The lobby is the hub of activity at the historic lodge. Game trophies hang on the paneled walls, which glow with a rich patina. On display are examples of Native American art, old and new, available for purchase in the gift shop. Guests cluster near the stone fireplace or in the section partitioned off as a small lounge beside the entrance to the restaurant. The casual dining room on the lodge's lake side serves three meals a day, specializing in Northwest seafood.

An enclosed sun porch, extending the length of the building, is a pleasant place to sit and write postcards or admire the reflections of trees and mountains in the ever-changing water.

The SeaSuns

1006 S. Lincoln
Port Angeles, WA 98362
360-452-8248

An inviting home in a residential neighborhood

Innkeepers: Bob and Jan Harbick. **Accommodations:** 4 rooms (2 with private bath). **Rates:** Summer, $85–$95; less in winter; $25 additional person in summer, $15 in winter. **Minimum stay:** None. **Payment:** MasterCard, Visa. **Children:** Over age 12, welcome. **Pets:** Not allowed. **Smoking:** Not allowed. **Open:** Year-round.

➤ **For authentic and excellent Italian cuisine, in a festive atmosphere, dine at Bella Italia, one of Port Angeles's best restaurants.**

Your first indication that the SeaSuns is a welcoming home comes with the hosts' warm greeting and offer to help with your baggage and dinner reservations and a ride to the ferry if you need it. The Harbicks, who've operated their B&B since 1996, do a lot for their guests. They bring morning coffee to your room on a silver tray, will pack a picnic lunch on request, provide snacks, and arrange fishing and riding trips. They serve a fine breakfast that often features salmon, and sometimes Dutch babies with fruit.

Guests rave about the place. "One of our best B&B experiences," "a great breakfast," and a "charming atmosphere" are a few of their comments.

The gracious Dutch Colonial home has a large living room with a fireplace. Several stuffed animals — not too many — are scattered around the house. Each guest room is named for a season. Winter, the largest, includes a sitting area and shares a bath with Spring, the smallest room, which features flowers and pastels and has a private deck. Summer, on the main floor, also has a deck, plus a private entrance and a jetted tub in the bath. Autumn, with a view of the mountains and water, reflects the season's colors. One room has a queen-size bed; the others have doubles.

After a day of exploring in Olympic National Park, it's a pleasure to relax under the vine-covered pergola in the garden and listen to the little waterfall.

The Tudor Inn

1108 South Oak Street
Port Angeles, WA 98362
360-452-3138

**A hospitable B&B on the
Olympic Peninsula**

Innkeeper: Jane Glass. **Accommodations:** 5 rooms (2 with private bath). **Rates:** $55–$85 single, $58–$90 double. **Included:** Full breakfast. **Minimum stay:** None. **Payment:** MasterCard, Visa (prefer cash or check). **Children:** Age 12 and older, welcome. **Pets:** Not allowed. **Smoking:** On porch only. **Open:** Year-round.

➤ **Port Angeles is a gateway to Olympic National Park on the south and a ferry terminal to Canada on the north.**

The Tudor Inn has been a popular stopping place on the north shore of the Olympic Peninsula since 1983, when it opened as a B&B. The rooms in the half-timbered, stucco inn are furnished with antiques from Jane Glass's collection and prettily decorated with hand-painted flowers and, in one room, a full landscape. The largest room has a king-size canopy bed; the others have queen-size. When winter's chill descends, you'll nestle under a Norwegian down comforter, which replaces the light covers used in summer. It's easy to sleep well, with no sound but the buoys and foghorns in the channel.

Views from the hillside home include glimpses of the Strait of Juan de Fuca and the Olympic Mountains as well as the inn's gazebo and terraced plantings of dahlias, wildflowers, and daisies.

On the main floor, guests relax in the living room by the white stone fireplace or in the den, which has shelves of books, a TV, and phone.

Breakfast is served in the dining room at two seatings, early for those catching the ferry to Victoria and later for those who want to sleep in. At a common table, guests compare travel and skiing notes while feasting on date muffins, raisin toast, scrambled eggs, bacon, and fresh fruit.

In the afternoon, you'll be offered tea, cider, or lemonade and cookies by a hostess who loves the region and enjoys sharing her wealth of information about it.

Port Ludlow

Inn at Ludlow Bay

One Heron Road
Port Ludlow, WA 98365
360-437-0411
Fax: 360-437-0310

A bayside inn with luxury and fine dining

Manager: David Holt. **Accommodations:** 37 rooms and suites. **Rates:** Summer, $165–$200 single or double; other seasons, $135–$195; $35 additional person; suites $300–$450. **Included:** Expanded Continental breakfast. **Minimum stay:** 2 nights in summer and on weekends and holidays. **Payment:** Major credit cards. **Children:** Welcome. **Pets:** Not allowed. **Smoking:** Outdoors only. **Open:** Year-round.

➤ **Guests have priority tee times and special rates at the 27-hole Port Ludlow Golf Course.**

The Inn at Ludlow Bay stands on a spit jutting into the bay, on the eastern shore of the Olympic Peninsula. It's part of the resort community of Port Ludlow, which has a 27-hole golf course and a full-service marina that rents seabikes, kayaks, and sailboats. The inn bears a resemblance to a New England coastal hotel with a wraparound verandah and Adirondack chairs, though the stone, shake, and painted peach of the exterior is less than ideal in the woodsy Northwest.

The rooms offer every comfort. They have fluffy duvets on firm beds, windows that open to the sea breeze, Jacuzzi tubs, good reading lamps, robes, and gas fireplaces. Each room has a coffeemaker and refrigerator. Best are the corner rooms with king-size beds; some have balconies.

Guests are treated well here, receiving preferred seating in the waterfront dining room, which is noted for outstanding cuisine. The chef, Joseph Merkling, has received national acclaim for his skill at blending Asian and Northwest flavors. Fresh seafood is a specialty. Another good dining spot, in a more casual setting (and less expensive) is the Library Room, offering a fireside menu. You might try coconut lime seafood chowder, peppercorn-crusted seared salmon with a cilantro-coconut sauce, or rice paper–wrapped summer rolls served with rare ahi.

A buffet breakfast is set out in the sun room, which has a fine view overlooking the lawn and rose bed, as well as the bay and the mountains.

Most guests come to this pleasant inn to relax, play golf, go boating, and venture into the green beauty of Olympic National Park. The hotel provides conference space for 10 to 75 people.

Port Ludlow Resort and Conference Center

200 Olympic Place
Port Ludlow, WA 98365
360-437-2222
800-732-1239
Fax: 360-437-2482

A waterside resort famed for outdoor recreation

General Manager: Bob Hobart. **Accommodations:** 188 rooms. **Rates:** Rooms: $90–$115 double, May–October; suites: $135–$420, 1–8 people; discounts and packages available. **Minimum stay:** None. **Payment:** Major credit cards. **Children:** Under age 12, free. **Pets:** Not allowed. **Smoking:** Nonsmoking rooms available. **Open:** Year-round.

➤ **Harbormaster Restaurant, overlooking the marina, has a bistro menu. The Wreck Room lounge is lively, with a big-screen TV and a sun deck.**

Above the waters of Port Ludlow Bay, one of the many inlets on the east side of the Olympic Peninsula, a group of boxy buildings stands among the native shrubbery and landscaped lawns. Visitors here enjoy modern, comfortable lodgings in one of Washington's prettiest waterfront settings. In recent years, the bayside location has become highly desirable, and a nearby development of condos and homes, called Port Ludlow Village, has grown into a major feature of the area.

Resort apartments are furnished in similar styles, with a blue and mauve decor and light oak furniture. They have kitchens, a TV, phones, and decks. The suites, with one to four bedrooms, have fireplaces. They all have access to the beach.

Building 18 is right above the water; in a loft room, doors to an angled balcony provide a fine vantage point for watching boats come and go. The lawn below extends as far as the thicket of blackberries, then the vine-covered bluff drops off to the water. The rooms, furnished in Northwest contemporary style, have a nautical flavor, with blue and gray colors and seashell-patterned fabrics. If a view is important, be sure to request one, as some rooms overlook only the parking lot or another building.

While Port Ludlow caters to groups, it also appeals strongly to families. As you stroll the grounds, you may see in one corner a basketball game in full swing; and in another, the small pitch-and-putt course in use. One group is holding a croquet match, another a picnic, another is out bicycling on the paths, while children are climbing on the playground. All this activity is going on at once, yet thanks to an intelligent layout there is no sense of crowding or undue noise.

Tennis is available, as are bicycles, volleyball, paddle boats and dinghies, badminton equipment, and fins and snorkels. The Beach Club has two swimming pools, one open in winter, the other in summer. The conference center opened in 1992.

Port Ludlow provides a shuttle to the 27-hole golf course, which has been rated by the American Society of Golf Course Architects as one of the best-designed courses in the country. Its challenging fairways undulate through woodlands with views of Admiralty Inlet. There's also a clubhouse with a restaurant, a pro shop, and a gift shop.

Port Townsend

Ann Starrett Mansion

744 Clay Street
Port Townsend, WA 98368
360-385-3205
800-321-0644
Fax: 360-385-2976

A grand Victorian home in a small seaside town

Innkeepers: Bob and Edel Sokol. **Accommodations:** 11 rooms and suites. **Rates:** Summer, $75–$225 double; other seasons, $70–$145; $20 additional person. **Included:** Full breakfast. **Minimum stay:** None. **Payment:** Major credit cards. **Children:** Over age 12, welcome. **Pets:** Not allowed. **Smoking:** Not allowed. **Open:** Year-round.

➤ **Port Townsend is a noted arts center with a number of yearly festivals; the main one is summer's Celebration of American Arts**

In the late 1800s George Starrett, a housebuilder from Maine, decided to construct a home in this burgeoning seaport town as a wedding gift for his wife, Ann. It would also showcase his building skills. The result was a magnificent example of Victorian style and workmanship that continues to draw admiring visitors.

The mansion bears the stamp of the craftsman, from the free-hanging circular stairway to the gabled widow's walk to the delicate carvings on the doorway lintels. The mahogany staircase winds to a third-story tower, where ceiling frescoes represent the seasons. When the sun's rays pass through the red window at the top at a solstice or equinox, light falls on the painting representing that period.

The rest of the house is also heavily ornamented with frescoes, predominantly the fruits and vines and flowers that were fashionable in 1890. The rooms are furnished with antiques the Sokols have collected.

Despite their opulence, the guest rooms have a homey feel. Ann's Parlor is the room where Ann Starrett greeted guests; now it's a comfortable bedroom with a four-poster bed, a private balcony, and a view of the sound. The Nursery, where the Starretts' son once slept, has a wooden bed and corner windows overlooking the quiet street. Next to it is Nanny's Room, with a brass bed and a rocking chair that belonged to Edel's mother. It's easy to imagine a Victorian nanny here, rocking her young charge to sleep.

From the sitting alcove in the Master Suite, views encompass Mount Rainier, the Olympic Mountains, and Port Townsend Bay. The Gables Suite, under the eaves on the third floor, has a sprightly, springlike atmosphere. The green walls are painted with birds, roses, and angels, and the furniture is white wicker.

Four guest rooms are in the basement, but there is no sense of being stuck in a cellar here. The Garden Suite is light, though not Victorian, with white wicker chairs and shutters. The brick-walled Amana Room, the least expensive, features antiques from the Amana Colony; it has a private entrance. The original carriage house door is now a wall in the Carriage Room, which contains a sleigh bed.

The cottage next door has been transformed into two spacious suites, one upstairs and one down.

The Sokols serve a satisfying breakfast promptly at 8:30. The choices may include crêpes, quiche, granola, yogurt and fruit, apple turnovers, and stuffed French toast. On Sundays, chocolates and champagne are offered as well.

Port Townsend, a designated National Historic District, has several other Victorian buildings that are open to the public. The Visitor's Center and Jefferson County Historic Museum can supply you with information.

Bishop Victorian Hotel

714 Washington Street
Port Townsend, WA 98368
360-385-6122
800-824-4738

A small hotel catering to families

Innkeepers: Joseph and Cindy Finnie. **Accommodations:** 14 suites. **Rates:** Summer: $79–$139 weekends, $69–$109 midweek; winter: $59–$109. **Included:** Continental breakfast. **Minimum stay:** 2 nights on holiday and festival weekends. **Payment:** Major credit cards. **Children:** Under age 12, free. **Pets:** Allowed with prior approval ($10). **Smoking:** Nonsmoking rooms available. **Open:** Year-round.

➤ **At Port Townsend Marine Science Center, visitors can touch sea cucumbers, starfish, and other sea creatures.**

In a town of Victorian homes filled with priceless antiques, it can be hard to find appealing lodgings suitable for families. The Bishop Victorian is an exception, providing a happy combination of comfort and style that reflects the local character.

The three-story brick building, a block inland from the waterfront, formerly housed apartments and a hotel. It was renovated in the early 1990s and now contains suites tastefully furnished with art and antiques as well as updated facilities. Each suite has a kitchenette and a sitting room with TV, phone, and sofa bed. The registration desk is one flight up from the street (no elevator), and the guest rooms are on the second and third floors. In keeping with the Victorian theme, artifacts of the period such as fans, boots, and gloves have been beautifully framed and hung in the rooms and hallways.

A Continental breakfast featuring fresh hot rolls and pastries is served buffet style in the upper level common area. You may take a tray to your room or eat in the lounge.

Guests have access to the Port Townsend Athletic Club facilities. Off-street parking is available.

James House

1238 Washington Street
Port Townsend, WA 98368
360-385-1238
800-385-1238
Fax: 360-379-5551

> **A classic Queen Anne on a bluff above the bay**

Innkeepers: Carol McGough. **Accommodations:** 12 rooms (10 with private bath), suites, and cottage. **Rates:** $60–$90 single, $75–$165 double. **Included:** Full breakfast. **Minimum stay:** None. **Payment:** MasterCard, Visa. **Children:**

Age 12 and older, welcome in cottage and garden suites. **Pets:** Not allowed. **Smoking:** Not allowed. **Open:** Year-round.

➤ **Port Townsend holds a Rhododendron Festival in May, the world-renowned Wooden Boat Festival in September, and a Summer Arts Festival.**

Since it opened in 1973, James House has maintained its tradition of hospitality in a stately setting. With rooms filled with antiques, parquet floors, and a carved staircase polished to a sheen, it represents the best of a bygone day.

The Queen Anne home, on a high bluff above the commercial district and busy Port Townsend Bay, was built in 1891 for Francis James, who came from England and worked as an Indian agent and assistant lighthouse keeper at Cape Flattery, on the western tip of the Olympic Peninsula. James was successful in real estate and built his $10,000 home (at the time, a good house could be constructed for $4,000) for his retirement. In his later years, he was often seen on the widow's walk off the master bedroom, watching the ships come and go.

Since then, the house has changed hands several times and now is a bit of living history, faded in spots but still expressing the gracious spirit of its time, formal without being somber.

The guest rooms vary in size and decor. (Some beds are soft; if you prefer a firm mattress, be sure to request it.) The Bridal Suite is especially popular for its working fireplace and four bay windows that overlook the landing for the Seattle ferry. One long window opens to a private balcony.

Room 2, on the third floor, has a bay view and a sleigh bed. Number 6 is a sunny corner room, while number 8 is an intimate space in pale violet, with a white wicker writing table, a brass and white iron bedstead, and a dressing table tucked into the closet.

At ground level there are two brick-walled garden suites. One has a parlor stove, a brass bed, and an eye-level view of the gardens. The other is furnished in antiques and wicker and has a fireplace.

James House is full of charming nooks, angles, and surprises. In the library, a display case holds James's beaver top hat, his satchel, and personal papers and geography books. In the Music Room, there's a quaint century-old music box from Germany.

Breakfast is served in the formal dining room or at an oak table in the kitchen. It consists of fresh fruit, granola and yogurt, homemade scones, and a main dish such as quiche or chile relleno casserole. Cookies and coffee are available all day, as well as a decanter of sherry on the dining room sideboard.

There's a strong sense of the past in Port Townsend, where so many ornate 19th-century buildings like the James House have been carefully preserved, but it's combined with the freshness of an active present.

Lizzie's

731 Pierce Street
Port Townsend, WA 98368
360-385-4168
800-700-4168

A historic home with a sense of place

Innkeepers: Patty and Bill Wickline. **Accommodations:** 7 rooms. **Rates:** $70–$135 single or double. **Included:** Full breakfast. **Minimum stay:** 2 nights in summer. **Payment:** Major credit cards. **Children:** Over age 10, welcome. **Pets:** Not allowed. **Smoking:** Not allowed. **Open:** Year-round.

➤ **Try the popular Fountain Café, Salal Café, and the Landfall. Bread & Roses is a great little bakery.**

Legend says there's a ghost at Lizzie's — the ghost of a lovely woman who once lived in the house. She's apparently a friendly sort, and once you have stayed at this pleasant guesthouse, you'll see why she would be reluctant to leave it.

Lizzie's is a gentle place, full of Victorian charm and the fabled slower pace of life. In fact, the owners call it "an anachronism — a thing out of harmony with the present time." In this case, the anachronism is intentional, befitting a 19th-century house built in a town that time passed by.

When the Union Pacific decided to end the railroad tracks at Seattle rather than Port Townsend, dreams of glory for the region faded. For a century the village slumbered, eking out a living as a minor seaport, until it struck gold with tourism. Now the romantic history and gingerbread homes draw visitors by the score, and places like Lizzie's allow them to step back in time for a night or two.

The blue-green frame house with white trim and bay windows is on a residential street behind a boxwood hedge. Period furnishings in its two red-carpeted parlors include a grand piano, cast-iron fireplaces, and a spinning wheel. You can see the original wallpaper (now faded) in the front parlor.

The guest rooms are decorated with individual flair, though all contain Victorian antiques. Lizzie's Room, on the first floor, has green wallpaper with exotic birds and flowers — a Victorian fantasy jungle — and a queen-size bed with a half canopy. It has a fireplace and a clawfoot tub in the bath. There are two more rooms on the main floor.

Upstairs, behind doors with lacy hearts and flowers, lie ornately carved beds, chaise longues, old-fashioned rocking chairs, and views of both town and bay. In Daisy's Room, look for Daisy's name on the wall. When the house was remodeled, the signature was framed rather than covered by wallpaper, and there it is today, with the date: 1894. Sarah's Room has the best view, overlooking the bay and the picturesque courthouse.

You'll have breakfast in Lizzie's big kitchen, around a long table shared with the other guests. Dutch babies and seasonal fruit from the inn's garden are often on the menu.

Palace Hotel

1004 Water Street
Port Townsend, WA 98368
360-385-0773
800-962-0741
palace@olympus.net

A historic hotel in a Victorian seaside town

Managers: Michael and Spring Thomas. **Accommodations:** 15 rooms (all with basins, 12 with private bath). **Rates:** $65–$139 single or double, $10 additional person; winter and weekly discounts. **Included:** Continental breakfast. **Minimum stay:** None. **Payment:** Major credit cards. **Children:** Under age 12, $5. **Pets:** Not allowed. **Smoking:** Nonsmoking rooms available. **Open:** Year-round.

➤ **The Jefferson County Museum has Native American artifacts, relics from a Chinese community, old firefighting equipment, Victorian toys and furniture, and photographs.**

In the heart of Port Townsend's downtown district, just a couple of blocks from the waterfront, the brick Palace Hotel provides comfortable, convenient lodging in a historic area.

From the lobby you climb wide, carpeted stairs to the landing and its life-size portrait of a Victorian lady dressed in blue. Light streams through the skylight to stained glass windows by the open stairs that lead up to the guest rooms.

Despite their age and history, the hotel's rooms are bright and inviting, with big windows that overlook Water Street and glimpse the harbor. Some rooms have kitchens, most with microwaves. All have antique furnishings and cable television. A phone is in the lounge off the landing. Coffee is provided, and juice and rolls are delivered to the door each morning.

The Palace has a colorful past. Constructed in 1889, when Port Townsend had high hopes of becoming a major seaport, it was a house of ill repute known for a time as the Palace of Sweets. The madam's room, now Marie's Suite, contains framed samples of the original red wallpaper and green woodwork. The corner room has a reproduction brass bed, a cast iron fireplace (logs are supplied), and an entire wall of windows above lively, shop-lined Water Street.

On the mezzanine and lobby levels is Blackberries, known for its excellent cuisine. Funds from the nonprofit restaurant are donated to the needy.

Quimper Inn

1306 Franklin Street
Port Townsend, WA 98368
360-385-1060
800-557-1060

A renovated home with up-to-date style

Innkeepers: Sue and Ron Ramage. **Accommodations:** 5 rooms (3 with private bath). **Rates:** Summer, $80–$140; winter, $75–$125. **Included:** Full Breakfast. **Minimum stay:** None. **Payment:** MasterCard, Visa. **Children:** Over age 12, welcome. **Pets:** Not allowed. **Smoking:** Not allowed. **Open:** Year-round.

➤ **For northern Italian food, don't miss Lanza's. The Silverwater Café is good for light meals, and Blackberries for innovative Northwestern cuisine.**

In the early years of the 20th century, Harry and Gertrude Barthrop bought a simple, square, two-story house in Port Townsend and remodeled it. They used gables and dormers to create a third floor, enlarged the windows, and put in bay windows, after the style of H. H. Richardson and Louis Sullivan, the forefathers of the Chicago School of Modern Architecture.

Many years later, after it had been a boarding house, a nurses' dormitory, and a warehouse, the home underwent two restorations. The last was by Bill Withers, a visual designer for Macy's, who furnished it with individual flair. The Ramages then took over and opened the B&B in 1991, maintaining its unusual style and charm.

The house contains some antiques and remnants of the Victorian ear, but it isn't the faithful replica commonly seen in Port Townsend. Dark woodwork contrasts with white walls in the large, inviting parlor. Beyond it is the dining room, with a bay window overlooking a sycamore tree, the lawn, and flowers. Here guests enjoy a breakfast of eggs, sausage and bacon, and muffins, though Sue is happy to adjust the menu to a guest's dietary needs.

The guest room called the Library, on the main floor, is the ideal spot for a book lover, with floor-to-ceiling bookshelves and a sliding ladder so that you can reach the books on the top shelves.

Harry's Room is an upstairs corner suite with rooms separated by pocket doors. From here you get terrific views of the Olympic Mountains, Admiralty Inlet, and the old red brick courthouse and clock tower.

Michele's Room, decorated in rose, gray, and white, has a bay view, a puffy down duvet on the queen-size bed, and an enormous bathroom with a clawfoot tub.

Christopher's Room, in the front corner, has twin beds and Eastlake furniture and shares a white tile bath with John's Room. John's is smaller, though not cramped, and has a double bed and large closet. You'll find morning coffee set on the old Victrola on the landing. You might carry your cup out to the balcony, where you can admire the flowers in window boxes and watch the boats come and go at the Port Townsend ferry landing.

Ravenscroft Inn

533 Quincy Street
Port Townsend, WA 98368
360-385-2784
800-782-2691
Fax: 360-385-6724
ravenscroft@olympus.net

**A B&B with views of the
Strait of Juan de Fuca**

Innkeeper: Leah Hammer. **Accommodations:** 6 rooms and 2 suites. **Rates:** Summer: $67–$165 double, $7.50 less single; winter: $65–$150. **Included:** Full breakfast. **Minimum stay:** 2 nights during summer and holidays. **Payment:** Major credit cards. **Children:** Age 12 and older, welcome. **Pets:** Not allowed. **Smoking:** Not allowed. **Open:** Year-round.

➤ **Fort Worden, a 446-acre estate of restored military barracks and Victorian officers' homes, is also the home of the Centrum Foundation for the arts.**

Almost every entry in the Ravenscroft guest book reads, "We'll be back," for this spacious, comfortable inn has the kind of atmosphere that makes you want to return.

Built in 1987 on a hillside with a view of Port Townsend and the water, the three-story rectangular inn has a classic, timeless style reminiscent of a Charleston mansion. A verandah and balcony extend across the front of the building. Greenery hangs in tall casement windows, and watercolors on the walls. Leah's talent as a creative decorator is evident throughout the B&B.

Breakfast is served at tables for two or four in the dining area next to a big, open kitchen that is every cook's dream. Fruit frappé, crustless quiche, a grapefruit half, muffins, and apple bread are some of the morning treats.

The guest rooms upstairs are well outfitted with comfortable beds, brass reading lamps, and clocks. Fireside Room has a brick fireplace, a four-poster bed, and a rose motif. French doors lead to a balcony with a view of the town and the Strait of Juan de Fuca. Bay Room, done in washed pine and Waverly fabrics, also has a balcony. Wicker Room contains wicker furniture and the whimsical touch of a bassinet holding teddy bears. The Admiralty Suite, done in yellow and blue, features a window seat with a view of Mount Baker. The suite has a clawfoot soaking tub on a raised platform.

On the third floor, along with the owner's quarters, is Rainier Suite, which has two rooms and two baths. It has a white wicker rocker and couch, pale green walls, and candles ready to light beside the double Jacuzzi. From the window, you can see the ferries come and go across the strait. The ferry blasts and seagulls' calls are almost the only sounds that interrupt the quiet in this peaceful inn.

The Swan

Monroe and Water Street
Port Townsend, WA 98368
360-385-1718
800-776-1718
Fax: 360-379-1010
swan@waypt.com

A small hotel in a Victorian seaport

Proprietors: Cindy and Joseph Finnie. **Accommodations:** 5 suites, 4 cottages. **Rates:** $80–$350, 2 to 6 people, discounts in winter. **Minimum stay:** None. **Payment:** Major credit cards. **Children:** Welcome. **Pets:** Allowed in cottages. **Smoking:** Allowed in 1 cottage. **Open:** Year-round.

➤ **Port Townsend lies in the rain shadow of the Olympic Mountains and so receives less rain than much of the peninsula.**

The Swan is close to Port Hudson Marina and a few blocks from Port Townsend's main shopping area. Built in 1989 to resemble a New Orleans hotel with balconies all around, it has spacious suites with kitchens.

The rooms have double and queen-size beds, sofa beds, and armoires. If you take the penthouse, you'll walk up outside stairs to the third floor, and then have a fine view of the water. The penthouse, with a large table in the dining area, is well suited to small conferences. It has two bedrooms (one with a king-size bed and Jacuzzi tub), a den with TV, and a loft with two more sleeping areas.

Across the parking lot from the hotel are the cottages, which date from the 1930s. They've been refurbished as small, cozy rooms, one with a water view. Rag rugs on hardwood floors, stencils on the walls, quilts, and checked curtains add to the ambience. Each cottage has a coffeemaker, microwave, refrigerator, and phone.

Poulsbo

Foxbridge Bed & Breakfast

30680 Highway 3 NE
Poulsbo, WA 98370
360-598-5599

A country manor on Kitsap Peninsula

Innkeepers: Bev and Chuck Higgins. **Accommodations:** 3 rooms. **Rates:** $85 single or double. **Included:** Full breakfast. **Minimum stay:** None. **Payment:** Visa, MasterCard. **Children:** Over age 16, welcome; any age if entire house is rented. **Pets:** Not allowed. **Smoking:** Outdoors only. **Open:** Year-round.

➤ **In mid-May, Poulsbo holds a Viking Fest. It features an arts and crafts show, food booths, a pancake breakfast, fun run, carnival, and parade.**

In the wooded countryside close to the Hood Canal Bridge, this Georgian Manor home sits on 5 acres, which include an orchard and a pond stocked with trout. The gracious hosts will encourage you to pick fruit from the trees and help you spot the bald eagles, blue heron, deer, and other wildlife on the property.

The Higginses built their large home as a bed-and-breakfast; their care is reflected in the superb quality of the place. It opened to guests in 1993 with a fox hunt theme that comes from the owners' days in Virginia. Guests are welcome to make themselves at home in several common areas: a sitting room, a cozy den with a fireplace and books, and a family room where you'll probably end up at the kitchen bar, chatting with the cook.

The three upstairs rooms, which overlook the gardens and cedar trees, have queen-size beds and different styles. Country Garden, in soft cream and rose, has a four-poster bed. The focus in the Old World Room is the sleigh bed, which is covered with a goosedown comforter. Foxhunt contains a four-poster oak bed, forest green and cranberry furnishings, and a fox or two. All the rooms and baths are immaculately clean and have good reading lamps and fresh flowers.

If you stay two weeks, you'll never have the same breakfast twice. The menu varies daily and usually includes fresh fruit and nuts from the orchard.

The Kitsap Peninsula is full of intriguing sights: the historic village of Port Gamble, the excellent Native American Suquamish

Museum, and Poulsbo, a delightful town that makes the most of its Norwegian heritage. Chuck and Bev have brochures and maps and will help you plan your route. But you may find it hard to go anywhere once you arrive at Foxbridge, with its peaceful atmosphere and lovely setting.

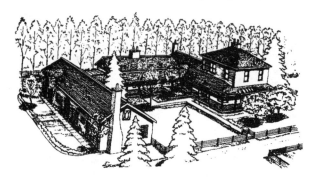

The Manor Farm Inn

26069 Big Valley Road N.E.
Poulsbo, WA 98370
360-779-4628
Fax: 360-779-4876

An estate in the country, near Hood Canal

Innkeeper: Jill Hughes. **Accommodations:** 7 rooms. **Rates:** $120–$170. **Included:** Full breakfast. **Minimum stay:** None. **Payment:** MasterCard, Visa. **Children:** Over age 16, welcome. **Pets:** Not allowed. **Smoking:** Not allowed. **Open:** Year-round.

➤ **Poulsbo is a pretty harbor town that honors its heritage with traditional festivals. Shops sell Scandinavian crafts, jewelry, and food.**

This is the picture that comes to mind when city folk dream of life in the country: a white frame house built in the 1890s, with roses climbing on a broad verandah and masses of tulips and daisies in bloom; fruit trees, vegetable and herb gardens; and a few sheep, a cow, some horses, and contented chickens. That's the Manor Farm Inn.

At this peaceful spot, the day begins with juice, hot scones, and coffee in your room. Later the full country breakfast is served in the dining room or on the lawn, with eggs from the farm's hens and fruit from its trees. You can spend the rest of the day wandering around the farm, sniffing the hay, watching the animals, listening to the wind in the poplar trees, or fly-fishing in the trout pond. Bicycles are available if you wish to explore the local byways. The quaint waterfront town of Poulsbo, 4 miles away, is an interesting place to visit: it has been turned into a little Scandinavia.

In the afternoon you can retire to the drawing room or courtyard for afternoon tea and crumpets with homemade raspberry jam. On Friday and Saturday nights, a five-course dinner is served at one seating in the dining room. The menu, which changes monthly, features three entrées. Specialties include grilled salmon and fennel, roast lamb with truffles, and scallops with raspberry-thyme butter. After dessert, coffee, and port, you'll perhaps stroll the grounds, stargazing, then turn in to sleep soundly under a down comforter.

The guest rooms are off a long verandah facing the lawn behind the main farmhouse. Wreaths of dried pine and juniper hang on the doors. Inside, white stucco walls and high angled ceilings lend a bright airiness to the country-luxury tone. Most rooms have pine antiques; some have fireplaces with copper andirons (baskets of wood are supplied). None has a phone or TV.

Prosser

Wine Country Inn

104 Sixth Street
Prosser, WA 99350
509-786-2855

A restored B&B in the wine country

Innkeepers: Chris Flodin and Audrey Zuniga. **Accommodations:** 4 rooms (2 with private bath). **Rates:** $65–$75, $15 additional person. **Included:** Full breakfast. **Minimum stay:** None. **Payment:** MasterCard, Visa. **Children:** Welcome. **Pets:** Allowed on leash outside. **Smoking:** Not allowed. **Open:** Year-round.

➤ **Wineries offering tastings are Yakima River Winery, Pontin Del Roza, Hinzerling Winery, Chinook Wines, and the Hogue Cellars.**

More than twenty wineries lie within 45 miles of Prosser, a small town at the southeastern end of the Yakima Valley. They're all easily reached from Wine Country Inn, an unassuming, cozy bed-and-breakfast on the bank of the Yakima River.

The restored turn-of-the-century home, furnished in a nostalgic country style, has a restaurant as well as guest rooms. The seasonal menu features Northwest cuisine served indoors or on the patio by the garden on Friday and Saturday nights and at brunch on Sundays. The wine list stars local labels.

One nicely furnished guest room, on the ground floor, has the disadvantage of being next to the kitchen. The biggest room, Riverside Romance, overlooks the shaded lawn, the Yakima River, and the bridge that spans it. Wicker furnishings and a rose color scheme lend a romantic mood. Warm woods and earth tones, greenery, and a cozy window seat make Chardonnay Room the homiest, and it has a private bath. Finally, the Country Kitchenette is just right if you want to do some light cooking. Its little kitchen area, defined by a border of heart stencils, has a hot plate, toaster oven, refrigerator, and dishes. The blue chairs and table are evocative of the 1940s. This room has a brass double bed and an old-fashioned window seat.

The country breakfast includes scrambled eggs, muffins, hash browns, sausage, and fruit.

Quinault

Lake Quinault Lodge

P.O. Box 7
South Shore Road
Quinault, WA 98575
360-288-2571
800-562-6672 in Washington
Fax: 360-288-2901

A historic lodge on the Olympic Peninsula

Manager: Russell Steele. **Accommodations:** 92 rooms. **Rates:** Rooms, $99–$140 double; $10 additional person; suites, $220; winter discounts available. **Mini-**

mum stay: None. **Payment:** Major credit cards. **Children:** Und\
Pets: Allowed ($10). **Smoking:** Allowed. **Open:** Year-round.

➤ **The park service maintains an interpretive Center in the H\
short distance from the lodge.**

Seven miles outside Olympic National Park but within the national forest, a two-story cedar lodge with green shutters and a great stone chimney sprawls across the lawn that slopes to Lake Quinault. This is vintage Northwest, a rustic hotel at the edge of the magnificent wilderness of the Olympic Peninsula. From here, west to the sea, the land is occupied by the Quinault Indian Reservation.

The lodge, now on the National Register of Historic Places, was built in 1926, but its history began much earlier. In 1896, Jack Ewell and James Ingram built a log hotel for those intrepid enough to cross the heavily forested peninsula. That building burned in 1923 and was replaced by the Lakeside Inn, which is part of the present lodge. Then, in 1925, another partnership obtained permission from the Forest Service to build a lodge. Round-the-clock labor completed the inn in ten weeks, even though materials had to be hauled over fifty miles of dirt road.

In 1937, Franklin D. Roosevelt toured the region; his stop at Lake Quinault helped convince him of the value of establishing Olympic National Park — 1,400 square miles of rain forest, hot springs, canyons, and snow-peaked mountains.

Popular as the lodge is today, and despite the sometimes overcrowded lobby and dining room, it retains its woodsy charm. Stenciled designs on the beamed ceiling, Native American art, hunting trophies, old wicker chairs, and an enormous fireplace in the lobby create an atmosphere the present owners work to continue. The guest rooms have an old-fashioned flavor, with brass and iron beds and clawfoot tubs. The beds are doubles or queen-size. Deluxe units, with a gas fireplace, are in a separate building. There are no kitchens, phones, or TV in the rooms.

As you drink in the view of gardens, lake, and trees from the dining room, you're likely to feel an urge to eat fresh, locally caught salmon, and the restaurant will happily oblige. The wine list includes Italian, French, and Northwest labels.

Although the lodge has a heated indoor pool, a sauna, horseshoes, canoes, and paddleboats, the overriding reason for coming here is the rain forest. Between 150 and 200 inches of rain fall on the western valleys of the peninsula, creating a lush green world. Hiking under the moss- and fern-laden trees of the Hoh River Valley trails is an extraordinary experience. The Hall of Mosses, a three-quarter loop, takes you past immense trees laden with shaggy moss. The Hoh River Trail extends deeper into the wilderness. There's a trail suitable for wheelchairs near the Visitors' Center.

Samish Island

Alice Bay Bed & Breakfast

982 Scott Road, Samish Island
Bow, WA 98232
360-766-6396
800-652-0223
Fax: 360-766-6396

One perfect, quiet suite by the bay

Innkeepers: Julie and Terry Rousseau. **Accommodations:** 1 suite. **Rates:** $90 double, $20 additional person. **Included:** Full breakfast. **Minimum stay:** None. **Payment:** MasterCard, Visa. **Children:** Welcome. **Pets:** Not allowed. **Smoking:** Not allowed. **Open:** Year-round.

➤ **In late summer, wild blackberries will be ripe along country roads. Picking them is one of the pleasures of life in the Pacific Northwest.**

Southwest of Bellingham and scenic Chuckanut Drive, Alice Bay Bed & Breakfast sits on a small bay that shelters a blue heron rookery. The large, graceful birds follow the tides. "When the tide is in, there will be at least a hundred of them here," says Julie, who provides a telescope for birders.

The suite is a restful room done in soft white and French country florals; you'll sleep on a feather bed, with Alice Bay just outside the window. From this vantage point or from a warm and watery perch in the outdoor hot tub, you can watch the tide move in and out, followed by blue herons feeding on saltwater delicacies.

In the summer kitchen, which faces the morning sun, Julie serves a satisfying breakfast that might include omelets, Dutch babies, French toast, or homemade scones with a hint of orange, along with fresh fruit. Julie, known for her cooking, has written the popular *Alice Bay Cookbook*, and she and Terry teach fall workshops on seafood preparation. Suppers are also available at their

B&B, as are private boat charters for fishing, crabbing, or picnicking on another island.

You can bicycle on the flat roads that circle the Skagit Valley tulip and daffodil fields, browse for antiques in nearby La Conner, wander along the beach with clam shovel in hand, or row the Rousseaus' boat when the tide is in.

San Juan Island

Friday Harbor House

130 West Street
P.O. Box 1385
Friday Harbor, WA 98250
360-378-8455
Fax: 360-378-8453

Fine-quality lodging and dining in a prime location

Manager: Jim Skoge. **Accommodations:** 20 rooms. **Rates:** May through October, $187–$277; November through April, $187–$257; additional person, $35. **Included:** Expanded Continental breakfast. **Minimum stay:** 2 nights on summer weekends and holidays. **Payment:** Major credit cards. **Children:** Welcome. **Pets:** Allowed by arrangement. **Smoking:** Not allowed. **Open:** Year-round.

➤ **Friday Harbor boasts several excellent art galleries.**

Location, location. If you like spectacular views, you won't find a better located hotel on San Juan Island. Friday Harbor House stands on a bluff above the busy marina, its windows overlooking the sailboats and yachts that fill the harbor, with an expanse of water and misty green islands beyond. The sunset views are a romantic's dream.

The architecture of the building itself, a three-story box, is less appealing, and parking in the narrow spaces provided is a challenge. Once inside, though, you encounter a plush little inn with many comforts and friendly, helpful service. Each room has a gas fireplace, TV, Jacuzzi tub, coffeemaker, and refrigerator. Toiletries are provided in the marble bathrooms, as well as magnifying mirrors, bathrobes, and hair dryers. Desks or writing tables aren't included, an indication that this is a spot for vacation rather than work, and you'll write nothing more than a postcard. Ground-floor rooms have sliding glass doors that open to a grassy area extending to the edge of the bluff.

Thoughtful amenities, such as the basket of apples at the reception counter, a stand of large, colorful umbrellas for guests' use, and complimentary island and Seattle newspapers, make visitors feel welcome.

The dining room at Friday Harbor House, open to the public, has earned a reputation for cuisine prepared by the noted chef Greg Atkinson. It's open nightly for dinner in summer and closed Tuesday and Wednesday in winter. The menu changes seasonally and features fresh local foods — greens from island farms, seafood from local waters. Recent winter choices included Shoal Bay mussels roasted with a black bean sauce, roasted vegetables and goat cheese on a freshly baked baguette, and warm spiced pork tenderloin with apple chutney. The wine list focuses on Northwest and California wines, plus a few select European labels. For a sweet touch, you might try the only local wine offered, Lopez Island Blackberry.

The serve-yourself breakfast, for hotel guests only, is also served in the light, attractive dining room. Tables for two or four are graced with fresh flowers. Guests may select from a variety of fruits, cereals, muffins, and scones, all to be enjoyed while admiring the lovely view.

Hillside House Bed & Breakfast

365 Carter Avenue
Friday Harbor, WA 98250
360-378-4730
800-232-4730
Fax: 360-378-3830

| **A homey retreat in the island's biggest town** |

Innkeepers: Dick, Cathy, and Megan Robinson. **Accommodations:** 7 rooms. **Rates:** Summer, $85–$175 double; winter, $65–$155; $25 additional person. **Included:** Full breakfast. **Minimum stay:** None. **Payment:** Major credit cards. **Children:** Over age 10, welcome. **Pets:** Not allowed. **Smoking:** Outdoors only. **Open:** Year-round.

➤ **Favorite activities are picking wild blackberries, boating, cycling, bird-watching, diving, fishing, kayaking, beachcombing, and whale-watching.**

Hillside House, less than a mile from downtown and the port of Friday Harbor, is a 4,000-square-foot contemporary home that has been remodeled as a B&B. When guests are not out exploring the island, they like to relax on the big deck, stroll around the four ponds, admire the flowers in the atrium, and chat with the friendly, outgoing Robinsons.

   Three of the guest rooms face east and have views of the harbor and Mount Baker. The largest, with the best view, is Eagle's Nest, on the third story, with a king-size bed, wet bar, TV, phone, balcony, and a spa for two. Captain's Quarters is also a large room, with a king-size bed and a 10-foot window seat. This room contains the Robinsons' memorabilia from their three-year sail on the *Vixen*. Ventana is the only room with a private entrance. It has a natural rock wall, a queen-size bed, and, a trademark of Hillside House, a window seat.

West-facing rooms, with floral comforters and lots of pillows, look into the two-story atrium and a stand of fir trees behind it.

A hearty breakfast is served buffet style in the sunny, open dining area at tables for two or four. Cathy and Dick whip up omelets to order, crêpes or a hot egg dish, along with juice and fresh fruit. If you pick the berries, they'll make hot berry cobbler for breakfast.

In addition to menus for nearby restaurants, the innkeepers have a list of island contacts for visitors; it's helpful when you want to rent a bicycle or kayak, go whale-watching or fishing, learn to dive, take a charter trip, buy fresh oysters, or go for a sail.

Lonesome Cove

5810-A Lonesome Cove Road
Friday Harbor, WA 98250
360-378-4477

| **Rustic cabins on north San Juan** |

Manager: Lawrence Penquite. **Accommodations:** 6 cabins. **Rates:** $95–$150 per cabin, 2–6 people. **Minimum stay:** 5 nights in summer, 2 nights in other months. **Payment:** MasterCard, Visa. **Children:** Welcome. **Pets:** Not allowed. **Smoking:** Discouraged. **Open:** Year-round.

➤ **Some 170 species of birds frequent the area. You may also see whales, and very likely seals, off the coast.**

This secluded retreat is on the north end of San Juan Island, facing Speiden Channel and Speiden Island, a wildlife preserve.

The red-trimmed, mossy-roofed log cabins were built by one man, Roy Durhack, in the 1940s. He built a cabin a year, cutting short logs that one person could handle, until they were completed. His intention was to create a fishing lodge, for the fishing is excellent here: red snapper, rock cod, sole, ling cod, and shark all frequent the waters off the cove, waiting for the right bait. Fishing is still one of the big draws at Lonesome Cove, but by no means the only one. Honeymooners love the place.

The cabins have no phones, TVs, or maid service; however, recent renovations have made them less rustic than in the past. They have electric heat, well-equipped kitchens, double beds, front decks with views, and stone fireplaces with firewood. They have been remodeled with hand-laid red cedar and new beds and carpeting but retain their 1940s character and charm. "I try to maintain a place that's clean and comfortable, but still a basic cabin at the beach," Larry says.

The Net Loft is popular with honeymooners. On the edge of the shore, it has a fireplace, a wet bar, and plenty of peace and privacy.

A good part of Lonesome Cove's appeal lies in its setting. There are 6 acres of lawn dotted with iris beds; an orchard with apple, plum, and cherry trees; and a lily pond with frogs and ducks. Picnic tables are scattered under the tall cedars, and a small curve of beach lies a few feet from the cabins. The pond is stocked with trout. Even the ducks are picturesque; they hastily waddle to Larry whenever he whistles.

Larry maintains a small library for guests that contains a wide range of subjects, from *The Life and Death of Ricky Nelson* to *Islam in Modern History.*

Reading by the fire is a pleasant prospect in the evenings, but during the day exploring the area is a must. Ten acres of forest are at your disposal. Boats may be rented, or you can bring your own and moor it at the 100-foot dock for a fee. Lonesome Cove is a special place, and very popular, so you won't have much luck getting a cabin on a weekend. Try for weekdays in the off-season.

Olympic Lights

4531-A Cattle Point Road
Friday Harbor, WA 98250
360-378-3186
Fax: 360-378-2097

A Victorian country farmhouse

Innkeepers: Christian and Lea Andrade. **Accommodations:** 5 rooms (1 with private bath). **Rates:** $65–$100 single, $70–$105 double, $20 additional person. **Included:** Full breakfast. **Minimum stay:** 2 nights in summer. **Payment:** Cash or check. **Children:** Not appropriate. **Pets:** Not allowed. **Smoking:** Not allowed. **Open:** Year-round.

➤ **The British Camp and American Camp, open to visitors, depict a time in the mid-1800s when Britain and the U.S. shared the island in an uneasy truce**

The old Johnson farm, 350 acres by the sea on San Juan Island, has undergone a transformation. In 1895, when cattle and chickens and a family with thirteen children lived here, it was probably jumping with activity, noise, and bustle. It's Olympic Lights now, a secluded, restful place with immaculate white carpets and subdued pastels on the walls. The cheerful guest rooms in the Victorian farmhouse are furnished with white wicker, simple shades, down comforters on queen-size beds, and flowery watercolors. The expanse of ivory walls and carpets and tile throughout the second floor makes every dash of color stand out. (You are asked to remove your shoes before going upstairs, to maintain the pristine whiteness.) The Ra Room is a favorite because of its sunny southeastern exposure and bay windows that view golden chain trees and, occasionally, a glimpse of Mount Rainier in the distance. Heart Room is largest, with a sitting area and queen-size and twin beds. The Garden Room, on the first floor, has a king-size bed and private bath.

You'll see numerous birds on the farm's 5 acres on this isolated corner at the southern tail of the island. Look for horned owls, hawks, and bald eagles, as well as the finches that flock to the bird feeder near the kitchen window.

Tea and sherry are offered in the living room, while sizable vegetarian breakfasts are served in the big, modern kitchen. Fruit, nut bread, juice, and a hot egg casserole constitute a typical breakfast, with the eggs fresh from the inn's chickens.

The innkeepers came from a faster-paced life in California. "It was one of the best choices we ever made," they say. Their ambition is to establish "a place of comfort and joy" that encourages contemplation. It's easy to slow down at this inn, a sure sign of their success.

Roche Harbor Resort and Marina

4950 Reuben Tarte Memorial Drive
Roche Harbor, WA 98250
360-378-2155
800-451-8910
Fax: 360-378-6809

An island resort with formal gardens

Resort Manager: Brent Snow. **Accommodations:** 20 hotel rooms (some with shared bath), 9 cottages, 22 condominiums. **Rates:** Hotel: summer, $79–$130; winter $55–$105. Condos: summer, $145–$245 (1–8 people); winter, $115–$195. Cottages (summer only): $130–$195 (up to 6 people). **Minimum stay:** 2 nights in cottages and condos. **Payment:** Major credit cards. **Children:** Welcome. **Pets:** Not allowed. **Smoking:** Not allowed. **Open:** Year-round.

➤ **Yachts dock regularly at the Roche Harbor marina; boaters consider the protected waters around San Juan Island to be prime cruising territory.**

Hotel de Haro, the centerpiece of this rambling resort, is a relic of an earlier day, when inns by the sea were white, with green roofs, towers, balconies, and gardens and arbors meant for strolling. The resort's restaurant, Roche Harbor Inn, has an equally classic design. Such establishments are more commonly found on the East Coast, but here the resort stands on the northwest corner of San Juan Island, tucked into a harbor that's closer to Canada than to the mainland U.S. Roche Harbor and Friday Harbor are U.S. customs ports of entry.

In the late 19th century, Roche Harbor was a company town, manufacturing limestone and its by-products. John S. McMillin's Roche Harbor Lime and Cement Company was the largest limeworks in the West, working thirteen quarries of rich deposits, and his fleet of cargo ships ranged the coast. The inn was built during this period.

Now it's a full resort with a little bit of everything: a marina, a private airfield, a general store, tennis, a swimming pool, and dancing in the lounge. There's even a chapel, and this is probably the only resort in the state with a mausoleum, a period piece erected in the woods for the McMillin family.

Lodgings include the museum-like hotel, where the floors are creaky, the steps crooked, and the bathtubs enormous; widely spaced cottages that were workers' homes in 1910; and modern condos. The aging but well-kept hotel rooms are furnished with antiques, although each has a telephone. If you stay in the Presidential Suite, where Theodore Roosevelt slept, you'll have a balcony with a view over a wisteria-covered trellis to the harbor. The furniture is red velvet Victorian, the fireplace polished wood and ceramic tile. There's a double bed, a sizable closet, and a private bathroom with a clawfoot tub and noisy plumbing.

The cottages down the road, some with sea views, have been updated but retain the atmosphere of old-fashioned summer houses, complete with screen doors, peeling paint, and swallows' nests in the eaves. They have kitchens and a hodgepodge of furnishings. The condos are typical modern apartments, with wall-to-wall carpeting, equipped kitchens, and TV. All have fireplaces and balconies with fine harbor views.

The restaurant — once McMillin's home — is directly above the water. It offers a standard American menu and is open daily from April through October and closed the rest of the year. The Lime Kiln Café is open year-round.

Trumpeter Inn

420 Trumpeter Way
Friday Harbor, WA 98250
360-378-3884
800-826-7926
Fax: 360-378-8235
swan@rockisland.com

> **A quiet country inn of charm and grace**

Innkeepers: Bobby and Don Wiesner. **Accommodations:** 5 rooms (all with private bath). **Rates:** Summer, $90–$115; winter, $70–$95 double; $25 additional person. **Included:** Full breakfast. **Minimum stay:** 2 nights on summer weekends. **Payment:** MasterCard, Visa. **Children:** Over age 12, welcome. **Pets:** Not allowed. **Smoking:** Outdoors only. **Open:** Year-round.

➤ **San Juan Island has several excellent restaurants. Springtree Eating Establishment, Roberto's, and Duck Soup Inn are considered the best.**

Trumpeter Inn, once a standard, two-story farmhouse, has been transformed into a first-rate hostelry that is perfect for travelers seeking a peaceful country retreat. It offers the personal touch of a B&B but has the atmosphere of an inn.

Many guests arrive by bicycle; it's an easy 2-mile ride from the ferry landing. The inn, named for the trumpeter swans that live on nearby ponds, sits on 5 acres. All the rooms, two downstairs and three upstairs, have a plant motif: Lavender, Sage, Rosemary, Yarrow, and Bay Laurel. They're furnished with king- and queen-size beds and down comforters. Bay Laurel, the largest, is a corner room in burgundy and green, with its own sitting area. This room has views of the pastures where horses graze, the ducks on the pond, and the Olympic Mountains.

Breakfast is served at separate tables in the light, open dining area or on the deck. A typical meal might be muffins, fruit, strawberry pancakes, and eggs laid by the farm's chickens. It will leave you well fortified for a day of exploring San Juan Island. Later you might relax in the outdoor hot tub or watch a video in the sitting room.

Westwinds Harmony Cottage

Mailing address:
685 Spring St. #107
Friday Harbor, WA 98250
360-378-5283

> **A secluded private home on the west shore**

Owner: Christine Durbin. **Accommodations:** 1-bedroom house. **Rates:** Summer, $225; winter, $150. **Minimum stay:** None. **Payment:** MasterCard, Visa. **Children:** Welcome. **Pets:** Allowed by arrangement. **Smoking:** Outdoors only. **Open:** Year-round.

➤ **For exciting whale-watching and bird-watching from the water, book a cruise aboard *Way to Go,* a 30-foot hydrofoil. Call 360-378-2826.**

When you seek seclusion, quiet, and natural beauty, come to Westwinds Harmony Cottage. A few doors away from the original Westwinds B&B, it too is perched on a rocky hillside high above the west shore of San Juan Island. The two-story private home on 4 acres is used exclusively by guests. It sleeps four, with a queen-size bed in the living room, but most visitors are couples seeking privacy in a scenic setting.

From the decks that surround the house you may see orca whales; binoculars are provided. In the living room there's a tape deck, a stereo system with CDs, a VCR, and a woodstove (wood is supplied). The bedroom has a queen-size bed. The cottage's most striking feature is its location. From this vantage point you can watch boat traffic, sea life, and the sun rise over Mount Rainier and set over Victoria.

Breakfast is no longer provided, but the cottage has a full kitchen and there is a barbecue.

Wharfside Bed & Breakfast

P.O. Box 1212
Friday Harbor, WA 98250
360-378-5661

A floating B&B off San Juan Island

Innkeepers: Clyde and Bette Rice. **Accommodations:** 2 rooms (1 with private bath). **Rates:** $90–$95 double, $15 additional person, winter discounts available. **Included:** Full breakfast. **Minimum stay:** None. **Payment:** MasterCard, Visa. **Children:** Welcome. **Pets:** Allowed. **Smoking:** Not allowed in cabins. **Open:** Year-round.

➤ **The best place to spy porpoises and whales is Whalewatch Park. The Whale Museum has life-size models of orca whales and children's activities.**

Living aboard a boat is just as romantic and adventurous as you thought it would be. Prove it by stepping aboard the *Jacquelyn*, a 60-foot motor sailer docked at Friday Harbor.

In the main salon are ashwood couches, a TV, and a polished trestle table where guests meet for breakfast. Under a curving skylight there is a tape deck and stereo, a wet bar, begonias, knick-knacks, and lots of books. (One of particular note is *A Heaven in the Eye*, the award-winning autobiography by Clyde's father.)

The forward cabin has a double bed and two bunks, a snug setup for a family. It will be a tight squeeze, though. The bathroom (or head, in sailing jargon) is next to the main salon, and unless you are familiar with boats you'll have to learn how to operate the mechanism — rest assured, it's easy. The aft cabin is larger, with a queen-size bed and a private half-bath.

What Bette calls a "hearty seaman's breakfast" is served in the main salon or, weather permitting, on the poop deck. And hearty it is — platters of fruit, bacon and eggs, muffins, and breads that will fortify you for a full day's sightseeing.

A family aboard the *Jacquelyn* could be a bit cramped for space, shipshape though she is, but the salon allows plenty of room to sprawl, and children love it here. Bette supplies coffee cans for found treasures, and white-bearded Clyde is the image of a salty sea cap'n. "We're 'Grandma and Grandpa Boat' to the kids," says Bette.

The Rices will recommend restaurants and places to see in Friday Harbor and the rest of San Juan Island.

Seattle

Alexis Hotel

1007 First Avenue
Seattle, WA 98104
206-624-4844
800-426-7033
Fax: 206-621-9009

**An elegant, small
downtown hotel**

General Manager: Michael DeFrino. **Accommodations:** 109 rooms and suites. **Rates:** Rooms: $175–$195 single, $190–$210 double; suites: $220–$370; weekend and corporate rates available. **Included:** Continental breakfast. **Minimum stay:** None. **Payment:** Major credit cards. **Children:** Welcome. **Pets:** Allowed. **Smoking:** Nonsmoking rooms available. **Open:** Year-round.

➤ **Public art is a part of life in Seattle: on the downtown streets, in the parks, on the university campus, and by the waterfront.**

Subtle elegance is the theme at the Alexis, where city noise fades as you enter the small lobby. There are no ornate chandeliers here. Recessed lighting, a few club chairs, and soft carpeting emphasize the understated motif. The hotel is a polished gem and has been recognized with numerous awards.

Built in 1901, the classic building went through several hands before it was renovated in the early 1980s. Everything in the present Alexis is new except the outside walls and courtyard. Now owned by the Kimpton Hotel Group, it's listed on the National Register of Historic Places.

In an area of downtown redevelopment, the Alexis is midway between Pike Place Market and historic Pioneer Square. It's a block from the ferry terminal and close to business centers and shopping. But when you enter the hotel, you leave all that bustle behind.

The rooms are quiet, air-conditioned (though the arched casement windows can be opened), and tastefully furnished in residential style. The suites are unusually spacious. Several have working fireplaces, oversize Jacuzzis, down comforters, and wet bars stocked with complimentary juices and sodas. Some afford glimpses of the sound; if you want a full water view, request Executive Suite 522 or 622. Six suites, on the 6th floor, are devoted to the Aveda spa experience, with massages, facials, and stress-relieving treatments available.

There's nothing pretentious here, and service is paramount. A no-tipping policy has not affected the staff's courtesy. Among the complimentary services are breakfast in the hotel restaurant or your room, a choice of morning newspaper, shoeshine, turndown service with chocolates, and evening sherry. The hotel has a steam room, in addition to the spa, and for a fee you may use the nearby Seattle Athletic Club.

The Bookstore Bar, at the First Avenue entrance, serves light lunches and appetizers in a bar with shelves of books (the site once held a bookstore). The hotel's main restaurant, the Painted Table, features Northwest cuisine with an Oriental touch. Places are set with large plates hand-painted in splashy designs.

Bellevue Place B&B

1111 Bellevue Place East
Seattle, WA 98102
206-325-9253
Fax: 206-455-0785

A large, classic home in a residential area

Innkeeper: Gunner Johnson. **Accommodations:** 3 rooms (share 2 baths). **Rates:** $85–$95 double. **Included:** Full breakfast. **Minimum stay:** 2 nights on weekends. **Payment:** Major credit cards. **Children:** Not appropriate. **Pets:** Not allowed. **Smoking:** Outdoors only. **Open:** Year-round.

➤ **The solarium is a favorite spot for breakfast, with views of the rose beds and landscaped garden.**

One of Seattle's landmark historic districts is Capitol Hill, northeast of the downtown area. A few years ago, Bellevue Place B&B opened in a quiet, residential section of the district. The pale gray and white 1905 home has a distinctive look, with its pillars, arabesque window, sailing ship weathervane, and panel of etched glass in the front door.

Inside, you immediately notice an Asian influence in the furnishings, which carries from the entrance through two parlors, one with a grand piano and one with a fireplace.

Upstairs, the guest rooms are stylishly decorated with Ralph Lauren linens, down comforters, and period pieces such as a burled wood dresser set from the 1920s and an unusual brass trumpet light fixture. One room has a balcony, another a tile fireplace. All three share a spotlessly clean divided bath on the second floor and another downstairs, off the kitchen.

Having lived in Hawaii and learned to love Kona coffee, the innkeeper serves it for breakfast, along with fruit, croissants or muffins, and a hot entrée such as pancakes with bacon or a baked strata.

The B&B caters to a mixed gay and straight clientele.

Chambered Nautilus Bed & Breakfast Inn

5005 22nd Avenue N.E.
Seattle, WA 98105
206-522-2536
800-545-8459
Fax: 206-528-0898

**A big, welcoming home
with a New England flavor**

Innkeepers: Joyce Schulte and Steve Poole. **Accommodations:** 6 rooms. **Rates:** $79–$110 double, $5 less single, $15 additional person. **Included:** Full breakfast. **Minimum stay:** None. **Payment:** Major credit cards. **Children:** Under age 12, by arrangement. **Pets:** Not allowed. **Smoking:** Not permitted. **Open:** Year-round.

➤ **Some good restaurants are within walking distance: the Italian Ciao Bella, the quiet and comfortable Queen Mary, and the Union Bay Café.**

This big blue Georgian Colonial is a casual, inviting home where guests help themselves to tea and cookies in the afternoon and linger over a buffet and the newspaper on Sunday mornings. Steve, the breakfast chef, prepares dishes such as French toast with homemade orange syrup, salmon quiche, and blueberry pancakes and serves them in the dining room or the light and airy sun porch.

The second-floor rooms are furnished with antiques. Most have queen-size beds; one has a king. They all have robes and teddy bears. Garden and Rose chambers share a flower-filled porch.

Up on the third floor, Crow's Nest is a fir-paneled hideaway with eyebrow windows above the antique bed. The bath has a clawfoot tub with a shower. Scallop Chamber is the spacious former library, which has a private porch that overlooks the maple trees and ferns on the hill behind the house. The third-floor rooms are the only ones that sleep more than two people.

The inn is half a block from the bus stop and a 20-minute bus ride to downtown Seattle.

Four Seasons Olympic

411 University Street
Seattle, WA 98101
206-621-1700
800-332-3442 in U.S.
800-268-6282 in Canada
Fax: 206-623-2681

A classic grand hotel in downtown Seattle

General Manager: Peter G. Martin. **Accommodations:** 450 rooms. **Rates:** Rooms: $245–$315 single, $285–$355 double; suite: $625–$1,470; seasonal rates and packages available. **Minimum stay:** None. **Payment:** Major credit cards. **Children:** Under 17, free with a parent. **Pets:** Allowed. **Smoking:** Nonsmoking floors available. **Open:** Year-round.

➤ **Services include interpreters, a pool, massages, a whirlpool and sauna, mending and pressing, and free shoeshine.**

There are many reasons for staying at this historic Seattle hotel — the rooms are comfortable, the lobby and ballroom are wonderfully opulent, and the list of amenities seems endless — but the best reason is the least tangible: consistently fine service. As one regular guest says, "I can arrive at any hour of the day or night, tired from traveling or a late meeting, and know I'll be taken care of perfectly, every time."

With a ratio of almost two staff members to every room and with a concierge on duty 24 hours a day, few mistakes are made in dealing with guests' needs.

You enter this major urban hotel from a brick circular driveway with a fountain and valet parking. At one end of the stately lobby, a curving staircase leads to the Spanish Ballroom, which has banquet seating for 400. The hotel's original chandeliers, dripping with crystal, hang from a 30-foot ceiling.

At the other end of the lobby are the Georgian Terrace and Georgian Room, where orchids sit on tables set in low alcoves with tall palms and Palladian windows. The Georgian is renowned for formal, classic dining and an extensive wine list. In 1990, the cuisine took an inspired turn with the arrival of award-winning chef Kerry Sears. His trend-setting menus have included such dishes as white truffle pasta with truffle sauce, abalone risotto, and curried banana strudel.

The chef works closely with all three hotel restaurants: the Georgian, Schucker's, and Garden Court. Shucker's is a more casual San Francisco–style eatery, where the specialty is oysters and seafood. The Garden Court is a green and glittery high-windowed room that is just right for a proper English tea or for a nightcap and whirl around the dance floor after an evening on the town.

When the Old Olympic Hotel opened in 1924, it was the hub of Seattle's social and cultural life, the place where benefits and banquets for heads of state were held. The Italian Renaissance building of buff brick was filled with crystal, antique mirrors, Italian and Spanish oil jars, and bronze statuary; the terrazzo floors were laid by Italian workers brought to Seattle for the project. But after those glory days, the Olympic, like so many big-city hotels, began to fade.

In the 1980s, after a $60 million restoration, the hotel reopened as part of the Four Seasons chain and again became a major site for social and business events. It is now listed on the National Register of Historic Places.

The guest rooms are commodious and uncluttered, mixing plain beige with splashy floral designs in residential furniture, thick carpets, and heavy drapes. A subdued Oriental theme is evident, with brass hardware, porcelain jars, Chinese paintings, and white chrysanthemums. Naturally there are televisions, telephones, and stocked mini-bars.

Along with careful attention to business travelers and tourists, the Four Seasons Olympic caters to children. There are children's menus and crayons to color them, clown dishes, finger foods, and drinks in oversize glasses in the Georgian Room. Child-size robes are available. Car seats, bottle warmers, games, babysitters, and even water wings at the pool are provided at this hotel worth visiting in all seasons.

Gaslight Inn

1727 15th Avenue
Seattle, WA 98122
206-325-3654

A city home with extra
amenities

Innkeepers: Trevor Logan, Steve Bennett, and John Fox. **Accommodations:** 9 rooms (5 with private bath) and 7 studios and suites. **Rates:** $74–$148 single or double. **Included:** Continental breakfast. **Minimum stay:** 2 nights on weekends. **Payment:** Major credit cards. **Children:** Not appropriate. **Pets:** Not allowed. **Smoking:** Not allowed. **Open:** Year-round.

➤ **The Capitol Hill neighborhood is a lively area, full of shops and restaurants. Look for the bronze Dancing Feet on the sidewalk on Broadway.**

Neither private home nor hotel, this urban inn fills the gap between the two. It's a blocky house, built as a family residence in 1906, with a sense of solidity that is emphasized by the furnishings.

In the wide entry hall is a big potted plant. Sitting rooms on either side contain sturdy oak antique furniture. The black leather couch, gramophone with wooden horn, fluted glass fixtures, and green tile fireplace add character. Art glass by a student of the famed Pilchuck School decorates the home.

All the guest rooms have sinks, TVs, and clock radios; some include refrigerators. Those with modern bedsteads are queen-size; the antiques are double beds. You can count on comfort, but the rooms differ in size and decor. Number 7 is the most whimsical, with a brass bed and frontier artifacts — heirlooms from Trevor's grandfather's cabin in the Yukon.

The Gaslight's newest accommodations are studios and suites next door. These blend antique and contemporary furnishings and have individual phones, TVs, wet bars, and coffeemakers. Off-street parking is a plus.

You'll be well cared for at the Gaslight, and the innkeepers enjoy visiting, but you shouldn't expect to be coddled. The inn, a handy headquarters for independent business travelers and tourists planning to explore Seattle, has many return guests. One attractive feature is the swimming pool in the enclosed backyard.

A buffet breakfast of croissants and fruit is served in the dining room, on a hand-carved table. Coffee and tea are available all day.

Hill House Bed and Breakfast

1113 E. John St.
Seattle, WA 98102
206-720-7161
800-720-7161
Fax: 206-323-0772
hillhouse@uspan.com

A superb B&B in the Capitol Hill district

Innkeepers: Ken Hayes and Eric Lagasca. **Accommodations:** 5 rooms (3 with private bath). **Rates:** May 15–November 14, $70–$105; November 15–May 14, $65–$95. **Included:** Full breakfast. **Minimum stay:** 2 nights on weekends, 3–4 nights on holidays. **Payment:** Major credit cards. **Children:** Over age 12, welcome. **Pets:** Not allowed. **Open:** Year-round.

➤ **Hill House keeps restaurant menus, including Jam Juree, a good Thai restaurant within walking distance.**

If you want to stay at Hill House on a summer weekend, better book your room two months in advance. When you first see the unassuming 2-story frame house on a fairly busy street, you may wonder why it's so popular, but it won't take long to understand the rave reviews. The owners know how to take care of their guests, providing lovely rooms, excellent breakfasts, and fine hospitality. As one visitor said, "We felt well cared for, but not fretted over."

The home is furnished with simple elegance and decorated in warm jewel tones. It has Oriental rugs on hardwood floors, plants in the corners, and fine art on the walls, along with select antiques in each room. It was not this inviting when Eric and Ken moved to Seattle from Washington, D.C., bought the place, and began remodeling. Now, it's a retreat that draws guests again and again.

The smallest room, Rose, is a snug spot best for a single traveler. It has rose walls, an embroidered duvet on the bed, and a basket of towels for the shared bath. Narcissus is a larger room with a brass bed covered by a comforter with ruffles and lace. The most spacious rooms are the suites downstairs. Bordeaux has a sitting room with a couch and TV, and a black and white tile bath with a shower but no tub. Madras, the largest suite, has a sitting room with a settee and a stylish tile bath with both tub and shower. In all rooms there are puffy pillows and plenty of mirrors and hooks.

An outstanding breakfast is served in the dining room or, if the weather allows, on the deck under the willow tree. Eric's creative outlet is cooking, and he does it with flair — "Martha Stewart breakfasts," as Ken says. You might have poached pears, melon balls in Riesling sauce, salmon quiche, crunchy French toast, marinated asparagus, omelets, fritattas, or eggs Benedict; guests never get the same meal twice.

Among their many services, the innkeepers lend umbrellas, put candies in the rooms, provide maps and restaurant recommendations, invite guests to make tea in the kitchen, and point out the intercom that connects with their home next door.

The inn is near Broadway, a lively area of shops and restaurants, and is a few minutes' drive or bus ride from downtown. A convenient location, comfortable rooms, friendly hosts, good food, and a sophisticated ambience make this B&B a treasure.

Hotel Monaco

1101 4th Avenue
Seattle, WA 98101
206-621-1770
800-945-2240
Fax: 206-621-7779

A sophisticated hotel in the heart of Seattle

Manager: Stan Kott. **Accommodations:** 189 rooms and suites. **Rates:** Rooms, $195–$210; suites, $235–$900. **Minimum stay:** None. **Payment:** Major credit cards. **Children:** Under age 17, free with a parent. **Pets:** Allowed. **Smoking:** Nonsmoking rooms available. **Open:** Year-round.

➤ **The hotel offers an unusual service: goldfish for any guest in need of a temporary pet.**

One of Seattle's newest fine hotels was once the office for the phone company. In 1997, after sitting vacant for several years, it was given a $29 million renovation by the Kimpton Group and became the Monaco. Cheryl Rowley, the interior designer, incorporated vivid color and classic forms into the decor because, she said, "Seattle's position as a center of commerce and technology made me think of ancient Greece, which, in its day, held a similar position." On the plaza level of the 11-story building is a mural with nautical imagery translated from the fresco at the Palace of Knossos. The lobby, with 22-foot-high ceilings, is enclosed by columns and has a white stucco fireplace, white quartzite floors, and bold accent colors — typical of the Kimpton Group's flair and style.

The guest rooms have a plush, residential feel, with provincial furnishings in fruitwood and antique pine; they're also configured for business use, with a sizable desk, data port, two-line phones, and voice mail. All the rooms and suites have stereos with CD players. Business services are available 24 hours a day — phones, fax, copier, computer, and printer. There are more than 6,000 square feet of meeting space. In the mornings, guests receive a complimentary newspaper and coffee in the lobby; wine is served in the evening. Same-day laundry service and dry cleaning are available, the concierge provides suggestions on getting around Seattle, you can always get room service with a smile — in other words, the Monaco provides all the comforts and amenities of a modern hotel with a savvy staff.

Adjacent to the hotel is the Sazerac restaurant, where Jan Birnbaum prepares southern-inspired cuisine. On the menu are intensely flavored dishes such as spicy garlic chili squid with white beans and olives, frog legs with garlic lime jalapeño sauce, and braised short ribs in red gravy. The Sazerac, named for a New Orleans cocktail, is a lively, energetic place, with an open kitchen and playful decor. In the bar area, flame-shaped lights appear as red fire balls, backed by a metal sculpture and fanciful chandeliers.

Hotel Vintage Park

1100 Fifth Avenue
Seattle, WA 98101
206-624-8000
800-624-4433
Fax: 206-623-0568

An urban hotel with a wine theme

General Manager: Tim Block. **Accommodations:** 126 rooms and suites. **Rates:** $185–$375 single or double. **Minimum stay:** None. **Payment:** Major credit cards. **Children:** Under 16, free with a parent. **Pets:** Not allowed. **Smoking:** Most rooms are nonsmoking. **Open:** Year-round.

➤ **To keep fit and learn your way around the city, join the outdoor guided exercise program offered to hotel guests.**

This classically European hotel appeals to those in search of a quiet retreat in the heart of the city. It's a renovated 1922 brick and terra cotta building that is close to the Seattle Art Museum, Pioneer Square, the Kingdome, the International District, and Pike Place Market.

The lobby is small and parlor-like, with a fireplace and plump sofas. There is no ballroom or swimming pool. In this hotel, the private spaces provide the amenities. The guest rooms, stylishly appointed and named for Washington wineries and vineyards, are designed for comfort. They have cherrywood furniture, original art, large desks, soundproofed walls, and computer-compatible phones. The most imposing is the Château Ste. Michelle Grand Suite, which has a theme of contemporary art and contains a four-poster bed and a fireplace. Services available include morning coffee and newspaper, shoeshine, portable headsets for walking or jogging, 24-hour room service, terrycloth robes, and valet parking. Business travelers have the use of a fax machine, copier, and meeting room.

Complimentary wine is served in the lobby, as in all hotels in the Kimpton Group, and notable Italian cuisine is served in the Tulio Ristorante. The 100-seat grill, next to the lobby, is a lively spot that draws Seattle residents as well as travelers in search of good pasta, pizza, risotto, fish, and authentic Italian desserts.

Inn at the Market

86 Pine Street
Seattle, WA 98101
206-443-3600
800-446-4484
Fax: 206-448-0631

One of Seattle's finest small hotels

GeneralManager: Joyce Woodard. **Accommodations:** 65 rooms, 10 suites. **Rates:** Summer, $140–$325 single or double; winter, $130–$175; $15 additional person. **Minimum stay:** None. **Payment:** Major credit cards. **Children:** Under 17, free with a parent. **Pets:** Not allowed. **Smoking:** Nonsmoking rooms available. **Open:** Year-round.

➤ **Pike Place Market has dozens of shops and cafés terraced down the steep hill by the waterfront.**

Open, airy, and designed with elegant simplicity, this inn overlooking Elliott Bay has become one of the region's great urban hostelries. A sense of festivity pervades, partly because the hotel is near one of Seattle's liveliest, most interesting attractions, Pike Place Market, and partly because of its fresh, bright decor.

You enter the inn through a brick courtyard edged with shops to a white-walled lobby with a fireplace and conversation area. For more casual chats, there's a deck on the fifth floor with a panoramic view of the bay where afternoon lemonade and tea are served under a wisteria-covered trellis.

The rooms overlook the city, the courtyard, or the bay; those with water views are the most expensive. There's a strong sense of balance and harmony in the decor. The furniture was designed to blend well with the sizes of the rooms, and there are few odd pieces or awkward angles. Some rooms have kitchenettes. Pickled pine armoires conceal TVs, and delicate watercolors and botanical prints hang on the walls.

Although it's a small hotel, Inn at the Market can provide a gratifying level of personal attention; in fact, the friendly staff enjoys it.

If you want an especially romantic setting, a party in a room with a private deck, or a catered celebration, the staff will oblige with imagination and verve.

Next door, in the Comfort Zone, weary travelers can get a massage or lie in the flotation tank. Floating in 150 gallons of water mixed with 800 pounds of Epsom salts is said to help recovery from jet lag; there is no doubt that it is relaxing.

Across the courtyard and overlooking Pike Place Market is an excellent dinner restaurant, Campagne, which serves French country cuisine. In its casual bar section, light entrées are offered until midnight. On the lower level, Café Campagne is a popular casual restaurant serving breakfast, lunch, and dinner.

MV Challenger

1001 Fairview Avenue North
Seattle, WA 98109
206-340-1201
Fax: 206-621-9208

A floating B&B on Lake Union

Owner/captain: Jerry Brown. **Accommodations:** 8 staterooms (5 with private bath). **Rates:** $55–$170 single, $80–$170 double. **Included:** Full breakfast. **Minimum stay:** 2 nights on weekends in summer. **Payment:** Major credit cards (discount for cash, check, or money order). **Children:** Welcome if well behaved. **Pets:** Not allowed. **Smoking:** Not allowed. **Open:** Year-round.

➤ **Several other tugboats and yachts are available for rent.**

The *MV Challenger* was built in 1944 as a tugboat for the army and then sold to a Victoria, B.C., tug company. The 96-foot vessel with a 765-horsepower engine was a working tug until 1981. Now restored and remodeled for "bunk and breakfast" guests, it's cabled to a wharf on Lake Union, in the heart of Seattle.

You'll never see a more luxurious tugboat. It has a mahogany and oak interior, carpeting, a cozy salon with a granite fireplace and conversation pit, a convivial bar, and comfortable cabins on two decks. Jerry Brown, who opened this waterfront hostelry in 1986, provides ice, glasses, and drink mixes at the bar; guests bring their own beverages. Weather permitting, you'll have breakfast on the deck; a crab omelet, French toast with "piggy parts" (bacon and sausage), and strawberry pancakes are among the dishes Jerry prepares.

The cabins are compact rather than spacious, but they have many comforts. The smallest are on the main deck. On the upper deck, which is reached by steep (though carpeted) stairs, are the bigger cabins, which have queen-size beds, TV, VCR, and phones. The Captain's Cabin, which has a sitting room filled with nautical gear in the former pilothouse, boasts an extra-long bed and a great view of the lake. The Admiral's Cabin, which is the most expensive, has a four-poster bed, a refrigerator, and a soaking tub, as well as views of the city, lake, and marina.

The *MV Challenger* has some 200 movies aboard; other entertainment includes an electric piano, guitar, and numerous books and brochures on Seattle attractions. Lake Union is 7.2 miles around and has many restaurants along its shores, some within easy walking distance.

Roberta's Bed & Breakfast

1147 16th Avenue East
Seattle, WA 98112
206-329-3326
Fax: 206-324-2149
robertasbb@aol.com

A homey spot in a peaceful neighborhood

Innkeeper: Roberta Barry. **Accommodations:** 5 rooms. **Rates:** $80–$105 single, $85–$125 double. **Minimum stay:** None. **Included:** Full breakfast. **Payment:** MasterCard, Visa. **Children:** Over age 10, welcome. **Pets:** Not Allowed. **Smoking:** Not allowed. **Open:** Year-round.

➤ **The site of the 1962 World's Fair, Seattle Center now has restaurants, theaters, carnival rides, and the Pacific Science Center.**

Staying at Roberta's is like going to a favorite aunt's home: you're greeted with enthusiasm, told to make yourself comfortable, and offered tea and conversation. This innkeeper loves people and knows what B&B visitors like: a quiet room, a good breakfast, someone who knows the area, and the chance to meet other, like-minded travelers.

The inn, a typical Seattle home with camellia bushes and flowers in the front yard, is in the Capitol Hill district, near downtown and within walking distance of Volunteer Park and several shops and cafés. Four of its guest rooms (Peach, Madrona, Plum, and Rosewood) are on the second floor, and the fifth, Hideaway, is under the eaves on the third floor. Hideaway is a cozy spot where you can curl up on the window seat with one of Roberta's many books.

Each room has its own bath (though Rosewood's is across the hall), some of them very small and cleverly designed to maximize the space. The rooms are furnished with antiques, but the decor is simple and homey.

Downstairs, in the parlor, there's a piano that guests are welcome to play. The *New York Times* is delivered daily, books and magazines fill the shelves, and there's a supply of brochures on Seattle sights. Talk is a big attraction here, for the outspoken, good-humored innkeeper enjoys sharing ideas with her guests.

Roberta serves a sizable, satisfying, meatless breakfast at the long dining room table. It often includes huge Dutch babies drizzled with powdered sugar and lemon along with baked apples and muffins or bread with homemade jam.

After breakfast, some guests hurry off to morning appointments; others linger over one more cup of coffee before heading out with a marked map and the cheery reminder to enjoy Seattle and come visit again.

Sorrento Hotel

900 Madison Street
Seattle, WA 98104
206-622-6400
800-426-1265
Fax: 206-343-6155
Telex: 244206 SORRUR

A hilltop gem on the edge of downtown

Managing Director: Jim Treadway. **Accommodations:** 76 rooms and suites. **Rates:** Rooms, $180–$220 single or double; $15 additional person; suites, $220–$425; penthouse suite $1,200; weekend and corporate rates available. **Minimum stay:** None. **Payment:** Major credit cards. **Children:** Under 18, free with a parent. **Pets:** Not allowed. **Smoking:** Nonsmoking rooms available. **Open:** Year-round.

➤ **The snazzy Seattle Art Museum has changing exhibitions and marvelous displays of North Coast Native American and African life.**

You know this hotel is different as soon as you see palm trees swaying in the breeze off Elliott Bay. The Sorrento keeps them growing by heating underground pipes in winter — an unusual solution typical of an unusual hotel.

The seven-story Italian Renaissance building stands on a hill a few blocks from the heart of downtown Seattle. Its octagonal lobby is quiet and dusky, with indirect lighting creating a relaxed mood.

A soft couch curves around a pillar by the Rookwood fireplace, an elaborate period piece of curved tiles with flowers and an Italian garden scene.

Off the lobby is the Hunt Club, a restaurant with brick walls, soft lighting, and intimate booths. It's considered one of the region's top dining spots, offering an imaginative Northwest menu that typically includes oyster mushroom timbales with smoked duck and hazelnuts, rack of Ellensburg lamb with loganberry wine demi-glace, and king salmon served with a ragout of rock shrimp and a corn, avocado, basil, and lobster sauce. The menu changes seasonally.

Antiques and art lend a European style to the romantic suites, which are decorated in burgundy, gold, and soft beige. Standard rooms have traditional residential furnishings, down pillows, bathrobes, oversize towels, and vases of flowers, creating an atmosphere of warm, understated luxury. In your room you'll find a jogging map, chocolates in the evening, and a bedwarmer for chilly nights. Business travelers like the complimentary limousine rides to the downtown area, morning newspaper, mobile cellular phones, and fax and modem capabilities.

The penthouse, with a view of and over the downtown skyscrapers, is a good spot for groups and meetings. It has pink walls and ceiling, walnut bookshelves backed by mirrors, a baby grand piano, and a powder room all in black with exotic pink flowers.

The Sorrento is a low-key, livable place, favored by those who like an intimate atmosphere and a staff that prides itself on personal yet unobtrusive service.

The concierge will supply courier, translation, babysitting, and secretarial services and handle more unusual requests, such as chartering an airplane, if need be. Whether you need a crib, a bedboard, dry cleaning, or party arrangements, the Sorrento is happy to oblige.

The Williams House

1505 4th Avenue North
Seattle, WA 98109
206-285-0810
Fax: 206-255-8526
innkeepr@wolfenet.com

A family B&B in the Queen Anne district

Innkeepers: Susan and Doug Williams. **Accommodations:** 5 rooms. **Rates:** $85–$150 single or double, $15 additional adult, $10 child; discounts for longer stays and in winter. **Included:** Full breakfast. **Minimum stay:** None. **Payment:** Major credit cards. **Children:** Welcome by arrangement (cribs, $7). **Pets:** Not allowed. **Smoking:** Not allowed in rooms. **Open:** Year-round.

➤ **The innkeepers keeps a box of cards with guests' opinions on nearby restaurants — a handy way to get honest reviews.**

Queen Anne is a hilly, residential neighborhood west of Lake Union and a few minutes' drive north of the downtown core. It's a convenient location, and for those who enjoy a family home, the Williams House is ideal.

The gracious old white and blue home, its broad verandah hung with wisteria, was built in 1905 of old-growth fir by a cart-builder from the Midwest. The plumbing has been modernized and the porch is now a sun room, but the Edwardian home remains as it was designed, although today it offers glimpses of skyscrapers and the Space Needle.

All the guest rooms are different, though each has antique furniture, a down comforter, and a souvenir sachet of flowers from Susan's lush garden. Three rooms have telephone jacks and some have desks. Cotton bathrobes and slippers are supplied. In the spotless bathrooms you'll find shampoo, razors, and other items you might have forgotten.

At breakfast, the emphasis is on fruit and homemade breads, served in the dining room. French toast, quiche, and coffee cakes are among the house specialties. The living room is a comfortable spot, with a Victorian settee, bay window, and baskets of ferns. There's a small piano, kept tuned so visitors will be tempted to practice. Some do, providing impromptu concerts for the delighted guests.

Seaview

The Shelburne Inn

P.O. Box 250
45th Street and Pacific Highway
Seaview, WA 98644
360-642-2442
800-INN1896

A Victorian hotel in an ocean resort

Innkeepers: Laurie Anderson and David Campiche. **Accommodations:** 15 rooms and suites. **Rates:** $99–$169 single or double, $10 additional person; group and midweek packages available. **Minimum stay:** 2 nights on weekends. **Included:** Full breakfast. **Payment:** Major credit cards. **Children:** Welcome. **Pets:** Not allowed. **Smoking:** Outdoors only. **Open:** Year-round.

➤ **Beyond seagrass-covered dunes, the beach is long, wide, and often windy, perfect for flying kites.**

In 1896, the Shelburne opened its doors to travelers, many of them Portlanders who sailed down the Columbia to Ilwaco, in southwestern Washington, and then rode a train up the Long Beach Peninsula. Seaview, a small town with a 28-mile strip of sand, forests, rhododendrons, cranberry bogs, and marshland, is a popular vacation spot. The inn quickly became popular and has remained so; it is the oldest continuously run hotel in Washington and now on the National Register of Historic Places.

The Shelburne stands behind gardens and a white picket fence a few blocks inland from the beach; unfortunately, it faces a noisy highway, so it's best to request a room away from the street.

The inn is a creaky old place, with slanting floors, halls that angle off in different directions, and a great deal of charm. Its flouncycurtained guest rooms are attractively furnished with antiques and porcelain pieces and lavish bouquets of flowers. Some have decks. The recently redone rooms on the third floor have queen beds, skylights, and watercolors by local artists. Homemade cookies are placed in all the rooms. "We try hard to give extra hospitality," says David Campiche.

David and his wife, Laurie, have accomplished a major feat. Not only do they maintain an extraordinary inn, preserving the past while updating the facilities to appeal to modern travelers, they have created a setting for a fine restaurant. Ann and Tony Kischner run the Shoalwater, just off the lobby of the Shelburne. In a classic atmosphere of dark paneled walls, tall windows at curved bays, and white and green linens, they serve excellent cuisine and wine.

The seafood, produce, and herbs come from local providers. The desserts, mostly made by Ann, are famous throughout the Northwest. Chocolate rum cake, fresh strawberry cheesecake, and homemade blackberry sorbet are examples. Tea is served in a pot covered by a knitted tea cosy.

The Shelburne's lobby glows in the light of large stained glass windows that came from a church in England. In the lobby, a country breakfast is served family-style at a large table. Typical dishes include a homemade sausage omelet prepared with herbs from the garden and fresh pastries. If you're in the honeymoon/anniversary suite, you can choose to have breakfast in your room.

After a day spent strolling on the beaches and exploring the peninsula, you'll enjoy relaxing in the Heron and Beaver Pub, off the lobby. Light fare, espresso, cocktails, regional beers, and wines are available.

Sou'Wester Lodge

Beach Access Road (38th Place)
Seaview, WA 98644
360-642-2542

A homey beach place with eclectic charm

Innkeepers: Leonard and Miriam Atkins. **Accommodations:** 8 rooms in lodge, 4 cabins, 10 trailers. **Rates:** Cabins: $81 double, $3–$5 additional person; lodge: $65–$109; trailers: $39–$95. **Minimum stay:** 2 nights on weekends. **Payment:** MasterCard, Visa. **Children:** Welcome. **Pets:** Allowed in cabins and trailers. **Smoking:** Not allowed in lodge, discouraged in cabins. **Open:** Year-round.

▶   **The Lewis and Clark Expedition of 1804–1806 ended at the southern end of Long Beach peninsula, where Fort Canby State Park now stands.**

Seaview is a village on the Long Beach Peninsula, a finger of land between Willapa Bay and the Pacific Ocean in Washington's southwestern corner. There are many surprises in the crannies of this historic spot, which was the summer playground of many 19th-century Portlanders, and one of them is this unique inn — "rather grandiosely called a lodge," as Leonard puts it. It's set in from the sea with a view of ocean and dunes.

The entrance is unpretentious. You drive west, almost to the end of the beach access road, until you glimpse a three-story red house among the trees and the sign: Sou'Wester Trailer Park and Motel. You enter through an enclosed front porch to a large living room that exudes homey comfort and a history of good conversation. It has a brick fireplace, usually a cat curled up on an armchair, and books scattered everywhere among the "early Salvation Army" furniture and the more valuable pieces collected during the Atkinses' travels. This room is where concerts and discussions often take place, both by and for the guests.

The lodge rooms are furnished with iron beds and handmade quilts, much as they were when the house was the summer estate of Henry Winslow Corbett, a banker, timber baron, shipping and railroad magnate, and U.S. senator. These rooms have kitchens, for this is, as Leonard says, a "B and M-Y-O-D B!" (Bed and Make-Your-Own-Damn Breakfast!) place.

The cabins, which face the dunes and the sea, are also simply furnished but are clean and roomy and have well-equipped kitchens. Then there are the trailers — genuine curved chrome trailers from the 1950s, fully furnished with kitchens, on the grass in a side yard. This is the Trailer Classic Hodgepodge (or "Tch-Tch"), bearing such names as Disoriented Express, Worst Western, and Royal Spartan Manor.

Leonard and Miriam are engaging hosts who love ideas, music, and people. Their seaside lodge is conducive not only to contemplation but to interesting chats by the fire. Their most recent addition to the property is a meditation garden.

Long Beach Peninsula is a noted historic site. Fort Canby State Park has a Visitors Center and two lighthouses, North Head and Cape Disappointment. The latter, built in 1856, is the oldest in the Pacific Northwest. The area is also the base of a cranberry industry, the home of the Willapa Bay oyster and a couple of great restaurants, and the site of a major kite festival.

Snohomish

Nita's on Ninth Street

425 Ninth Street
Snohomish, WA 98290
360-568-7081
Fax: 360-568-7081

> **An inviting home in a small town**

Innkeepers: Anita Steigerwald. **Accommodations:** 3 rooms (1 with private bath). **Rates:** $85–$95. **Included:** Full breakfast. **Minimum stay:** None. **Payment:** MasterCard, Visa. **Children:** Over age 12, welcome. **Pets:** Not allowed. **Smoking:** Outdoors only. **Open:** Year-round.

➤ **Snohomish offers a tour of showplace gardens in July and a tour of historic homes every September. Nita's is a highlight of both tours.**

Snohomish, northeast of Seattle on the Snohomish River, bills itself as the antiques capital of the Northwest. Scores of antiques shops dot the well-preserved downtown district of brick-fronted stores and cafés. In the outlying residential areas, Victorian homes have been restored and are carefully maintained.

One of them is Nita's, a hillside estate built in 1884 by A. H. and Charlotte Eddy. The blue and white home is surrounded by lovely gardens where lilacs, roses, and wisteria grow in profusion. There's an orchard of dwarf fruit trees and a swimming pool that is open in summer.

Indoors, there's a light-filled front parlor with a few antiques and a second parlor with a bay window facing the side garden. Victorian lace curtains hang at the windows of these bright, cheerful rooms.

Sooner or later, most guests end up in the big, open kitchen, where the coffeepot is on and a fire burns in the brick hearth on cool days. The innkeeper serves breakfast at 9:00 A.M. at one table in the dining room. Fresh fruit, an omelette, and homemade pastries are a typical morning meal.

The guest rooms have clock radios, TVs, reading lamps, plenty of drawers, handmade quilts, night lights, and windows overlooking the lawns and flowers. The largest room has a queen-size Victorian four-poster bed and a private bath. Another room also has a four-poster bed with a fringed canopy and a rocker by the window. It shares a large, clean bathroom with the third room, which has antique twin beds.

Recommended restaurants in Snohomish are Venus, serving Italian and Greek food, Mardini's, and Collector's Choice, in the large antiques mall.

Snoqualmie

The Salish Lodge and Spa

37807 Southeast Fall City/
  Snoqualmie Road
P.O. Box 1109
Snoqualmie, WA 98065
206-888-2556
800-826-6124
Fax: 206-888-2533

A classic, restored lodge at the edge of a waterfall

GeneralManager: Loy Helmley. **Accommodations:** 91 rooms and suites. **Rates:** Rooms, $165–$269 double; $25 additional person; suites, $375–$599. **Minimum stay:** 2 nights on weekends in summer. **Payment:** Major credit cards. **Children:** Welcome. **Pets:** Allowed ($50). **Smoking:** Nonsmoking rooms available. **Open:** Year-round.

➤ **Not far from the lodge is The Old Winery, an outdoor amphitheater where musical performances and shows are presented on weekends.**

Thirty miles east of Seattle, Snoqualmie Falls plunges in a roaring cascade 268 feet past sheer cliffs to a misty pool. For centuries it was a place of awe to the Native Americans who lived on the banks of the Snoqualmie River, and many tribes came to the falls to trade and hold council. Now the thundering torrent draws crowds of sightseers, who follow the fenced paths to an observation viewpoint.

Perched at the brink of the falls is Salish Lodge, built in 1988 as a major expansion of the original Snoqualmie Falls Lodge. It has an excellent dining room, a peaceful library with a fireplace, a gift shop, and fine service. Complimentary tea and cookies are served in the library every afternoon. The 4,000-square-foot spa on the fourth floor offers two hydrotherapy pools, two saunas, massage, and body treatments.

All the guest rooms have king-size beds or two doubles, down comforters, handsome furniture, stone fireplaces, and two-person whirlpool tubs. Soaps and shampoos are tucked into Shaker wooden boxes, the refrigerator is stocked with goodies, and the fire is ready to light (a chimney sweep, dressed in top hat and tails, will build the fire for you). Most rooms have balconies or patios with a view of the river. Some look out on power transmitters, since the falls serves as a power source. The rooms with fine vistas are numbers 316–323 and 416–423. An even better view of the falls and forested hills can be had from the cozy Attic Lounge, on the top level.

The entrance, flagstone lobby, and restaurant are on the third level, with two floors of rooms against the hillside below. Notable meals are served in the dining room, which features Northwest cuisine that emphasizes regional produce, game, and fish. Special touches are Indian-style potlatch salmon, which is roasted slowly over an open fire, and farm-raised game meats smoked with apple and cherry woods.

The Country Celebration Breakfast is a four-course extravaganza. Among the items served are pastries, fruit parfait with Devonshire cream, stuffed French toast on grilled pineapple, salmon with wild rice, and Dungeness crab strudel. After this feast you might want to take a ride on one of the hotel's mountain bikes or borrow fishing gear and try for steelhead in the river below the falls. Other activities include golfing at any of four nearby courses, rock climbing, and riding. In winter, you can go downhill and cross-country skiing. From the quaint, restored train depot in the village of Snoqualmie, a train rides the rails through the scenic valley on summer weekends.

Spokane

Cavanaugh's Inn at the Park

West 303 North River Drive
Spokane, WA 99201
509-326-8000
800-843-4667
Fax: 509-325-7329

> **A riverside hotel in a convenient location**

GeneralManager: Jeff Fox. **Accommodations:** 402 rooms. **Rates:** Rooms, $99–$149; suites, $185–$850; corporate rates available. **Minimum stay:** None. **Payment:** Major credit cards. **Children:** Under 17, free with a parent. **Pets:** Small pets permitted. **Smoking:** Nonsmoking rooms available. **Open:** Year-round.

➤ **Among Spokane's attractions are Manito Park, a showcase of lilacs, roses, and Japanese gardens, and a skywalk linking the downtown stores.**

The park of the inn's name is Riverfront Park, a Spokane showcase and legacy from the Expo '74 World's Fair; but Cavanaugh's itself has parklike qualities. The outdoors comes in at the Atrium, a greenery-filled courtyard just inside the entrance. Sun streams through skylights, and a tropical jungle surrounds the tables and rattan chairs of the Atrium, where breakfast, lunch, and light dinners are served.

Windows of the Seasons is the hotel's formal dining room. River and park views, white and blue linens, and flowers and hanging ferns make this a pleasant dinner setting. Specialties are rack of lamb, prime rib, and seafood.

The hotel has two lounges: Park Place, off the lobby, offers entertainment and dancing, while Cesare's, on the top floor of the executive wing, is a quiet, intimate setting for cocktails or a buffet lunch.

The guest rooms have comfortable beds and the usual extras, including TVs, phones, and individual heat control. The executive wing, geared to the business traveler, offers work space and wet bars. A recent expansion added a 17-story tower to the inn.

Business travelers will appreciate the Constant Traveler program for regular customers. It grants useful privileges such as express check-in and check-out, discounts on meeting rooms, a complimentary Continental breakfast, and a morning paper. The fitness center has a workout room, whirlpool, sauna, and indoor lap pool.

Outdoors, lawns curve between the walkway by the river and the free-form swimming pool, where a bar extends into the pool. Underwater stools allow you to obtain refreshments without leaving the water.

Behind the hotel's blocky white buildings, a footbridge leads to Riverfront Park, 100 acres of hills and meadows on the Spokane River at the center of the business district. The park has an opera house, convention center, carousel, and entertainment pavilion and holds hundreds of events during the year.

Waverly Place

West 709 Waverly Place
Spokane, WA 99205
509-328-1856

A homey B&B in a historic
district

Innkeepers: Marge and Tammy Arndt. **Accommodations:** 4 rooms (2 with private bath, 2 share 2 baths). **Rates:** $75–$105 double, $10 additional person; discounts for longer stays. **Included:** Full breakfast. **Minimum stay:** 2 nights on Bloomsday Weekend and college graduation weekends. **Payment:** Major credit cards. **Children:** Welcome (no cribs available). **Pets:** Not allowed. **Smoking:** Not allowed. **Open:** Year-round.

➤ **Spokane, the largest city in the inland Northwest, is nicknamed the Lilac City. In the spring there's a week-long Lilac Festival.**

This Queen Anne house on a corner of a quiet residential neighborhood is run by a mother-daughter team. Calm Marge and ebullient Tammy welcome guests to their gracious home furnished with heirlooms, reminders of a bygone period and a family's treasures.

Hand-painted blue Delft vases stand on the mantel of the blue brick fireplace in the large living room. Beside the wide staircase, old-fashioned storybook dolls are displayed. Marge's Scandinavian heritage is evident in such touches as the red wooden candleholders in the entry hall, a tray with tea or coffee and cookies, and in the quiet, friendly welcome she extends. If your visit marks an anniversary or other special occasion, she'll bring out sparkling cider and (with advance notice) make a heart-shaped cake.

Upstairs, Anna's Room has a four-poster queen-size bed and a turret with a window seat overlooking Corbin Park. Skinner Suite is larger and has an oak queen-size sleigh bed, a couch, and a round table and chairs for those who prefer breakfast in their room. Mill Street Room is festive with yellow walls and flower stencils. It has bird's-eye maple furniture and a walk-in closet. The newest addition is the Waverly Suite. It's on two levels, with the sitting area above, offering a good view of the park. The large bath holds a clawfoot tub. The rooms are air-conditioned.

You'll find coffee on the landing outside your room in the morning. Breakfast is served on a Duncan Phyfe table in the dining room or, if you like, by the pool. Classical music plays softly while the Arndts serve their special Swedish breakfast. Kringla, a flaky, glazed pastry with almond filling, is a big favorite. Fruit, Swedish pancakes, homemade huckleberry and elderberry jam, quiche with wild mushrooms, and egg-baked tomatoes are a few of the other dishes that may be offered.

For other meals, Marge and Tammy can recommend several Spokane restaurants, from elegant dining at Patsy Clark's, in a historic mansion, to neighborhood cafés. The Corbin Park Historic District is pleasant for evening strolls; for a more aerobic experience, a running path circles the park.

Stehekin

Silver Bay Inn

10 Silver Bay Road
Stehekin, WA 98852
509-682-2212
(weekdays, 8:30 A.M.–5:00 P.M.)
800-555-7781

| **Lakeside cabins in the wilderness** |

Innkeepers: Kathy and Randall Dinwiddie. **Accommodations:** 4 cabins. **Rates:** $105–$150 double; $20 additional person. **Included:** Expanded Continental breakfast in River View Room only. **Minimum stay:** 3 nights in Headwaters Cabin, 5 nights in cabins (summer only). **Payment:** Cash or check. **Children:** Over age 8, welcome. **Pets:** Not allowed. **Smoking:** Not allowed. **Open:** Year-round.

➤   **Don't miss Rainbow Falls, a 312-foot torrent in spring that becomes a mere ribbon ending in a swimming hole later in the year.**

When they say this inn is a getaway, they really mean it. At Silver Bay, you are getting away from phones, TV, radio, credit cards, and traffic. (One 25-mile road serves the community, but you won't have a car.) It can be reached only by plane or boat or on foot, as no roads reach this part of the North Cascades wilderness. A passenger and mail boat, *Lady of the Lake,* runs regularly between Chelan, at the southern end of the narrow 55-mile lake, to Stehekin at its northern tip, a 4-hour scenic ride. Stehekin and Chelan Airways fly in, a trip that takes half an hour and provides views of rugged mountains rising above a slender ribbon of blue water.

Don't expect rusticity in the living quarters, however. The Dinwiddies call them cabins, but these are beautifully designed homes that are light, comfortable, clean, and furnished with sophistication. There's even a hot tub.

Kathy or Randall will pick you up at the landing and drive you to their property, which stands just at the point where glacier-fed Stehekin River runs into Lake Chelan. They built the place in 1977 as part of their plan to live close to nature.

The Headwaters Cabin, formerly their own glass-fronted, solar-heated home, is now used exclusively by guests. It has two bedrooms and two baths and accommodates up to 4 adults. One bedroom has a queen-size bed and a deck with skylights in the upper sunroom – a fine spot for stargazing. Its bathroom, with pine walls and a Persian carpet, has a deep soaking tub, a shower, and a sink set in an antique sideboard.

In the private sitting area off the upstairs landing, you can browse through the many books or step onto the deck for a view of the icy rushing river. Watch for the harlequin ducks that travel in pairs; they look as if they've been splashed with white paint. On the main floor is a sunroom, a kitchen, and a wide deck overlooking the lake.

Adjoining the house, with a private entrance, is the River View Room. It's a cozy place with quilts on the double bed, big windows, and a kitchenette with a microwave, a toaster, a coffeemaker, and a refrigerator stocked with breakfast makings.

The other cabins are pine homes, one with a view of the bay and the other the lake. In one, sliding glass doors open from a wraparound deck to a living room with braided rugs (made by Kathy), a rocking chair, a soft couch, and an efficient wood stove with a copper bucket full of wood. Tall windows face a lawn shaded by cottonwood trees. The kitchen includes a microwave and dishwasher. (You should bring groceries from Chelan, as the store at the boat landing is not always open.) The queen-size and twins beds are in a loft with a sky and mountain view.

The cabin next door has a similar layout but has two queen-size beds on the main level and a double bed and two twins in the loft. It sleeps up to six people.

Outdoor recreation is abundant in North Cascades National Park. You can go horseback riding, river running, canoeing, and fishing for trout and salmon. If you like to hike, ask your hosts about the unmarked trail that leads to an overlook with spectacular views of the lake and woods.

Stevenson

Skamania Lodge

P.O. Box 189
Stevenson, WA 98648
509-427-7700
800-221-7117
800-376-9116
Fax: 509-427-2547

A luxurious lodge and conference center above the river

Manager: Ian Muirden. **Accommodations:** 195 rooms and suites. **Rates:** Rooms, $110–$240 single or double; suites, $280; $15 additional person; packages available. **Minimum stay:** None. **Payment:** Major credit cards. **Children:** Under age 12, free. **Pets:** Not allowed. **Smoking:** Nonsmoking rooms available. **Open:** Year-round.

➤ **The Columbia Gorge Interpretive Center provides 11,000 square feet of exhibits that bring to life the natural and cultural history of the region.**

This impressive lodge opened in 1993 on a hillside overlooking the Columbia River near the little town of Stevenson, 45 minutes from Portland. It was established through an unusual three-way partnership among Skamania County, Salishan Lodge, and the federal government to improve the local economy, boost tourism, and fill a need for a conference and lodging facility.

The builders' plan was to blend the resort with the environment, comprising two wetlands and two lakes. An old landfill was transformed into a wildflower meadow; the golf course layout follows a natural line; and native plantings were used in the landscaping. The quality throughout is outstanding, the 175-acre setting glorious.

Through a covered walkway on the north side, you enter the lobby, which has a floor of Montana slate. Here the U.S. Forest Service provides visitors with information on the Columbia River Gorge area. Off the lobby, on the other side of an 85-foot-tall rock fireplace, is the Gorge Room, a relaxing common space with sturdy Mission furniture and windows framing the lovely river view.

Several touches are reminiscent of turn-of-the-century lodges: heavy timbers, black wrought-iron, native stone, locally produced artwork. The petroglyph rubbings on the walls were taken from cliffs in the gorge, many in areas now submerged by dams.

Light meals are served in the River Rock Lounge and on the terrace, or you can eat in the dining room, which is open all day and serves innovative Northwest cuisine. The atmosphere is casual, with a lighthearted, holiday feel; the service is both friendly and polished. One wing of the lodge, with 12,000 square feet of meeting space, is the Conference Center. It can hold groups up to 700. There's a fitness center at the opposite end of the lodge, with an indoor pool, exercise equipment, massage service, and a pretty outdoor whirlpool spa set against natural rock.

The guest rooms, with contemporary furnishings and warm natural wood, have views of the river or forest. Most expensive are the four Parlor Rooms, which have fireplaces, wet bars, and balconies, and the Hood River Suite.

When you're not exploring the Gorge and watching windsurfers, you might like to play the scenic golf course, follow the forest trails behind the lodge, and relax in a lawn chair as you watch the moon rise above the mountain on the far side of the river.

Sumas

Silver Lake Park Cabins

9006 Silver Lake Road
Sumas, WA 98295
360-599-2776

Rustic cabins on the lake shore

ParkManager: Mike Barnes. **Accommodations:** 6 cabins (shared bathhouse) and lodge. **Rates:** Cabins: Whatcom County residents, $40–$50 double; nonresidents, $50–$60 double; $5 additional adult. Lodge: $150 for residents, $170 nonresidents. **Minimum stay:** 2 nights on weekends. **Payment:** MasterCard, Visa. **Children:** Under age 18, free. **Pets:** Allowed on leash, not allowed inside cabins. **Smoking:** Not allowed. **Open:** Year-round.

➤ **All along the highway there's captivating scenery: waterfalls, tumbling streams, and thick forests, with the looming presence of the mountain.**

Silver Lake Park is a rambling, grassy, wooded park near Sumas, a small town just south of the Canadian border. The park is about 35 miles west of Mount Baker, a recreational magnet for skiers in winter and hikers in summer. Those who enjoy deep forests and misty waterfalls love the area at any time of year.

The well-kept park, which is maintained by the Whatcom County Park and Recreation Board, has stables, bridle and hiking trails, a play area, campsites, and a pretty lake with a boat launch. Bring your own horse; rowboats and pedal boats can be rented.

Rustic cedar cabins in the trees edge the lakefront. Each cozy cabin has the basic necessities: a stove and oven, refrigerator, gas heater, and double beds. They also have cold running water, no hot water and no bathrooms. There are two outhouses and a bathhouse with showers, all kept clean by the staff. You bring your own bedding, towels, and cooking utensils.

The largest cabins, which contain three double beds and sleep six people, have a separate bedroom. Others consist of a single room. Three have stone fireplaces. Wood is available for a fee.

The three-bedroom lodge, which accommodates up to 8 people, is a good choice for a group. It has a fireplace and an equipped kitchen.

Tacoma

Chinaberry Hill

302 Tacoma Avenue North
Tacoma, WA 98403
206-272-1282
Fax: 206-272-1335

| **Historic hillside home above Commencement Bay**

Innkeepers: Cecil and Yarrow Wayman. **Accommodations:** 5 rooms. **Rates:** $95–$125 double, $25 additional person over age 2. **Included:** Full breakfast. **Minimum stay:** None. **Payment:** Major credit cards. **Children:** Welcome in cottage. **Pets:** Not allowed. **Smoking:** Outdoors only. **Open:** Year-round.

➤ **Point Defiance, one of America's most beautiful urban parks, has 689 acres of forest, gardens, beaches, and trails, plus an outstanding aquarium and zoo.**

Formerly the Lucius Manning Estate, built in 1889, Chinaberry Hill is on the National Register of Historic Places. The mansion has been lovingly restored and furnished with antiques and modern conveniences (phones, modem hookups, fax service, videos), along with a few oddities the Victorians, who were drawn to whimsy, would appreciate. Crimson velvet curtains frame the entrance to the living room, where a wooden bear stands with a fishing pole. An old steamer trunk serves as a table, a harp stands in one corner, and the bookshelves are filled with bestsellers of the 1800s. Solar-powered spinning crystals cast prisms across the walls.

The friendly hosts live on the third floor, and their guests have the rest of the house — including the big kitchen, where juice and soft drinks are chilling in the refrigerator and the cookie jar is always full. Breakfast, served in the dining room at the time you request it, is ample. Cecil prepares salmon quiche with black bean salsa, fruit with lemon yogurt, blueberry pancakes, eggs and bacon, and other dishes.

An ornate staircase leads to three of the rooms. Garden Room is the smallest. Once the children's room, it now sleeps two comfortably. There's a down comforter on a queen-size bed; windows overlook the garden. In the bathroom is a clawfoot tub with ring shower. Pantages Suite offers the most dramatic bay views and has a four-poster bed. Its sitting area, which the original owners used as a nursery, holds a Jacuzzi tub. Wild Rose Suite, the former master bedroom, has a white tile fireplace, a queen-size four-poster bed, and a dressing room with an oversized tub.

Each room displays stage memorabilia, reflecting the owners' interest in Tacoma's theater history.

The Carriage Suite and Hay Loft are in a separate cottage, the estate's carriage house. It has a curved four-poster iron bed, a quaint Victorian Murphy bed, and a step-up Jacuzzi in the bath (caution is required climbing into this tub; you need a good sense of balance). The second story has a sitting room, a bedroom with a queen-size bed, and a private bath. Families and friends traveling together often rent the entire cottage.

The Villa

705 North 5th Street
Tacoma, WA 98403
206-572-1157
888-572-1157
Fax: 206-572-1805
villabb@aol.com

| A Mediterranean mansion in a historic district |

Innkeepers: Becky and Greg Anglemyer. **Accommodations:** 2 rooms, 2 suites. **Rates:** $85–$135 single or double, $15 additional person. **Included:** Full breakfast. **Minimum stay:** None. **Payment:** MasterCard, Visa. **Children:** Over age 12, welcome. **Pets:** Not allowed. **Smoking:** Not allowed. **Open:** Year-round.

➤ **Dale Chihuly is a well-known artist from Tacoma. His stunning glass creations can be seen in the restored Union Station.**

In 1925 a noted local architect, Ambrose Russell, designed a home for James McCormack, a Tacoma businessman. Russell had just returned from traveling in the Mediterranean and incorporated the features he admired most in Italy: huge arched windows, verandahs, spacious common rooms, and light, bright colors. The result was a mansion that today brings admirers from around the world. What they find at the Villa is a B&B fantasy come true.

In addition to large, comfortable rooms and a good breakfast, guests are treated like visiting royalty. Not that this is a formal place; on the contrary, the Anglemyers are casual, friendly folk who want their guests to feel at home. They've provided each room with a CD player, hair dryer, Almond Roca snacks, art from their world travels, and fresh flowers. They invite guests to bring friends or family in for breakfast or evening appetizers. They launder clothes, carry luggage, and have even been known to wash honeymooners' cars.

The Villa is in Tacoma's North End, site of a number of grand homes and gardens, and is listed on the National Register of Historic Homes. On the main floor you first see a foyer where white pillars and arches frame an oak staircase. There's a pink and white living room with a fireplace, a dramatic kitchen, a dining room with a 10-foot pine table, and a tranquil, light-filled sun room. White wicker furniture, orchids, vines, and three walls of windows give the sun room a sense of the outdoors.

Upstairs, each guest room has individual character. Bay View Suite offers sweeping views of Commencement Bay and the Olympic Mountains. It has a king-size four-poster bed draped with muslin, soft couches, and a private verandah. The Rice Bed Room is named for the carved four-poster queen-size bed. The Garden Suite has a sitting room, fuchsia walls, a queen-size bed, and a verandah overlooking the sunken garden. The fourth room, tucked away on the top floor, is the Maid's Quarters, cozy and romantic with white lace linens on an iron bed, a verandah, and a bird's-eye view.

The innkeepers' quarters are on the lower level, so guests have no sense of intruding on their privacy. The entire main floor is for the guests' use. A breakfast of muffins, scones, fruit, and egg dishes is served in the dining room between 7:00 and 10:00 A.M.

Vashon Island

Artist's Studio Loft B&B

16529 91st Avenue SW
Vashon Island, WA 98070
206-463-2583
Fax: 206-463-3881
medowart@asl-bnb.com

| A country inn on an island

Innkeeper: Jacqueline Clayton. **Accommodations:** 3 rooms. **Rates:** $85–$105 single or double. **Included:** Expanded Continental breakfast. **Minimum stay:** 2 nights on weekends and holidays. **Payment:** Major credit cards. **Children:** Not appropriate. **Pets:** Not allowed. **Smoking:** Not allowed. **Open:** Year-round.

➤ **Vashon has several antiques shops, art galleries, and casual restaurants.**

When an artist opens an inn, you can expect some interesting room decor. Jacqueline Clayton's artistic skills (and hard work) have made this 1920s farmhouse and separate cottage a retreat of beauty. She blended the old with the new by using such techniques as rag painting, sponging, and marbling. Her own stained glass works hang in the rooms. If time permits, she'll show you the barn studio where she creates her works of art.

The B&B stands on five acres of fields, woods, and flower gardens. Bird houses hang in the trees and gravel paths wind around islands of colorful blooms, a wishing well, and a pond. Intricate wrought-iron fences made by Lance Gaut form trellises and fences. You won't find a place in the Northwest with more peace and charm.

Each guest room has a private entrance and a queen-size bed. The Aerial Cottage, Jacqueline's former studio, is a large, second-story room with a vaulted ceiling and windows all around. It has a woodstove, a TV and VCR, and a small kitchen with a refrigerator, microwave, and stovetop. Juice, cereals, coffee, and tea are placed in the kitchen before you arrive, and in the morning Jacqueline comes to the door with a basket of hot scones.

Downstairs is the Ivy Room, warm and homey with rag-painted walls, Mexican tile floors, and a wicker rocker. The entrance to the Master Suite, upstairs in the main house, is from a balcony, through lace-curtained French doors. This spacious room has an 8-foot mirrored wall, skylights, and glass block dividers in the bath. The woodwork on drawers, cabinets, and doors in the suite is remarkable. The Ivy Room and Master Suite do not have kitchen facilities; guests take breakfast in the sunny eating area in the main house.

Between the two buildings, under a vine-covered tree, is a gazebo with a hot tub. After watching the sunset, perhaps from Lisabeula Beach Park, it's pleasant to relax in the hot tub and listen to the night birds and frogs.

AYH Ranch Hostel

12119 Southwest Cove Road
Vashon, WA 98070
206-463-2592

Budget lodgings in a country hostel

Managers: Judy Mulhair and Gwen Duckworth. **Accommodations:** 2 bunk rooms, 1 lodge room, 9 tepees, 4 covered wagons (shared baths). **Rates:** $9 per person for AYH members, $12 nonmembers, children half-price; private room, $35–$45. **Minimum stay:** None. **Payment:** Major credit cards. **Children:** Welcome. **Pets:** Not allowed. **Smoking:** Outdoors only. **Open:** May through October.

➤ **A summer highlight on the island is the Strawberry Festival in mid-July, with food, music, and arts and crafts sales.**

The hostel movement originated in Germany more than 75 years ago, providing inexpensive lodging to young travelers. Now there are hostels all over the world, still based on low cost and cooperation. There's no age limit; you'll meet people of all ages and nationalities.

You don't have to be a member of American Youth Hostel to stay at the ranch on rural Vashon Island. Here you get a taste of frontier life (updated with electricity and running water) by sleeping in a handmade log lodge, a canvas tepee, or a covered wagon. These accommodations stand on 10 acres of pasture, woodland, and apple orchards.

The two-story lodge, made from thirty 100-foot trees taken from the property, was built by the energetic proprietors. Its large common room has a sitting area with comfortable couches, a kitchen that guests may use, and bulletin boards filled with bus schedules and requests for rides. One room has bunks for eight men, the other, for seven women. There's a bathroom for each side. Upstairs is a private bedroom for two.

Scattered across the grounds are white Sioux Indian–style tepees. Stretched around poles made from local trees, they have low entrances, folding army beds, and Indian designs painted on the canvas walls. Tepee guests use the outside bathhouses. The covered wagons each sleep two on wall-to-wall mats.

A hostel is not a formal place. Guests make friends quickly, trading travel tips, and a cooperative spirit prevails. You're expected to clean up after yourself and perhaps do a little extra. In the kitchen you'll find free buttermilk pancake mix (Judy Mulhair's old family recipe) and, Judy says, "one of the last 10-cent cups of coffee in the West."

Staples such as eggs, tuna, and soup may be purchased. No alcohol or drugs are allowed in the hostel. Linens and towels can be rented, and bikes may be borrowed (helmets rent for $1). There are three barbecues, a volleyball court, and a bonfire area in the pasture.

Back Bay Inn

24007 Vashon Highway S.W.
Vashon, WA 98070
206-463-5355

An intimate country inn on a pastoral island

Innkeepers: Don and Stacy Wolczko. **Accommodations:** 4 rooms (all with private bath). **Rates:** $103–$118 single or double, $10 additional adult, $4 child. **Included:** Full breakfast. **Minimum stay:** None. **Payment:** Major credit cards. **Children:** Welcome. **Pets:** Not allowed. **Smoking:** Not allowed. **Open:** Year-round.

➤ **In autumn, cyclists enjoy the peace of Vashon's country roads. From the shore you can see great blue herons, bald eagles, seals, and sea lions.**

Back Bay Inn is fresh and new, though it was designed around a turn-of-the-century private home on the same corner location and has a Victorian flavor. The owners have created a blend of old and new that emphasizes fine quality in every respect.

This place will improve with age, especially as the landscaping matures. Its gardens, planted with seasonal color and scent, provide not only a scenic backdrop to the inn but flowers for the guest rooms and herbs for the kitchen. The restaurant, previously serving notable Northwest cuisine, at this writing is open only for breakfast. Early risers may enjoy coffee and newspapers in the library by the fireplace before breakfast is served.

The clean and well-decorated guest rooms have antique furnishings and views of the harbor. For other perspectives on the inner harbor and a view of the distant lights of Seattle, take a walk through the garden to the top of the hill behind the hotel.

Winthrop

Sun Mountain Lodge

P.O. Box 1000
Winthrop, WA 98862
509-996-2211
800-572-0493
Fax: 509-996-3133
smtnsale@methow.com

> **An award-winning
> mountain resort**

GeneralManager: Brian Charlton. **Accommodations:** 115 rooms, suites, and cabins. **Rates:** Summer: rooms, $140–$510 single or double; less other seasons. **Minimum stay:** 2 nights on weekends, 3 nights on holidays. **Payment:** Major credit cards. **Children:** Under 13, free. **Pets:** Not allowed. **Smoking:** Nonsmoking rooms available. **Open:** Year-round.

➤ **The Sun Mountaineers Program in summer keeps kids occupied with games, arts and crafts, nature activities, fishing, and field trips.**

Sun Mountain Lodge is one of Washington's premier resorts, worthy of its magnificent surroundings in the North Cascades. Reflecting its mountain setting, the lodge is built from massive timbers and stone native to the area. It stands high above the Methow Valley on 2,000 acres of woodland, meadows, trails, and streams.

Outdoor recreation of all kinds is available on your own or through the resort's many programs. In summer you can go riding, whitewater or scenic rafting, boating, and hiking. You might rent a mountain bike, play tennis or golf, swim in the resort pool, or shop in the nearby town of Winthrop, which has an Old West theme.

In winter, the Methow Valley draws skiers from around the world for cross-country fun on 175 kilometers of trails. The lodge rents skis and equipment and provides lessons from top instructors. Ice skating and sleigh rides are also available.

The restaurant has received acclaim for its French-based cuisine. The classical cooking shows a regional flair in such dishes as poached Chinook salmon wrapped in spinach and layered with Dungeness crab and scallop mousselline. The Eagles Nest Café and Lounge offers live entertainment and after-dinner relaxation by the split-log bar.

The dining room overlooks the panorama of the Methow Valley and rugged mountains. In fact, almost every room in the lodge, including the exercise room, has a breathtaking view. Some guest rooms are in the lodge, others in outlying buildings. Handmade quilts cover the beds, and original works by regional artists hang on the walls. Several rooms feature lava rock fireplaces and hand-hewn birch furnishings. The nine cabins, which have kitchenettes and queen-size and sofa beds, are on the quiet shore of Lake Patterson.

What's What

A cross-reference to accommodation types and special interests

Bicycling

British Columbia
River Run Floating Cottages, 27
Oregon
Black Butte Ranch, 190
The Resort at the Mountain, 297
Salishan Lodge, 221
Sunriver Resort, 286
The Woods House, 178
Washington
Inn at Semi-Ah-Moo, 327
MacKaye Harbor Inn, 369
The Manor Farm Inn, 412
Orcas Hotel, 386
Port Ludlow Resort and Conference Center, 398
Run of the River, 360
Silver Bay Inn, 454
Turtleback Farm Inn, 390

Boating

British Columbia
The Boathouse, 13
Clarion Lakeside Resort, 45
Hatheume Lake Resort, 22
Lowe's Resort, 30
Oak Bay Beach Hotel, 98
River Run Floating Cottages, 27

Children Welcome

Golf

Hot Springs

Idaho
Gunter's Salmon River Cabins, 135
Oregon
Kah-Nee-Ta, 295
Washington
Carson Hot Mineral Springs Resort, 329

Ice Skating

Idaho
Idaho Country Inn, 140
Sun Valley Lodge, 141
Oregon
The Inn of the Seventh Mountain, 185
Sunriver Resort, 286
Washington
Freestone Inn, 373

Kitchen or Cooking Facilities

British Columbia
Corbett Lake Country Inn, 36
Lowe's Resort, 30
Sea Breeze Lodge, 23
Point-No-Point Resort, 60
Ponderosa Point Resort, 25
River Run Floating Cottages, 27
Strathcona Park Lodge, 62
Victoria Regent Hotel, 104
Idaho
Heidelberg Inn, 123
Gunter's Salmon River Cabins, 135
Redfish Lake Lodge, 137
Oregon
Argonauta Inn, 196
Hallmark Resort, 198
Heather Cottage, 294
House on the Metolius, 194
The Inn at Face Rock, 183

Near University

Pets Allowed with Permission

Rafting

Restaurant Open to the Public

Swimming

Tennis

Wheelchair Access

Windsurfing

British Columbia
 Clarion Lakeside Resort, 45
 Sooke Harbour House, 61
 Tyax Mountain Lake Resort, 20
Idaho
 The Coeur d'Alene Resort, 121
 Idaho Rocky Mountain Ranch, 136
 Redfish Lake Lodge, 137
Oregon
 Ayers' Cottage, 254
 Columbia Gorge Hotel, 232
 Hood River Hotel, 234
 Inn at Manzanita, 245
 Lakecliff Estate, 235

Recommended Guidebooks

These books are excellent sources of information for sightseeing, restaurant suggestions, and regional history.

Pacific Northwest

Fodor's Pacific North Coast. Fodor's Travel Guides, $17. Solid, practical information on what to see and do in Oregon, Washington, British Columbia, and southeast Alaska. Includes some historical and geographical background.

Let's Go: Pacific Northwest, Western Canada & Alaska. Harvard Student Agencies, $16.99. Overview on what to see and where to stay on a budget. A few maps, small print.

Sierra Club Guide to the Natural Areas of Oregon & Washington. John Perry and Jane Greverus Perry, Sierra Club Books, $12. Detailed descriptions of camping, fishing, hiking, and boating opportunities in 250 outdoor areas.

Northwest Best Places. David Brewster and Stephanie Irving, Sasquatch Books, $19.95. Capsule reviews of restaurants and lodgings in Washington, Oregon, and British Columbia.

Exploring the Seashore in B.C., Washington & Oregon. Gloria Snively. ProStar Publications, $17.95. Readable field guide to shorebirds and intertidal plants and animals. Illustrations and color photos.

Journals of Lewis & Clark. Bernard DeVoto, editor, American Heritage Library, $14.95. Excerpts from the journals of members of the Lewis and Clark Expedition of 1804–1806.

Hidden Pacific Northwest. Ulysses Press, $16.95. Short descriptions of what to see and do and how to get around in Oregon, Washington, and B.C. Emphasizes the offbeat, adventurous, and low-priced, but has standard information as well.

British Columbia

Adventuring in British Columbia. Isabel Nantow and Mary Simpson, Sierra Club Books, $16. Outdoor activities in B.C. Readable guide with history, wildlife information, tips, addresses, map.

Michelin Green Guide. Michelin Tires, Ltd., $14.95. The familiar long green Michelin guide, a sound and thorough resource covering all Canada. History, travel routes, sights, festivals; includes regional maps and illustrations plus separate road map.

The British Columbia Handbook. Jane King, Moon Publications, $15.95. Capsule information on what to see and do throughout the province.

The Vancouver Guide. Terri Wershler, Chronicle Books, $10.95. How to get around in Vancouver and make the most of your visit.

Idaho

Idaho for the Curious. Cort Conley, Backeddy Books, $15.95. Thick, 685-page guide to 14,000 miles of Idaho roads. Includes history, geography, road map.

Sawtooth National Recreation Area. Luther Linkhart, Wilderness Press, $14.95. Thorough descriptions of SNRA in Sawtooth, White Cloud, and Boulder Mountains. Photos and separate map.

River of No Return. Johnny Carrey and Cort Conley, Backeddy Books, $11.95. Historical guide to travel on the Salmon River, with black-and-white photos.

Snake River of Hells Canyon. Johnny Carrey, Cort Conley, and Ace Barton, Backeddy Books, $12.95. Stories of Indians, explorers, trappers, and homesteaders along the Snake River. Includes black-and-white photos.

The Hiker's Guide to Idaho. Jackie Maughan and Ralph Maughan, Falcon Press, $12.95. Idaho hikers describe 78 favorite backcountry trails. Photos, simple maps.

Oregon

The Oregon Desert. E. R. Jackman and R. A. Long, The Caxton Printers, $19.95. A combination of folklore, natural history, science, and eastern Oregon atmosphere. Includes photos.

Oregon Handbook. Stuart Warren and Ted Long Ishikawa, Moon Publications, $16.95. Cultural and recreational activities, history, attractions. Very informative. Maps, photos, small print.

Exploring the Oregon Coast by Car. Marje Blood, Image Imprints, $9.95. Comprehensive descriptions of sights and activities along Highway 101.

Washington

The Hiker's Guide to Washington. Ron Adkison, Falcon Press, $14.95. Accurate information on 75 backcountry hikes. Detailed maps.

The Seattle Guidebook. Archie Satterfield, Globe Pequot Press, $12.95. What to see and do, how to get around, shopping, and a bit of history.

The San Juan Islands Afoot & Afloat. Marge and Ted Mueller, The Mountaineers, $14.95. Concise descriptions of what to expect and how to get around in the San Juans. Includes maps and numerous photos.

Washington Handbook. Dianne J. Boulerice Lyons and Archie Satterfield, Moon Publications, $16.95. Detailed guide to outdoor activities, historic sites, culture, entertainment, and accommodations. Regional maps, some photos.

Index

Best Places Report

Authors of the Best Places to Stay series travel extensively in their research to find the best places for all budgets, styles, and interests. However, if we've missed an establishment that you find worthy, please write to us with your suggestion. Detailed information about the service, food, setting, and nearby activities or sights is most important. Finally, let us know how you heard about the place and how long you've been going there.

Send suggestions to:

> The Harvard Common Press
> Best Places to Stay Suggestions
> 535 Albany Street
> Boston, Massachusetts 02118

NAME OF HOTEL_____

TELEPHONE_____

ADDRESS_____

_____ ZIP _____

DESCRIPTION_____

_____

_____

_____

_____

_____

_____

YOUR NAME_____

TELEPHONE_____

ADDRESS_____

_____ ZIP _____

Best Places Report

Authors of the Best Places to Stay series travel extensively in their research to find the best places for all budgets, styles, and interests. However, if we've missed an establishment that you find worthy, please write to us with your suggestion. Detailed information about the service, food, setting, and nearby activities or sights is most important. Finally, let us know how you heard about the place and how long you've been going there.

Send suggestions to:

> The Harvard Common Press
> Best Places to Stay Suggestions
> 535 Albany Street
> Boston, Massachusetts 02118

NAME OF HOTEL_____

TELEPHONE_____

ADDRESS_____

_____ ZIP _____

DESCRIPTION_____

_____

_____

_____

_____

_____

_____

YOUR NAME_____

TELEPHONE_____

ADDRESS_____

_____ ZIP _____

Best Places Report

Authors of the Best Places to Stay series travel extensively in their research to find the best places for all budgets, styles, and interests. However, if we've missed an establishment that you find worthy, please write to us with your suggestion. Detailed information about the service, food, setting, and nearby activities or sights is most important. Finally, let us know how you heard about the place and how long you've been going there.

Send suggestions to:

> The Harvard Common Press
> Best Places to Stay Suggestions
> 535 Albany Street
> Boston, Massachusetts 02118

NAME OF HOTEL _____

TELEPHONE _____

ADDRESS _____

_____ ZIP _____

DESCRIPTION _____

_____

_____

_____

_____

_____

_____

YOUR NAME _____

TELEPHONE _____

ADDRESS _____

_____ ZIP _____

Best Places Report

Authors of the Best Places to Stay series travel extensively in their research to find the best places for all budgets, styles, and interests. However, if we've missed an establishment that you find worthy, please write to us with your suggestion. Detailed information about the service, food, setting, and nearby activities or sights is most important. Finally, let us know how you heard about the place and how long you've been going there.

Send suggestions to:

The Harvard Common Press
Best Places to Stay Suggestions
535 Albany Street
Boston, Massachusetts 02118

NAME OF HOTEL _____

TELEPHONE _____

ADDRESS _____

_____ ZIP _____

DESCRIPTION _____

_____

_____

_____

_____

_____

_____

YOUR NAME _____

TELEPHONE _____

ADDRESS _____

_____ ZIP _____

Best Places Report

Authors of the Best Places to Stay series travel extensively in their research to find the best places for all budgets, styles, and interests. However, if we've missed an establishment that you find worthy, please write to us with your suggestion. Detailed information about the service, food, setting, and nearby activities or sights is most important. Finally, let us know how you heard about the place and how long you've been going there.

Send suggestions to:

> The Harvard Common Press
> Best Places to Stay Suggestions
> 535 Albany Street
> Boston, Massachusetts 02118

NAME OF HOTEL_____

TELEPHONE_____

ADDRESS_____

_____ ZIP _____

DESCRIPTION_____

_____

_____

_____

_____

_____

_____

YOUR NAME_____

TELEPHONE_____

ADDRESS_____

_____ ZIP _____

Best Places Report

Authors of the Best Places to Stay series travel extensively in their research to find the best places for all budgets, styles, and interests. However, if we've missed an establishment that you find worthy, please write to us with your suggestion. Detailed information about the service, food, setting, and nearby activities or sights is most important. Finally, let us know how you heard about the place and how long you've been going there.

Send suggestions to:

> The Harvard Common Press
> Best Places to Stay Suggestions
> 535 Albany Street
> Boston, Massachusetts 02118

NAME OF HOTEL_____

TELEPHONE_____

ADDRESS_____

_____ ZIP _____

DESCRIPTION_____

_____

_____

_____

_____

_____

_____

YOUR NAME_____

TELEPHONE_____

ADDRESS_____

_____ ZIP _____

Best Places Report

Authors of the Best Places to Stay series travel extensively in their research to find the best places for all budgets, styles, and interests. However, if we've missed an establishment that you find worthy, please write to us with your suggestion. Detailed information about the service, food, setting, and nearby activities or sights is most important. Finally, let us know how you heard about the place and how long you've been going there.

Send suggestions to:

> The Harvard Common Press
> Best Places to Stay Suggestions
> 535 Albany Street
> Boston, Massachusetts 02118

NAME OF HOTEL _____

TELEPHONE _____

ADDRESS _____

_____ ZIP _____

DESCRIPTION _____

_____

_____

_____

_____

_____

_____

YOUR NAME _____

TELEPHONE _____

ADDRESS _____

_____ ZIP _____